Wild Flowers
of Britain and Europe

Wild Flowers
of Britain and Europe

BOB PRESS and BOB GIBBONS

The publishers, authors and photographic consultant gratefully acknowledge the assistance of all those involved in the compilation of this book. All photographs, with the exception of those listed below, were taken by Bob Gibbons.

Natural Image: P. Brough 125tr; Paul Davis 57tr, 71tl,mr, 81tr, 103br, 143ml, l93mr, 207ml, 217tr, 227mr, 259bl, 271tr, 295tr,br, 297tr, 311tl,br, 317ml,mr,bl,br; Charles Marden Fitch 279bl; Robin Fletcher 307tl; Liz Gibbons 75tr, 253mr; Jean Hall 283mr; T. McCathie 89bl, 105tr, 239br, 261ml; F. B. Macdonald 85mr; S. R. Martin 75tl; D.& M. Nesbitt 191tr; P. R. Perfect 265br; E.H. Sawford 79bl, 273ml; H. Schrempp 57br, 77mr, 121tr, 123tl,bl, 131mr, 161mr, 187mr,bl, 215br, 229tr, 245t; David Sutton 63b; Nick Turland 55ml, 65ml, 69mr, bl, 73br, 77tr,bl, 85tl, ml, bl, 87mr, br, 89br, 91tl, 95tl, 97ml, 99bl, 103mr, 105ml, 115br, 117ml, 121bl, 133tl,br, 137mr,br, 139ml, 143mr, 151mr,br, 153tr,bl, 159ml, 161bl, 171br, 173mr, 175br, 177tl,tr, 181tl,br, 195br, 207tl,mr, 215ml, 227bl, 231tl, 233br, 235d, 137tl, 243tl, 249tl,bl, 251tl, 253tr, 259tl, 267br, 271bl, 275bl, 277tl,tr, 287tr, 293br, 297br, 303tl,ml,br, 305tr, 307ml,bl, 309mr, 311bl, 313br; D.Westerhoff 149tl; Peter Wilson 81mr, 107ml, 135ml, 145tl, 151tl, 157tl, 169mr, 185bl, 189t1, 193bl, 195tr, 213br, 227ml, 241bl, 247mr,br, 249tr, 251mr,bl, 293tl, 297mr, 309bl,br; Michael Woods 87bl.

Nature Photographers: S. C. Bisserot 157tr; F. V. Blackburn 165bl, 167ml, 263tl, 281tr; Idris Bowen 289tl; Brinsley Burbidge 81tl, 117bl, 149mr, 209mr, 221mr, 245bl, 273mr, 275br, 285mr; Robin Bush 83mr, l0lbr, 171tl, 261tr; A. A. Butcher 227tl; Kevin Carlson 151bl, 157mr; Andrew Cleave 53bl, 65bl, 67tl, 117tr, 131ml, 173tr, 185br, 203tr, 215tl, 249ml, 269mr; C. H. Gomersall 149tr; Jean Hall 223tr, 229mr, 231tr, 253bl, 273br, 291tl, 309tl,tr; James Hyett 163tl, 219br; E. A. Janes 71tr, 265ml; D. Osborn 179bl; Paul Sterry 56ml, 59ml,mr,br, 65br, 67tr, 69tr, 81bl, 83tr, 107tr, 119tr,br, 127br, 129mr, 131bl, 171ml, 173tl, 177bl, 213mr, 227tr, 243mr,bl,br, 279tl, 289ml.

Andrew N. Gagg 57tl,ml, 59tl,tr, 61tl,mr,br, 63tr, 69br, 71br, 73mr, 85br, 93br, 97tl, 103ml, 125br, 141tr, 163tr,br, 165tl,ml, 175mr, 181tr, 193br, 195mr, 205tl, 213bl, 219ml, 231ml,br, 251br, 265tr, 285br, 287br.

(tl = top left; tr = top right; ml = middle left; mr = middle right; bl = bottom left; br = bottom right.)

This edition published by Connaught
an imprint of New Holland Publishers (UK) Ltd
Garfield House, 86-88 Edgware Road, London W2 2EA
www.newhollandpublishers.com

First published in 1993

10 9 8 7 6 5 4 3 2 1

ISBN 978 1 84517 188 9

Commissioning Editor: Charlotte Parry-Crooke
Project Manager: Ann Baggaley
Editorial Assistant: Charlotte Fox
Design: ML Design, London
Artwork: Margaret Tebbs

Cover image © Paul Brough/NHPA

Typeset by ML Design, London
Printed and bound in Singapore by Tien Wah Press (Pte) Ltd

CONTENTS

INTRODUCTION

Plants are one of the most important elements of the natural world and hold a fascination beyond that of their mere usefulness. This is especially true of the largest and most numerous group of plants – those which bear flowers. This group includes annuals, herbaceous perennials, shrubs and trees, but to most of us the term 'wild flowers' implies the smaller plants and bushes, and it is these which are covered here.

Bluebell wood in late spring

A basic requirement for any study of or interest in wild flowers is the ability to put a name to the different kinds encountered. This book is aimed at fulfilling that requirement, enabling you to identify the plants you see in the wild, and providing information on their structure, habitats and distribution which will lead you to a better understanding of the plants themselves.

The book covers the wild flowers of Europe. The number of species recorded for this area has been variously estimated but, excluding trees, is certainly in excess of 10,000, unfortunately far too many to be contained in a single volume. In any case, many are extremely restricted in distribution and often found only in the most inaccessible places, or are identifiable only with expert help. The species included here have therefore been selected to include all of those which are most widespread or likely to be encountered, those which are striking or well known for some reason, and those which are representative of a group of similar species or of particular habitats. All are found in the wild, even if they were originally introduced to Europe from other parts of the world as garden or crop plants and still principally occur in cultivation.

Plants are constrained by physical boundaries such as oceans and mountain ranges rather than by political or economic divisions, so although Europe in a floristic sense has some resemblance to the political outline of the continent there are some major differences. As defined in this book, Europe extends from the Arctic tundra south to the Mediterranean Sea, and from the Atlantic Ocean eastwards to a line running down the Ural mountains to the Caspian Sea, including the Crimean Peninsula but excluding the Caucasian mountains, Anatolian Turkey and the countries south of it as well as the islands of Cyprus and Rhodes. The Atlantic islands of the Azores, Madeira and the Canaries have a distinctive flora of their own and are also omitted.

The main guide runs from pages 52 to 317 and contains photographs and descriptions of the plants. Each species is illustrated – and described on the page opposite in detail. Since it is likely you will be attempting to identify a specimen in flower the plants are mostly depicted in this condition. The descriptions however give additional data on leaves, fruits and general appearance, particularly where these are needed for positive identification. Where similar species exist these are also described and may be illustrated with a marginal drawing to show the differences. How to use this guide is explained in the next section.

The remaining introductory sections provide further information about wild flowers. *How to Identify Wild Flowers* explains the different structures that make up a plant, their variety, how to interpret them correctly, and which are the most useful in identifying wild flowers. The *Glossary* explains any unfamiliar terms which are used in the text. *Classification and Names* deals with the application and usage of both scientific and common names, how plants are classified and how this classification provides information to the user. *History* gives a brief account of the history of the flora in Europe and *Wild Flower Habitats* describes some of the major types of modern vegetation that occur here. The essential diagnostic characters of 97 families are summarised in *Wild Flower Families*. These characters are not always repeated in the individual species descriptions, so in cases of doubt it is worth checking the appropriate family description to be sure no conflicting characters are mentioned there. Finally, the *Key* will help you to determine the species or group of species to which a particular plant belongs before turning to the descriptions to confirm your choice.

The final part of the book contains sections on the *Equipment* you will find useful for observing and recording wild flowers in the field and on the *Conservation* of plants in Europe. *Where to see Wild Flowers in Europe* lists some of the best reserves and protected areas in which to see wild flowers and the particular wild flowers for which they are notable. *Organisations* gives the names and addresses of groups and societies concerned with various aspects of wild flowers. Finally, the *Bibliography* provides a selected list of references which will lead you further into the study of wild flowers.

How to Use this Guide

The species in this guide are arranged in the same order as the families on pages 27 to 39. The order groups closely related families together so in general plants with similar characteristics appear near each other in the book. Occasionally plants which are superficially similar but not at all related will be found on widely separated pages.

Each of the main species covered is illustrated by a photograph and described in detail in the accompanying text. Where a plant is described as 'Resembles **x**', it matches species **x** except for the differences stated in the description. Additional species at the end of some of the descriptions are included when they are either very similar to, or much less common and widespread than the main species. Diagnostic features for these additional species are usually depicted in detailed drawings in the page margin.

Detailed text describes the plants, their flowering periods and distribution.

Marginal figures illustrate additional species, showing the main distinguishing features.

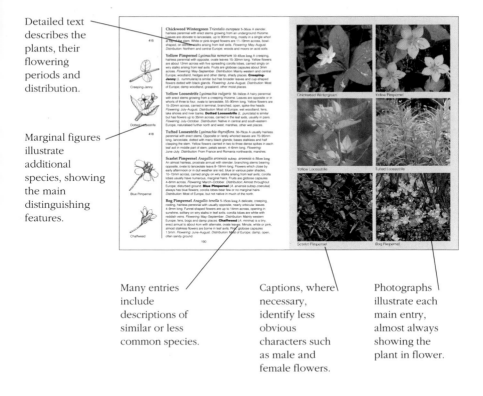

Many entries include descriptions of similar or less common species.

Captions, where necessary, identify less obvious characters such as male and female flowers.

Photographs illustrate each main entry, almost always showing the plant in flower.

The Photographs and Captions

Bog
Pimpernel

Each main entry is illustrated with a photograph. In almost all cases the plant is shown in flower, since this is the stage at which it is most obvious and when you are most likely to want to identify it. Only a few species are shown at the fruiting stage, usually those which have highly visible, distinctive or noteworthy fruits. The species covered in this book range in size from tiny annuals to large perennials and shrubs several metres high. For the larger plants it would be quite impossible always to show both the whole plant and details of its various parts in a single photograph. Every attempt has been made to select photographs which show diagnostic features or which convey the overall character of the plant. Structures such as male and female flowers, fruits which are immature or not otherwise readily recognisable are identified in the captions. All of the plants were photographed in natural habitats.

The Marginal Figures

Grecian
Foxglove: fruit

Further, detailed illustration is provided in the marginal figures. These nearly always relate to the additional species mentioned at the ends of the main descriptions. Normally they show a particular feature or features which allow you to distinguish the additional species from the main one. Occasionally the main differences between the species are solely those of size or colour, neither of which can be shown in this way. In these few cases, the marginal figure shows another character which will help you to identify the plants. As with the photographs less obvious structures are identified in the captions.

The Descriptions

The descriptions provide more detailed information about the plant. Of necessity in a book this size, they are brief, concentrating on those characters which will help you to identify the plant. The common name is printed in **bold**. This is followed by the Latin name in *italics*. For the most part common names are taken from *English Names of Wild Flowers*. The species and their Latin names are essentially those given in *Flora Europaea* but where more up-to-date names are available these are used. The height is the range or upper limit which the plant normally attains. It is, however, only an indication of the size of plant you might expect to find. Growth rates and final size vary considerably with factors including the age of the plant, soil type, and degree of exposure, and exceptions frequently occur. For prostrate species which always grow along the

9

ground, length may be substituted for height.

The order of the text is the standard one found in most botanical descriptions: stems, leaves, inflorescence and flowers, fruits. This makes it easier to compare different descriptions. Not all of these parts are described in every case; those which provide no clues to identity or which contribute little to the overall image of the plant are often excluded. The family descriptions on pages 27 to 39 provide additional characters as well as a more general overview of the species in each family. Although the photographs concentrate on plants which are in flower, the text frequently contains a description of the fruits too. Fruits, at least young ones, often develop while the plant is still flowering, and these can be very helpful in identification.

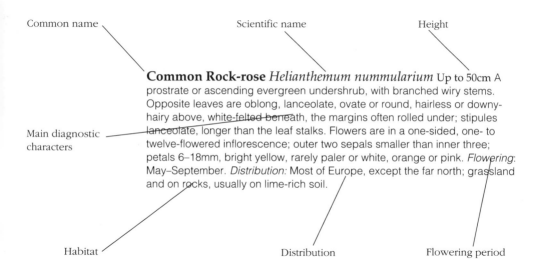

Common name

Scientific name

Height

Common Rock-rose *Helianthemum nummularium* Up to 50cm A prostrate or ascending evergreen undershrub, with branched wiry stems. Opposite leaves are oblong, lanceolate, ovate or round, hairless or downy-hairy above, white-felted beneath, the margins often rolled under; stipules lanceolate, longer than the leaf stalks. Flowers are in a one-sided, one- to twelve-flowered inflorescence; outer two sepals smaller than inner three; petals 6–18mm, bright yellow, rarely paler or white, orange or pink. *Flowering*: May–September. *Distribution*: Most of Europe, except the far north; grassland and on rocks, usually on lime-rich soil.

Main diagnostic characters

Habitat

Distribution

Flowering period

Like the height, the flowering period is an indication only and should be treated with some care. Flowering times within a species may vary widely depending on both local fluctuations in the timing and climate of the seasons from year to year and where in Europe a particular individual is growing. An early spring may affect the flowering times by several weeks. The greatest variation tends to be in species with a broad north-south distribution, with plants in the south flowering in advance of those to the north. The description ends with a brief summary of the distribution of the species in Europe, the habitats in which it commonly occurs and any special ecological factors or points of interest.

How to Identify Wild Flowers

Overall, wild flowers show an enormous range of variation in their habit and in their different parts, leaves, flowers and fruits. At the same time, closely related species may be very similar, differing only in small details, so accurately identifying wild flowers can be quite a challenge. It is important to be sure you are comparing like with like – the 'leaves' of Butcher's-broom for example are actually flattened stems and cannot be compared to the true leaves of its relatives the onions. Characters which are important for distinguishing between the species of one group may be of little or no use when considering the species of a different group. There are no substitutes for accurate observation and experience, but a good understanding of the different structures which make up a wild flower and the range of variation they show is an excellent basis from which to start. This section explains what the different structures are, and how to interpret and compare them. For explanations of some of the less familiar terms see the glossary on page 15.

Type

This refers to whether the plant is annual, biennial or perennial. Annuals complete their life cyle from germination to producing seeds – after which they die – in a single year, although plants which germinate late in the season may occasionally overwinter, flowering and fruiting early in the following year. Biennials usually take two years to complete their life cycle. In the first year they germinate and produce stems and leaves and often lay down large food reserves. In the second year they flower and produce seeds after which, like annuals, they die. A few plants are like biennials but grow for several years before they flower and subsequently die. Perennials do not die after producing seeds but grow and flower year after year. Some are relatively short-lived, gradually declining and eventually dying; others are very long-lived. In species which spread vegetatively to form clumps, the oldest part of the plant, often the centre, may die but it survives as the more recent parts of the clump forming a ring of more vigorous growth. Woody perennials have aerial stems and branches which survive and grow from year to year. They include, of course, shrubs. In herbaceous perennials, the aerial parts die back to ground level in winter, the plant surviving in the form of underground storage organs such as bulbs, corms or fleshy rhizomes.

Habit

This is the term for the growth form of a plant, whether it is erect, ascending, spreading, or prostrate. It is usually a general description, since a plant may have spreading or even prostrate stems with erect branches. The habit may also be affected by the conditions in which the plant is growing such as exposure to wind which can produce stunted plants, especially in shrubs and woody perennials.

Hairs, Scales and Glands

Many plants have a covering of hairs or sometimes scales, called the indumentum. The exact make-up of the indumentum can be very important in identification. You should examine the whole plant carefully with a hand lens, noting whether the hairs occur over the whole plant or just certain parts of it, if they are sparse or dense, long or short, as well as the shape of the hairs and presence or absence of glands at their tips. Hairs can be branched or unbranched. T-shaped hairs are common in members of the Cabbage family while star-shaped or stellate hairs occur in the Mallow family. Gland-tipped hairs may make the plant sticky to the touch as in some Catchflys and Sundews. Stalkless glands on the leaf surface often appear as dark or shiny dots. Examples are found throughout the St John's-wort and Mint families. Some species, notably the Goosefoots and some members of the Primrose family, have a mealy-white covering (actually composed of modified hairs) which is easily rubbed off with a finger.

Stems

Stems offer a number of useful characters, including robustness, colour and degree of hairiness. The shape of the stem in cross-section can be strongly indicative of some groups or even individual species. Square stems are typical of Mints, some Figworts and St John's-worts. Ridged or angled stems occur in Asparagus and Stinking Iris. This book includes various shrubs and these have woody stems, sometimes with well-developed and distinctive bark. We think of shrubs as large plants but many comparatively small plants have woody stems, particularly at the base. These are referred to here as dwarf shrubs. It is important to check whether the stem is truly woody, as these dwarf shrubs are often very small and easily mistaken for herbaceous, i.e. non-woody, perennials.

The degree and pattern of branching of the stem can be significant. The stem may be completely unbranched, or branched only from the base or in the upper half. Some species such as Mistletoe have distinctive, regularly forked stems.

Leaves

Leaves are very variable and provide a multitude of characters which aid in identification. The leaves may be arranged alternately on the stem, in pairs with successive pairs sometimes at ninety degrees to each other, or in whorls. When all confined to the base of the stem, the leaves may form a dense basal rosette.

Size is generally only useful in the crude sense of leaves being very small, small, large or very large. Leaf-size varies with the conditions in which the plant is growing and even with the age of the plant and is difficult to quantify with any degree of precision. The sizes given in the descriptions here are for mature leaves on well-grown plants and are usually expressed as a range, and unless otherwise stated include both blade and stalk. Even so, leaves which fail to reach, or else exceed the sizes given, will sometimes be found. Far more reliable are the overall shape and degree of dissection of the leaf blade.

The overall shapes of leaf blades range from very narrow to circular and may be lobed, cut or divided in a variety of ways. Pinnate leaves have the blade completely divided into two parallel rows of usually paired leaflets. An important character is whether it is terminated by a pair of leaflets, a single leaflet, or sometimes a tendril or spine. Pinnately lobed or cut leaves are similar but with the blade not completely divided. The depth of lobing, expressed as one third of the way to the mid-rib, halfway to the mid-rib and so on, can be diagnostic. Palmate leaves are also completely divided, but with the leaflets radiating from the tip of the leaf stalk, rather like the fingers of a hand. Palmately lobed leaves are similar but, again, incompletely divided. Leaves which have only three leaflets are termed trifoliate; they are common in the Pea family but occur in other groups as well. The margins of leaves and leaflets may be entire (i.e. unbroken), toothed or spiny. If the teeth themselves bear teeth, the leaf is referred to as doubly toothed. Plants of dry or exposed habitats frequently have leaf margins which are rolled under to protect the more vulnerable lower surface. In such cases the leaf may appear to be much narrower than it really is.

Leaf texture can be split into three simple types. The normal type can be thought of as thin. Thicker, leathery leaves occur in many evergreens while others have fleshy, succulent leaves. Leaf colour shows a wider range of variation but, like leaf size, can be dependent on the age of the leaves or the health of the plant. Leaves which are just unfolding are often pinkish or bronzed while markedly yellowish leaves may indicate a sickly plant. The upper leaf surface is often darker than the lower one, and the indumentum may alter the colour, making the leaf appear grey or white if the hairs are very dense. Some species, especially those of coastal habitats, have a distinctive bluish-green coloration to the leaves or even the whole plant.

Stipules are leaf-like growths borne at the base of the leaf stalk. They are not present in all species but when they are can be quite large, in extreme cases even replacing the leaves as the main photosynthetic organs.

Inflorescences

An inflorescence is the arrangement of the flowers and any associated structures such as bracts in plants which have more than one flower. Crowding small flowers together makes them more visible and attractive to pollinators. Bracts are small, leaf-like structures usually found at the base of the flower stalks; bracteoles are additional small bracts. There are many types of inflorescence, classified by their branching patterns and the sequence in which the flowers develop. However they can be grouped into a few broad types. Spikes are generally long, narrow and unbranched. Clusters are broader, often branched and irregular; they may be very dense or open and diffuse. Umbels are a specialised type of cluster in which the flower stalks all arise from the same point and are usually of equal length, giving a more or less flat-topped inflorescence. It is typical of the Carrot family but is also found in other groups such as the Spurges and Onions.

In the Daisy and Teasel families, the inflorescence is called a capitulum and resembles a single large flower. Spurges also have a specialised inflorescence, the cyathium, resembling a single flower. In this case, the individual flowers are reduced to the sexual organs – stamens and ovary.

Flowers

The flowers, together with the leaves, are often the most visible and obvious parts of a plant and are composed of successive whorls of sepals, petals, stamens, and carpels, although any of them may be missing or highly modified.

The sepals – collectively the calyx – protect the flower in bud and are generally green but are sometimes brightly coloured and petal-like. In some species they fall very soon after the flower opens. Sometimes there is an additional whorl of segments, the epicalyx, outside the sepals. The petals collectively form the corolla and are usually brightly coloured to attract pollinating insects. Where the sepals and petals are indistinguishable, they are referred to as perianth segments – collectively the perianth. The perianth segments may be all green and sepal-like or all coloured and petal-like. The shape and especially the number of both sepals and petals are important for identification, as is the degree of fusion of the parts of each whorl.

The overall shape of the flower is largely determined by the petals. It may be regular (radially symmetrical) as in Geraniums or irregular (bilaterally symmetrical) as in Mints and Orchids. Regular flowers may be almost flat or bowl-, cup- or bell-shaped and so on. In many species the lower parts of the petal form a tube with the upper parts wide-spreading. Irregular flowers frequently have the petals fused into a long or short tube with two lobed lips. Flower shape is often a very useful character for assigning plants to their correct families.

The stamens are the male organs of the flower and consist of a sac-like anther containing the pollen on a slender stalk. They may be hidden inside the corolla or project beyond it. The female organs of the flower are carpels. These contain ovules which, after fertilisation, form the seeds. In some families such as the Buttercups the carpels are numerous and remain separate. In others the carpels are few and fused to form a single compound ovary. At the tip of each carpel is a style, a slender stalk bearing the stigma which receives the pollen. In flowers where the carpels are fused the styles are often fused too, only their tips remaining free.

Fruits

The fruits of wild flowers are very varied, ranging from small, single-seeded nutlets to many-seeded berries and large spiny capsules. A simple and practical classification is to divide the fruits into two categories, dry, and juicy or fleshy. Dry fruits can be subdivided into those which open in some way to release the seeds and those which remain closed, releasing the seeds only as they decay. Dry fruits which open include pods and most types of capsule. Dry fruits which remain closed include nuts and the seed-like fruits of families such as the Daisies. Note the structures which may be associated with fruits, such as parachutes of hairs or wing-like bracts and, on fleshy fruits the persistent remains of sepals or petals. These can be helpful in identifying the specimen.

Glossary

Anther	Fertile part of a stamen, containing pollen.
Appendix	Naked and fleshy upper portion of the flower spike in members of the Arum family (Araceae).
Bract	Usually small, leaf-like organ beneath a flower or inflorescence.
Bracteole	Small bract.
Bulb	Underground storage organ composed of fleshy, scale-like leaves.
Calyx	All the sepals of a flower.
Carpel	Female organ of a flower consisting of an ovary, style and stigma.
Corm	Underground storage organ formed from a swollen stem base.
Corolla	All the petals of a flower.
Cyathium	Specialised inflorescence typical of the Spurges, consisting of a cup-shaped structure containing a single, stalked ovary and several stamens.
Disc floret	Very small, tubular flower with equal lobes; typical of members of the Daisy family (Compositae).
Epicalyx	Additional whorl of sepal-like segments lying outside the true sepals.
Hemiparasite	Parasitic plant which obtains some of its food from another plant (the host); it has green pigment and its own root system and is often capable of living completely independently.
Inflorescence	A group of flowers and their particular arrangement, eg. a spike or cluster.
Involucral bract	One of the bracts surrounding a head of small flowers or florets; typical of the Daisy family (Compositae).
Keel	Boat-shaped structure formed by the two lower petals in members of the Pea family (Leguminosae).
Labellum	Lowermost petal of an orchid flower, often specially modified to aid insect pollination; it may be variously shaped, coloured or ornamented.
Lanceolate	Shaped like the blade of a spear, widest below the middle.
Linear	Very narrow, with parallel sides.
Ob-	Prefix applied to shapes, and meaning inverted; thus ob-ovate means egg-shaped but widest above the middle, not below the middle as in ovate.
Ovate	Egg-shaped, widest below the middle.
Palmate	With lobes or leaflets spreading from a single point.
Parasite	Plant completely lacking green pigment and obtaining all its food from another plant (host) via specialised roots called haustoria.
Perianth	All the sepals and petals of a flower.

Pinnate	With two parallel rows of lobes or leaflets.
Ray floret	Very small tubular flower with one side of the apex extended into a long, petal-like strap; typical of the Daisy family (Compositae).
Rhizome	Horizontal, underground stem, sometimes forming a storage organ.
Runner	Slender stem growing along the ground and rooting at intervals to form new plants.
Saprophyte	Plant lacking green pigment and feeding entirely on decaying matter.
Silicula	Pod-like fruit of the Cabbage family that is less than three times as long as wide; it has two halves and a persistent central partition.
Siliqua	A silicula that is more than three times as long as wide.
Spathe	Large, leaf-like bract, often papery or fleshy and brightly coloured.
Standard	Upper petal in members of the Pea family (Leguminosae); often erect.
Stellate	Star-shaped.
Stipule	Usually small, leaf-like organ at base of a leaf-stalk.
Trifoliate	With three leaflets.

Eastern Larkspur:

a) spur

Greater Musk Mallow:

a) sepal; b) epicalyx

Onopordum illyricum:

a) involucral bract

Snowdrop Windflower:

palmate leaf

Ononis arvensis:

trifoliate leaf with a) stipule

Anthyllis barba-jovis:

pinnate leaf

Classification and Names

Classification

This is the process by which plants are divided into a hierarchy of groups. A useful classification system reflects the natural relationships of the plants to each other and provides a rapid and effective means of identifying them. Of the various hierarchical ranks, the most commonly used are family, genus and species. The largest of these is the family. Members of a family all share some common characteristics, such as leaf or flower arrangement, petal number and so on but some families such as the Carrots are more homogenous and easy to recognise than others, for example the Pinks. A family contains a number of similar genera.

A genus is a group of species which are obviously similar and generally share quite a large number of common characters. Genus is an important rank in the hierarchy and often reflects useful data on distribution and ecological preferences.

The lowest of the three ranks is that of species, the basic unit of both classification and the study of its principles and practice – taxonomy. A species includes all populations of a single breeding group of plants which, in normal circumstances, remains separate from other such groups. Members of a species are very similar, sharing many characteristics. Interbreeding between different species of plants takes place much more often than between animal species but the hybrids which result are often sterile or do not breed true. Two further categories below that of species are subspecies and variety. These are used for groups of plants which differ from the rest of the species in usually only one or two characters.

The order of families, genera and species followed here is that used in *Flora Europaea*, the major taxonomic work for European plants.

Names

All plants known to science are given a Latin name consisting of two parts – a binomial. The first part applies to the genus to which the plant belongs eg. *Papaver*, the Poppy genus. The second part denotes the particular species to which the plant belongs. Thus *Papaver somniferum* is the Opium Poppy while *Papaver rhoeas* is the Common Poppy. A major advantage of this system is the inherent implication of relationships and therefore of similarities. Common names, though often charming and evoking an appropriate image of the plant, can also be very confusing. Marsh Marigold and Corn Marigold might be members of the same group and therefore similar. In fact they belong to completely unrelated families (the Buttercups and Daisies respectively) and are very different in appearance. Red Bartsia and Hen-gorse are very different-sounding names for the same plant (*Odontites verna*). Further confusion comes when a name applied in one area refers to another plant altogether in a second area. The Bluebell in Scotland is the moorland Harebell in England, not the more familiar plant of English woodlands which is also called Bluebell. Finally, not all plants have a common name. For these plants there is no other alternative but to use the Latin name.

History

The geologically recent history of plants in Europe is tied to the climate of the continent and to the history of man. The last ice age, which began about one million years ago, brought severe conditions to much of Europe, driving most plants far to the south. Only with the final retreat of the ice around 11,000 years ago were plants able to migrate north again, with cold-tolerant species being the first to re-colonise old ground. Plants of course are unable to move around but, like animals, they do migrate, via their seeds. Small, light air-borne seeds and those carried by birds can be dispersed rapidly over great distances. Larger, heavier seeds are carried for correspondingly short distances and the plants which produce them migrate much more slowly. Rising sea-levels associated with melting glaciers at the end of the ice age caused some areas of Europe such as the British Isles to become isolated as low-lying land was inundated by the sea. Faster-moving species had reached all suitable areas exposed by the retreating ice but slow-moving species did not reach some areas before they were cut off from the main continent.

As southern regions became warmer, plants adapted to cool conditions would have moved northwards following the retreating ice or, where possible, higher into mountain regions since an increase in altitude is accompanied by a decrease in temperature. This explains why many species found today at low altitudes in the far north also occur on mountains in the south. Plants thus isolated in mountain ranges and those confined to islands or other small areas may become cut off from the rest of the population. Over long periods of time, enforced inbreeding causes such small populations to diverge from the more widespread plants and acquire different characteristics until they become recognisable as different subspecies, species or even genera. Species which occur naturally in an area are referred to as native plants. Those which are found in a single, usually restricted, area are known as endemic species. The greatest influence on plants in modern times has undoubtedly been the activities of man. From earliest times, the clearing and draining of land for agriculture, building and development have destroyed many plants and reduced the habitats of others and this destruction has increased. But man has influenced the flora of Europe in other ways too. Many species have been introduced from other parts of the world, some intentionally like ornamental garden flowers, others unintentionally as with many weeds of crops. When such species escape and establish themselves in the wild, becoming fully integrated in the native flora, they are said to be naturalised. Anciently introduced species may have been brought here so long ago that their origins are difficult or impossible to trace. Some never become widespread, occurring only sporadically or as short-lived escapes. Many introduced crops which require a minimal level of cultivation fall into this category. Others have succeeded almost too well, becoming rampant invaders competing aggressively with native species. In a few cases hybrids have appeared between a native species and an introduced species when, in nature, the parents would have remained widely separated. An interesting phenomenon is the introduction of some native species to areas outside Europe followed after a period of time by their inadvertent return to Europe but in a form differing slightly from the native stock.

Wild Flower Habitats

Plants will grow wherever conditions will sustain them, even in very marginal habitats where survival is difficult. They occur from the hottest, driest deserts of the world to the frozen wastes of Antarctica. Most species will tolerate a variety of conditions but nearly all show some degree of preference and some are quite specific in their requirements. Plants with the same preferences are frequently found together, forming recognisable communities. The complete list of species within a community may vary somewhat from place to place, but overall such plant groupings tend to be very similar. Habitats are also seldom homogeneous over a large area. Rather they are mosaics made up of many small or even tiny areas which vary according to local conditions. A knowledge of the major types of habitat and of the plant communities which inhabit them can help in predicting which species will be encountered.

Mountains and Tundra

Wolf's-bane, Yellow Monkshood and Adenostyles in the Italian Alps

Arctic and alpine regions share many plant species and can be treated together, although it is only the higher, colder altitudes of mountains which closely resemble the arctic tundra. Both are harsh habitats in which the major factors affecting plants are low temperatures, exposure and drought. Despite often copious quantities of snow and ice, free water is often in short supply for much of the year, and arctic-alpine species show many adaptations to drought conditions. These include fleshy leaves for storing water, with thick and waxy coatings to reduce water loss. Extensive root systems allow the plants to take advantage of what water is available as well as providing strong anchorage in thin soils or rock crevices of steep cliffs. Biting winds may cause physical damage as well as increased water loss and many arctic-alpines adopt a low-domed or creeping habit to avoid the wind as much as possible. An added advantage is that the air temperature within a tight leafy cushion is slightly higher than that of the surrounding air, helping to prevent the frost damage which occurs when ice crystals form in the plant's cells and rupture them. Dense hairs on leaves and stems also provide protection from the cold.

The weight of heavy snow falls can break the branches from trees, causing severe damage. By contrast deep snow can be advantageous to low-growing plants by providing an insulating blanket. A number of alpine species are specialised 'snow-patch' plants, found where snow lies late in the season and provides protection from late bursts of bad weather. Snowbells are typical snow-patch plants. Early flowerers, their flower stalks generate heat, melting a passage through the covering snow so that the blossoms can emerge undamaged.

Summers in mountains and tundra are short, giving plants little time to grow and they may have to complete their reproduction in as little as a few weeks, from flowering through to seed dispersal. Arctic-alpines are mostly perennials, and use food reserves built up in the previous year to burst quickly into growth. In order to flower rapidly, flower buds may be formed at the end of the season but remain dormant and unopened until the next year when they can mature and bloom with great speed. The flowers of arctic and alpine plants are often disproportionately large and colourful and may offer attractions for pollinators besides nectar. Mountain Avens is only one example where the flowers act as parabolic mirrors. They reflect and concentrate the sun's rays within the bowl of the flower so that the temperature there is higher than the ambient. Insects alighting in the flowers are warmed, aiding their metabolism and encouraging them to seek the next floral 'hot-spot', effecting cross-pollination. Another flowering strategy encountered in these habitats is vivipary, in which small plantlets are produced in place of some or all of the flowers in the inflorescence. When the plantlets fall from the parent they can grow into new individuals faster than can seeds.

Woodlands

This is really a group of habitats, differing from each other depending on the type of trees forming the wood. Deciduous woods and evergreen woods provide quite different conditions while mixed woods combine some of the characters of each.

Coniferous woods such as pine or spruce woods have little or no ground flora or understorey of shrubs. The dense canopy of evergreen foliage means light levels within the wood are too low for any but the most shade-tolerant species to survive. This is especially true of many plantations, where the trees are deliberately planted close together. The needles of coniferous trees are highly resistant to decay. Over the years they build up to form a deep litter on the woodland floor, further discouraging the growth of herbs. There are some plants which grow in these conditions, particularly saprophytes such as Yellow Bird's-nest which do not rely on photosynthesis.

Broad-leaved evergreen woods of the Mediterranean, dominated by Evergreen Oak (*Quercus ilex*) are also dark and densely canopied, with some tall shrubs and many climbers but few ground dwelling herbs. However, little of the original dense forest remains in these regions, most of the woods nowadays being much thinner and more open. These have a well-developed flora of both shrubs and herbs, mostly those typical of maquis and garigue habitats.

Deciduous woods show a much greater variety. Shrubs form an understorey to the main canopy while herbs provide the ground flora. Shade-loving plants of course abound, but many woods support a diverse and quite different spring flora. This consists of flowers which bloom and grow early, before the trees reach full leaf and light levels are still high. By the time the canopy is complete in summer their main growth is over and they are already becoming dormant until the next spring. Similarly woodland margins, glades and rides are richer in ground species because light is able to penetrate to the woodland floor. This effect is seen to perfection in

Ransoms in a hazel coppice

woods which are still coppiced. In this woodland management system suckers are allowed to grow from the stumps of felled trees. After a few years, the suckers have developed into sizeable trunks and are in turn harvested, starting the cycle again. When the trees are first felled, there is an explosion of flowers as light reaches the newly cleared woodland floor. This profusion lasts until the tree suckers have grown sufficiently to provide some shade, when the numbers and diversity of flowers begins to dwindle until, when the suckers are mature, only typical shade-loving woodland species remain. When the trees are next felled, the whole process is repeated.

Beech woods are something of an exception. On rich soils they have a ground flora typical of deciduous woodland. On poor soils a deep layer of undecayed leaves accrues on the floor and smothers most flowers, and beech woods have a characteristic bare look between the trees.

Ancient woods are very stable plant communities and some flowers are good general indicators of age. Ramsons (*Allium ursinum*) for example, only occurs in old, undisturbed woods. Hedgerows, which are effectively narrow, linear woods, may show similar signs. Bluebells are woodland flowers. When found in a hedgerow, they indicate that the hedge is a remnant of an older and once more extensive wood.

Heaths and Moors

European heathlands and moors occur in the regions bordering the Atlantic and North Sea coasts. They are essentially similar habitats, heathlands being dry while moorlands are wet. However the two types intergrade and the distinction is not always clear cut; in any case many species occur in both habitats. Heaths are generally tree-less and exposed places, always with very peaty soil. Peat makes the soil acid, even when the underlying rock is neutral or basic. It is mineral-deficient and poorly aerated.

The vegetation is dominated by dwarf, twiggy shrubs with small evergreen leaves. They are typically members of the Heath family but many other, unrelated, heathland plants have evolved similar 'ericoid' features. The dwarf habit is a useful adaptation to the exposed, windswept conditions. The small, often needle- or scale-like evergreen leaves cut down water loss. The roots of all members of the Heath family form an association (termed mycorrhiza) with a fungus which allows them to grow well in the poor soil and most species are adapted to and indeed require very acid conditions. The most common species on heaths and moors is Heather, but on higher and more exposed sites Bilberry may become the dominant shrub, producing Bilberry moors. Although low and rather open, the shrubs form a canopy and the large stands of similar sized and often crowded plants act as a windbreak.

Heathland is a natural habitat, but heaths have also been deliberately extended in suitable areas by felling woodland and allowing the heath and moorland vegetation to develop in their place. Heathland provides grazing for stock and for game birds such as the Red Grouse which is endemic to Scotland. Such areas are managed by periodic burning of old stands of Heather, usually every ten years or

so. Heather seeds need bare ground on which to germinate. Burning clears the ground, allowing new Heather plants to become established and produce plenty of new growth as food and cover for animals and birds.

Moorlands can occur in upland or lowland regions, wherever the combination of water and peaty soil is right. Upland moors are usually wet due solely to high rainfall. Lowland moors may be wet because drainage is poor. In moorland areas

Bell Heather on Dartmoor, south Devon

which are even wetter than usual bogs can form. These are areas dominated by the moss *Sphagnum*, a plant which to some extent controls and maintains the high acidity of the surroundings. These bogs are very poor in nutrients, especially nitrogen, and it is here that carnivorous plants such as Sundews and Bladderworts are most common. By supplementing the available nutrients by trapping and digesting insects, they are able to make a home where other species cannot.

Maquis

Garigue: southern France

This habitat is typical of the Mediterranean and southern Europe and contains some of the most striking and colourful plant communities. Like the heathlands of northern Europe it is dominated by evergreen shrubs, though these are of a very different type to those found on heaths. As with the northern heathlands, many areas of maquis reflect man's interference with nature. Maquis occurs naturally on the margins of evergreen forests and coasts but can also be the first stage in the degeneration from forest to bare ground. As the Mediterranean forests are cleared they are replaced by maquis which is now the more widespread community in this region. Maquis vegetation consists principally of dense, twiggy shrubs with small, leathery and often aromatic leaves. Intense sunshine builds up the levels of essential oils in the plants and on a hot summer day the air may be heavy with their scent. Characteristic and common species include members of the Rockrose and Pea families, especially Brooms.

Maquis can be subdivided into several types of plant community, but the two most commonly recognised are high maquis and low maquis. High maquis is exactly that, with the shrubs growing as much as five metres tall. Scattered among the shrubs are occasional trees, particularly Evergreen and Kermes Oaks (*Quercus ilex* and *Q. coccifera*). In low maquis the shrubs seldom top two metres and trees are conspicuously absent.

Maquis species provide many exploitable products and if further interference is too great the maquis degenerates into garigue. This degraded form of maquis consists of low and often spiny or densely hairy shrubs generally less than half a metre tall interspersed with rocks and patches of bare ground. It is a community rich in species. Members of the Mint family are common here, particularly those we recognise as culinary plants such as Thyme and Sage, and there are large numbers of herbs, especially bulbs and orchids. Garigue, also known as phrygana in the east and tomillares in the west, is extensive in the hottest and driest parts of the Mediterranean region. Most garigue species are early-flowering and by summer are largely over. Soil-type has a greater effect on garigue than on maquis and local variations can produce markedly different plant communities.

Further degradation, usually by overgrazing, destroys the remaining shrubs and causes soil erosion. Only annuals and deep-rooted perennials survive. These regions, called steppe, have an extremely brief flowering period in spring then turn sere and parched until the autumn rains fall.

Grasslands

Like woodlands, grasslands are a mixture of related habitats, including upland and lowland meadows, steppes and even lawns and verges. They vary considerably in terms of geology, soil chemistry and water content for example and therefore in species composition but all are open habitats dominated, of course, by grasses. Except for mountain meadows above the tree-line and some areas where the soil is very thin, most grasslands are unnatural habitats and would eventually revert to woodland unless tree and shrub seedlings are prevented from establishing themselves by continuous grazing by wild animals such as rabbits, or by domesticated ones such as cattle.

Grasses are unique in having their growing points situated at the bases of the leaves and stems. Removal of the tips does no irreparable damage to the plant which quickly recovers and continues to grow. Not so other plants, which have their growing points at the tips of the shoots. Loss of the upper portions of the leaves and stems greatly restricts further growth and may prevent flowering and thus seed production, or even kill the plant. Grassland flowers have various strategies for overcoming this problem. One solution is to develop some form of protection such as the spines of thistles or poisons. Buttercups contain poisonous alkaloids and are unpalatable to animals. Another solution is to have leaves grouped in low-growing rosettes. Many species have adopted this habit, including plantains and members of the Pink and Daisy families. The buds of grassland flowers are usually produced at or near soil-level, well out of harm's way. However, the flowers must be raised to at least the height of the surrounding vegetation in order to be visible to pollinators. Rosette plants tend to have their flowers grouped at the top of a long, bare stem.

Grassland with Bunch-flowered Daffodils

Newly established grasslands are species-poor but old ones can be very rich in wild flowers. There are many species which are good indicators of particular conditions and even of the age of the grassland. Horse-shoe Vetch and the Milkweeds are lime-loving species or calcicoles found in chalky areas such as downland while Sheep's-bit is lime-hating or calcifuge and only occurs in neutral or acid grassland. The presence of Kidney-vetch is a good sign of an old, well-established turf. Competition is fierce, with little room in the crowded turf for new plants to establish so most species are perennials, the few annuals appearing in very small areas such as hoof-prints and old cowpats. Land use is also a major factor influencing the diversity of flowers. Modern, intensively farmed grasslands are generally poorer in species than those managed by traditional methods. Conversely some plants benefit from an intense regime of regularly mowing. Daisies and Dandelions for example grow best in short turf; they are soon swamped if the grass is left uncut.

Disturbed Sites

Any area where the soil has been turned counts as a disturbed site. They can have rich or poor soil, are often rubble-strewn and occur in towns as readily as in the countryside. Arable land, gardens, waste ground, demolition sites and even rubbish dumps all qualify. These are frequently rich areas for wild flowers. They may contain many introduced and even exotic species, but the majority are those usually regarded as 'weeds'. These are opportunistic plants superbly adapted to compete in a challenging and changing environment. Most have high reproductive rates, and may exhibit a range of other adaptations to ensure success.

In greatly disturbed sites, such as freshly ploughed land, all previous plant residents may have been swept away, leaving a completely bare habitat. Subsequent colonisation by plants follows a quite well defined succession. The first plants to appear are generally annuals with light seeds which are easily dispersed or those, like poppies, whose seeds have remained buried in the soil from the last period of disturbance. These early pioneers have rapid life-cycles, germinating, flowering and setting seed in a very short time. By producing several generations within a season, they can quickly cover large areas before competition from other species becomes too intense.

Following behind are slower-growing annuals and the first perennials. The perennials are often species which spread vegetatively, by means of runners, creeping rhizomes, rooting stems or similar means which allow them to quickly establish large patches.

Colonisation continues as more perennials invade. Competition for space increases and the earliest invaders gradually become squeezed and shaded out. Eventually the number of new arrivals decreases and the community becomes more stable, taking on the characteristics of the habitat it will eventually become, whether grassland, woodland or any other. The succession may be interrupted at any point by further disturbance of the soil, when the cycle begins again.

Coastal Habitats

Coasts embrace a range of habitats but all of them have high levels of salinity, both of the water and of the soil. Plants which can tolerate such salty conditions are called halophytes. Most can cope with salt-laden winds and spray or occasional immersion in sea water. A few withstand periodic immersion and a very few, such as the Sea-grasses, live completely submerged in the sea. Terrestrial halophytes are often stiff plants with a waxy coating on their leaves to prevent damage and salt absorption. This gives them the bluish appearance seen in many coastal plants. A dense layer of hairs serves a similar purpose. Somewhat paradoxically water, i.e. fresh water, is precious here and coastal plants show many of the features normally associated with desert plants. Succulence is a common feature of

A species of Sand Crocus (*Romulea revelierei*) on a Corsican beach

halophytes, with water stored in fleshy leaves and stems, and the waxy coating which keeps salt out also helps to keep water in. A reduction in the surface area of the leaves is another water-retention feature commonly found in coastal plants.

Cliff plants have strong roots to provide a firm anchorage on the often precarious surfaces where they grow. They tolerate salt spray carried on the wind but their seeds may need to be more resistant and capable of surviving in the sea for some time as this is often the only practical method of dispersal to new sites.

Salt-marsh plants grow on accreting areas of mud below the level of the highest tides. They too must be securely rooted and able to tolerate periodic immersion in sea water and withstand mechanical damage caused by waves. Species which need the least time between immersions in which to germinate grow nearest the water. Those needing most time to become established grow furthest up the marsh.

Shingle banks and shorelines support a variety of plants. A major problem here is the poor water-retention of gravel. Shingle plants typically have long or extensive root systems to offset this and to provide anchorage in the shifting soil. Similar adaptations are found in dune plants which must also withstand occasional burial by wind-blown sand. Annuals find such conditions difficult and most species encountered are perennials which spread vegetatively. This movement of substrate is similar to that found in disturbed sites and both habitats often have a high organic content – manure on arable land, rotting seaweed on coasts. It is not surprising that a number of plants familiar as arable weeds are also seen along shorelines.

Wild Flower Families

The species covered in this guide are grouped into 97 families whose essential characteristics are described here. Not all of the family names may be familiar but the European genera within each family are listed at the end of the description. Some of the families also contain tree species but the description applies only to the herbaceous and shrubby members of the family.

Willows Family Salicaceae p.52
Mainly deciduous trees or large shrubs but a few arctic and alpine species are extremely dwarfed, with creeping or even underground stems. Leaves are alternate. The flowers lack a perianth and are borne in catkins, males and females on different plants. The seeds, tufted with white hairs, are wind-dispersed. Genera: *Salix*.

Bog-myrtles Family Myricaceae p.52
A small family represented in Europe only by shrubs. They have alternate leaves and are densely dotted with aromatic yellow oil glands. The male and female flowers lack sepals and petals. The fruit is slightly fleshy. Genera: *Myrica*.

Birches Family Betulaceae p.52
A family of deciduous trees and tall shrubs and, in Europe, one dwarf shrub. Leaves alternate. The flowers lack a perianth; male and female catkins are borne on the same plant. Female catkins are cylindrical and cone-like in fruit, consisting of winged nutlets and lobed scales. Genera: *Betula*.

Nettles and Hops Families Urticaceae and Cannabidaceae pp.52–54
Plants with stipules at the base of the leaf stalks and unisexual flowers lacking petals. Nettles are herbs or sometimes shrubs, often armed with numerous stinging hairs. The leaves may be opposite or alternate. Male and female flowers in the same cluster, in different clusters or on different plants. Males have four sepals, females sometimes lack sepals. Hops are twining climbers with opposite, palmately lobed leaves. Male and female flowers borne on different plants, males in branched clusters, females in papery, cone-like heads. Urticaceae. Genera: *Parietaria, Urtica*. Cannabidaceae. Genera: *Humulus*.

Sandal-woods Family Santalaceae p.54
A family of mostly perennial and sometimes woody herbs, shrubs and (outside Europe) trees. Many species are semi-parasitic on the roots of other plants. In European species the leaves are alternate and narrow. Small flowers often greenish, with a three-, four- or five-lobed perianth. The fruit is either a small stone-fruit or a small nut. Genera: *Osyris, Thesium*.

Mistletoes Family Loranthaceae p.54
A family of semi-parasitic plants including trees, shrubs and climbers but represented in Europe by small shrubs which grow on tree branches. They have regularly forked stems and opposite leaves. Unisexual flowers are yellowish-green. The fruit is usually a berry. Genera: *Loranthus, Viscum*.

Rafflesias Family Rafflesiaceae p.54
A very small and mainly tropical family of totally parasitic plants. Perennials lacking chlorophyll and with scale-like leaves, they have unisexual flowers in dense spikes. The fruit is a berry. Genera: *Cytinus*.

Birthworts Family Aristolochiaceae p.56
A mostly tropical family with two genera extending into the warmer parts of Europe. They

are rhizomatous perennials or climbers with alternate leaves. Flowers are tubular, often S-shaped and in some species smell of rotten meat. The fruit is a slightly fleshy capsule. Genera: *Aristolochia, Asarum.*

Knotweeds Family Polygonaceae pp.56–58
A family of herbs and a few climbers, widespread in temperate regions. The distinctive character of the family is the presence of an ochrea (*plural* ochreae) - a membranous sheath enclosing the stem at each of the joints. The size, shape and colour of the ochreae are important in identification. Small flowers usually have six perianth segments, often arranged in two whorls of three. The inner whorl may enlarge in fruit, enclosing the three-sided nutlet. Genera: *Fagopyrum, Fallopia, Persicaria, Polygonum, Rumex.*

Goosefoots Family Chenopodiaceae pp.58–62
This family contains many coastal and arid-zone plants, as well as common weeds and a few well-known vegetables. Mostly herbs or shrubs, their stems are often fleshy and jointed. Leaves are alternate, rarely opposite. Small green flowers usually have a calyx but no corolla. In many species the whole plant is covered with a farina – a mealy white coating easily rubbed off with a finger. Genera: *Atriplex, Beta, Chenopodium, Halimione, Salicornia, Salsola, Sarcocornia, Sueda.*

Pigweeds Family Amaranthaceae p.62
Mostly herbs with a few climbers. Leaves are alternate or opposite. The inflorescences are often long and bristly with pointed bracts which may be brightly coloured. Small flowers have three to five sepals but petals are absent. Genera: *Amaranthus.*

Mesembryanthemums Family Aizoaceae p.62
In Europe a very small family though widespread in warmer regions, especially South Africa. They are herbs with thick fleshy leaves. Flowers superficially resemble those of the daisy family, with numerous strap-shaped, petal-like segments. The fruit is enclosed in the persistent, fleshy calyx. Genera: *Carpobrotus, Mesembryanthemum.*

Portulaccas Family Portulacaceae p.62
Annuals and perennials, usually succulent and occasionally aquatic, with alternate or opposite leaves. The flowers may be solitary or in clusters. Each has two sepals, and five petals which may be joined. The fruit is a capsule containing often shiny seeds. Genera: *Claytonia, Montia.*

Pinks Family Caryophyllaceae pp.64–72
Most species of this family are herbaceous but a few form small shrubs. The leaves are nearly always opposite with the pairs alternating on different sides of the stem and are usually entire. Flowers are frequently borne in a regularly forked inflorescence. There are four to five sepals often fused to form a tubular calyx, and the same number of petals (petals rarely absent). The number of styles, ranging from two to five, is important in identifying different genera. Fruit usually a capsule, rarely a berry. Capsules have either the same number of teeth as there are styles, or twice as many. A large and widespread family containing many ornamentals and a number of common weeds. Genera: *Agrostemma, Arenaria, Cerastium, Cucubalus, Dianthus, Gypsophila, Herniaria, Honkenya, Illecebrum, Lychnis, Minuartia, Moehringia, Paronychia, Petrorhagia, Sagina, Saponaria, Scleranthus, Silene, Spergula, Spergularia, Stellaria, Vaccaria.*

Water-lilies Family Nymphaeaceae p.72
Aquatic perennials, principally found in still and slow-moving water. Rhizomes bear large, broadly oval to circular and long-stalked leaves which float on the surface. Numerous spirally arranged petals are not clearly differentiated from the stamens, the one gradually passing into the other. Genera: *Nymphaea, Nuphar.*

Buttercups Family Ranunculaceae pp.74–84

A very large family of temperate and arctic herbs, some aquatic, with a few woody climbers. The leaves are usually alternate and often deeply lobed or divided into leaflets. The flowers are regular or irregular. The perianth segments may be all petal-like, or the outer whorl of green or coloured and petal-like sepals, the inner whorl of petals or of variously shaped nectar-bearing structures sometimes called honey-leaves. Genera: *Aconitum, Adonis, Anemone, Aquilegia, Caltha, Clematis, Consolida, Delphinium, Eranthis, Helleborus, Hepatica, Myosurus, Nigella, Pulsatilla, Ranunculus, Thalictrum, Trollius.*

Peonies Family Paeoniaceae p.84

A small family of perennial herbs with woody stems, outside Europe also shrubs, sometimes evergreen. The large, alternate leaves are much divided into lobes. Flowers are solitary, large and showy with four to five sepals and five to eight or more petals. There are numerous stamens. Dry, pod-like fruits form a head. Various species and cultivars are grown as ornamentals. Most of the European species have very restricted distributions. Genera: *Paeonia.*

Barberries Family Berberidaceae p.84

Perennial herbs and shrubs, some of them spiny. Leaves are alternate or whorled and often divided into segments. The flowers typically have two whorls of sepal-like perianth segments and four to five whorls of petal-like segments. Many species are grown as ornamentals. Genera: *Berberis, Leontice.*

Poppies Family Papaveraceae pp.86-88

Annual or perennial herbs, usually exuding white or coloured latex from broken or cut stems. The alternate leaves are often deeply lobed or divided. Most species have two sepals which fall soon after the four crumpled petals unfold. The fruit is a capsule containing numerous small seeds. It is either narrow and opens by valves or pepper-pot shaped with a ring of pores beneath the rim. Most of the family have showy flowers and many species are grown as ornamentals. Genera: *Chelidonium, Escholtzia, Glaucium, Meconopsis, Papaver, Roemeria.*

Fumitories Family Fumariaceae p.88

Annual and perennial herbs with often brittle stems. Some species scramble up through surrounding vegetation. The alternate leaves are much divided into small segments. The flowers, borne in spikes or clusters, are irregular, usually with one or both of the outer petals having a sac-shaped spur at the base and the inner two petals often joined together. The fruit is a small many-seeded capsule or a single-seeded nutlet. Genera: *Corydalis, Fumaria, Hypecoum.*

Capers Family Capparidaceae p.88

Annuals or shrubby perennials with alternate leaves. The flowers have four sepals and four petals; there are either six or many stamens. The fruit is either a berry or a dry capsule. Genera: *Capparis.*

Cabbages Family Cruciferae pp.90–104

A very large family distributed world-wide. It contains mostly herbs and a few small shrubs. The leaves are alternate and the flowers are usually borne in long spikes or clusters. The four sepals, though not joined, form a tube. The four petals each have a narrow lower portion and a broad upper portion which spreads above the sepal tube, forming the characteristic cross shape for which the family is named. There are usually six stamens. The fruit is a capsule which is usually divided internally by a thin wall or septum. The relative dimensions of the fruit and orientation of the septum are particularly important for identification. Fruits which are more than three times as long as wide are called siliquas; those which are less than three times as long as wide are called siliculas. Many members of the family are of economic importance, either as vegetables and salad plants or as ornamentals such as annual bedding plants. Others are widespread weeds, particularly annual species. Genera: *Aethionema, Alliaria, Alyssum, Arabidopsis, Arabis, Armoracia, Barbarea, Berteroa, Biscutella, Brassica, Bunias, Cakile, Camelina, Capsella, Cardamine, Cardaria, Cochlearia, Coronopus, Crambe, Diplotaxis, Draba, Erophila, Eruca, Erucastrum, Erysimum, Hesperis, Hornungia, Hutchinsia, Iberis, Isatis, Lepidium, Lobularia, Lunaria, Matthiola, Moricandia, Petrocallis, Raphanus, Rhyncosinapis, Rorippa, Sinapis, Sisymbrium, Teesdalia, Thlaspi.*

Mignonettes Family Resedaceae p.104
A small family of annual, biennial and perennial herbs with alternate leaves. Flowers are borne in spikes at the tips of the stems. They have four to eight sepals and the same number of petals but these may be so deeply divided or fringed as to appear more. The fruit is usually a capsule. Genera: *Reseda.*

Sundews Family Droseraceae p.106
A small family of insectivorous perennials. The leaves, which are used to catch and digest prey, are often arranged in a basal rosette. They are either active traps which respond to trigger-hairs by snapping shut or bear long, sticky, gland-tipped and mobile hairs. Flowers have parts in fives. Plants of nutrient deficient, usually wet and acidic habitats. Genera: *Aldrovanda, Drosera.*

House-leeks Family Crassulaceae pp.106–108
Annuals, biennials and perennials, all with thick fleshy and succulent leaves. The leaves are opposite or alternate, often in rosettes. The flowers are borne in clusters or spikes. There may be three to 20 sepals and an equal number of petals but usually twice as many. The fruits are pod-like. Most species grow in rocky places, often at high altitudes; many are grown as ornamentals. Genera: *Crassula, Jovibarba, Sedum, Sempervivum, Umbilicus.*

Saxifrages Family Saxifragaceae pp.108–110
Herbs, mostly perennials and many of them succulent. The leaves are alternate, often in basal rosettes. The flowers have four or five sepals and petals and usually twice as many stamens. The fruit is a capsule containing numerous seeds. Genera: *Chrysosplenium, Parnassia, Saxifraga.*

Currants Family Grossulariaceae p.112
Small shrubs with alternate, palmately lobed leaves. The five sepals and five petals sit on a special cup-shaped structure (the *hypanthium*) joined to the ovary. The fruit is a berry. Genera: *Ribes.*

Roses Family Rosaceae pp.112–118
A family containing a wide range of herbaceous plants as well as many shrubs and trees. The alternate leaves may be undivided, lobed, pinnate or rarely palmate. The often showy flowers usually have five sepals and five petals, often seated on a cup-shaped structure (the *hypanthium*). The fruits are structurally very diverse, from dry or pod-like fruits to burrs, berries, stone-fruits and firm fleshy fruits such as apples. This very large family occurs worldwide but especially in the temperate northern hemisphere. It includes some of the most widely cultivated ornamentals and fruits in the world. Genera: *Agrimonia, Alchemilla, Aphanes, Aruncus, Dryas, Filipendula, Fragaria, Geum, Potentilla, Rosa, Rubus, Sanguisorba, Sarcopoterium, Spiraea.*

Peas Family Leguminosae pp.120–138
Herbaceous plants, shrubs and trees with alternate, frequently trifoliate or pinnate leaves.

Many species climb, some by twining stems, others by means of tendrils. The five-petalled flowers have a very characteristic structure; the upper petal (*standard*) is erect, the side pair (*wings*) spreading while the lower pair are fused to form a boat-shaped structure (*keel*) enclosing the stamens and ovary. The fruit is a dry, slender, usually many-seeded pod called a legume. A very large family containing many ornamentals and one of the most important families for crop and fodder plants. In addition, almost all species develop root nodules containing nitrogen-fixing bacteria which help the plants grow and make them valuable as green manure. Genera: *Anthyllis, Astragalus, Chamaecytisus, Chamaespartium, Colutea, Coronilla, Cytisus, Dorycnium, Galega, Genista, Hedysarum, Hippocrepis, Lathyrus, Lotus, Lupinus, Medicago, Melilotus, Onobrychis, Ononis, Ornithopus, Oxytropis, Psoralea, Tetragonolobus, Trifolium, Trigonella, Spartium, Ulex, Vicia.*

Crane's-bills Family Geraniaceae pp.140–142
Annuals and perennials, usually softly glandular-hairy, many of them aromatic. Leaves are usually alternate and palmately or pinnately divided into lobes or separate leaflets. The flowers have parts in fives and are frequently pink, reddish or purplish. The fruit consists of five single-seeded segments joined at the base of a column – the characteristic 'bird's beak' of the family name – formed by the persistent stigmas. These roll upwards towards the tip of the column or coil spirally when the ripe segments separate. Genera: *Erodium, Geranium.*

Caltrops Family Zygophyllaceae p.142
In Europe a small family of herbs and shrubs often growing in arid places. The leaves are pinnate, with paired, often persistent and spiny stipules. The flowers have parts in fours or fives. Genera: *Fagonia, Tribulus.*

Flaxes Family Linaceae p.142
All European members of this family are slender herbs or small shrubs. The leaves are usually alternate, narrow and entire. The flowers are four- or five-petalled. The fruit is a rounded capsule. Genera: *Linum, Radiola.*

Wood Sorrels Family Oxalidaceae p.144
Small herbs, often with bulbs or creeping rhizomes. Leaves trifoliate, often folding downwards at night. The solitary or clustered flowers are five-petalled, yellow, pink to purple, rarely white. The fruit is a capsule. Genera: *Oxalis.*

Spurges Family Euphorbiaceae pp.144–146
A very large and widespread family. The majority of species are herbs, some of them succulent, a few are shrubs and (outside Europe) trees. Most species exude a milky latex when cut or broken. Leaves are alternate, opposite or in whorls. Unisexual flowers are usually borne in separate clusters and sometimes on different plants or together in specialised inflorescences. There may be three, four, five or six sepals depending on the genus; petals, if present, equal the number of sepals. In the Spurge genus (*Euphorbia*) the 'flowers' actually represent modified and much reduced inflorescences called *cyathia*. Each cup-shaped cyathium has a central, stalked ovary (representing the female flower) surrounded by several stamens (the reduced male flowers) and four horn-shaped glands on the rim. The whole may be enclosed by several green, petal-like bracts. The shape and colour of the glands are important diagnostic features. The fruit is a usually capsule. Genera: *Euphorbia, Mercurialis, Ricinus.*

Rues Family Rutaceae pp.146–148
Herbs, shrubs and trees, often with evergreen and aromatic foliage dotted with oil glands. Flower parts in fours or fives. This family contains commercially important plants, notably the citrus fruits. Genera: *Dictamnus, Ruta.*

Milkworts Family Polygalaceae p.148

Small herbs or occasionally small shrubs, usually of grassland and open places. Leaves are mostly alternate. The irregular flowers have three small outer sepals and two much larger, petal-like inner sepals. The three petals are partially joined into a crested tube which is partially or wholly concealed by the inner sepals. The stamens are also joined to form a tube. Genera: *Polygala.*

Balsams Family Balsaminaceae p.148

Only six species of this mainly tropical family occur in Europe; five of them are introductions. They are herbs with translucent stems and mostly alternate leaves. The flowers hang from slender stalks and are strongly irregular. There are three sepals, the lower one large and petal-like and forming a backward pointing spur. The lower four petals are united in two pairs so the flower appears to have only three petals, not the true number of five. The fruit is a capsule which opens explosively when ripe. Genera: *Impatiens.*

Mallows Family Malvaceae pp.148–150

A very large family, mostly of herbs and small, soft-wood shrubs but with a few tree species. The alternate leaves are often palmately lobed. The showy flowers have an epicalyx as well as usually five sepals and five large petals. The sepals are fused for part or most of their length. The numerous stamens are fused to form a long central column. The fruit is variable, depending on the genus. This family includes many well-known ornamentals. Genera: *Abelmoschus, Alcea, Althaea, Hibiscus, Lavatera, Malva.*

Spurge-laurels Family Thymelaeaceae pp.150–152

In Europe, small deciduous or evergreen shrubs and a few herbs, all containing poisonous compounds. Leaves are usually alternate, sometimes very small. Flowers have a sometimes coloured tube bearing the four petal-like sepals at the rim. The fruit may be dry or fleshy and berry-like. Genera: *Daphne, Thymelaea.*

St John's-worts Family Hypericaceae p.152

Herbs, usually perennials, and small shrubs with stalkless leaves dotted with translucent glands. Showy flowers always yellow, usually in clusters at the tips of stems and branches, with five petals and numerous stamens grouped into bundles. The fruit is a dry capsule or a berry. In Europe the family is represented only by the St John's-wort genus itself. Genera: *Hypericum.*

Violets Family Violaceae p.154

A large and widespread family but only the Violet genus (*Viola*) occurs in Europe. They are annuals or perennials with alternate leaves and often conspicuous, leafy stipules. The flowers are irregular, with five sepals and five petals, the sepals with backward-pointing flaps and the lowermost petal also extended backwards to form a nectar-filled spur. Small, self-pollinated flowers which never open are sometimes produced towards the end of the flowering period. The fruit is a capsule. Many species are cultivated as garden ornamentals or as a source of perfumed oils. Genera: *Viola.*

Rock-roses Family Cistaceae pp.156–158

Shrubs and herbs, many from the Mediterranean region. The leaves are usually opposite, only occasionally alternate or whorled in a basal rosette; at least the underside has a dense covering of starry hairs. Sepals three, or five with the two outer often smaller than the three inner. The five petals are often crumpled and quickly fade. The fruit is a capsule. Genera: *Cistus, Fumana, Halimium, Helianthemum, Tuberaria.*

Sea-heaths Family **Frankeniaceae** p.158

A small family of annuals and woody perennial herbs typically growing in saline habitats. Small, opposite leaves are often hairy and inrolled. Small five-petalled flowers are solitary at tips and in forks of branches. The fruit is a capsule enclosed in the persistent calyx. Genera: *Frankenia*.

Gourds Family **Cucurbitaceae** p.158

Climbing or trailing herbs, often with coiled tendrils and palmately lobed leaves. Flowers are unisexual, the sexes sometimes borne on different plants; they have a deeply five-lobed corolla. The fruit is a berry, often with a hard rind. This family contains numerous fruits and vegetables such as cucumbers, marrows and melons, many of them grown on a large scale outdoors in the warmer parts of Europe and under glass in cooler areas. Genera: *Bryonia, Ecballium.*

Cacti Family **Cactaceae** p.160

Shrubby plants with succulent green stems often spiny and with tufts of short barbed hairs. The leaves are either absent or small and soon shed. Flowers have numerous perianth segments and stamens surmounting a fleshy base. The fruit is a berry and often spiny. A very large family typical of arid regions in the New World; there are no native European species but several are widespread as introductions. Many species are grown as indoor plants. Genera: *Opuntia.*

Loosestrifes Family **Lythraceae** p.160

Annual or perennial herbs with opposite or sometimes whorled leaves. The four to six petals are pink or purple and crumpled in bud and the flowers are often heterostylous, with the stamens all being placed at any one of three different levels in a flower. The fruit is a capsule. Genera: *Lythrum.*

Water-chestnuts Family **Trapaceae** p.160

Aquatic annuals, with floating leaves and short-lived submerged leaves. The floating leaves form a rosette. Flowers have four petals. The fruit is a woody nut with the four sepals persisting on it as horny spines. Only one species occurs in Europe. Genera: *Trapa.*

Myrtles Family **Myrtaceae** p.160

A very large family which includes the Eucalyptus trees of Australia. The only native European members are evergreen shrubs. Opposite leaves, aromatic, flowers with five petals and numerous stamens. Fruit is a berry. Genera: *Myrtus.*

Willowherbs Family **Onagraceae** pp.160–164

Mostly perennial herbs with opposite or alternate leaves. Flowers are solitary, in spikes or in clusters. Sepals usually four, rarely two or five, and often seated on a long and brightly coloured tube. Petals the same number as the sepals, rarely absent. The fruit is a capsule, a berry or a burr; some species have plumed, wind-dispersed seeds. A number of species are popular ornamentals, others are invasive weeds. Genera: *Chamerion, Circaea, Epilobium, Ludwigia, Oenothera.*

Water-milfoils and *Mare's-tails* Families **Haloragidaceae** and **Hippuridaceae** p.164

Two very small families of aquatic plants with whorled leaves and tiny, inconspicuous flowers. Water-milfoils have pinnate leaves with thread-like segments. Mare's-tail has undivided, strap-shaped leaves. Haloragidaceae. Genera: *Myriophyllum*. Hippuridaceae. Genera: *Hippurus.*

Dogwoods Family Cornaceae p.164

Mostly deciduous shrubs or small trees with a few perennial herbs. The leaves are opposite and entire, with conspicuous veins. Small four-petalled flowers are borne in heads; in some species the heads are surrounded by four showy, petal-like bracts. The berry-like fruit has a single stone. Genera: *Cornus.*

Ivies Family Araliaceae p.166

Species of *Hedera* are the only European members of this essentially tropical family. They are woody climbers with evergreen leaves, umbels of greenish flowers and berry-like fruits. Genera: *Hedera.*

Carrots Family Umbelliferae pp.166–180

A very large family of annuals, biennials and perennials. Many are aromatic; a number are poisonous. The leaves are alternate, usually large and much-divided, the stalk often broad at the base and sheathing the stem. The small flowers are frequently white, purplish or yellow, with five petals; sepals are usually absent or very small. The flower stalks all arise from the same point and are of equal length, giving a characteristic flat-topped cluster called an umbel. In many species these simple umbels are themselves arranged in larger or compound umbels. There may be a number of bracts at the base of the compound umbel, with smaller bracteoles at the bases of the constituent simple umbels. The presence or absence of bracts and bracteoles can be important for identification. The fruits consist of two single-seeded segments united along their inner faces and variously ornamented with hairs, spines, grooves and ridges. Ripe fruits are of particular diagnostic importance. The family provides many culinary herbs and spices and several well-known vegetables. Genera: *Aegopodium, Aethusa, Angelica, Anthriscus, Apium, Astrantia, Berula, Bunium, Bupleurum, Carum, Chaerophyllum, Conium, Conopodium, Coriandrum, Crithmum, Daucus, Eryngium, Falcaria, Ferula, Foeniculum, Heracleum, Hydrocotyle, Meum, Myrrhis, Oenanthe, Orlaya, Pastinaca, Petroselinum, Peucedanum, Physospermum, Pimpinella, Pseudorlaya, Sanicula, Scandix, Seseli, Silaum, Sison, Sium, Smyrnum, Tordylium, Torilis, Trinia.*

Diapensias and *Wintergreens*
Families Diapensiaceae and Pyrolaceae p.182

Two small families of mostly perennial herbs and dwarf shrubs with rosettes of leaves. In Diapensias both calyx and corolla are deeply five-lobed. In Wintergreens the flowers are drooping and often somewhat urn-shaped, the five short sepals joined at the base and the five petals free. Most species occur on acid soils. Diapensiaceae. Genera: *Diapensia.* Pyrolaceae. Genera: *Moneses, Monotropa, Pyrola.*

Heaths Family Ericaceae pp.182–186

A very large family of dwarfed or low shrubs and trees. Most species are evergreen. The alternate or whorled leaves may be small and narrow to needle-like or broader and leathery. The flowers range from small to very large and are urn-shaped or funnel-shaped with five free or fused petals. The fruit is a dry capsule or a berry. Most members of the family require acid soils. Many are typical of and dominant on north temperate moorland and heathland. Others are Mediterranean plants and occur in southern Europe, North Africa and the Cape. Most species are ornamental. Genera: *Andromeda, Arctostaphyllos, Cassiope, Calluna, Erica, Loiseluria, Rhododendron, Vaccinium.*

Primroses Family Primulaceae pp.186–192

Annual and perennial herbs, sometimes tufted, one species aquatic, a few dwarf shrubs. Leaves are often in a basal rosette, otherwise opposite, whorled or alternate. The flowers usually have parts in fives, the sepals joined to form a bell-shaped or tubular calyx, the petals also joined to form a corolla which is bell- or funnel-shaped, or tubular with wide-spreading lobes. The fruit is a capsule. This family contains many well-known alpine and garden plants, including many cultivars. Genera: *Anagallis*, *Androsace*, *Coris*, *Cortusa*, *Cyclamen*, *Glaux*, *Hottonia*, *Lysimachia*, *Primula*, *Samolus*, *Soldanella*, *Trientalis*.

Sea-lavenders Family **Plumbaginaceae** p.192
Herbs and small shrubs. The leaves are alternate or more frequently in basal rosettes. Flowers are borne in sprays or tight heads, with parts in fives; the persistent calyx is often papery. Most are species of coastal habitats including salt-marshes. Genera: *Armeria*, *Limonium*, *Limoniastrum*, *Plumbago*.

Olives Family **Oleaceae** p.192
Mostly trees and shrubs but with a few woody climbers. The leaves are opposite and, in Jasmines, trifoliate or pinnate. Flowers have four petals joined to form a tube. The family contains commercially important trees such as Ash and Olive as well as ornamentals. Genera: *Jasminum*.

Gentians Family **Gentianaceae** pp.194–198
Annual, biennial and perennial herbs, hairless and bitter-tasting. Leaves are almost always opposite and stalkless, those of each pair frequently joined at the base. The flowers have a bell-shaped, funnel-shaped or tubular corolla, sometimes with wide-spreading lobes often with small lobes between the main ones or scales or hairs in the throat of the tube. Many species are alpines and prized as ornamental plants; some species are used medicinally. Genera: *Blackstonia*, *Centaurium*, *Cicendia*, *Exaculum*, *Gentiana*, *Gentianella*.

Bog-beans Family **Menyanthaceae** p.198
A very small family of aquatic perennials. At least some of the leaves are alternate. Both calyx and corolla are deeply five-lobed, the corolla lobes fringed. The fruit is a capsule. Genera: *Menyanthes*, *Nymphoides*.

Periwinkles and *Milk-weeds*
Families **Apocynaceae** and **Asclepiadaceae** p.198
In Europe both of these mainly tropical families are represented by perennial herbs and shrubs. The leaves are opposite, rarely whorled and the flowers have parts in fives. In addition to the corolla lobes, Milk-weeds have one or two whorls of fused segments at the base of the stamens. Family Apocynaceae. Genera: *Nerium*, *Vinca*. Family Asclepiadaceae. Genera: *Vincetoxicum*.

Bedstraws Family **Rubiaceae** pp.200–202
A very large family distributed world-wide and containing large trees, shrubs and herbs but in Europe only herbs and dwarf shrubs. The leaves are opposite but may appear to be whorled in species where the stipules and leaves are identical. Flowers small, borne in heads, spikes or clusters. The fruit is usually dry and separates into two single-seeded halves. Genera: *Asperula*, *Cruciata*, *Galium*, *Rubia*, *Sherardia*.

Jacob's-ladders Family **Polemoniaceae** p.202
Only four members of this family occur in Europe. They are annuals or perennials with alternate leaves. Calyx bell-shaped and deeply-lobed; corolla bell-shaped, or with a narrow tube and spreading lobes. Genera: *Polemonium*.

Bindweeds Family **Convolvulaceae** pp.202–204
A family of herbs, often climbing by means of twining stems, and small shrubs. Dodders (species of *Cuscuta*) are parasitic. Leaves alternate. Flowers are often large and showy, with five sepals and a five-lobed or five-angled, tubular, funnel- or bell-shaped corolla. The fruit is a capsule. Genera: *Calystegia*, *Convolvulus*, *Cuscuta*, *Ipomoea*.

Forget-me-nots **Family Boraginaceae** pp.206–210

A large family of usually bristly herbs and dwarf shrubs with alternate leaves. Flowers typically borne in coiled, one-sided sprays which unfurl as the flowers progressively open; they are often pink in bud but open bright blue. The corolla usually has a distinct tube with wide-spreading lobes but may also be bell-shaped or funnel-shaped; there are often scales or hairs at the mouth of the tube. The fruit consists of four small nutlets within the persistent calyx. Genera: *Alkanna, Anchusa, Borago, Buglossoides, Cerinthe, Cynoglossum, Echium, Heliotropium, Lithospermum, Mertensia, Myosotis, Onosma, Pulmonaria, Symphytum, Trachystemon.*

Vervains **Family Verbenaceae** p.210

Herbs, shrubs and (outside Europe) many trees. Herbaceous species have square stems and resemble members of the Mint family. Leaves opposite or whorled. Flowers borne in spikes or clusters. Corolla tubular with the five lobes forming two lips. The fruit is two or four small nutlets. Genera: *Verbena.*

Water-starworts **Family Callitrichaceae** p.210

A very small family of usually annual herbs. Mostly aquatic or found growing on wet mud. Leaves are opposite but in aquatic plants the floating leaves form a rosette on the water surface. Minute unisexual flowers consist of only a single stamen or an ovary with two slender styles. Genera: *Callitriche.*

Mints **Family Labiatae** pp.210–224

A large family of herbs and shrubs, many of them dotted with glands containing aromatic essential oils. Stems are typically square in cross-section and the leaves are opposite. Flowers are borne in axillary clusters forming whorls around the stem, the whorls sometimes crowded together to form a spike. The pairs of bracts beneath each whorl may resemble the leaves or differ in shape, size or colour. The corolla is usually two-lipped, the lower lip three-lobed, the upper two-lobed or entire and sometimes forming a hood over the four stamens. The fruit consists of four small nutlets at the base of the style and within the persistent calyx. A family best known for its numerous culinary and medicinal herbs; other species are important sources of oils and perfumes. Genera: *Acinos, Ajuga, Ballota, Calamintha, Clinopodium, Galeopsis, Glechoma, Hyssopus, Lavandula, Lamiastrum, Lamium, Leonurus, Lycopus, Marrubium, Melittis, Mentha, Origanum, Phlomis, Prasium, Prunella, Rosmarinus, Salvia, Satureja, Scutellaria, Stachys, Teucrium, Thymus.*

Potatoes **Family Solanaceae** pp.224–226

Herbs, climbers, shrubs and a few trees. The leaves are variable but usually alternate, and entire, lobed or pinnate. Flowers have five petals forming either a spreading corolla or a tubular one. The fruit is a berry or a dry capsule. This family contains many fruit and vegetable crops such as tomatoes, peppers and potatoes, plus various ornamentals as well as some highly poisonous species. Genera: *Atropa, Datura, Hyoscyamus, Lycium, Mandragora, Solanum, Withania.*

Figworts **Family Scrophulariaceae** pp.228–244

A large family often confused with the Mints but readily distinguished by the fruits which are dry capsules with a persistent style. Most species are herbs, some of them parasitic; a few are shrubs. The stems are often square in cross-section and the leaves are alternate or opposite. Like the Mints, the flowers often have a two-lipped corolla; the lips may be closed over the corolla tube and pollinating insects force them apart to reach nectar, brushing against the stamens and style as they do so. A widespread family but particularly numerous in temperate regions and containing many well-known garden ornamentals. Genera: *Anarrhinum, Antirrhinum, Asarina, Bartsia, Bellardia, Chaenorhinum, Cymbalaria, Digitalis, Erinus,*

Euphrasia, Kickxia, Lathraea, Linaria, Melampyrum, Mimulus, Misopates, Odontites, Parentucellia, Pedicularis, Rhinanthus, Scrophularia, Sibthorpia, Verbascum, Veronica.

Globularias Family **Globulariaceae** p.244
A very small family of perennial herbs and small shrubs. Leaves are alternate or in basal rosettes. Flowers have five unequal blue petals and four stamens, and are borne in dense heads surrounded by a ring of bracts. The fruit is dry and enclosed in the persistent calyx. Genera: *Globularia.*

Gloxinias and *Bear's-breeches*
Families **Gesneriaceae** and **Acanthaceae** p.244
Two large families almost entirely confined to the tropics and subtropics with a few isolated herbaceous perennial species in Europe. Gloxinias have leaves in a basal rosette and a bare stem bearing tubular flowers with spreading, usually unequal corolla lobes. Bear's-breeches are robust, with mostly basal leaves and flowers in a spike, each with a four- or five-lobed calyx and a tubular corolla with an upper and lower lip or with the upper lip absent. Gesneriaceae. Genera: *Ramonda.* Acanthaceae. Genera: *Acanthus.*

Broomrapes Family **Orobanchaceae** pp.244–246
A small family very closely related and similar to Figworts, but with all members completely parasitic on the roots of other plants. They are totally lacking in chlorophyll, being usually yellowish or reddish- to violet-tinged, with alternate, scale-like leaves. Genera: *Orobanche.*

Butterworts Family **Lentibulariaceae** p.246
Small carnivorous plants which capture insects by means of leaf-traps. The leaves are either alternate, divided, with bladder-traps or basal, undivided and sticky. The flowers are two-lipped and spurred, solitary or in short spikes. All species are aquatic or found on wet soils. Genera: *Pinguicula, Utricularia.*

Plantains Family **Plantaginaceae** p.248
Mostly herbs with a few dwarf shrubs and one aquatic perennial, typically with the leaves in a basal rosette and a naked stem bearing a dense head of small, brownish, four-petalled flowers. Flowers, which open from the bottom of the head upwards, have long, pale stamens. Genera: *Litorella, Plantago.*

Honeysuckles Family **Caprifoliaceae** p.250
Woody climbers, shrubs and small trees, rarely herbaceous perennials. The opposite leaves range from undivided to deeply lobed or pinnate. Flowers are borne in clusters; they are small with five spreading petals in *Sambucus* but larger and tubular in Honeysuckles (*Lonicera* species). The fruit is a berry. Many species are ornamentals. Genera: *Linnaea, Lonicera, Sambucus.*

Moschatels Family **Adoxaceae** p.250
A family containing only three species, one of which occurs in Europe and is remarkable for its flower head, fancifully thought to resemble a clock face. It is in the form of a rough cube, with a five-petalled flower forming each of the sides and a four-petalled flower on the top. Genera: *Adoxa.*

Valerians Family **Valerianaceae** pp.250–252
A widespread family of annuals and perennials with opposite, whorled or basal leaves. The flowers are borne in dense clusters and have a tubular, often unequally lobed and spurred corolla. Small fruits may have a parachute formed by the persistent calyx teeth. Genera: *Centranthus, Valeriana, Valerianella.*

Teasels Family **Dipsacaceae** pp.252–254

A family of herbs and occasionally shrubs, concentrated in the Mediterranean region. They have opposite or whorled leaves and dense heads of flowers with a ring of bracts immediately beneath, the whole head often giving the appearance of a single flower. Flowers have an epicalyx of narrow segments, a small calyx sometimes with bristle-like teeth and a four- to five-lobed corolla. Stamens two or four. Genera: *Dipsacus, Knautia, Pterocephalus, Scabiosa, Succisa.*

Bellflowers Family **Campanulaceae** pp.254–256

A large and widespread family of mainly herbs. They usually have alternate leaves and spike-like or branched inflorescences. The showy flowers are frequently blue and typically have parts in fives; sometimes the corolla is two-lipped. The fruit is a capsule, usually opening by means of pores or valves to release the numerous small seeds. Many species are grown as ornamentals. Genera: *Campanula, Jasione, Legousia, Lobelia, Phyteuma, Wahlenbergia.*

Daisies Family **Compositae** pp.258–286

The largest of all plant families and occurring in every part of the world. The characteristic feature of this family is the flower, which represents a complete inflorescence and is composed of one or two types of small, unisexual or hermaphrodite florets. *Disc florets* have a tubular, five-lobed corolla; *ray florets* are similar but have the corolla extended on one side into a strap-like extension resembling a single petal. There may be only disc florets present (eg. Edelweiss), only ray florets (eg. Dandelion) or both types with ray florets surrounding the central disc florets (eg. Daisy). The florets are crowded together on a button-like receptacle with a ring of *involucral bracts* immediately below it, the whole structure forming the 'flower'. Genera: *Achillea, Adenostyles, Antennaria, Anthemis, Arctium, Arnica, Artemisia, Aster, Asteriscus, Bellis, Bidens, Calendula, Carduncellus, Carduus, Carlina, Carthamus, Centaurea, Chamomilla, Chrysanthemum, Cicerbita, Cichorium, Cirsium, Crepis, Cynara, Doronicum, Echinops, Erigeron, Eupatorium, Filago, Galactites, Galinsoga, Gnaphalium, Helianthus, Helichrysum, Hieracium, Hypochoeris, Inula, Lactuca, Lapsana, Leontodon, Leontopodium, Leucanthemum, Matricaria, Mycelis, Notobasis, Onopordum, Otanthus, Pallenis, Petasites, Picris, Prenanthes, Pulicaria, Saussurea, Scolymus, Scorzonera, Senecio, Serephidium, Serratula, Silybum, Solidago, Sonchus, Tanacetum, Taraxacum, Tragopogon, Tripleurospermum, Tussilago.*

Water-plantains and *Flowering-rushes*
Families **Alismataceae** and **Butomaceae** p.288

Plants of wet places or aquatics. The leaves have sheathing bases. The flowers have parts in threes, the petals white, pink or purplish, those of Water-plantains soon falling. Alismataceae. Genera: *Alisma, Baldellia, Damasonium, Sagittaria.* Butomaceae. Genera: *Butomus.*

Frogbits Family **Hydrocharitaceae** pp.288–290

A small family of free-floating aquatics, some of them completely submerged. The flowers have parts in threes and are usually unisexual, the males often breaking free and floating so that pollination occurs at the water surface. Genera: *Hydrocharis, Stratiotes.*

Pondweeds Family **Potamogetonaceae** p.290

Aquatic plants with narrow, often translucent submerged leaves, sometimes also with broader, green floating leaves. Inconspicuous greenish flowers with four perianth segments are borne in an aerial spike. Genera: *Potamogeton.*

Lilies Family **Liliaceae** pp.290–302

Perennials arising from a bulb, corm, tuberous root or other fleshy storage structure. The leaves are often narrow and strap-like. The flowers have a perianth of two whorls of three segments, all of them petal-like and sometimes joined. There are usually six stamens. A large family, many of the species familiar as garden ornamentals. Genera: *Allium, Anthericum, Asparagus, Asphodeline, Asphodelus, Bellevalia, Bulbocodium, Colchicum, Convallaria, Dipcadi, Fritillaria, Hyacinthoides, Lilium, Merendera, Muscari, Narthecium, Ornithogalum, Paradisea, Paris, Polygonatum, Ruscus, Scilla, Smilax, Tulipa, Urginea, Veratrum.*

Yams Family Dioscoriaceae p.302
A tropical family with only four species in Europe. These are usually non-woody climbers with clusters of small, unisexual flowers. The perianth has six segments and the fruit is usually a berry. Genera: *Tamus.*

Daffodils Family Amaryllidaceae pp.302–304
Bulbous perennials with strap-shaped leaves, often arranged in a flat fan. The solitary- to many-flowered inflorescence is enclosed in a papery sheath when young. As well as six petal-like perianth segments, the flowers may have a coloured, inner tube, the *corona*. There are six stamens. The fruit is dry or fleshy. Genera: *Galanthus, Leucojum, Narcissus, Pancratium, Sternbergia.*

Irises Family Iridaceae pp.304–306
Similar to the Daffodil family but sometimes arising from rhizomes or corms. The flowers sometimes have unequal perianth segments and may be quite complex in structure, especially in the genus *Iris* which has petal-like styles as well as six coloured perianth segments. There are three stamens. Genera: *Crocus, Gladiolus, Iris, Romulea.*

Duckweeds Family Lemnaceae p.306
Very small, free-floating aquatics. The plant body is reduced to a green thallus, sometimes with a few thread-like roots on the underside. The minute flowers are borne in a pouch on the edge of the thallus but many species reproduce by budding new plants. Genera: *Lemna, Spirodela.*

Arums Family Araceae p.308
A large and mainly tropical family of perennial herbs. They are distinguished by the structure of the inflorescence in which the small flowers are crowded into a dense spike, which often has a naked, fleshy portion – the appendix – towards the tip. The spike is enfolded within a very large sheathing bract – the spathe – which is often spotted or brightly coloured. The inflorescence often smells of rotting meat to attract pollinating flies. Genera: *Acorus, Arisarum, Arum, Biarum, Calla, Dracunculus.*

Orchids Family Orchidaceae pp.310–316
One of the largest of plant families and spread throughout the world. European species are perennial herbs or sometimes saprophytes, the stems swollen at the base to form a bulb-like structure. The flowers are always irregular, with two whorls of three perianth segments and are sometimes spurred. The middle, inner segment – the *labellum* – is usually larger and of a diferent shape to the others. In many species it is also intricately and even bizarrely coloured and lobed, fringed or otherwise decorated, sometimes resembling a particular species and even sex of insect. This mimicry attracts insects of the same species which, in attempting to copulate with the simulacrum, pollinate the flower. The anthers and stigma are borne on a single column and the pollen is bound into packets called *pollinia*. Genera: *Aceras, Anacamptis, Calypso, Cephalanthera, Cypripedium, Dactylorrhiza, Epipactis, Epipogium, Goodyera, Gymnadenia, Himantoglossum, Listera, Limodorum, Neottia, Ophrys, Orchis, Platanthera, Serapias, Spiranthes.*

Key to Wild Flowers

The following pages contain a series of keys to help you identify wild flowers. The keys deliberately utilise very few characters, relying mainly on those provided by flowers, leaves and the more obvious aspects of habit. Such simplification occasionally causes large groups of similar species to key out together, but it is hoped that this disadvantage is outweighed by the benefit of a system accessible to less experienced users. In most cases where a plant does key out to a large group, rapid 'picture-spotting' through the relevant pages will quickly yield a suitable candidate species.

Using the Keys

Every step in the keys consists of two (occasionally three or four) contrasting statements. Look at your specimen and decide which is true. The next stage is indicated at the end of the line and may be another key, the next numbered section in the same key (set in **bold** type) or a name and page reference. Follow the series of correct statements until you arrive at a name and page number where you can check your identification. The first key leads to a number of secondary keys, and these to species. Sometimes a plant will fit both statements and in some cases, especially in species with different male and female plants, two specimens of the same species will each fit one of the contrasting statements. In these instances, simply follow whichever statement you feel is most apt; all such plants are keyed out twice, or even several times, so it does not matter which path you follow. After using the key, turn to the appropriate page and use the photograph and description to confirm your selection. With a little experience you may be able to go directly to those pages showing the most likely group of plants. Until then, make full use of the keys. They are an essential tool for identification.

MAIN KEY

1   Aquatic plants, all but the flowering
stems usually submerged or floating   *Key 1*
Terrestrial plants though sometimes
rooted in water margins   **2**

2   Flowers packed into a cylindrical spike
enveloped by a large, leafy, greenish,
whitish or purple-brown spathe   Arums p. 308

Flowers variously arranged but never in a
spike with a single spathe   **3**

3   Plant wholly lacking chlorophyll,
usually creamy-white or pinkish in colour
and with leaves reduced to scales or
absent   *Cytinus* p.54; Yellow
Bird's-nest p.182; Dodder
p.202; Toothwort, Broomrapes
pp.244–246; Limodore, Bird's-
nest Orchid, Ghost Orchid p.310

Plant with at least some green pigment;
leaves usually present   **4**

4	Flowers or florets small, crowded in dense heads each with a ruff of sepal-like bracts beneath, the whole head usually resembling a single flower	*Key 2*
	Individual flowers distinct, however arranged, the inflorescence not resembling a single flower	**5**
5	Flowers arranged in umbels – broad, usually flat-topped clusters with the stalks all arising from the same point at the stem tip	*Key 3*
	Flowers variously arranged but never in umbels	**6**
6	Flowers irregular, the petals unequal	**7**
	Flowers regular, the petals all equal	**8**
7	Petals free to the base	*Key 4*
	Petals joined above the base	*Key 5*
8	Perianth of two whorls differing markedly in size, colour or shape	**9**
	Perianth of one whorl, or two very similar whorls	**10**
9	Petals free to the base	*Key 6*
	Petals joined above the base	*Key 7*
10	Perianth segments all petal-like, white or brightly coloured	*Key 8*
	Perianth segments all sepal-like, greenish	*Key 9*

KEY 1
Aquatic plants

1	Shoreline plant submerged by tides	Glasswort p.62
	Freshwater plants	**2**
2	At least some leaves emerging above the water	Mare's-tail p.164; Bog-bean p.198; Water-plantains p.288
	Leaves all submerged or floating on the surface	**3**
3	Leaves all submerged	**4**
	At least some leaves floating on the surface	**5**
4	Leaves divided into numerous fine segments	Thread-leaved Water-crowfoot p.84; Spiked Water-milfoil p.164; Water-violet p.188; Bladderwort p.246
	Leaves narrow but undivided	Mare's-tail p.164;

		Shoreweed p.248; Fennel Pondweed p.290

| 5 | Plant less than 10mm, consisting of a single green plate-like body | Common Duckweed p.306 |
| | Plant much bigger, with leaves and stems | **6** |

| 6 | Flowers inconspicuous, lacking petals | Water-starwort p.210; Broad-leaved Pondweed p.290 Hampshire Purslane p.162 |
| | Flowers conspicuous; petals white, yellow or lilac | **7** |

7	Petals 3	Frogbits pp.288–290
	Petals 4	Water-chestnut p.160
	Petals 5	Water-lilies p.72; Pond Water-crowfoot p.84; Fringed Water-lily p.198

KEY 2
Flowers or florets small, in dense heads which have a ruff of sepal-like bracts beneath, the head often resembling a single flower

1	Flowers or florets with an obvious calyx, at least the teeth green	Dwarf Cornel p.164; Astrantia, Sea-hollies p.166; Thrift p.192; Globularias p.244; Round-headed Rampion, Sheep's-bit p. 256
	Flowers or florets without a calyx though sometimes with a whorl of hairs or scales at the base of the corolla	**2**

| 2 | Stamens free, conspicuously projecting well beyond the corolla | Valerians, Teasels pp.250–254 |
| | Stamens fused to form a tube, not projecting well beyond the corolla | **3** |

| 3 | Plant with spiny or prickly leaves, stems or flower heads | Daisies p.262, 272–280 |
| | Plant without spines or prickles | **4** |

| 4 | Flower heads composed entirely of ray florets | Daisies pp.280–286 |
| | Flower heads composed entirely of long or short disc florets | Hemp-agrimony, Sea Aster p.258; Daisies pp.260–262; Pineappleweed, Cottonweed p.266; Daisies p.268; p.270; Alpine Saw-wort p.274; Saw-wort p.276; Knapweeds p.278 |

Flower heads with a ring of ray florets
(sometimes very short) surrounding the
central disc florets   Daisies pp.258–272

KEY 3
Flowers arranged in umbels with all the stalks arising from the same point at the stem tip

1	Petals and sepals absent, flowers consisting of a cyathium with curved glands around the rim	Spurges pp.144–146
	Flowers with petals or sepals	**2**
2	Plant an evergreen climber	Ivy p.166
	Plant not climbing	**3**
3	Leaves opposite	Dogwoods p.164; Valerians pp.250–252
	Leaves alternate or basal	**4**
4	Sepals 4, yellow; petals absent	Alternate-leaved Golden-saxifrage p.110
	Sepals 3, 5 or absent; white pink or purplish petals present	**5**
5	Petals 3 or 6	Flowering-rush p.288; Garlics p.298; Daffodils pp.302–304
	Petals 5	**6**
6	Petals joined above the base to form a tube with 5 spreading lobes	Primroses p.188
	Petals free to the base	Carrots pp.166–180

KEY 4
Flowers irregular, variously arranged but not in umbels or ruffed heads; petals unequal, free to the base

1	Petals or petal-like segments 3 or 6	**2**
	Petals or petal-like segments 4 or 5	**3**
2	Leaves opposite or whorled	Balsams p.148
	Leaves alternate or basal	Mignonettes p.104; Gladiolus p.306; Orchids pp.310–316
3	Flowers with a backward pointing spur	**4**
	Flowers without a spur	**5**
4	Plant tall, erect, up to 100cm high	Lice-bane, Larkspur p.76
	Plant low or spreading, usually less than 50cm high	Fumitories p.88; Violets p.154

5	Petals all spreading	Candytufts p.102; Burning-bush p.148; Rosebay Willowherb p.162
	Petals not all spreading	**6**
6	Upper petal forming a helmet-like hood	Monk's-hood p.76
	Upper petal usually erect, not hooded, two side petals spreading, two lower petals fused to form a boat shape	**7**
7	Leaves ending in a tendril	Vetches and Vetchlings pp.124–128
	Leaves lacking a tendril	**8**
8	Leaves entire or absent or trifoliate	Peas p.120, 124, Common Restharrow p.128, Peas pp130–140
	Leaves pinnate or palmate	Peas pp. 122–124, 134–140

KEY 5
Flowers irregular, variously arranged but not in umbels or ruffed heads; petals unequal, joined above the base

1	Shrubs or woody climbers	Alpenrose p.184; Germanders p.212; Prasium, Jerusalem Sage p.214; Lavenders p.222; Rosemary p.224; Honeysuckles p.250
	Herbs, sometimes woody at the base	**2**
2	Petals joined near the base, forming a short, inconspicuous tube	Mulleins p.228; Speedwells, Cornish Moneywort pp.236–238; Gladiolus p.306
	Petals joined above the base, forming a distinct tube	**3**
3	Leaves all basal, flowering stem naked	Louseworts p.242; Butterworts p.246
	Stems leafy	**4**
4	Corolla with a slender spur	Toadflaxes and Fluellens pp.232–234, Valerians p.252
	Corolla not spurred	**5**
5	Flowers in forks of branches and in dense, terminal heads; stamens three	Narrow-fruited Cornsalad p.250
	Flowers usually in terminal spikes; stamens four or five	**6**
6	Stems always square, leaves always opposite; flowers usually several in axil of each leaf or bract, forming a whorled spike	Vervain and Mints pp.210–224

Stems often cylindrical, leaves opposite or alternate; flowers usually one in axil of each bract; fruit a capsule		*Coris* p.192; Monkeyflower p. 228; Figworts to Snapdragons pp.230–232; Foxgloves pp234–236; Cow-wheats to Rattles pp.240-242; Bear's-breeches p.244; Heath Lobelia p.256

KEY 6
Flowers regular, variously arranged but not in umbels or ruffed heads; perianth in two whorls which differ in size, shape or colour; petals free to the base

1	Leaves or stems very thick and fleshy, sometimes lime-encrusted or with glistening, red or crystalline hairs	**2**
	Leaves and stems not or little fleshy, without encrustations or glistening hairs	**3**
2	Petals 8 to 10	Sundews, House-leeks and Saxifrages pp.106–110
	Petals numerous	Mesembryanthemums p.62; Barberry-fig p.160
3	Petals 2	Enchanter's-nightshade p.160
	Petals 4	**4**
	Petals 3, 5 or more	**7**
4	Leaves in whorls of 4 or more	Bedstraws pp.200–204; Herb-Paris p.300
	Leaves basal or opposite, rarely in whorls of 3	**5**
5	Flowers with sepals and petals seated on a long, narrowly cylindrical and often coloured ovary-tube	Willowherbs pp.162–164
	Flowers without a long ovary-tube below the sepals and petals	**6**
6	Sepals 2, usually falling as flower opens	Poppies, Hypecoum pp.86–88
	Sepals 4, persisting after flower opens	Caper p.88; Cabbages pp.90–104; Rue p.146; Sea-heath p.158
7	At least some leaves opposite	**8**
	Leaves all basal or alternate	**10**
8	Leaves deeply divided	Crane's-bills, *Fagonia* Small Caltrops pp.140–142
	Leaves entire or slightly toothed	**9**
9	Stamens up to 12; herbs	Springbeauty, Pinks pp.62–72;

	Stamens numerous; mostly shrubs	Fairy Flax p.142; Sea–heath p.158; Loosestrifes p.160 St John's-worts p.152; Rockroses pp.156–158; Myrtle p.160
10	Stamens united into a column	Mallows pp. 148–150
	Stamens not united	**11**
11	Shrubs (sometimes dwarf and evergreen) or perennials with prickly stems	Currants p.112; Roses p.114; Mountain Avens p.116; Burning-bush p.148; Butcher's-broom p.300
	Unarmed herbs	**12**
12	Leaves deeply lobed or divided	Buttercups p.82; Paeony p.84; Roses p.112, 116–118; Wood Sorrels p.144
	Leaves not deeply lobed or divided	**13**
13	Petals 3 or 6	Docks p.58; Water-plantains p.258; Daffodils and Irises pp.302–304
	Petals 5	**14**
14	Flowers white	Sundews p.106; Saxifrages pp.108–110; Wintergreens p.182
	Flowers yellow, pink or blue	Lesser Celandine, Lesser Spearwort p.82; Perennial Flax p.142

KEY 7
Flowers regular, variously arranged but not in umbels or ruffed heads; perianth in two whorls which differ in size, shape or colour; petals joined above the base

1	Shrubs, sometimes dwarf evergreens with leathery or needle-like leaves	Diapensia, Heathers pp.182–186; Jasmine p.192; Lesser Periwinkle, Oleander, p.198 China Teaplant p.224
	Herbs, leaves rarely evergreen	**2**
2	Leaves opposite or whorled	Primroses p.190; Gentians, Swallow-wort pp.194–198; Glandular Plantain p.248; Dwarf Elder, Twinflower p.250
	Leaves alternate or basal	**3**
3	Leaves all basal; flowering stem, if present, naked	**4**

	Flowering stem with at least a few leaves	**5**
4	Petals 4; flowers greenish or brownish	Plantains p.248
	Petals 5; flowers usually brightly coloured	Primroses pp.186–188; Sea-lavender p.192; Mandrake p.226; *Ramonda* p.244
	Petals 6, surrounding a central, trumpet-shaped corona	Daffodils p.304
5	Leaves pinnate	Jacob's–ladder p.202
	Leaves sometimes deeply lobed but not divided into separate leaflets	**6**
6	Flowers in coiled sprays; plant typically bristly hairy	Borages pp.206–210
	Flowers in terminal spikes	Navelwort p.106; Mulleins p.228; Bellflowers pp.254–256
	Flowers solitary or in clusters	Squirting Cucumber p.158; Bindweeds p.204; Potatoes pp.224–228; Ivy-leaved Bellflower p.256

KEY 8
Flowers regular, variously arranged but not in umbels or ruffed heads; perianth in one, or two similar whorls, all segments petal-like and coloured

1	Shrubs	Barberry p.84; Spurge-laurels p. 152; Butcher's-broom p.300
	Climbers	Black-bindweed p.58; *Clematis* p.80; *Smilax*, Black Bryony p.302
	Herbs	**2**
2	Leaves deeply lobed or divided	**3**
	Leaves undivided	**5**
3	Leaves either two- or three-lobed, or palmately divided	Hellebores, Winter Aconite p.74; Globe-flower p.76; Anemones, Liverleaf p.78; *Leontice* p.84
	Leaves pinnately divided	**4**
4	Stem leaves opposite	*Clematis recta* p.80; Danewort, Moschatel p.252
	Stems leaves alternate	Columbine p.76; Pasque-flowers p.78; Pheasant's-eye, Lesser Meadow-rue p.80
5	Petals 5	**6**
	Petals 6, sometimes in two whorls of 3	Mousetail p.80; Lilies pp.290–300; Daffodils p.302; Crocuses p.306

| 6 | Flowers yellow | Marsh Marigold p.76 |
| | Flowers white or pink | **7** |

7	Stems with a papery sheath (ochrea)	
	at the base of each leaf stalk	Knotweeds p.56
	Stems without a papery sheath	Bastard-toadflax p.54;
		Sea- milkwort p.190

KEY 9
Flowers regular, variously arranged but not in umbels or ruffed heads; perianth in one, or two similar whorls, all segments green and sepal-like

1	Climber with twining stems	Hop p.54; Black-bindweed
		p.58; *Smilax*, Black Bryony p.304
	Plant not climbing	**2**

2	Flowers each a cup-shaped cyathium	
	with curved glands around the rim	Spurges pp.144–146
	Flowers not cyathia	**3**

3	Flowers borne singly in leaf axils	Asarabacca p.56;
		Procumbent Pearlwort p.64;
		Fagonia p.142
	Flowers variously grouped together	**4**

4	Flowers or groups of flowers arranged in	
	narrow spikes, catkins or dense cylindrical heads	**5**
	Flowers or groups of flowers arranged in	
	axillary clusters or in broad, spreading heads	**9**

5	Plant woody	Dwarf Willow, Bog-myrtle,
		Dwarf Birch p.52; Sea-purslane p.60;
		Spiny Burnet p.116;
		Castor-oil-plant p.142
	Plant herbaceous	**6**

6	Leaves opposite	Nettles p.52;
		Annual Mercury p.144
	Leaves alternate, basal or absent	**7**

| 7 | Leaves with up to 12 pairs of leaflets | Salad Burnet p.116 |
| | Leaves not divided into leaflets | **8** |

8	Stems with a papery sheath (ochrea) at	
	the base of each leaf stalk	Docks p.58
	Stems without a papery sheath	Sea–beet, Goosefoots pp.58–60;
		Amaranth p.62; Sweet-flag p.308

9	Shrubs	*Osyris*, Mistletoe p.54;Spurge-laurels
		pp.150–152; Butcher's-broom p.300
	Herbs	**10**

10	At least some leaves opposite	Spear-leaved Orache p.60; Annual Knawel p.66; Paronychia p.68; Hampshire Purslane p.162
	Leaves all alternate or basal	**11**
11	Leaves palmately divided	Stinking and Green Hellebore p.74; Alpine Lady's-mantle p.118
	Leaves not divided	Pellitory-of-the-wall, Bastard-toadflax p.54; Saltwort p.60; Annual sea-blite p.62; Alternate-leaved Golden-saxifrage p.110

WILD FLOWERS
OF BRITAIN AND EUROPE

Creeping Willow: ♂ flower

Dwarf Willow *Salix herbacea* Up to 3cm A dwarf creeping shrub with long underground stem but few aerial branches, often forming large patches. Leaves are 6–20mm, on short branches, ovate, bright green and shiny, with conspicuous veins. Flowers are in small catkins, males and females on different plants, appearing after the leaves. *Flowering*: June–July. *Distribution:* Northern Russia to the Pyrenees, in arctic regions and on mountains.
Creeping Willow *(S. repens)* is more vigorous, up to 150cm long, erect or prostrate, with catkins appearing before the elliptical leaves. *Flowering:* April–May. *Distribution:* Damp places from Scandinavia to northern Italy.

Bog-myrtle *Myrica gale* Up to 250cm A deciduous shrub, the twigs and leaves dotted with resinous glands and fragrant when crushed. Leaves are 20–60mm, lanceolate, toothed at tip. Flowers are very small, in catkins at the tips of shoots; plants are usually male or female but sometimes bear catkins of both sexes. Small fruits are rather waxy. *Flowering:* June–July. *Distribution:* Western Europe, from Scandinavia to Portugal; boggy areas on moors and heaths.

Dwarf Birch *Betula nana* Up to 100cm A small deciduous shrub, usually prostrate or ascending with stiff, spreading branches. Leaves 5–15mm, rounded, deeply toothed, dark green. Flowers in small, male and female catkins. Fruiting catkins cone-like, composed of small, narrowly winged nutlets and lobed scales. *Flowering:* May. *Distribution:* Arctic and northern Europe, restricted to mountains further south.

Small Nettle

Common Nettle *Urtica dioica* Up to 150cm A coarse perennial covered with stinging hairs. It has tough yellow roots and often forms large patches. Four-angled stems have opposite, ovate, pointed and toothed leaves, the lower with blades longer than their stalks. Flowers small, in loose axillary spikes, males and females on separate plants; greenish petals four. Fruit small, about 1.2mm, ovoid, flattened. *Flowering:* June–August. *Distribution:* Throughout Europe; hedges, woods and near buildings, on nitrogen-rich soils. **Small Nettle** *(U. urens)* is a smaller annual, up to 60cm, the lower leaves with blades shorter than their stalks. Short flower spikes contain both male and female flowers. *Flowering:* June–September. *Distribution:* Absent only from the far north.

Large-leaved Nettle *Urtica dubia* 15–80cm Similar in general appearance to Common Nettle, this species has leaves with stalks the same length as the blades. Female flowers borne in short, ovoid spikes in the axils of the lower leaves; long horizontally spreading male spikes in axils of upper leaves are swollen, with flowers all arranged on the upper side. *Flowering:* May–August. *Distribution:* Mediterranean region; cultivated ground and waste places.

Roman Nettle *Urtica pilulifera* Up to 100cm. An annual or sometimes a biennial with opposite, toothed, ovate leaves and the most vicious sting of any European nettle. Male and female flowers borne in separate clusters; males branched; females clusters spherical, up to 10mm diameter in fruit and most noticeable then. Fruit about 2.4mm. *Flowering:* May–August. *Distribution:* Native to southern Europe but often found as a casual elsewhere; woods and waste ground.

Dwarf Willow: fruiting catkins

Bog-myrtle: ♀ catkins

Dwarf Birch

Common Nettle

Large-leaved Nettle

Roman Nettle: ♀ flower heads

Pellitory

Thesium arvense: leaf

Loranthus europaeus

Cytinus ruber

Pellitory-of-the-wall *Parietaria judaica* Up to 40cm A perennial with prostrate or ascending much branched stems. Alternate, ovate and shortly pointed leaves up to 50mm are softly hairy. Small greenish flowers in clusters in leaf axils are either unisexual or hermaphrodite; perianth four-lobed. *Flowering:* June–October. *Distribution:* Western and southern Europe; in rocky areas, and particularly on walls. **Pellitory** *(P. officinalis)* is taller, up to 100cm, with upright, at most slightly branched stems. Leaves are long-pointed, the stalk shorter than the blade. *Flowering* June–October. *Distribution:* Central and southern Europe; walls and rocky areas.

Hop *Humulus lupulus* Up to 600cm A far-spreading perennial climber, bristly with downward-pointing, stiff hairs. Stems twine clockwise. Leaves are opposite, large, ovate, usually three- or five-lobed. Plants are either male or female; small, stalked male flowers in branched clusters; female flowerhead cone-like, becoming papery in fruit. *Flowering:* July–August. *Distribution:* Throughout most of Europe; extensively cultivated for the brewing industry.

Osyris alba Up to 120cm A spreading evergreen shrub with numerous slender branches. Leathery leaves linear to lanceolate, with pronounced mid-rib. Male and female flowers on different plants, males in few-flowered clusters, females solitary on short branches. Perianth is three-lobed. Fruit red when ripe. *Flowering:* April–June. *Distribution:* Southern Europe; hemiparasite growing on roots of other plants.

Bastard-toadflax *Thesium humifusum* Up to 20cm A perennial, often forming hummocks in dry situations, and often woody at the base. Leaves are linear with a single vein. Small, greenish-white flowers in small clusters; perianth usually four-lobed. *Flowering:* June–August. *Distribution:* Endemic to western Europe, from Belgium to Spain; chalk and limestone grassland. Hemiparasitic on roots of various plants. **T. arvense** is 10–30cm, upright or ascending, with wider leaves and flowers in a long loose inflorescence. *Flowering:* June–August. *Distribution:* grassland in eastern and central Europe; hemiparasite.

Mistletoe *Viscum album* Up to 100cm An evergreen shrub with green, regularly forked branches, parasitic on the branches of trees. Leaves are leathery, 20–80mm, yellowish-green, obovate. Flowers small, in cluster of three to five, males and females on different plants; sepals absent; four petals greenish and sepal-like. Fruit a sticky white berry. *Flowering:* February–May. *Distribution:* Throughout most of Europe; on many types of trees, including conifers. **Loranthus europaeus** is smaller, up to 50cm, with smaller dull-green leaves. Flowers have small calyx teeth, and four to six petals. Berry pear-shaped, yellow and sticky. *Flowering:* May–June. *Distribution:* South-eastern Europe, north to Germany; parasitic on members of the beech and oak families.

Cytinus hypocistus Up to 7cm A parasitic perennial, without any chlorophyll, the leaves scale-like, yellow, orange or scarlet. Flowers up to 10 in a dense spike, the lower female, the upper male, tubular, bright yellow. *Flowering:* April–June. *Distribution:* Southern and western parts of the Mediterranean, up into western France; on the roots of members of the genus *Cistus*. **C. ruber** is similar, but with stems up to 12cm, crimson scale leaves, and whitish or pale pink flowers. *Flowering:* March–May. *Distribution:* Mediterranean region; parasitic on the pink-flowered Cistus species.

Pellitory-of-the-wall

Hop

Osyris alba

Bastard-toadflax

Mistletoe

Cytinus hypocistus

Asarabacca *Asarum europeaum* Up to 5cm A creeping evergreen perennial. Stems short, usually with just two kidney-shaped, dark glossy green leaves, 25–100mm, their stalks much longer than their blades. Solitary, brownish, tubular flowers are borne at the ends of branches. *Flowering:* April–May. *Distribution:* southwards from Scandinavia to southern France and central Italy, occasionally naturalised elsewhere; woods, rocks and walls.

Birthwort *Aristolochia clematitis* Up to 80cm A creeping, evil-smelling plant with numerous upright stems. Leaves are alternate, broadly ovate and finely toothed. Dull yellow flowers, four to eight together in leaf axils, are cylindrical with a swollen base; tube curved with long flap at the tip. Fruit pear-shaped. *Flowering:* June–September. *Distribution:* Probably native only in eastern and south-eastern Europe, but quite widely naturalised. **A. longa** is usually branched, with triangular-ovate leaves and larger brownish- or yellowish-green flowers, with a purple-brown flap. *Flowering:* May–July. *Distribution:* Mediterranean region and Portugal, rarer in the east. **A. pallida,** up to 50cm, has ovate to kidney-shaped leaves, and green, pale-brown or yellow flowers, striped with brown or purple. *Flowering:* June–August. *Distribution:* Southern Europe, absent from the west.

Aristolochia longa: flower

Knotweed *Polygonum aviculare* Up to 200cm A straggling and usually prostrate annual, with alternate, lanceolate to ovate leaves, much larger on the main stems. Each leaf-base is enclosed in a papery sheath (ochra). Flowers are small, in small spikes of up to six, usually in leaf-axils. Fruit three-sided, often extending beyond the flower. *Flowering:* June–October. *Distribution:* Throughout Europe, on waste and arable ground. **Lesser Red Knotgrass** (*P. arenarium*) differs in having pointed, very narrowly lanceolate leaves, conspicuous pink and white flowers, and smaller, usually glossy fruit. *Flowering:* June–October. *Distribution:* Southern, eastern and central Europe.

Lesser Red Knotgrass: leaf and ochrea

Common Bistort *Polygonum bistorta* Up to 100cm A patch-forming perennial, with unbranched stems. Lower leaves are ovate, blunt, with winged leaf-stalks, the upper triangularly lanceolate; basal sheath (ochra) deeply fringed. Flowers bright pink, in a dense terminal spike. *Flowering:* June–October. *Distribution:* Damp grassland throughout Europe, except Scandinavia, where it occurs in mountains in the south. **Alpine Bistort** (*P. vivipara*) up to 40cm, is more slender, with smaller, oblong-lanceolate leaves. Flowers are pinkish to white, in a less dense spike, the lower flowers replaced by dark brown bulbils. *Flowering:* June–August. *Distribution:* Grassland and wet rocks in northern Europe, on mountains in central and southern Europe.

Alpine Bistort: bulbils

Redshank *Polygonum maculosa* Up to 80cm A weedy annual, usually erect or ascending, often reddish-tinged. Leaves are lanceolate, hairless, often with a black spot; basal sheath (ochra) with long-haired margin. Numerous flowers densely crowded into a spike, each one pale pink. *Flowering:* May–October. *Distribution:* Throughout mainland Europe; a weed of cultivated and waste ground.

Buckwheat *Fagopyrum esculentum* Up to 60cm An erect little-branched annual, usually hairless, with a red tinge to the mature stems. Leaves are triangular, dark green, the lower stalked, the upper stalkless. Flowers form short compact inflorescences, at tips of stems or in axils of leaves. Each flower has five petal-like segments. *Flowering:* June–August. *Distribution:* Most of Europe except Scandinavia; cultivated for grain-like fruits.

Asarabacca

Birthwort

Knotweed

Common Bistort

Redshank

Buckwheat

Copse-bindweed: fruit

Black-bindweed *Fallopia convolvulus* Up to 100cm A vigorous, fast-growing, trailing or climbing annual. Leaves are triangular-ovate. Flowers are small, in spike-like inflorescences; petal-like perianth segments five, inner three narrowly winged in fruit. Fruit 4–5mm, dull black. *Flowering:* July–October. *Distribution:* Throughout Europe, introduced in the north; cultivated and waste ground. Similar **Copse-bindweed** (*F. dumetorum)* has narrower leaves and perianth segments broadly winged in fruit. Fruit up to 3mm, shiny. *Flowering:* July–October. *Distribution:* Europe, absent from the north; hedgerows.

Horned Dock *Rumex bucephalophorus* Up to 40cm An annual or occasionally perennial, with one or more slender stems, and very small ovate leaves. Flowers small, two or three in each cluster. Fruits very variable, the persistent inner perianth segments triangular or oblong, toothed or not, the stalk short and slender or long and flat. *Flowering:* April–June. *Distribution:* Mediterranean and south-west Europe; usually near the sea.

Sheep's Sorrel

Common Sorrel *Rumex acetosa* Up to 100cm A perennial, with acid-tasting foliage. Leaves are arrow-shaped, the basal leaves two to four times as long as wide, with backward-pointing lobes, upper leaves clasping the stem. Flowers in a branched inflorescence, sexes on different plants. Inner three perianth segments 3–4mm in fruit, broad, papery, reddish. *Flowering:* May–August. *Distribution:* throughout most of Europe, more rare in the south; grassland and woodland areas; very variable. **Sheep's Sorrel** (*R. acetosella),* is a slender plant with narrow, arrow-shaped basal leaves, the lobes pointing outwards or forwards; upper leaves stalked. *Flowering:* May–August. *Distribution:* Acid soils throughout Europe.

Broad Leaved Dock: leaf and fruit

Clustered Dock *Rumex conglomeratus* Up to 100cm A short-lived perennial, with oblong leaves, wedge- or nearly heart-shaped at the base. Flowers in whorls in sparse, widely branched inflorescence. Inner three perianth segments 2–3mm in fruit, narrow, each with a large, swollen protuberance. *Flowering:* June–August. *Distribution:* Throughout most of Europe, but absent from parts of Russia; damp places, especially by rivers and ponds, and waste ground. **Broad Leaved Dock** (*R. obtusifolius)* is up to 120cm, with large oblong leaves, the lower heart-shaped at the base. Fruiting perianth segments 5–6mm, triangular, toothed, usually only one with a protuberance. *Flowering:* June–October. *Distribution:* Europe, except the extreme north and south; streamsides, wood margins and waste places.

Curled Dock *Rumex crispus* Up to 150cm An invasive perennial weed, with basal leaves about four times as long as wide, narrowly lanceolate, with wavy margins, the stalk shorter than the blade. Flowers in whorls in dense, narrow, branched inflorescence. Inner three perianth segments 3.5–5.5mm in fruit, broad, net-veined, at least one with a swollen protuberance. *Flowering:* June-October. *Distribution:* Throughout Europe; coasts.

Sea Beet *Beta vulgaris* subsp. *maritima* Up to 80cm An annual, biennial or perennial, sprawling or erect, often reddish. Leaves are shiny-green, ovate, heart- or wedge-shaped at the base; stem leaves lanceolate. Small flowers greenish, in clusters of one to three, forming a branched spike. *Flowering:* June–September. *Distribution:* Coasts of southern and western Europe. **Beet** (*B. vulgaris* subsp. *vulgaris)* is larger, up to 200cm, with a conspicuously swollen root. *Flowering:* June–September. *Distribution:* Widely cultivated in Europe for sugar and for fodder, often naturalised.

Black-bindweed

Horned Dock

Common Sorrel

Clustered Dock

Curled Dock:fruiting plant

Sea Beet

Good-King-Henry *Chenopodium bonus-henricus* Up to 80cm
An erect or ascending perennial, triangular leaves with wavy margins and
prominent lobes at the base. Mealy white when young, they turn green later.
Flowers are very small, greenish, usually hermaphrodite, many together on a
long tapering spike, leafless at the top. *Flowering:* May–August. *Distribution:*
Throughout Europe, except the east and parts of the south; roadsides, fields
and especially areas which are nitrogen-rich, such as farmyards.

Fat-hen *Chenopodium album* Up to 150cm Resembles Good-King-Henry
but is an annual, taller, often with reddish stems and usually covered with a
white powdery meal. Leaves are 10–80mm, very variable in shape but usually
ovate to lanceolate, often toothed, and lacking lobes. Flowers in a more open,
leafy spike with long branches. Perianth segments have a raised ridge on the
back. *Flowering:* June–October. *Distribution:* Throughout Europe; often very
abundant as a weed of waste ground.

Stinking Goosefoot *Chenopodium vulvaria* Up to 65cm An annual
with stems branching from the base and usually ascending. It smells very
strongly of rotten fish. Ovate leaves up to 25mm are covered in white meal.
Flowers are greenish, crowded in small leafy spikes, at the tips of stems, or in
leaf axils. Perianth segments rounded and lacking a ridge on the back.
Flowering: July–October. *Distribution:* Throughout most of Europe; salt
marshes, waste ground by the sea, and also as a casual weed inland.

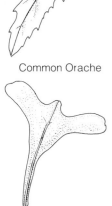

Common Orache

Atriplex pedunculata:
fruit

Spear-leaved Orache *Atriplex prostrata* Up to 100cm An erect or
prostrate annual, with white- or red-striped stems. Lower leaves are triangular
and lobed at the base, green or mealy white only beneath. Flowers in
clusters, small, unisexual. Male flowers have a five-lobed perianth; female
flowers enclosed by two small bracts which greatly enlarge to cover the fruit
as it develops. *Flowering:* June–October. *Distribution:* Throughout Europe;
waste ground, especially near the coast. **Common Orache** (*A. patula*) is
the same size, but has more lanceolate lower leaves and is usually
completely white-mealy. The stem is strongly ridged. Flowers are in clusters
in axils, or on long spikes. *Flowering:* July–October. *Distribution:* Throughout
Europe; a common weed.

Sea Purslane *Atriplex portulacoides* Up to 100cm A sprawling,
branched shrub, covered with silvery meal. Stems often root from the nodes.
Lower leaves are opposite, elliptical, thick and fleshy. Flowers are small, in
short, branched inflorescences, males and females on different plants. Fruits
unstalked. *Flowering:* July–October. *Distribution:* Mediterranean, Atlantic and
North Sea coasts, and the south-west shore of the Black Sea; salt–marshes,
especially on the edges of channels. **A. pedunculata** is smaller, up to
50cm, annual, and erect, with all leaves alternate. Fruits have short stalks.
Flowering: July–October. *Distribution:* Shores of northern and north-western
Europe; drier parts of salt–marshes.

Annual Sea-blite *Sueda maritima* Up to 75cm A very variable annual,
often much branched, occasionally woody at the base. Leaves are alternate,
fleshy, semi-cylindrical but flat on the top, with a pointed tip and tapering
base. Flowers small in clusters of one to three, either hermaphrodite or female
only. *Flowering:* August–October. *Distribution:* Throughout coastal Europe,
except the north-east and the far north; salt–marshes, but usually on the
seaward side.

Good-King-Henry

Fat-hen

Stinking Goosefoot

Spear-leaved Orache

Sea Purslane

Annual Sea-blite

Saltwort *Salsola kali* Up to 100cm A prickly, prostrate or erect, untidy annual. Leaves are linear, flattened cylindrical, stalkless, fleshy, usually with a sharp spine at the tip. Flowers are small, green, each with two small green leaf-like bracts, which are often spiny, enclosing them. *Flowering:* July–October. *Distribution:* Throughout Europe, more or less confined to coastal areas in the north; a plant of waste, sandy places.

Glasswort *Salicornia europea* Up to 40cm A much-branched annual with opposite leaves fused to give the appearance of leafless, fleshy stems made up of short segments. Flowers borne one to three together, at the joints of segments, often somewhat sunken in the stem and difficult to distinguish. Whole plant usually turns reddish or purple in fruit. A very variable species. *Flowering:* August–October. *Distribution:* Most of coastal Europe; salt–marshes, usually on bare mud. Similar **Perennial Glasswort** *(S. perennis)* is perennial, with creeping mat-forming stems. *Flowering:* July–September. *Distribution:* South-west Europe north to Britain.

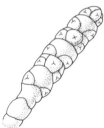
Perennial Glasswort: flowering stem

Amaranthus blitum: flowers and fruit

Common Amaranth *Amaranthus retroflexus* Up to 100cm An upright, almost unbranched annual, covered in dense hairs towards the top. Leaves are alternate, more or less ovate. Flowers are small, in a short dense spike, with five dry narrow and pointed perianth segments. *Flowering:* July–October. *Distribution:* A North American species, naturalised throughout Europe. **A. blitum** is similar, but hairless, the leaves ovate to round, with spots on the upper surface, and the flowers have wider perianth segments. *Flowering:* July–September. *Distribution:* Waste places, mainly in southern Europe, but as a casual elsewhere.

Hottentot Fig *Carpobrotus edulis* Up to 300cm long A prostrate, woody perennial. Fleshy leaves are opposite, 40–90mm long, three-angled, of equal thickness for most of their length but tapering to the tip. Flowers reach 100mm across, borne on the tips of stems; sepals five; petals numerous, narrow strap-shaped, yellow or purple; stamens yellow. *Flowering*: June–August. *Distribution:* A South African species widely naturalised on the coasts of southern and western Europe north to Ireland; dunes, rocks.

Mesembryanthemum nodiflorum: leaves

Ice-plant *Mesembryanthemum crystallinum* Up to 20cm A prostrate annual, densely covered in shiny crystalline hairs. Leaves are ovate, flat. Flowers are both axillary and at the tips of stems, with yellowish petals longer than sepals. *Flowering:* June–August. *Distribution*: Mediterranean region and Portugal; salt marshes and sandy areas by the sea. **M. nodiflorum** is similar, but has narrow, oblong leaves, only a slight peppering of crystalline hairs, and petals shorter than the yellow or whitish sepals. Flowering times and distribution are the same as for Ice-plant.

Blinks

Spring Beauty *Claytonia perfoliata* Up to 30cm An annual with a rosette of basal leaves, and conspicuous fleshy stem leaves joined at the base to encircle the stem. White flowers emerge in loose, few-flowered clusters from axils of stem leaves; petals 2–3mm, slightly longer than sepals. Flowering: April–July. *Distribution:* A native of western North America, naturalised in western Europe; dry sandy soils. **Blinks** *(Montia fontana)* is sometimes perennial, reaching 50cm or more when growing in water but far shorter on land. Leaves are opposite, narrowly ovate or spoon-shaped. Flowers in small clusters at the end of stems. *Flowering:* April–October. *Distribution:* Throughout most of Europe; in water or on muddy areas.

Saltwort

Glasswort

Common Amaranth

Hottentot Fig

Ice-plant

Spring Beauty

Slender Sandwort: fruit

Three-nerved Sandwort

Annual Pearlwort

Lesser Stitchwort

Thyme-leaved Sandwort *Arenaria serpyllifolia* Up to 30cm A very variable, greyish annual or rarely a biennial, usually much branched at base with ascending stems. Leaves are broadly ovate to lanceolate-ovate, pointed, the lower stalked, the upper stalkless. Flowers form a loose inflorescence; sepals three or four 4mm, petals shorter. Capsule flask-shaped. *Flowering:* April–November. *Distribution:* Throughout Europe; dry sandy places. **Slender Sandwort** (*A. serpyllifolia* subsp. *leptoclados*) is a more delicate plant; sepals usually less than 3mm; capsule straight-sided. *Flowering:* April–November. *Distribution:* Southern, western and central Europe.

Fine-leaved Sandwort *Minuartia hybrida* Up to 20cm An erect, slender annual, branched from the base and above the middle, usually hairless, with opposite linear leaves. Flowers white, in a loose inflorescence, with petals slightly shorter than sepals of 2–4mm. *Flowering:* May–September. *Distribution:* Southern and western Europe, extending north to Britain, central Germany and the Ukraine; dry bare sandy places, and walls. **Three-nerved Sandwort** (*Moehringia trinervia*) to 40cm, is a larger, downy straggling annual. Leaves are opposite, ovate, with three to five prominent veins. Flowers solitary in axils, or in loose inflorescences, the white petals shorter than the sepals. *Flowering:* May–June. *Distribution:* Throughout Europe; woods and hedge banks, in shady places.

Sea Sandwort *Honkenya peploides* Up to 25cm A creeping perennial, with glossy green, ovate or oblong, fleshy leaves. Flowers greenish-white, up to 10mm across, in axils, or one to six together at the end of a stem. Male and female flowers are on different plants; sepals equalling petals in male flowers, longer than petals in females. *Flowering:* May–August. *Distribution:* Northern and western Europe and the Urals; coastal sand or shingle, rarely inland.

Procumbent Pearlwort *Sagina procumbens* Up to 20cm long A perennial with ascending stems that root at the nodes, forming a dense mat. Leaves are 5–12mm, linear and pointed. Small, solitary flowers are greenish; four sepals 1–2.5mm, blunt; petals rarely as large as sepals, more usually minute or absent. *Flowering:* May–September. *Distribution:* Throughout Europe; common weed of cultivated areas, especially in paths, lawns and short turf. Very similar **Annual Pearlwort** (*S. apetala*) is a much branched annual. Flowers have minute petals but these usually fall early. *Flowering:* April–August. *Distribution:* Throughout Europe except for parts of the far north; dry bare waste or cultivated ground.

Chickweed *Stellaria media* Up to 90cm An untidy much branched annual but often overwintering. Lower leaves are ovate, pointed, long-stalked, the upper more or less stalkless. Flowers in few- or many-flowered inflorescences; sepals 3–7mm, slightly longer than deeply-divided white petals. *Flowering:* All year. *Distribution:* Common weed throughout Europe.

Greater Stitchwort *Stellaria holostea* Up to 60cm A perennial, with weak, usually sharply four-angled rough stems. Leaves are lanceolate, pointed, rough on margins and underside of midrib. Flowers 15–30mm wide, in loose inflorescences; white petals cut to half-way. *Flowering:* April–June. *Distribution:* Most of Europe, rare in Mediterranean regions; woods and hedgerows. **Lesser Stitchwort** (*S. graminea*) is very similar, with smooth leaves and flowers 5–12mm. *Flowering:* May–August. *Distribution:* Throughout Europe, except the far south; grassy places.

Thyme-leaved Sandwort

Fine-leaved Sandwort

Sea Sandwort

Procumbent Pearlwort:fruiting plant

Chickweed

Greater Stitchwort

Field Mouse-ear *Cerastium arvense* Up to 30cm A variable perennial, forming loose mats, with prostrate or ascending, usually downy branches. Leaves are linear to elliptic-lanceolate. Flowers are 12–25mm across, one to three at tips of stems; white deeply notched petals twice as long as sepals. *Flowering:* April–August. *Distribution:* Most of Europe, except far north; dry open places, often on lime-rich soil.

Sticky Mouse-ear *Cerastium glomeratum* Up to 45cm Low annual covered with sticky glandular hairs. Leaves are hairy, the lower ovate, the upper elliptic to ovate. Flowers about 10mm, in tight clusters; white petals the same length as sepals. *Flowering:* April–October. *Distribution:* Throughout Europe, except the north-east; open places, in both natural and man-made habitats. **Common Mouse-ear** (*C. fontanum*) is a very variable, often downy perennial, with lanceolate, stalkless leaves. Flowers small, white, in dense heads; petals notched, the same length as sepals. *Flowering:* April–November. *Distribution:* Almost throughout Europe; waste and cultivated ground, and grassland.

Common Mouse-ear

Corn Spurrey *Spergula arvensis* Up to 70cm An annual, branching from the base, with ascending, stickily hairy stems. Leaves are whorled, linear, blunt at the tips, channelled on the underside. Flowers are 4–10mm; petals white, slightly larger than sepals. *Flowering:* May–September. *Distribution:* Almost throughout Europe; weed of cornfields and cultivated ground, usually on sandy, lime-free soils. **Pearlwort Spurrey** (*S. morrisonii*) to 30cm, is smaller, with more rigid, generally hairless stems, and leaves without channels on the underside. Flowers smaller, with equal petals and sepals. *Flowering:* April–June. *Distribution:* Central Europe, south to Spain and Portugal, north to central Sweden.

Pearlwort Spurrey

Greater Sea-spurrey *Spergularia media* Up to 40cm An almost hairless perennial, with prostrate or ascending stems. Leaves are opposite, linear, with short points. Flowers are 8–12mm, in a loose inflorescence; petals pink or white, shorter than the sepals. *Flowering:* May–September. *Distribution:* European coast and inland saline areas, except the north-east; maritime sand or mud, salty areas inland.

Lesser Sea-spurrey *Spergularia marina* Up to 35cm Resembles Greater Sea-spurrey but is a more slender perennial, with glandular hairs on the inflorescence, and often on the stem. Leaves are fleshy. Flowers have sepals of 2.5–4mm, longer than the petals which are pink with a white base. *Flowering:* May–September. *Distribution:* Throughout most of Europe; coastal sand and mud, and inland salty areas. **Sand Spurrey** (*S. rubra*) is annual or perennial, covered with glandular hairs; flowers are 3-8mm, with rose-pink petals longer than the sepals. *Flowering:* May–September. *Distribution:* Throughout Europe; sandy soils, not in limy or salty conditions.

Sand Spurrey

Annual Knawel *Scleranthus annuus* Up to 25cm An annual or biennial with ascending stems. Leaves are linear, joined at the base in pairs. Flowers in clusters at tips of stems or in leaf axils lack petals; sepals greenish with a white border. *Flowering:* May–October. *Distribution:* Throughout Europe, except the far north; sandy ground. **Perennial Knawel** (*S. perennis*) is a generally stouter perennial with some sterile shoots. Flowers with much blunter green sepals, with a broader white margin than those of Annual Knawel. *Flowering:* June–October. *Distribution:* Throughout most of Europe.

Perennial Knawel

Field Mouse-ear

Sticky Mouse-ear

Corn Spurrey

Greater Sea-spurrey

Lesser Sea-spurrey

Annual Knawel

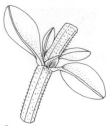

Smooth
Rupture-wort

Paronychia argentea Up to 30cm A usually prostrate perennial, much branched and matted. Leaves are ovate to lanceolate, about as long as the distance between nodes. Flowers small, in clusters, usually in leaf axils. Each flower is surrounded by a pair of silvery leaf-shaped bracts, forming a distinctive inflorescence. Petals usually absent. *Flowering:* May–September. *Distribution:* Southern Europe; open sandy or rocky ground. **Smooth Rupture-wort** (*Herniaria glabra)* is similar, but sometimes annual, with short hairs all around the stem and elliptic-ovate leaves. Flowers in small clusters, without silvery bracts; petals shorter than sepals. *Flowering:* May–October. *Distribution:* Most of Europe except far north; dry sandy ground.

Coral-necklace *Illecebrum verticillatum* Up to 30cm A hairless, usually prostrate annual, with slender, branched or unbranched, four-angled stems often rooting at the nodes, and occasionally reddish in colour. Leaves are opposite, linear-ovate. Each node has two clusters of four to six small flowers. Petals are much shorter than white, fleshy sepals. *Flowering:* June-October. *Distribution:* Western and central Europe to Russian and Italy; damp, sandy and gravelly areas.

Annual Gypsophila *Gypsophila muralis* Up to 30cm A short, normally hairless, branched annual. Leaves are linear, pointed, grey-green. Flowers are about 4mm across, in a loose cluster; pink petals about twice as long as sepals, with darker veins. *Flowering:* June–October. *Distribution:* Central and eastern Europe, extending to north-west Spain, Sweden and central Greece; meadows and damp woodlands.

Sticky Catchfly

Ragged-robin *Lychnis flos-cuculi* Up to 90cm A perennial, with branched or unbranched, usually rough stems and ragged-looking pink flowers. Basal leaves are oblong, stalked, stem leaves linear-lanceolate, stalkless. Flowers are loosely clustered on long stalks, with bright pink, usually four-lobed petals. *Flowering:* May–August. *Distribution:* Throughout Europe, but rare in the south; damp areas. **Sticky Catchfly** (*L. viscaria)* is similar, but very sticky below each leaf node. Flowers in a more dense spike, pink with notched petals. *Flowering:* May–August. *Distribution:* Most of Europe, but rare in south-west; cliffs and rocky places.

Corn-cockle *Agrostemma githago* Up to 100cm A tall, hairy annual with linear opposite leaves, their bases joined around the stem. Flowers are solitary on long stalks; calyx hairy, forming a tube; petals reddish-purple, notched, shorter than the narrow calyx teeth. *Flowering:* May–August. *Distribution:* Throughout Europe, but probably only native in the eastern Mediterranean; weed of cultivated land.

Berry Catchfly

Bladder Campion *Silene vulgaris* Up to 60cm A hairless greyish perennial, with ascending or erect stems, sometimes woody at the base. Leaves are ovate to linear, often wavy-edged. Flowers in a loose spike, often unisexual; calyx forming an inflated tube; large white petals deeply divided. *Flowering:* May–September. *Distribution:* Throughout Europe; arable land, waste ground and grassland. **Berry Catchfly** (*Cucubalus baccifer)* up to 120cm, is similar, with ovate leaves and much-branching stems. The flowers are smaller and drooping; fruit is a black berry. *Flowering:* July–September. *Distribution:* Southern and eastern Europe, northwards to the Netherlands and Russia; grassy places.

Paronychia argentea

Coral-necklace

Annual Gypsophila

Ragged-robin

Corn-cockle

Bladder Campion

Moss Campion *Silene acaulis* Up to 20cm across A bright green, moss-like perennial, forming mats with short, upright flowering stems. Leaves are linear, pointed, with tough leathery margins. Profuse flowers are 5–10mm in diameter, rose-pink, hermaphrodite or occasionally males and females on different plants. *Flowering:* June–August. *Distribution:* Arctic Europe and higher mountains of western and central Europe.

Red Campion *Silene dioica* Up to 100cm A downy perennial, occasionally glandular or hairless. Leaves are ovate or lanceolate-ovate, those on the stem stalkless. Flowers form a loose inflorescence at the end of the stem, large, bright pink, occasionally paler, with deeply notched petals, the sexes on different plants. *Flowering:* March–November. *Distribution:* Throughout most of Europe, but rare in the south; usually in woodlands or hedgerows. **White Campion** *(S. latifolia)* is very similar, but often annual, and more glandular-hairy. Flowers larger, white, opening fully in the evenings. Hybridises with Red Campion. *Flowering:* May–October. *Distribution:* Almost throughout Europe; disturbed or cultivated ground. **Night-flowering Catchfly** *(S. noctiflora)* up to 40cm, is an annual, very sticky, with more pointed ovate leaves. Flowers large, hermaphrodite, opening in the evening, normally rolled up during the day. *Flowering:* June–October. *Distribution:* Throughout Europe, but only a casual in the north; bare and arable ground.

Night-flowering Catchfly

Small-flowered Catchfly *Silene gallica* Up to 45cm A softly hairy, sticky annual, with a simple or branched stem and downy lanceolate leaves. Flowers are small, in a loose, more or less one-sided inflorescence, with the lower flower stalks longer than the upper; petals often blotched pink. *Flowering:* June–October. *Distribution:* Southern and central Europe, north to Poland, Denmark and Russia; sandy places and waste ground.

Sand-catchfly *Silene conica* Up to 35cm A softly hairy, sticky annual, greyish-green, with narrowly lanceolate leaves and only a few small pink flowers. Calyx tube becomes more or less oval. *Flowering:* May–June. *Distribution:* Central and southern Europe, north to Britain and the Ukraine; sandy places, especially by the sea.

Soapwort *Saponaria officinalis* Up to 90cm A hairless perennial, usually unbranched, with ovate or elliptical three-veined leaves, ending in a point. Large flowers in a compact inflorescence; calyx cylindrical, often reddish; petals pale pink. Plants escaped from gardens may have double flowers. *Flowering:* June–September. *Distribution:* From Belgium, north Germany and central Russia southwards; roadsides, hedges, waste ground and grassy places, often an escape from gardens. **Rock Soapwort** *(S. ocimoides)* up to 50cm, is downy hairy, with narrowly elliptical leaves, and pale purple flowers 10mm across, in a loose inflorescence. *Flowering:* May–September. *Distribution:* South-west and south-central Europe; rocky areas, much grown in gardens and occasionally escaping elsewhere.

Rock Soapwort

Cowherb *Vaccaria hispanica* Up to 60cm A hairless, grey-green, branched annual, with ovate or lanceolate leaves. Flowers are 10–15mm across, on long stalks, froming a loose inflorescence; pale pink petals notched. The calyx becomes inflated and bladdery after flowering. *Flowering:* June–October. *Distribution:* Southern and central Europe, to Belgium and central Russia, often as a casual elsewhere; weed of arable lands.

Moss Campion

Red Campion

Small-flowered Catchfly

Sand-catchfly

Soapwort

Cowherb

Petrorhagia prolifera

Tunic-flower *Petrorhagia saxifraga* Up to 45cm A roughly hairy or hairless perennial with opposite, linear leaves 10mm long, their bases fused into a sheath around the stems. Flowers are about 10mm across, solitary or in loose clusters at the tips of stems, each flower surrounded by four brownish, papery bracts; notched petals white or pink. *Flowering:* June–August. *Distribution:* Central and southern Europe, to central France and eastwards to the Ukraine; open places on dry soils and on walls. **P. prolifera** is similar, but has broader leaves and pinkish or purplish flowers in tight clusters; petals heart-shaped at tips. *Flowering:* May–September. *Distribution:* Central Europe and mountains in the south; dry open ground.

Large Pink *Dianthus superbus* Up to 90cm A grey-green perennial, often prostrate at the base, with branched, erect flowering stems. Leaves are opposite, linear-lanceolate. Fragrant flowers are 30–50mm across, purplish or pink, rarely white; petals many times divided, giving a deeply fringed edge. *Flowering:* June–September. *Distribution:* Throughout Europe, except the far west and south, and the islands; dry, often shady places.

Cheddar Pink

Maiden Pink *Dianthus deltoides* Up to 45cm A tufted green or grey-green perennial, with rough stems. Leaves are linear-lanceolate and blunt on non-flowering shoots, narrower and pointed on flowering shoots. Flowers are 12–20mm across, white to deep pink. *Flowering:* June–September. *Distribution:* Most of Europe, but very rare in the Mediterranean area; dry, grassy or sandy areas. **Cheddar Pink** (*D. gratianopolitanus*) up to 25cm, is more mat-forming, with longer leaves, and solitary fragrant pink flowers, with shortly fringed petals. *Flowering:* May–July. *Distribution:* Western and central Europe, to the west Ukraine; rocks, usually in full sun, often on limestone.

Deptford Pink *Dianthus armeria* Up to 60cm An upright, green downy annual or biennial with oblong, blunt basal leaves, and linear stem leaves, all flat and thin. Unscented flowers up to 15mm across, form clusters at the stem apex; petals bright pink, usually spotted. *Flowering:* June–August. *Distribution:* Throughout Europe, but rare in the north; dry sandy grassland.

Nymphaea candida

White Water-lily *Nymphaea alba* An aquatic plant, with round floating leaves up to 40cm across, the lobes of the leaves not overlapping at the base. Top of leaf is glossy, dark green; underside often reddish. White flowers floating, 50–200mm in diameter, scented, with up to 25 petals; numerous stamens; nine to 25 yellow stigmas on top of the ovary. *Flowering:* June–September. *Distribution:* Throughout most of Europe; still shallow water. **N. candida** is smaller, and has the basal leaf lobes overlapping, flowers with fewer petals, and deeper yellow stamens. *Flowering:* June–September. *Distribution:* Scattered throughout northern, central and eastern Europe.

Least Water-lily

Yellow Water-lily *Nuphar lutea* Similar to White Water-lily but with thinner, wavy-edged submerged leaves, the floating leaves more oval, up to 40 x 30cm. Yellow flowers up to 60mm across have up to seven yellow-green sepals, shorter petals, and 15–20 stigmas. Fruit is flask-shaped. *Flowering:* June-September. *Distribution:* Throughout Europe; still or flowing water. **Least Water-lily** (*N. pumila*) has smaller leaves, and flowers up to 30mm across, with more widely-spaced petals, and eight to ten stigmas. *Flowering:* June–July. *Distribution:* Northern and central Europe to central France, Yugoslavia and south-east Russia.

Tunic-flower

Large Pink

Maiden Pink

Deptford Pink

White Water-lily

Yellow Water-lily

Stinking Hellebore *Helleborus foetidus* 20–80cm A sombre green perennial with more or less upright, leafy stems which persist over winter. Leaves have seven to 11 narrow, toothed lobes from the base. Nodding flowers are bell-shaped; five perianth segments green with a purplish edge. Fruits have three pod-like parts, each opening to release several seeds. *Flowering:* January–April. *Distribution:* South-western and western Europe north to Britain and Germany; woodland and scrub.

Lenten Rose

Christmas Rose *Helleborus niger* 15–30cm A winter-flowering perennial which dies back to an underground stem. Leaves arise from the base, lasting over winter, each with seven to nine toothed lobes. Flowers in groups of two to three, 30–100mm, bowl-shaped; perianth segments white or pink-tinged; stamens numerous. Fruit has about seven pod-like parts, joined at the base, each with several seeds. *Flowering:* January–April. *Distribution:* Eastern Alps and mountains of central Italy; woodland or scrub, mainly in mountains on lime-rich soils. **Lenten Rose** (*H. purpurascens*) differs in having leaves usually with five lobes and purplish flowers. *Flowering:* March–April. *Distribution:* Native to eastern central Europe.

Green Hellebore *Helleborus viridis* 20–40cm A perennial dying back to an underground stem in winter. Basal leaves usually two, each with seven to 13 radiating, toothed lobes. Flowers in clusters of two to four, 40–50mm across, bowl-shaped; oval perianth segments yellowish-green; stamens numerous. Fruit has three to eight pod-like parts, joined at the base, each containing several seeds. *Flowering:* February–April. *Distribution:* Western and central Europe extending eastwards to Italy and Austria; woodland, scrub and rocky places on lime-rich soil.

Winter Aconite *Eranthis hyemalis* 5–20cm A small, early-flowering perennial. Basal leaves are deeply divided into many lobes; three stem leaves similar but smaller, forming a ring near top of flowering stem. Solitary flower at stem tip is 20–30mm across, bowl-shaped, usually with six narrowly oval yellow perianth segments. Fruit usually has six separate pod-like parts. *Flowering:* February–March. *Distribution:* Southern Europe from France to Bulgaria; often cultivated.

Fennel-flower

Love-in-a-mist *Nigella damascaena* 10–15cm A delicate annual with finely divided leaves cut two- to three times into very slender segments. Short-stalked blue flowers are 20–30mm across with a ring of small, finely divided leaves immediately beneath; perianth segments usually five, oval; blue stamens numerous; ovary has five long styles. Smooth fruit, almost globular and swollen, opens to release many seeds. *Flowering:* June–September. *Distribution:* Mainly southern Europe, naturalised elsewhere; cultivated fields, waste ground. Similar **Fennel-flower** (*N. sativa*) differs in the absence of a ring of finely divided leaves surrounding each of its whitish flowers. *Flowering:* August–September. *Distribution:* South-eastern Europe, naturalised elsewhere.

Nigella arvensis 10–30cm An annual with leaves finely divided into very slender segments. Distinctly stalked flowers are 20–30mm across; perianth segments pale blue, sometimes green-veined. Fruit has five pod-like segments, joined for about half their length, each containing many seeds. *Flowering:* June–July. *Distribution:* Much of Europe except for the north; cornfields and disturbed ground.

Stinking Hellebore

Christmas Rose

Green Hellebore

Winter Aconite

Love-in-a-mist

Nigella arvensis

Globe-flower *Trollius europaeus* Up to 70cm A hairless perennial, with long-stalked, three- to five-lobed basal leaves, and more or less stalkless, divided stem leaves. Flowers are up to 50mm across, globular, with ten lemon-yellow, curved perianth segments, the outer ones occasionally green-tinged. Stamens and carpels are numerous. *Flowering:* May–August. *Distribution:* Throughout Europe, only on mountains in the south; damp grassy areas, woods, and on rocks.

Marsh Marigold *Caltha palustris* Up to 60cm A creeping, hairless perennial with hollow stems, and heart-shaped, long-stalked dark green basal leaves; stem leaves are smaller with shorter stalks. Large flowers in a loose inflorescence are 15–50mm across with five glossy yellow perianth segments. Stamens numerous; carpels five to 15. *Flowering*: March–August. *Distribution:* Most of Europe, but rare in the Mediterranean; in wet places, from lowlands to mountain tops.

Columbine *Aquilegia vulgaris* Up to 60cm A branched perennial, with leaves divided into three lobes, each lobe itself three-lobed, usually hairy on the underside. Flowers are nodding; petal-like sepals five; petals five, each with a backwardly directed, curved spur. All flower segments are usually violet, but occasionally white or reddish. *Flowering:* May–July. *Distribution:* Western, central and southern Europe; woods and scrubland, usually on lime-rich soils.

Wolf's-bane

Yellow Monk's-hood *Aconitum anthora* Up to 100cm A poisonous, hairless perennial, with long-stalked basal leaves, deeply divided into narrow segments. Flowers in a simple or branched inflorescence; perianth segments five, yellow or occasionally blue, the upper one forming a hood. *Flowering:* July–September. *Distribution:* Southern, central and eastern Europe; rocky places, usually in mountains, up to 700m. **Wolf's-bane** (*A. vulparia*) up to 200cm, has dark-green leaves that are three times divided to the middle. Flowers small, yellowish or rarely blue, in a few-flowered inflorescence. *Flowering:* July–August. *Distribution*: France and Netherlands eastwards to Russia and Poland; dry grassland, and on rocks up to 800m.

Alpine Larkspur

Lice-bane *Delphinium staphisagria* Up to 100cm A stout-stemmed annual or occasionally a biennial, with hairy, five- to seven-lobed leaves, each lobe entire or three-lobed, the lobes ovate-lanceolate or blunt. Flowers deep blue; perianth segments 13–20mm, the upper with a backwardly directed spur. *Flowering:* May–July. *Distribution:* Mediterranean region; rocky or stony areas. **Alpine Larkspur** (*D. elatum*) is a perennial up to 200cm, with flowers that are usually dirty blue or blue-violet, but occasionally deep blue. *Distribution:* Central Europe and Yugoslavia; in meadows, and on rocks up to 700m.

Eastern Larkspur

Larkspur *Consolida ajacis* Up to 100cm An downy annual, with a simple or branched stem, and basal leaves deeply cut into narrow segments. Flowers in a loose inflorescence, deep blue, the upper petal with a backwardly projecting spur 12–18mm long. *Flowering:* June–August. *Distribution:* Mediterranean region, locally naturalised elsewhere; usually on disturbed ground. Similar **Eastern Larkspur** (*C. orientalis*) has stickily hairy branches and petals with spurs less than 12mm. *Flowering:* June–August. *Distribution:* Southern and eastern Iberian Peninsula and south-east Europe.

Globe-flower

Marsh Marigold

Columbine

Yellow Monk's-hood

Lice-bane

Larkspur

Wood Anemone *Anemone nemorosa* Up to 30cm A creeping, hairless perennial, with upright flowering stems with a whorl of three leaves two-thirds up the stem; two large basal leaves appear after the flowers. Leaves are usually palmately three-lobed, the lobes toothed. Flowers are solitary, up to 40 mm across; perianth segments five to nine, white, usually pinkish or purple on the back; stamens numerous. *Flowering:* March–May. *Distribution:* Most of Europe, but rare in the Mediterranean; woodland or alpine meadows.

Yellow Anemone *Anemone ranunculoides* Up to 30cm Similar to Wood Anemone but usually with only one basal leaf, and short-stalked, deeply divided stem leaves. Flowers up to 20mm across, single or occasionally two or more, with five yellow perianth segments. *Flowering:* March–May. *Distribution:* Most of Europe, but rare in the Mediterranean area; woodlands. **Snowdrop Windflower** (*A. sylvestris*) up to 50cm, is downy-hairy, with deeply lobed basal leaves on long stalks. Stem leaves are smaller. Flowers solitary or rarely two, 40–70mm, across, with five white perianth segments. *Flowering:* April–June. *Distribution:* Central and eastern Europe to Sweden and France; dry woods on lime-rich soils.

Snowdrop
Windflower: basal leaf

Blue Anemone *Anemone apennina* Up to 15cm Similar to Wood Anemone but with leaves downy-hairy beneath and the main leaf-divisions stalked; stem leaves borne near the middle of the stem. Flowers are 25–35mm across; perianth segments eight to 14, blue or rarely white. *Flowering:* March–April. *Distribution:* Southern Europe; open woodland and scrubby areas.

Pasque-flower *Pulsatilla vulgaris* Up to 12cm A low, hairy perennial with basal leaves silky-hairy when young, pinnately divided into feathery segments, and not fully opening until the plant is in flower. Flowering stem has three leaf-like bracts just below the flower. Flowers are 55–85mm across, made up of six pale- to dark-purple perianth segments. Stamens numerous. *Flowering:* March–May. *Distribution:* England and western France northwards to Sweden, and eastwards to the Ukraine; old grassland, on lime-rich soil. **Small Pasque-flower** (*P. pratensis*) is very like Pasque-flower but with smaller flowers, rarely over 40mm across, always drooping, more or less cylindrical, and dark purple, violet, greenish-yellow or white. *Flowering:* May. *Distribution:* Central and eastern Europe, westwards to south-east Norway, Denmark and Yugoslavia; meadows.

Small Pasque-flower

Pale Pasque-flower *Pulsatilla vernalis* Up to 15cm Similar to Pasque-flower but with much less divided, short-stalked, evergreen basal leaves. Flowers are 40–60mm across, at first nodding, becoming erect; perianth segments pink, violet or blue on the outside, white on the inside. *Flowering:* April–June. *Distribution:* Scandinavia southwards to Spain, northern Italy and Bulgaria; meadows, especially in mountains.

Liverleaf *Hepatica nobilis* Up to 15cm A perennial with very distinctive, evergreen, three-lobed leaves, heart-shaped at the base and purplish beneath. Flowers are 15–25mm across, solitary at the tips of stems, with three sepal-like bracts below the flower; perianth segments six to nine, blue-violet, purple, pink or white. *Flowering:* March–April. *Distribution:* Most of Europe, except the far north and south; woody and scrubby areas on lime-rich soil.

Wood Anemone

Yellow Anemone

Blue Anemone

Pasque-flower

Pale Pasque-flower

Liverleaf

Traveller's-joy: fruiting head

Virgin's Bower *Clematis flammula* Up to 500cm A more or less woody climber, often forming large hummocks growing over low vegetation. Both stems and leaf stalks twine. Leaves are twice-pinnate; leaflets narrow-oblong or rounded, sometimes three-lobed. Flowers up to 20mm across in dense clusters, very fragrant; perianth segments four, creamy white. Fruits are tipped with the long-plumed style. *Flowering:* July–September. *Distribution:* Southern Europe; scrub and woodland. **Traveller's-joy** (*C. vitalba*) up to 30m, is similar, but much more vigorous, often covering large trees. Fragrant flowers are about 20mm across. Fruits are feathery. *Flowering:* July–September. *Distribution:* Southern, western and central Europe; woodland, hedges and scrub, usually on lime-rich soils.

Alpine Clematis *Clematis alpina* Up to 200cm A scrambling woody climber, with twining stems and flower stalks. Leave are divided into three segments, each segment with three ovate-lanceolate, toothed leaflets. Flowers are usually solitary, terminal, nodding; four perianth segments blue, violet or white. Fruits tipped with the long-plumed style. *Flowering:* May–July. *Distribution:* Northern Europe and central and southern mountains, woods.

Clematis recta Up to 150cm An upright, herbaceous plant, with pinnate leaves, the leaflets ovate, stalked. Flowers about 20mm across, in clusters at the stem-tips, fragrant; four perianth segments white. Fruits tipped with the long-plumed style. *Flowering:* May–June. *Distribution:* Central, southern and eastern Europe; dry hillsides, and in open woodland.

Summer Pheasant's-eye: fruiting head

Pheasant's-eye *Adonis annua* Up to 40cm An annual with much divided leaves, the final segments linear with a pointed tip. Flowers are 15–25mm across; sepals ovate, hairless; petals five to eight, oblong, longer than the sepals, bright scarlet with a dark spot at the base. Fruits are 3.5–5mm. *Flowering:* June–July. *Distribution:* Southern Europe, north to southwards Switzerland, a casual elsewhere; weed of arable ground, on lime-rich soils. **Summer Pheasant's-eye** (*A. aestivalis*) is very similar to Pheasant's-eye, but the flowers are sometimes yellow and the fruits are 5–6mm long, ridged around the middle. *Flowering:* June–July. *Distribution:* Most of Europe, except the north; fields, on limestone. **Yellow Pheasant's-eye** (*A. vernalis*) is a perennial, with divided leaves. Flowers are 40–80mm; sepals half as long as the 10 to 20 elliptical yellow petals. *Flowering:* April–May. *Distribution:* Eastern, central and southern Europe, north to Sweden; grassland.

Alpine Meadow-rue

Lesser Meadow-rue *Thalictrum minus* Up to 150cm A hairless or glandular-hairy, branched perennial, with basal leaves much divided into round or ovate, irregularly toothed lobes. Flowers small, yellowish, with perianth segments that fall soon after the bud opens. *Flowering:* June–August. *Distribution:* Throughout most of Europe; wet areas, dry grassland and mountains. **Alpine Meadow-rue** (*T. alpinum*) up to 20cm, is smaller and unbranched, with purplish-green flowers. *Flowering:* June–August. *Distribution:* Arctic and subarctic Europe, southwards to the Pyrenees, Alps and East Carpathians; damp grassland, and rock ledges.

Mousetail *Myosurus minimus* Up to 12cm A small hairless annual, with a basal rosette of linear leaves. Flower are 8mm, solitary on long stalks, the five to seven shortly spurred perianth segments greenish-yellow. Central part of the flower elongates in fruit. *Flowering:* April–July. *Distribution:* Most of Europe, rare in the far north, south, and the islands; arable fields and damp ground.

Virgin's Bower

Alpine Clematis

Clematis recta

Pheasant's Eye

Lesser Meadow-rue

Mousetail

Lesser Celandine *Ranunculus ficaria* Up to 30cm A hairless, glossy or dark green perennial, with a rosette of ovate, long-stalked leaves, heart-shaped at the base. Flowers are 15–50mm, solitary; sepals three; eight to 12 narrow petals yellow, turning white with age; stamens numerous. *Flowering*: March–May. *Distribution:* Throughout most of Europe; hedges, woodland, and on damp open ground.

Meadow Buttercup *Ranunculus acris* Up to 100cm A perennial, downy-hairy with stiff hairs on the stem. Lower leaves are deeply divided into three to seven, ovate or wedge-shaped and toothed or further divided segments; stem leaves similar but smaller. Flowers are 15–25mm across; five sepals erect; five petals glossy yellow; stamens numerous. *Flowering:* May–July. *Distribution:* Throughout most of Europe; meadows and damp grassland.

Hairy Buttercup *Ranunculus sardous* Up to 45cm A downy-hairy annual, with basal leaves divided into three, often shiny leaflets, each with three, toothed lobes; central leaflet long-stalked. Flowers are 12–25mm across; sepals bent back; petals pale yellow. Fruits have small warts and a conspicuous green border. *Flowering:* May–October. *Distribution:* Most of Europe; grassland, and damp, cultivated ground.

Bulbous Buttercup *Ranunculus bulbosus* Up to 50cm A downy-hairy perennial with a bulbous base to the stem. Lower leaves are divided into three leaflets, the central one long-stalked; each leaflet is further divided or lobed. Bright yellow flowers are 20–30mm across; five sepals bent back. *Flowering:* March–June. *Distribution:* Most of Europe, except for parts of the east; dry grassland, generally on lime-rich soils. **Creeping Buttercup** (*Ranunculus repens*) is similar but lacks a bulb. Instead it has long, creeping runners. Sepals are not bent back. *Flowering:* May–September. *Distribution:* Most of Europe; damp areas, both grassy and bare.

Creeping Buttercup

Corn Buttercup *Ranunculus arvensis* Up to 60cm An annual, hairless or occasionally downy-hairy, with entire lower leaves; upper leaves are three-lobed, often with each lobe further divided. Flowers are 4–12mm across; five sepals spreading; five petals greenish-yellow. *Flowering:* May–July. *Distribution:* Southern, western and central Europe; a weed of arable land, often in damp areas.

Glacier Crowfoot *Ranunculus glacialis* Up to 25cm A nearly hairless perennial, with prostrate or ascending, simple or branched stems. Basal leaves are fleshy, three-lobed, each lobe stalked and further divided into oblong or elliptical lobes; stem leaves similar but smaller and stalkless. Flowers are 25–40mm; five sepals covered in red-brown hairs; five petals white. *Flowering:* June–August. *Distribution:* Northern Europe, mountains of central Europe, Pyrenees and Sierra Nevada; near the snow-line, on stony areas, avoiding lime-rich soils. **Pyrenean Buttercup** (*R. pyrenaeus*) is a bluish-green, perennial with basal leaves linear to broadly lanceolate, stalkless. Flowers are 20mm across; white sepals hairless; occasionally some petals absent. *Flowering:* May–July. *Distribution:* Alps, Pyrenees and mountains of Spain and Corsica, to 2800m; meadows and limestone slopes.

Pyrenean Buttercup: basal leaf

Lesser Celandine

Meadow Buttercup

Hairy Buttercup

Bulbous Buttercup

Corn Buttercup

Glacier Crowfoot

Greater Spearwort: basal leaf

Common Water-crowfoot: submerged leaf

River Water-crowfoot: submerged leaf

Paeonia officinalis

Lesser Spearwort *Ranunculus flammula* Up to 80cm A hairless perennial with erect stems or creeping and rooting at the nodes. Leaves are lanceolate or elliptical, the lower stalked, the upper stalkless. Flowers are 7–20mm, yellow, solitary or several together, on furrowed stalks. *Flowering:* June–October. *Distribution:* Throughout Europe, but rare in the Mediterranean; wet areas. Similar **Greater Spearwort** (*R. lingua*) up to 120cm, is more robust, with long-stalked ovate or heart-shaped basal leaves that soon wither, and oblong-lanceolate stem leaves. Flowers are 20–50mm, few on smooth stalks. *Flowering:* June–September. *Distribution:* Throughout Europe, but rare in the Mediterranean; marshes, fens, ponds and ditches.

Water-crowfoot *Ranunculus peltatus* Up to 100cm An aquatic annual or perennial, usually with both floating and submerged leaves. Broad, rounded floating leaves have three to seven toothed lobes; submerged leaves are globose clusters of narrow segments. Flowers are 20mm across; five petals white. Fruit stalk is usually more than 50mm long. *Flowering:* June–September. *Distribution:* Throughout most of Europe; ponds, ditches and slow-moving rivers. Similar **Common Water-crowfoot** (*R. aquatilis*) sometimes lacks floating leaves, and the fruit-stalk is less than 50mm long. *Flowering:* April–September. *Distribution:* Most of Europe.

Thread-leaved Water-crowfoot *Ranunculus trichophyllus* Up to 100cm An aquatic annual or perennial, with submerged leaves only, the segments short and stiff. Flowers are 5–10mm across; five petals white. Fruit stalk is usually less than 40mm. *Flowering:* May–September. *Distribution:* Most of Europe; ditches, canals, ponds and slow rivers, sometimes in brackish water. **River Water-crowfoot** (*R. fluitans*) is similar but with longer submerged leaves, the segments collapsing when taken out of water. Flowers are 20–30mm. *Flowering:* May–September. *Distribution:* Western and central Europe.

Peony *Paeonia mascula* Up to 60cm A perennial, usually with several erect stems and large, showy flowers. Basal leaves are divided into three segments, each with nine to 16 elliptical or ovate leaflets, hairless or downy-hairy beneath. Flowers are 8–14cm across; five to ten petals red; stamens numerous; carpels up to eight. *Flowering:* May–June. *Distribution:* Southern Europe, northwards to France and Austria, introduced elsewhere; rocky areas. Similar **P. officinalis**, has hairless basal leaves shiny above, segments divided into 17 to 30 leaflets. Stamens have red filaments; carpels two to three. *Flowering:* May–June. *Distribution:* Southern and south-central Europe; woods and fields.

Leontice leontopetalum Up to 50cm An upright, branched perennial with leaves up to 200mm wide, the lower stalked, the upper stalkless, all two- or three-lobed. Flowers are 16mm, 15 to 40 together on long stalks in the axils of upper leaves. Perianth segments six to eight, yellow. Inflated, leathery fruit of 25–40mm rots to release seeds. *Flowering:* March–April. *Distribution:* South-eastern Balkan Peninsula, Aegean Islands; arable and waste places.

Barberry *Berberis vulgaris* Up to 300cm A shrub with usually erect branches and yellowish, spiny and ridged twigs. Spines usually with three equal prongs. Leaves are 25–55mm, elliptical or ovate, finely toothed. Flowers are 10mm, hanging in clusters; perianth segments normally nine, yellow. Fruit is a bright red berry. *Flowering:* May–June. *Distribution:* Most of Europe but rare in the Mediterranean, often introduced; woods.

Lesser Spearwort

Water-crowfoot

Thread-leaved Water-crowfoot

Peony

Leontice leontophyllum

Barberry

Common Poppy *Papaver rhoeas* 25–90cm An erect, branching, coarsely hairy annual with leaves divided into toothed segments. Red flowers, 60–90mm across, are bowl-shaped or flattened, carried singly at stem tips; two green sepals fall off as flower opens; four petals nearly circular, often with a dark spot at base; numerous purplish filaments bear bluish anthers; disc-like stigma usually has eight to 12 rays. Fruit is a globose, hairless capsule, opening by pores below the flattened top to release many small, bluish-black seeds. *Flowering*: April–August. *Distribution:* Almost throughout Europe, doubtfully native in northern part of range; disturbed ground.

Rough Poppy *Papaver hybridum* 10–50cm A bristly annual similar to Common Poppy but smaller with crimson flowers 20–50mm across; petals are obovate with a dark spot at base. Oval capsule is stiffly bristly. *Flowering*: April–July. *Distribution:* Native in southern Europe, naturalised further north, in disturbed ground. **Prickly Poppy** (*Papaver argemone*) is very similar but has longer, almost cylindrical capsules. *Flowering:* April–July. *Distribution:* Native in southern Europe, naturalised further north; disturbed ground.

Prickly Poppy: fruit

Opium Poppy *Papaver somniferum* 30–100cm An erect, bluish-green, almost hairless annual with pinnately lobed leaves. Bowl-shaped flowers are usually 70–100mm across; petals almost circular; white, pink or purple, sometimes with a dark spot at base. Capsule is large, globose and hairless. *Flowering:* April–August. *Distribution:* Widely naturalised in Europe as an escape from cultivation, growing on disturbed ground.

Welsh Poppy *Meconopsis cambrica* 30–60cm A sparsely hairy perennial with leaves divided into toothed segments, green above, glaucous beneath. Bright yellow flowers are carried on erect, slender stalks; petals lack basal markings. Ovoid, hairless capsule opens near the apex by four to six pores. *Flowering:* June to August. *Distribution:* Western Europe; in shady, often damp and rocky places; sometimes naturalised.

Violet Horned-poppy *Roemeria hybrida* 20–40cm A spasely hairy annual with leaves divided three times into narrow segments. Flowers are violet, 30-60mm across; petals each have a dark spot at base. Fruit is a slender, bristly capsule, 50–100mm long, opening from tip almost to base by two to four slits. *Flowering:* April–June. *Distribution:* Native in Southern Europe, locally introduced further north; disturbed ground. **Californian Poppy** (*Eschscholzia californica*) is sometimes perennial, lacks hairs and has bright yellow to orange flowers 20–120mm across; petals are darker at base. Capsule is hairless. *Flowering:* June–September. *Distribution:* Native to south-western U.S.A., naturalised in western and central Europe.

Californian Poppy

Yellow Horned-poppy *Glaucium flavum* 30–90cm A sparsely hairy, bluish-green biennial or perennial with basal rosettes of pinnately lobed leaves. Branching stems end in solitary, yellow flowers, 60–80mm across; petals sometimes have a dark spot at base. Capsule is 150–300mm long, slender, curved and hairless, opening from tip almost to base by two slits. *Flowering:* April–September. *Distribution:* Native on coasts of western and southern Europe, naturalised in central Europe; maritime sand and shingle and on disturbed soils. **Red Horned-poppy** (*G. corniculatum*) is similar but annual or rarely biennial, with orange or reddish flowers and hairy capsules. *Flowering:* April–September. Distribution: Native in southern Europe, naturalised further north; disturbed ground.

Red Horned-poppy: fruit

Common Poppy

Rough Poppy

Opium Poppy

Welsh Poppy

Violet Horned-poppy

Yellow Horned-poppy

Greater Celandine *Chelidonium majus* 30–90cm A bluish-green, sparsely hairy perennial with basal rosettes of pinnate leaves and erect, branching stems. Yellow flowers are up to 20mm across, carried in clusters of two to six; four petals are unspotted. Capsules are 30–50mm long, slender, straight and hairless, opening from below by two pores. *Flowering:* May–August. *Distribution:* Almost throughout Europe, but only naturalised from cultivation in some areas; hedges, on walls and in waste areas.

Hypecoum procumbens 10–40cm long A sprawling, hairless annual with bluish-green leaves pinnately cut into narrow lobes. Yellow flowers are 5–15mm across; outer two petals each have a large central lobe and small lateral lobes; inner two petals are deeply three-lobed. Fruits are 4–6cm long, slender, curved, held erect, falling apart when ripe into one-seeded segments. *Flowering:* March–May. *Distribution:* Southern Europe, growing on maritime sands and other sandy soils.

Hollow-root: fruit

Bird-in-a-bush *Corydalis solida* 10–20cm An erect perennial with solid tubers and one to three leaves normally twice divided into small, toothed segments. Ten to 20 flowers are carried in a short, cylindrical, terminal spike-like head; four narrow, usually purplish petals form a tube 15–25mm long; inner two petals are oblong; outer two with broadened lip at apex, the upper with a spur at base. Fruit is an oblong, two-valved capsule, 10–25mm long. *Flowering:* March–May. *Distribution:* Native in most of Europe, naturalised in Britain, Denmark and Norway; woodland, scrub and hedges. Similar **Hollow-root** (*C. cava*) has hollow tubers. *Flowering* and *Distribution* as for Bird-in-a-bush but absent from much of the Mediterranean.

White Ramping-fumitory *Fumaria capreolata* Up to 100cm long

A robust, climbing annual with leaves pinnately cut into fine segments. Cylindrical spike-like clusters of about 20 flowers are carried on slender stems arising from leaf axils. Flowers are similar to Bird-in-a-bush in structure, 10–14mm long, usually creamy-white or pinkish with a blackish-red tip. Fruit-stalks turned downwards; fruit is small, globular, dry when ripe, remaining closed, containing one seed. *Flowering:* April–September. *Distribution:* Western, central and southern Europe; scrub, hedges and similar habitats.

Tall Ramping-fumitory

Common Ramping-fumitory *Fumaria muralis* A slender annual similar to White Ramping-fumitory but not climbing. Flowers about 12 in each cluster, 9–12mm long, pink with dark tip; lower petal with narrow, upturned margin. Fruit stalks are not turned downwards. *Flowering:* April–October. *Distribution:* Western Europe, growing on disturbed ground. **Tall Ramping-fumitory** (*Fumaria bastardii*) is very similar but with 15 to 25 flowers in each cluster and lower petal with flat margin. *Flowering:* April–October. *Distribution:* Western and southern Europe; disturbed ground.

Caper *Capparis spinosa* Up to 150cm long A deciduous, shrubby perennial with straggly, sometimes spiny stems branching from the base. Leaves are circular to ovate and rather fleshy. Flowers are carried singly in the leaf axils, opening flat, 50–70mm across; four petals are white or purplish-tinged; stamens are numerous, long and projecting, the filaments purplish. Fruit is a rounded berry, about 20mm across, splitting open when ripe to reveal numerous seeds embedded in a sticky mucilage. *Flowering:* April–September. *Distribution:* Mediterranean region; limestone cliffs, in rocky places and waste areas.

Greater Celandine

Hypecoum procumbens

Bird-in-a-bush

White Ramping-fumitory

Common Ramping-fumitory

Caper

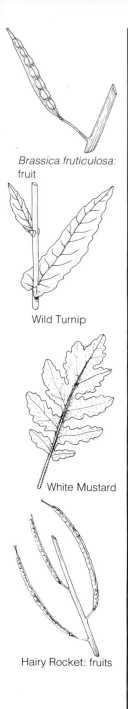

Brassica fruticulosa: fruit

Wild Turnip

White Mustard

Hairy Rocket: fruits

Black Mustard *Brassica nigra* Up to 100cm An erect, branching annual with slender stems. Lower leaves are bristly, pinnately cut, the terminal lobe much larger than the others. Small, yellow flowers are carried at the stem-tips; petals are 7–9mm long. Fruits are small, very slender, beaked siliquae, 10–20mm long, pressed against the stems. *Flowering:* April–September. *Distribution:* Almost throughout Europe, growing on disturbed ground. **B. fruticulosa** is usually biennial to perennial, woody at base; petals are 9–10mm long; fruits 15–40mm, not pressed against the stem. *Flowering:* February–June. *Distribution:* Native in the Mediterranean region.

Wild Cabbage *Brassica oleracea* Up to 300cm A hairless, branching biennial or perennial with stems becoming woody near base. Lower leaves up to 400mm long, with lobed margins and thick texture. Yellow petals are 15–20mm long. Fruits are 50–70mm long siliquae, carried on spreading stalks. *Flowering:* May–August. *Distribution:* Native on coasts of Britain, France, Spain and Italy; maritime cliffs. The ancestral cabbage. **Wild Turnip** (*Brassica rapa*) is somewhat similar but annual or biennial, with upper leaves clasping stem. *Flowering:* June–August. *Distribution:* Throughout much of Europe; disturbed ground.

Charlock *Sinapis arvensis* Up to 80cm An erect annual with hairy, lobed lower leaves, toothed at margins. Yellow flowers are 15–20mm across. Fruits are 25–45mm long siliquae, spreading from the stem, hairless or with short, stiff, downward-pointing hairs, the beak half as long as the lower part. *Flowering:* May–August. *Distribution:* Probably native in Mediterranean region, introduced in most of the rest of Europe; disturbed ground. **White Mustard** (*Sinapis alba*) differs in having more distinctly lobed leaves and beak of fruit as long or longer than the lower part containing seeds. *Flowering:* April–August. *Distribution:* As for Charlock.

Wallflower Cabbage *Rhynchosinapis cheiranthos* 15–30cm An erect annual or short-lived perennial with hairy leaves usually pinnately cut into lobed or toothed segments. Petals are bright yellow with darker veins. Fruits are slender siliquae, 30–80mm long, held upright, spreading or downward-pointing. *Flowering:* June–August. *Distribution:* Native to western Europe and Italy, introduced in Britain, Holland and Switzerland; growing mainly in mountains, but also in waste areas. **Hairy Rocket** (*Erucastrum gallicum*) is a similar, densely hairy annual with fruits less than 40mm long. *Flowering:* June–August. *Distribution:* Native in south-western and central Europe, introduced further north; waste areas and dry rocks.

Perennial Wall-rocket *Diplotaxis tenuifolia* 20–80cm An ascending, almost hairless perennial with stems woody at the base. Lower leaves pinnately divided, rather fleshy. Yellow flowers have petals 7.5–14mm long. Fruits are slender siliquae, 20–60mm long, carried erect on spreading stalks. *Flowering:* May–September. *Distribution:* Native in most of Europe, introduced in northern and eastern parts; waste areas and on old walls.

Violet Cabbage *Moricandia arvensis* Up to 65cm A short-lived perennial with branched stems and smooth, rounded, somewhat fleshy, bluish-green leaves clasping the stem. Rather large, showy, violet-purple flowers are carried near the stem tips; petals are about 20mm long. Fruits are slender, flattened, four-angled siliquae 30–80mm long. Flowering: March–June. Distribution: Mediterranean region, preferring lime-rich soils.

Black Mustard

Wild Cabbage

Charlock

Wallflower Cabbage

Perennial Wall-rocket

Violet Cabbage

Sea Rocket *Cakile maritima* 15–60cm An ascending, hairless annual with often branching stems and shiny, fleshy leaves, which vary from pinnately cut to unbroken at the margins. Flowers are carried towards the stem-tips; petals are 4–14mm long, variable in colour, ranging from violet, through pink, to white. Fruits are jointed siliculae, in two segments, the lower smaller than the rather conical, pointed upper portion. *Flowering:* April–September. *Distribution:* Coasts of most of Europe, growing on maritime sands.

Sea-kale *Crambe maritima* 30–75cm A stout, hairless perennial forming clumps of large, leathery, bluish leaves with lobed, wavy margins. Repeatedly branching, ascending stems terminate in a mass of white flowers; petals are 6–10mm long. Fruits are jointed siliculae, in two segments, the larger, globose to ovoid upper portion 7–12mm long containing one seed. *Flowering:* June-August. *Distribution:* Native on shores of Atlantic, Baltic and Black Sea, growing on maritime shingle and sand. **White Ball-mustard** (*Calepina irregularis)* is a more openly branched annual or biennial with upper leaves clasping stem. Petals are smaller, unequal, the outer about 2mm, the inner 2.5–3mm. *Flowering:* May–June. *Distribution:* Native in western, central and southern Europe, and naturalised in some areas including Britain; waste areas on lime-rich soils.

White Ball-mustard

Garden Rocket: fruit

London-rocket: fruits
and flowers

Wild Radish *Raphanus raphanistrum* 15–150cm A bristly annual with erect, branching stems and pinnately lobed lower leaves. Different races have differently coloured flowers; petals are 10–20mm long and may be yellow, white, lilac or violet, sometimes dark-veined. Fruits are ascending, slender, beaked siliquae, constricted between the seeds and breaking into segments. *Flowering:* April–September. *Distribution* Throughout Europe; waste areas, as a weed in fields, and on sandy and rocky sea-shores. **Garden Rocket** (*Eruca vesicaria)* is very similar but with fruits opening by two valves. *Flowering:* February–June. *Distribution:* Mainly southern Europe, naturalised further north; disturbed ground and often cultivated.

Hedge Mustard *Sisymbrium officinale* 5–90cm An erect, branching, bristly annual with pinnately cut lower leaves, oval in outline with large terminal lobe. Very small yellow flowers are grouped at the stem-tips; petals are 2–4mm long. Fruits are small, slender, erect siliquae, 1–2cm long, tightly pressed against the stem. *Flowering:* April–August. *Distribution:* Almost throughout Europe, growing on disturbed ground. **London-rocket** (*S. irio)* grows up to 60cm; fruits are 2.5–6.5cm long, erect but not pressed to the stem, overtopping flowers at stem tips. *Flowering:* May–October. *Distribution:* Almost throughout Europe; disturbed ground.

Garlic Mustard *Alliaria petiolata* Up to 120cm An erect biennial with distinctive, heart-shaped leaves toothed at the margins and smelling of garlic when crushed. Flowers are white, carried at stem-tips; petals are 4–6mm long. Fruits are slender, ascending siliquae 6–20mm. *Flowering:* April–July. *Distribution:* Most of Europe; open woodland, scrub and hedges, especially on lime-rich soils.

Thale Cress *Arabidopsis thaliana* 5–50cm An erect annual or biennial forming a rosette of often toothed, basal leaves from which arises the erect leafy flowering stem. Flowers are small and white; petals 2–4mm long. Fruits are 5–20mm long, ascending, carried on wiry, spreading stalks. *Flowering:* April–May. *Distribution:* Almost throughout Europe; dry, sandy, open ground.

Sea Rocket

Sea-kale

Wild Radish

Hedge Mustard

Garlic Mustard

Thale Cress

Perennial Honesty: fruit

Treacle Mustard: fruits

Sad Stock: fruit

Southern Warty-cabbage *Bunias erucago* 30–60cm A roughly glandular-hairy, branching annual or biennial with pinnately lobed lower leaves. Flowers are yellow; petals 8–13mm long. Fruits are very distinctive, 10–12mm long, four-sided, with irregularly toothed wings on the angles, and a straight, terminal beak. *Flowering:* March–July. *Distribution:* Native in southern Europe, introduced further north; disturbed ground.

Honesty *Lunaria annua* Up to 100cm An erect biennial with roughly hairy, heart-shaped to lanceolate leaves, toothed at the margins and drawn to a point at the tip. Showy flowers are reddish-purple, rarely white; petals 5–25mm long. Distinctive fruits are very strongly flattened, disc-like to oblong-elliptical, 20–70mm long. *Flowering:* March–June. *Distribution:* Native in south-eastern Europe, naturalised elsewhere, growing in partially shaded places such as open woods and scrub. **Perennial Honesty** (*L. rediviva*) differs in being perennial, with elliptical fruits 35–90mm long. *Flowering:* May–July. *Distribution:* Native through most of Europe, introduced in Britain; damp woodland, preferring lime-rich soils.

Dame's-violet *Hesperis matronalis* 40–120cm A hairy biennial or perennial with lanceolate, toothed leaves. Showy flowers are purple or white, strongly fragrant; petals 14–25mm long. Fruits are long, slender, upcurved siliquae 25–100mm. *Flowering:* May–August. *Distribution:* Native in central and southern Europe, and widespread as an escape from cultivation; damp and shaded habitats, and on roadsides and waste ground.

Wallflower *Erysimum cheiri* 20–90cm A woody-based or shrubby, greyish perennial bearing narrow leaves covered with minute hairs. Flowers are yellow; petals 15–25mm long. Fruits are narrow, slightly flattened siliquae 25–75mm long, held erect and minutely hairy. *Flowering:* March–June. *Distribution:* Native only in the Aegean region, widely naturalised elsewhere in Europe, growing on limestone cliffs and old walls. Naturalised plants, of garden origin, are hybrids with other species of Erysimum and usually have darker flowers. **Treacle Mustard** (*E. cheiranthoides)* is an annual or rarely biennial, quite unlike Wallflower, growing up to 100cm tall. Small yellow flowers have petals 3–6mm long. Fruits are slender siliquae, 10–50mm long, ascending from spreading stalks. *Flowering:* June–September. *Distribution:* Widespread in Europe except for most of the south; disturbed ground.

Sea Stock *Matthiola sinuata* 8–60cm A stout, woody-based plant, usually biennial, rarely annual or perennial, with basal rosettes of narrow leaves, usually white-hairy and conspicuously wavy-edged. Erect stems carry showy, pinkish-purple flowers; petals 17–25mm long. Fruits are narrow, flattened, stickily hairy siliquae, 50–150mm. *Flowering:* April–August. *Distribution:* Along coasts of western and southern Europe; cliffs and maritime sands. **Sad Stock** (*M. fruticulosa*) is perennial with yellow to reddish-purple flowers and cylindrical siliquae, sometimes tipped with horns up to 3mm long. *Flowering:* May–August. *Distribution:* Southern Europe, often in mountainous areas.

Winter-cress *Barbarea vulgaris* Up to 100cm A stout, hairless biennial or perennial with upright branches and pinnately lobed, deep green, glossy lower leaves. Yellow flowers are grouped at the stem tips; petals 5–7mm long. Fruits are narrow, four-angled, ascending siliquae, 15–30mm long. *Flowering:* May–August. *Distribution:* Almost throughout Europe; hedges and wet or waste places.

Southern Warty-cabbage

Honesty

Dame's-violet

Wallflower

Sea Stock

Winter-cress

Horse-radish *Armoracia rusticana* Up to 125cm A robust perennial with stout tap-roots, used as a condiment. Large, stalked leaves are oblong to ovate, glossy dark green, with indented margins. Leafy flowering stems are erect and branching. White flowers have petals 5–7mm long. Fruits are globose to ovoid siliculae, 4–6mm long. *Flowering:* May–August. *Distribution:* Native in Russia, cultivated and naturalised in most of Europe; roadsides and in waste areas.

Creeping Yellow-cress

Marsh Yellow-cress *Rorippa palustris* 10–60cm An almost hairless annual or biennial with pinnately lobed lower leaves. Small, yellow petals are 2–3.5mm long, equal to or shorter than sepals. Fruits are short, slightly curved siliquae, 4–12 x c. 2mm. *Flowering:* June–October. *Distribution:* Most of Europe, growing in wet places. **Creeping Yellow-cress** (*R. sylvestris*) is perennial, 20–50cm, spreading by runners. Petals 4–5mm, twice as long as sepals. Fruit is longer and narrower, 6–18mm. *Flowering:* June–September. *Distribution:* Almost throughout Europe; wet places, often on bare ground.

Water-cress *Rorippa nasturtium-aquaticum* 10–60cm A more or less hairless perennial with initially creeping, rooting stems which grow upwards to flower. Leaves are dark green, glossy, pinnate, with rounded leaflets. Flowers are small, white, carried at stem tips. Fruits are ascending siliquae, 13–18mm long, with seeds visible in two rows on each side. *Flowering:* April–October. *Distribution:* Throughout Europe except the far north; shallow, usually running water. **Narrow-fruited Water-cress** (*R. microphylla*) is very similar but has siliquae 16–24mm long, with seeds in only one row on each side. *Distribution:* Mainly in western Europe, growing in the same habitat as Water-cress. The two species hybridise.

Narrow-fruited Water-cress: fruit

Coral-root *Cardamine bulbifera* 35–70cm A perennial with slender, erect, unbranched stems from a creeping rhizome covered with fleshy scales. Lower leaves pinnate, with lanceolate, toothed leaflets; upper leaves simple, their axils bearing reddish-brown bulbils, by which the plant increases. Short-lived flowers are carried in a terminal cluster; petals are pale purple, 12–16mm long. Fruits ripen only in southern areas. *Flowering:* April–May. *Distribution:* Most of Europe; woodland with well-drained soil.

Wavy Bitter-cress *Cardamine flexuosa* 10–50cm A slender biennial or perennial with an erect, sinuous stem. Leaves are pinnate; leaflets ovate to rounded, those of upper leaves narrower. Flowers are small, white; petals 2.5–3mm; stamens six; anthers pale. Fruits are narrow, ascending siliquae, 12–25mm long, bursting open explosively when ripe, like other Bitter-cresses. *Flowering:* March–September. *Distribution:* Most of Europe; damp places and on disturbed ground. **Hairy Bitter-cress** (*C. hirsuta*) is very similar but annual, with straight stems and four stamens with pale anthers.

Hairy Bitter-cress

Cuckooflower *Cardamine pratensis* 30–55cm A perennial with an erect stem and a well-defined basal rosette, sometimes producing stolons. Leaves pinnate, the basal with one to seven pairs of rounded leaflets; stem leaves with narrower, more numerous leaflets. Flowers are pink, purplish or white; notched petals 8–13mm. Fruit is 25–40mm. *Flowering:* April–July. *Distribution:* Throughout most of Europe; damp grassland and wet places. **Narrow-leaved Bitter-cress** (*C. impatiens*) is annual or biennial with a pair of small lobes at the base of each leaf-stalk; leaflets distinctly lobed. Petals are 2–3mm or absent. *Flowering:* May–August. *Distribution:* Most of Europe.

Narrow-leaved Bitter-cress

Horse-radish

Marsh Yellow-cress

Water-cress

Coral-root

Wavy Bitter-cress

Cuckooflower

Annual Rock-cress

Hairy Rock-cress *Arabis hirsuta* 10–60cm A short-lived, hairy perennial forming basal rosettes of oblong-ovate leaves and erect, slender flowering stems with smaller, often clasping leaves. Small, white flowers are carried at the stem tips; petals 4–5.5mm long. Fruits are erect, narrow, flattened siliquae, 1.5–35mm long. *Flowering:* May–August. *Distribution:* Most of Europe; grassland, on bare ground, rocks and sand-dunes, preferring lime-rich conditions. **Annual Rock-cress** *(A. recta)* is annual with a short-lived, basal rosette of untoothed leaves; petals 2–3.5mm. *Flowering:* April–June. *Distribution:* Most of Europe, except the north; rocky places in mountains.

Alpine Rock-cress *Arabis alpina* 5–40cm A coarsely hairy perennial with few rosettes of leaves forming loose mats. Basal leaves are oblong to obovate, with a few coarse teeth on each side; stem leaves with clasping bases.Flowers are white or, rarely pink; outer sepals with conspicuous sac-like bases; spreading petals 6–10mm long. Fruits are slender siliquae 20–35mm long. *Flowering:* June–August. *Distribution:* Most of Europe; rocky and gravelly places in mountainous and arctic areas.

Tower Mustard: fruits

Tower Cress *Arabis turrita* 20–80cm A hairy biennial or perennial similar to Hairy Rock-cress but more robust, with long-stalked basal leaves. Flowers are larger, pale yellow; petals 6–8mm long. Fruits are very long, 100–140mm, all turned to one side, downcurved when ripe. *Flowering:* April–July. *Distribution:* Native in central and southern Europe, naturalised in Britain, growing on rocks and walls. **Tower Mustard** *(A. glabra)* is biennial, 60–120cm, with short-lived basal leaves in a rosette, and hairless, bluish-green leaves on the stem. Fruits are shorter, 40–70mm long, held erect. *Flowering:* May-July. *Distribution:* Most of Europe; dry banks, roadsides and in open woodland.

Small Alison *Alyssum alyssoides* Up to 30cm A greyish-hairy annual or biennial with small, obovate to oblanceolate leaves. Small, pale yellow flowers are clustered at the stem tips; sepals persist in fruit; petals are 3–4mm long. Fruits are small, flattened, disc-like siliculae, 3–4mm across. *Flowering:* April–June. *Distribution:* Most of Europe, growing in sandy fields, often on lime-rich soils. **Mountain Alison** *(A. montanum)* is a green to white-hairy perennial with creeping to erect, branching stems bearing rosettes of leaves. Flowers are larger, bright yellow. *Flowering:* April–July. *Distribution:* Most of Europe, except the north and south-west; rocky and gravelly places in the mountains.

Golden Alison *Alyssum saxatile* 10–40cm An often woody-based perennial, similar to Mountain Alison, but with larger leaves, sometimes with wavy margins. Flowers are yellow; petals 3–6mm long. Fruits are disc-like siliculae, sometimes longer than wide. *Flowering:* March–May. *Distribution:* Native in central and south-eastern Europe, introduced locally elsewhere; limestone rocks and cliffs.

Sweet Alison *Lobularia maritima* 10–40cm An often greyish-hairy perennial with stems branching from the base, bearing narrowly lanceolate leaves. Small, white flowers are grouped in compact clusters at the tips of the branches; petals are about 3mm long. Fruits are small, disc-like siliculae, 2–3.5mm across. *Flowering:* April–September. *Distribution:* Native in southern Europe, widely cultivated for ornament elsewhere and frequently escaping; dry, sunny places, especially near the coast.

Mountain Alison

Hairy Rock-cress

Alpine Rock-cress

Tower Cress

Small Alison

Golden Alison

Sweet Alison

Common
Whitlowgrass

Danish Scurvygrass

Pink Shepherd's-
purse

Yellow Whitlowgrass *Draba aizoides* 5–10cm A dwarf, tufted perennial with rosettes of stiff, narrow leaves, bristly at margins. Erect, slender flowering stems terminate in a cluster of yellow flowers, with petals 4–6mm long. Fruits are small, flattened, elliptical siliculae, 6–12mm long. *Flowering:* March–May. *Distribution:* Mountains of central and southern Europe, and in South Wales; limestone rocks and walls. **Common Whitlowgrass** (*Erophila verna*) is a tiny annual with basal rosettes of lanceolate or spoon-shaped leaves. Petals 1–6mm, white or reddish, deeply notched. *Flowering:* March–May. *Distribution:* Throughout Europe, except the arctic; dry, open, often sandy ground, rocks and walls.

Pyrenean Whitlowgrass *Petrocallis pyrenaica* 2–3cm A dwarf, densely tufted or cushion-forming perennial with rosettes of stiff, greyish, wedge-shaped leaves, 4–6mm long, cut into finger-like lobes. Short, erect stems bear clusters of pink to lilac flowers, with petals 4–5mm long. Fruits are small, obovate to elliptical siliculae. *Flowering:* June–August. *Distribution:* Pyrenees, Alps and Carpathians; limestone rocks and screes.

Common Scurvygrass *Cochlearia officinalis* 5–50cm An ascending, hairless biennial or perennial with long-stalked, usually kidney-shaped, basal leaves in a loose rosette. Upper leaves are stalkless, clasping, fleshy. White, rarely lilac flowers are grouped at stem tips; petals 3–7mm. Fruits are ovoid to globose siliculae, 4–7mm long, rounded at both ends. *Flowering:* April–August. *Distribution:* Mainly on coasts of north-western Europe, and in the Alps up to 2200m; salt-marshes, cliffs, rocks and in grassy places. **Danish Scurvygrass** (*C. danica*) is a lower-growing annual or biennial, up to 20cm, with most upper leaves stalked. Flowers are white or purplish; fruits often narrowed at both ends. *Flowering:* January–September. *Distribution:* Western and northern Europe; coasts or disturbed ground inland.

Hoary Alison *Berteroa incana* Up to 70cm A hairy, erect annual or perennial with leafy stems. Leaves are lanceolate to oblong, usually untoothed, more or less stalkless and grey-hairy. Flowers are white, the petals 4.5–6mm and deeply notched at the tips. Fruits are elliptical or ovate siliculae 4.5–8mm long, hairy and inflated with convex sides. *Flowering:* June–September. *Distribution:* Central and eastern Europe, naturalised in the north and parts of the west; waysides and waste ground.

Woad *Isatis tinctoria* 50–120cm An bluish-green biennial with erect stems bearing clasping, arrow-shaped, hairless leaves. Flowers are yellow, with petals 2.5–4mm. Fruits are oblong, dark brown, winged siliculae, 11–27mm, pendulous. *Flowering:* June–August. *Distribution:* Native in central and southern Europe, long cultivated for dyeing and widely introduced; dry, often rocky places.

Shepherd's-purse *Capsella bursa-pastoris* 3–40cm An erect, slender annual or biennial with a basal rosette of pinnately lobed leaves. Upper leaves clasp stem. Small, white flowers have normally green, hairy sepals; petals are twice as long, 2–3mm. Fruits are heart-shaped siliculae, 6–9mm long, held erect on spreading stalks. *Flowering:* All year. *Distribution:* Throughout Europe; waste areas and disturbed ground. **Pink Shepherd's-purse** (*C. rubella*) has hairless sepals, usually reddish at tips and scarcely shorter than the reddish petals. *Distribution:* Mainly in southern Europe, extending northwards to Britain.

Yellow Whitlowgrass

Pyrenean Whitlowgrass

Common Scurvygrass

Hoary Alison

Woad

Shepherd's-purse

Shepherd's Cress: fruits

Hutchinsia *Hornungia petraea* 3–15cm A slender annual producing a basal rosette of pinnately cut leaves and an ascending, branching, sparsely leafy stem. Tiny, white flowers have petals 0.75–1mm long. Fruits are flattened, narrowly elliptical to ovate siliculae, 2–2.5mm long. *Flowering:* March–May. *Distribution:* Most of Europe; bare, sandy ground, rocks and dunes, preferring lime-rich conditions. **Shepherd's Cress** (*Teesdalia nudicaulis*) is similar, but with the flowering stem simple or branched from base, usually leafless. *Flowering:* April–October. *Distribution:* Mainly western and central Europe; bare, open, often sandy ground, avoiding lime-rich soil.

Chamois Cress *Hutchinsia alpina* Up to 10cm A hairless or sparsely hairy, mat- forming perennial. Leaves are mostly in basal rosettes, pinnately cut with five to nine ovate-lanceolate lobes; flowering stems are usually leafless. Flowers are white, the petals 3–5mm long. Fruits are elliptical to lanceolate siliculae 3.5–6mm long. *Flowering:* May–August. *Distribution:* Central and southern Europe; limestone rocks and screes in the mountains.

Field Penny-cress *Thlaspi arvense* 10–60cm An erect, branching, hairless annual with oblong, often toothed leaves clasping the stem. Flowers are white; petals 3–4mm long. Fruits are disc-like, winged siliculae, 10–15mm across, notched at apex, held on ascending stalks. *Flowering:* May–August. *Distribution:* Most of Europe, growing on disturbed ground. **Garlic Penny-cress** (*T. alliaceum*) is similar but garlic-scented, with narrower fruits. *Flowering:* April–June. *Distribution:* Central and southern Europe, introduced in Britain; disturbed ground.

Burnt Candytuft *Aethionema saxatile* Up to 30cm A hairless annual or perennial with ascending, often branching stems bearing oblong to ovate leaves, the upper ones narrower. Small, white, lilac or purplish flowers have petals 2–5mm long. Fruits are disc-like, winged siliculae, 5–9mm across, notched at apex. *Flowering:* March–July. *Distribution:* South-central and southern Europe, mainly in the mountains; often on limestone.

Wild Candytuft *Iberis amara* 10–40cm An erect, branched annual with spoon-shaped, usually toothed, glossy leaves. Small, white or purplish flowers are carried in terminal, flat-topped clusters which become longer in fruit; petals are unequal, the two closest to the outside of the inflorescence much longer than inner two. Fruits are small, winged, disc-like siliculae, 4–5mm across, notched at apex. *Flowering:* May–September. *Distribution:* Mainly western Europe; bare and disturbed ground, often on lime-rich soils.Similar **Garden Candytuft** (*I. umbellata*) is hairless, with narrower, more or less untoothed leaves; heads of pink or purplish flowers remain compact and flat-topped in fruit. *Flowering:* April–September. *Distribution:* Native in the Mediterranean region; rocky and bushy places.

Garden Candytuft

Buckler-mustard *Biscutella laevigata* 10-50cm A hairy or hairless perennial, and one of the most variable plants in Europe. Basal leaves sometimes forming a rosette, ovate to narrowly lanceolate, the margins toothed or unbroken; upper leaves smaller, sometimes linear and untoothed. Yellow flowers are clustered at the stem tips; petals 4–8mm long. Fruits are flat siliculae, wider than long, 8–14mm across, each shaped like a figure-of-eight on its side. *Flowering:* April–August.*Distribution:* Mainly in central and southern Europe, often in the mountains.

Hutchinsia

Chamois Cress

Field Penny-cress

Burnt Candytuft

Wild Candytuft

Buckler-mustard: fruits

Field Pepperwort *Lepidium campestre* 20–60cm A densely hairy annual or biennial. Basal leaves are ovate to obovate, sometimes slightly lobed, withering before the flowers open; middle and upper stem leaves triangular, clasping. Flowers are white; petals 2mm long. Fruits are broadly elliptical, winged siliculae, 5–6mm long, covered with white scales and deeply notched at apex. *Flowering:* May–August. *Distribution:* Throughout most of Europe; waste and disturbed ground.

Dittander *Lepidium latifolium* 50–130cm A stout, hairless perennial with erect, much-branched stems. Lower leaves are long-stalked, ovate, toothed or pinnately lobed, leathery; upper leaves stalkless, smaller, narrower. Masses of tiny, white flowers are borne at stem tips. Fruits are small, rounded siliculae, 2mm across, with no wings or notch. *Flowering:* May–August. *Distribution:* Most of Europe; damp and waste areas, often near the sea.

Hoary Cress *Cardaria draba* 15–90cm A greyish-hairy perennial spreading underground to form patches, producing erect stems bearing oblong, pointed, clasping leaves. Stems branch above, terminating in clusters of small, white flowers, the petals about 4mm long. Fruits are heart-shaped siliculae, broader than long, 3.5–5mm across. *Flowering:* April–June. *Distribution:* Probably native in southern Europe, widely naturalised elsewhere; waste areas, on roadsides and disturbed ground.

Lesser Swine-cress: fruits

Swine-cress *Coronopus squamatus* 10–60cm long A prostrate annual or biennial with pinnately cut leaves, the lobes themselves toothed or lobed. Tiny, white flowers are carried at stem tips and in leaf axils, in small clusters which remain crowded in fruit; petals 1–1.5mm long. Fruits are small, rounded, two-lobed siliculae, wider than long, 3.5–4mm across. *Flowering:* June–September. *Distribution:* Most of Europe, characteristically growing on trodden ground. **Lesser Swine-cress** (*C. didymus*) is more delicate with creeping or ascending stems up to 30cm. Flower-clusters elongate in fruit; petals shorter than sepals, about 0.5mm long, or absent. Fruits are smaller, 2–3mm across. *Flowering:* June–September. *Distribution:* Native to South America, widely naturalised in Europe; waste areas and on disturbed ground.

White Mignonette: fruit

Weld

Wild Mignonette *Reseda lutea* 30–75cm A bushy, hairless annual or perennial with leaves mostly once- or twice-pinnate, the segments linear. Yellow flowers are small, 6mm across, carried in terminal, spike-like heads; sepals six; petals six, lobed. Erect, oblong, warty capsules are 7–12mm long. *Flowering:* April–October. *Distribution:* Native in western and southern Europe, naturalised further north and east; grassland and on disturbed, lime-rich ground. **White Mignonette** (*R. alba*) is very similar but has white flowers, with five or six sepals and petals. *Distribution:* Native in southern Europe, locally naturalised further north; disturbed ground.

Corn Mignonette *Reseda phyteuma* 10–50cm A hairy annual or biennial, rather like Wild Mignonette, branching from near base with ascending stems. Leaves are 50–100mm long, spoon-shaped, sometimes lobed. Flowers are white, followed by drooping capsules. *Flowering:* June–August. *Distribution:* Native in southern Europe, naturalised further north; disturbed, lime-rich ground. **Weld** (*R. luteola*) is an erect, scarcely branched biennial, 50–130cm, with narrowly lanceolate, wavy-edged leaves in a basal rosette and up the stem. Flowers are yellow, with four sepals and petals. *Flowering:* June–September. *Distribution:* Most of Europe.

Field Pepperwort

Dittander

Hoary Cress

Swine-cress

Wild Mignonette

Corn Mignonette

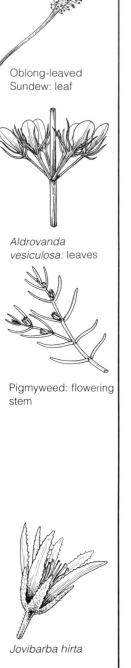

Oblong-leaved Sundew: leaf

Aldrovanda vesiculosa: leaves

Pigmyweed: flowering stem

Jovibarba hirta

Great Sundew *Drosera anglica* 10–18cm A reddish carnivorous perennial with a basal rosette of long-stalked, erect or slightly spreading leaves. Oblanceolate leaf blades are 30mm long and covered with long red, gland-tipped hairs which move to envelop and digest any insect which becomes stuck to them. Flowering stem bears six to 10 flowers, only open for a short time; five white petals, about. 6mm long. *Flowering:* July–August. *Distribution:* Northern and central Europe, occasionally in the south; peat bogs, usually in the wetter parts. Similar **Oblong-leaved Sundew** (*D. intermedia*) is only 2–3cm high, the leaves with broader blades 7mm long. *Flowering:* June–August. *Distribution:* Northern, western and central Europe.

Round-leaved Sundew *Drosera rotundifolia* 4–8cm Similar to Great Sundew but smaller and with the leaves spread flat. Leaf blades are circular, 5–8mm diameter, and both blade and stalk bear gland-tipped hairs. *Flowering:* June–August. *Distribution:* Most of Europe but absent from most Mediterranean islands and southern Balkan Peninsula; peat bogs.
Aldrovanda vesiculosa is a slender, rootless, submerged aquatic. Small narrow whorled leaves each end in a circular lobe hinged down the centre which rapidly closes on insects. *Flowering:* June–August. *Distribution:* Mainly central and eastern Europe; still, shallow water.

Mossy Stonecrop *Crassula tillaea* 1–5cm A tiny, moss-like annual with spreading densely-leaved stems. Leaves 2mm, thick, fleshy and joined in pairs, often reddish-tinged. Tiny flowers are usually solitary in leaf axils; sepals three; petals three, white or pink. *Flowering:* June–July. *Distribution:* Mainly southern and western Europe, scattered further north; bare ground, especially where winter-flooded. Similar **Pigmyweed** (*C. aquatica*) has narrower leaves 3–6mm long, not crowded on the stems, and flowers with four petals. *Flowering:* June–July. *Distribution:* Northern and central Europe.

Navelwort *Umbilicus rupestris* 20–50cm An erect perennial with fleshy, parasol-like leaves. Blade circular, dished in the centre where stalk joins, the margin shallowly toothed or wavy. Pendulous flowers in a long spike; corolla 8–10mm, tubular with five short lobes, whitish-green. *Flowering:* June–August. *Distribution:* Central and western Europe, northwards to Scotland; cracks in walls and rocks, especially acid ones.

Cobweb House-leek *Sempervivum arachnoideum* 4–12cm A low perennial spreading by stolons and with numerous small, crowded rosettes of fleshy leaves covered with a cobweb-like veil of hairs. Leaves are 7–12mm long, oblanceolate, fine-pointed and hairy, those on the stem, which only elongates in flower, often tinged red. Petals eight to ten, narrow, reddish-pink, each with a purple central vein; stamens purple. *Flowering:* July–September. *Distribution:* Mountain species endemic to the Alps, Apennines, Pyrenees.

Mountain House–leek *Sempervivum montanum* 5–10cm Similar to Cob-web Houseleek but resin-scented, the leaves sticky and lacking a cobweb-like veil. Petals are usually reddish, occasionally yellowish; stamens are pale. *Flowering:* July–September. *Distribution:* Endemic to the Alps, Apennines, Carpathians, Pyrenees and mountains of Corsica; avoids limestone rocks. ***Jovibarba hirta*** has leaves 15–20mm in rosettes 3–7cm across. Bell-shaped flowers have six pale yellow, fringed petals. *Flowering:* August–September. *Distribution:* Endemic to mountains of central Europe and the north-western Balkan Peninsula.

Great Sundew

Round-leaved Sundew

Mossy Stonecrop

Navelwort

Cobweb House-leek

Mountain House-leek

White Stonecrop: leaves

Rock Stonecrop: sterile shoot

Biting Stonecrop *Sedum acre* 5–12cm A loosely tufted evergreen perennial with thick, fleshy, bright green leaves 3–6mm long and elliptical in cross-section. They are crowded and overlapping on short sterile shoots, more widely spaced on longer flowering ones. Flowers borne in small clusters with spreading branches. Bright yellow petals are spreading. *Flowering:* June–July. *Distribution:* Almost throughout Europe; typically on dry, alkaline soils, dunes and walls. **White Stonecrop** (*S. album*) has more cylindrical, often reddish leaves 4–12mm long and white flowers. *Flowering:* July–August. *Distribution:* as for Biting Stonecrop.

Reflexed Stonecrop *Sedum reflexum* 15–35cm A creeping and mat-forming evergreen perennial with ascending flowering shoots and much shorter sterile shoots. Leaves are 8–20mm, narrow, more or less cylindrical, often bluish-green; the upper may curve away from the stem. Inflorescence has drooping branches bearing numerous bright yellow flowers. Pod-like fruits are also yellow. *Flowering:* June–August. *Distribution:* Central Europe extending to Finland, western France, Sicily and Greece, introduced elsewhere; rocks and walls. Similar **Rock Stonecrop** (*S. forsteranum*) has leaves flat on the upper side and forming rosettes at the tips of sterile shoots with only dead leaves below. *Flowering:* June–July. *Distribution:* Western Europe; in damper habitats than Reflexed Stonecrop.

Thick-leaved Stonecrop *Sedum dasyphyllum* 3–8cm A fleshy, evergreen perennial tinged greyish-pink with a whitish bloom. Leaves are mostly opposite, 3–5mm, ovoid to orbicular and flattened on the upper side, glandular hairy. Loosely overlapping on sterile shoots they readily fall and may root to form new plants. Flowers have five to six petals, each 3mm, white with pink streaks. *Flowering:* June–July. *Distribution:* Native in southern and parts of central Europe, naturalised in the north; rocks and old walls.

Orpine *Sedum telephium* 15–80cm A fleshy perennial with tuberous roots and erect or somewhat sprawling, annual stems. Leaves of 20–100mm range from almost circular to narrowly oblong, toothed or not, the base sometimes encircling the stem. Alternate, opposite or whorled, they may be green, bluish or red-tinged. Greenish, white, lilac or purplish-red flowers 9–12mm across are borne in large clusters at tips of stems. *Flowering:* July–September. *Distribution:* More or less throughout Europe.

Roseroot *Sedum rosea* 5–35cm A fleshy perennial with annual stems arising from a scaly crown at the tip of a thick, fragrant rhizome. Thick bluish-green leaves are alternate with toothed margins, the bases often encircling the stem. Flowers with four short, dull yellow petals borne in dense clusters at tips of stems. Plants are male or female; male flowers sometimes have sepals and petals tinged purple beneath and have conspicuous but abortive female parts. *Flowering:* May–August. *Distribution:* Northern Europe and in mountains south to the Pyrenees, Apennines and Bulgaria.

Starry Saxifrage *Saxifraga stellaris* 4–20cm A tufted perennial with rosettes of obovate to spoon-shaped, sparsely hairy and slightly fleshy leaves. Leafless flowering stems have more or less erect branches in the upper half. Sepals are down-curved; petals of 3–7mm are narrow, white with two yellow spots. *Flowering:* June–August. *Distribution:* A mountain species, found in all the major European ranges, also in lowlands in the far north; stream banks and wet rocks.

Biting Stonecrop

Reflexed Stonecrop

Thick-leaved Stonecrop

Orpine

Roseroot

Starry Saxifrage

Livelong Saxifrage *Saxifraga paniculata* 12–30cm An evergreen

perennial with tufts of rosettes of oblong, bluish and lime-encrusted leaves 12–60mm long. Flowering stems branch in the upper third; spreading branches with one to three flowers. Petals are 4–6mm, white or pale cream, sometimes flecked with red. *Flowering:* May–August. *Distribution:* Mountains of central and southern Europe, from France and Poland south to Spain, Italy and Greece; also in Norway.

Meadow Saxifrage *Saxifraga granulata* Up to 50cm A summer-

dormant perennial overwintering by means of bulbils. Basal leaves kidney-shaped, toothed, hairy and often fleshy; stem leaves few or absent. Small brown bulbils are borne underground in axils of basal leaves. Flowers in a loose cluster. Petals are 9–16mm, white. A very variable plant. *Flowering:* May–July. *Distribution:* Northern, central and western Europe; typically in dry, rocky places in the south, in damp grassland elsewhere. **Bulbous Saxifrage** (*S. bulbifera*) has bulbils in axils of glandular-hairy basal leaves and of the many stem leaves; flowers with shorter petals are in small compact clusters. *Flowering:* April–June. *Distribution:* Central and southern Europe.

Bulbous Saxifrage:
bulbil

Yellow Saxifrage *Saxifraga aizoides* Up to 25cm A loosely tufted

evergreen perennial with ascending flowering stems and much shorter sterile stems. Fleshy, stalkless leaves are 10–25mm, narrowly oblong, the margins sometimes with a few teeth. Flowers in a leafy, terminal cluster. Petals of 3–6mm are yellow to orange, often flecked with red; they do not touch. *Flowering:* June–September. *Distribution:* Arctic regions and mountains south to Pyrenees, central Italy and Albania; damp habitats.

Purple Saxifrage *Saxifraga oppositifolia* 2–6cm A low evergreen

perennial forming loose mats or compact flat cushions. Thick, opposite leaves are 2–6mm, narrowly obovate to almost circular, dull bluish-green. Flowers are solitary on short, leafy stems; petals 5–15mm pale pink to deep purple; anthers bluish. Very variable in size, petal colour and leaf characters. *Flowering:* March–May. *Distribution:* Arctic Europe and mountains to the south.

Alternate-leaved Golden-Saxifrage *Chrysosplenium*

alternifolium Up to 20cm A somewhat hairy perennial with three-angled stems and creeping, leafless stolons. Basal leaves are rounded kidney-shaped, toothed or shallowly lobed; stem leaves are alternate. Flowers are borne in terminal clusters with leafy, yellowish bracts; four sepals yellowish, blunt, spreading; petals absent. *Flowering:* April–July. *Distribution:* Throughout most of Europe except the far north and west, and most of the Mediterranean region; damp, shady habitats. **Opposite-leaved Golden-saxifrage** (*C. oppositifolia*) has opposite, dark bluish-green leaves, finely toothed or wavy at the edges, and pointed sepals. *Flowering:* April–June. *Distribution:* Western and central Europe.

Opposite-leaved
Golden-saxifrage

Grass-of-Parnassus *Parnassia palustris* 5–40cm A perennial with a

basal rosette and erect stems with a single, stalkless leaf. Basal leaves long-stalked, ovate to very broadly rounded-triangular, heart-shaped at the base and often red-spotted beneath. Solitary, terminal flowers are 15–30mm across; five petals white with darker veins; five stamens alternate with five nectary-bearing structures fringed with long narrow lobes tipped with yellowish glands. *Flowering:* June–September. *Distribution:* Throughout most of Europe but rarer in the south; damp or wet places.

Livelong Saxifrage

Meadow Saxifrage

Yellow Saxifrage

Purple Saxifrage

Alternate-leaved Golden-saxifrage

Grass-of-Parnassus

Blackcurrant

Mountain Currant *Ribes alpinum* 100–200cm A deciduous shrub with deeply palmately three-lobed leaves 20–60mm long. Plants are male or female. Greenish flowers 4–6mm, each with a small but conspicuous bract, in erect spikes; petals very small. Scarlet berries are insipid. *Flowering:* April–May. *Distribution:* Northern and central Europe, and mountains south to northern Spain, central Italy and Bulgaria. **Blackcurrant** (*R. nigrum*) has aromatic five-lobed leaves, drooping spikes of hermaphrodite purplish-green flowers and black sweet-tasting fruits. *Flowering:* April–May.

Gooseberry *Ribes uva-crispa* 100–150cm A small deciduous, much-branched shrub with stout spines in groups of three on stems and twigs. Palmately three- to five-lobed leaves are 20–50mm wide; flowers one to three hanging from the axils. Pale green or pinkish sepals are 5–7mm, longer than the white petals. Juicy berry of 10mm or more is ovoid or globose, green, yellow or purplish when ripe; it is normally bristly. *Flowering:* March–May. *Distribution:* Native to western, central and southern Europe but widely grown and naturalised in other areas.

Bridewort *Spiraea salicifolia* 100–200cm A deciduous shrub with upright branches and flowers in spikes at tips of long twigs. Short-stalked alternate leaves are 40–80mm, elliptical-oblong, finely and often doubly toothed. Branched inflorescence is 4–12cm long, cylindrical. Flowers are about 8mm across with pink or sometimes white petals. *Flowering:* June–September. *Distribution:* Somewhat scattered in central and parts of eastern Europe but widely cultivated elsewhere and naturalised in some places.

Buck's-beard *Aruncus dioicus* Up to 200cm A tall perennial with unbranched stems and large leaves up to 100cm long, twice-pinnately divided. Leaflets are oval with doubly toothed margins. Branched, pyramidal inflorescence has numerous white or yellowish flowers each about 5mm across. Flowers are usually unisexual, the sexes borne on the same or different plants. Small dry fruits are pendent. *Flowering:* June–August. *Distribution:* An upland species from Belgium and the Pyrenees eastwards to Poland, Ukraine and Albania; damp, shady places.

Dropwort

Meadowsweet *Filipendula ulmaria* 50–200cm A tall perennial with leafy stems and non-tuberous roots. Leaves are pinnate, the pairs of large, toothed leaflets interspersed with pairs of much smaller ones. Basal leaves have up to five pairs of large leaflets, each leaflet 20–80mm. Inflorescence is up to 25cm, longer than wide, with numerous creamy flowers. Petals five, rarely six, each 2–5mm. Tiny dry fruits are spirally twisted. *Flowering:*June–September *Distribution:* Common except for most of the Mediterranean region; generally in damp places. **Dropwort** (*F. vulgaris*) has roots with strings of bead-like tubers, basal leaves with eight to 25 pairs of large leaflets each 5–20mm long and flowers with six petals purplish beneath. *Flowering:* May–August. *Distribution:* Dry grassland in much of Europe.

Cloudberry *Rubus chamaemorus* 5–20cm Perennial with a creeping rhizome producing thornless annual stems. Wrinkled, kidney-shaped leaves have five rounded, toothed lobes. Flowers are unisexual, males and females on different plants, at tips of shoots. Flower stalks and pointed sepals are glandular; petals five or more, white and hairy. Large edible fruit, orange when ripe, has few segments. *Flowering:* June–August. *Distribution:* Mountains of northern Europe; moors and bogs.

Mountain Currant

Gooseberry

Bridewort

Buck's-beard

Meadowsweet

Cloudberry: fruits

Stone Bramble

Dewberry *Rubus caesius* 30–80cm A perennial with biennial stems, sprawling, rooting, covered with a white bloom and few, scattered prickles. Leaves are divided into three doubly-toothed leaflets, the central one sometimes three-lobed, the laterals usually two-lobed. White flowers are 20–25mm across on shortly hairy stalks, two to five in a cluster. Large fruit black with a white bloom, composed of few segments. *Flowering:* May–June. *Distribution:* Most of Europe, usually on lime-rich soils. **Stone Bramble** (*R. saxatilis*) has stems armed with small straight prickles, toothed leaves, small flowers, and red fruits. *Flowering:* June–August.

Bramble *Rubus fruticosus* Up to 100cm A group of non-outbreeding species very difficult to tell apart and often treated, as here, as a single aggregate. Biennial stems usually sharply angled and prickly, often arching and rooting at tips. Leaves of non-flowering stems are usually palmate, with five, toothed leaflets. Flowers borne in branched inflorescences; petals white or pink. Ripe fruit is black and shiny, with many small segments. *Flowering:* May–September. *Distribution:* Common in most habitats throughout Europe.

Raspberry *Rubus idaeus* 100–150cm A perennial with erect, biennial woody stems produced as suckers from the roots, armed with numerous weak prickles and densely covered with a white bloom. Pinnate leaves have five to seven leaflets, white-hairy beneath. Nodding flowers are about 10mm across, few in each cluster; narrow petals white, erect. Ripe fruit is red or orange. *Flowering:* June–August. *Distribution:* Most of Europe but confined to mountains in the south.

Evergreen Rose:
young fruit, petals
fallen

Field Rose *Rosa arvensis* 200cm A deciduous shrub with long trailing stems and branches armed with scattered, hooked and slender prickles. Pinnate leaves have five to seven ovate, dull green leaflets. Flowers one to three, rarely as many as five, together. Sepals are pinnately lobed, bent backwards after flower opens; petals 15–25mm, white; styles are fused into a single naked column. Globose to ovoid fruit is red. *Flowering:* June–July. *Distribution:* South-western and central Europe. Similar **Evergreen Rose** (*R. sempervirens*) has shiny, leathery evergreen leaves, sepals with stalked glands and a hairy or naked stylar column. *Flowering:* June–July. *Distribution:* Mediterranean and Iberia, north to France; naturalised in Britain.

Burnet Rose *Rosa pimpinellifolia* Up to 100cm A deciduous shrub with erect stems, often forming large, dense patches. Stems armed with numerous dense, straight prickles and with sharp, bristly hairs. Pinnate leaves have five to 11 broad leaflets 5–15mm long. Flowers are solitary. Sepals are erect and entire; petals 10–20mm, white or rarely pink; woolly styles form a compact head. Small fruit is globose, black. *Flowering:* May–July. *Distribution:* Most of Europe except the north-east, far south-west and Mediterranean islands.

Harsh Downy Rose:
leaf, underside

Dog Rose *Rosa canina* Up to 500cm A deciduous shrub with green, erect or arching stems with stout, hooked prickles. Pinnate leaves have five to seven leaflets. Flowers are solitary or two to five together. Sepals are pinnately lobed, bent back after the flower opens; petals 15–25mm, pink or white; loosely arranged styles are hairy or naked. Fruit of 10–20mm is globose, ovoid or ellipsoid, red. *Flowering:* June–July. *Distribution:* Throughout Europe except for the far north. Similar **Harsh Downy Rose** (*R. tomentosa*) has leaves downy on both sides. *Flowering:* June–July. *Distribution:* As for Dog-rose.

Dewberry

Bramble: ripe and unripe fruits

Raspberry: fruits

Field Rose

Burnet Rose

Dog Rose

Fragrant Agrimony: fruit

Great Burnet: flower head

Agrimony *Agrimonia eupatoria* 15–150cm An erect perennial with a long spike of yellow flowers, the pinnate leaves often mostly basal. There are two to three pairs of small leaflets between each of the three to six pairs of main leaflets; all are toothed, dark green above and white- or grey-hairy beneath. Flowers have four to five golden yellow petals. Top-shaped fruit is grooved for most of its length, with hooked bristles at the upper end. *Flowering:* June–August. *Distribution:* Throughout Europe except for the far north; hedgerows, fields and grassy places. **Fragrant Agrimony** (*A. procera*) is more robust with leaves green on both sides, fragrant; fruit grooved for only half its length. *Flowering:* June–August. *Distribution:* Mostly in western, central and southern Europe.

Salad Burnet *Sanguisorba minor* 10–90cm A rhizomatous perennial with basal rosettes and leafy flowering stems. Pinnate leaves have three to twelve pairs of toothed leaflets, each 5–20mm. Globose or ovoid heads 10–30mm long at the tips of stems contain a mixture or male, female and hermaphrodite flowers. Sepals four, green; petals absent; stamens numerous. Fruit is hard, dry and four-angled. *Flowering:* May–August. *Distribution:* Western, central and southern Europe, as a casual elsewhere; dry grassland, especially on chalk and limestone. **Great Burnet** (*S. officinalis*) is a generally larger plant, with dull red sepals and only four stamens. *Flowering:* June–September. *Distribution:* Much of Europe except the Mediterranean; damp grassland.

Thorny Burnet *Sarcopoterium spinosum* Up to 60cm An intricately branched, spiny shrub with densely hairy shoots. Pinnate leaves have four to seven pairs of hairy leaflets. Globose or oblong heads up to 30mm long have female flowers in the upper part, male flowers below. Calyx has four spreading teeth which soon fall; petals absent. The flower becomes swollen, fleshy and red in fruit, resembling a berry. *Flowering:* March–April. *Distribution:* Dry places in the Mediterranean from Sardinia eastwards.

Mountain Avens *Dryas octopetala* Up to 50cm An evergreen dwarf shrub with branched, low-spreading stems. Leaves are oblong to ovate with rounded teeth or shallow lobes and densely white-hairy beneath. Showy flowers are solitary; sepals seven to ten; eight petals are white, 7–17mm, oblong; stamens numerous. Dry fruits in a head, each with a hairy style 20–30mm long. *Flowering:* June–July. *Distribution:* Mountain species extending southwards to a line from northern Spain to southern Bulgaria.

Water Avens *Geum rivale* 20–30cm. A perennial with pinnate basal leaves and deeply three-lobed stem leaves. Stem is erect and branched. Leaflets of basal leaves in three to six differently-sized pairs; terminal leaflet largest, 20–50mm. Flowers borne in clusters of two to five, bell-shaped and hanging, with dark brownish-purple calyx and cream to pink petals 8–15mm long. Fruits are small, dry with a long hooked beak, 100 to 150 in an ovoid head. *Flowering:* May–September. *Distribution:* Everywhere except the Mediterranean region.

Wood Avens *Geum urbanum* 20–60cm. A plant similar in general appearance to Water Avens but for the flowers. Basal leaves have one to five pairs of leaflets, the terminal one 20–100mm, almost circular and deeply lobed; stem leaves are deeply three- to five-lobed. Flowers are held erect; spreading yellow petals 4–7mm long. Fruits are hairy, only about 70 in each head. *Flowering:* June–August. *Distribution:* Most of Europe.

Agrimony

Salad Burnet

Thorny Burnet: fruiting plant

Mountain Avens

Water Avens

Wood Avens: fruiting heads

Marsh Cinquefoil *Potentilla palustris* Up to 45cm A perennial with far-creeping rhizomes and a loose terminal cluster of purple flowers. Pinnate leaves have five to seven leaflets each 30–60mm, oblong and coarsely-toothed. Flowers have a whorl of narrow epicalyx segments; purple sepals 10–15mm, about twice length of the five persistent purple petals. *Flowering:* May–July. *Distribution:* Northern and central Europe; wet, acid places.

Silverweed *Potentilla anserina* Up to 80cm A silvery silky-hairy perennial with a rosette of pinnate leaves. Leaflets seven to 25, each 10–40mm, oblong to ovate, sharply toothed. Flowers are solitary in leaf axils. Epicalyx segments are narrow; five yellow petals 7–10mm, about twice length of sepals. *Flowering:* June–August. *Distribution:* Most areas but absent from much of the south.

Tormentil

Creeping Cinquefoil *Potentilla reptans* 30–100cm A perennial with a rosette of persistent leaves and sprawling, rooting flowering stems. Leaves have five obovate, toothed leaflets 5–70mm long, spreading like the fingers of a hand. Solitary, axillary flowers have five yellow petals 8–12mm and twice length of sepals. *Flowering:* June–September. *Distribution:* All of Europe except the far north. **Tormentil** (*P. erecta*) has leaves with three to five leaflets and clusters of four-petalled flowers. *Flowering:* June–September. *Distribution:* Most areas. **Alpine Cinquefoil** (*P. crantzii*) also has clusters of flowers but they are five-petalled. *Flowering:* June–July. *Distribution:* Chalky soils of northern Europe, central and southern mountains.

Hautbois Strawberry

Strawberry *Fragaria vesca* 5–30cm A perennial with basal leaf-rosettes and long stolons rooting at intervals and producing new plants. Trifoliate leaves have ovate to obovate, coarsely-toothed leaflets 10–60mm long. Erect stem, little longer than the leaves, carries a loose cluster of white flowers each about 15mm across. Bright red 'fruit' is the swollen and fleshy base of the flower bearing the true fruits as small dry pips on its surface. *Flowering:* April–July. *Distribution:* More or less all of Europe. Similar **Hautbois Strawberry** (*F. muricata*) has few, if any, stolons and flowering stems conspicuously longer than leaves. *Flowering:* May–July. *Distribution:* Native to central Europe but widely cultivated and naturalised in northern areas.

Intermediate Lady's-mantle

Alpine Lady's-mantle *Alchemilla alpina* 10–20cm An often yellowish-green perennial with ascending stems little longer than the leaves. Leaves are palmately divided into five to seven narrow leaflets silvery-silky beneath. Branched inflorescence composed of many dense clusters of green or yellowish flowers. Flowers small, only 3mm long, with an epicalyx and four sepals but no petals. *Flowering:* June–August. *Distribution:* Northern, western and parts of central Europe, almost always in mountains. **Intermediate Lady's-mantle** (*A. xanthochlora*) has kidney-shaped to almost circular leaves with nine to 11 shallow, toothed lobes. *Flowering:* May–August. *Distribution:* Western and central Europe north to southern Sweden.

Parsley-piert *Aphanes arvensis* Up to 30cm, often much smaller A small, easily overlooked annual with deeply lobed leaves and minute flowers. Plant pale or greyish-green, much-branched. Leaves of 2–10mm are divided into three segments each with three to five oblong lobes at the tip. Leafy, lobed stipules are joined in pairs about the stem. Flowers are less than 2mm, borne in dense clusters half enclosed in the cup formed by the stipules. *Flowering:* April–October. *Distribution:* Almost all of Europe; disturbed ground.

Marsh Cinquefoil

Silverweed

Creeping Cinquefoil

Strawberry: fruits

Alpine Lady's-mantle

Parsley-piert

Cytisus villosus: fruit

Broom *Cytisus scoparius* Up to 200cm A much–branched shrub with long, straight, green, five-angled twigs, erect or sometimes prostrate in coastal areas. Simple or trifoliate leaves have leaflets 6–20mm long. Yellow flowers are about 20mm long, borne on young twigs. Fruits are flattened, oblong pods, 25-40mm long, hairy at margins, ripening black. *Flowering:* April–June. *Distribution:* Most of Europe; open woodland, scrub, on heaths and coastal cliffs, on acid soils. **C. villosus** is an erect shrub with trifoliate leaves and yellow flowers streaked red. Fruits are densely hairy. *Flowering:* April–May. *Distribution:* Southern Europe; acid woodland and scrub.

Hairy Broom *Chamaecytisus hirsutus* 20–100cm A small, hairy shrub with slender branches usually erect or ascending. Small leaves are trifoliate, the leaflets 6–20mm long. Yellow or pinkish-yellow flowers, 20–25mm long, are carried in clusters of one to four in leaf axils; standard sometimes has brown spots. Fruits are linear pods, 25–40mm long, hairy all round or only at margins. *Flowering:* April–June. *Distribution:* Central and eastern Europe; grassy places and scrub.

Hairy Greenweed: leaf and fruit

Dyer's Greenweed *Genista tinctoria* 10–200cm A variable shrub with creeping to erect stems and hairy or hairless, often lanceolate leaves. Yellow flowers, about 15mm long, are carried in mostly terminal, spike-like heads. Fruits are flattened, narrowly oblong pods, hairy or not, blunt at apex. *Flowering:* June–August. *Distribution:* Most of Europe; open woodland, scrub, grassland and on heaths. **Hairy Greenweed** (*G. pilosa)* is similar but more frequently prostrate, with leaves densely hairy below. Flowers are smaller, about 10mm long, hairy. Fruits are hairy, pointed. *Flowering:* April–June. *Distribution:* Mainly western and central Europe; heaths and coastal cliffs.

Winged Broom *Chamaespartium sagittale* 10–50cm A dwarf shrub with creeping, mat-forming branches and normally erect, herbaceous flowering stems with prominent, green wings. Leaves are few, elliptical. Yellow flowers, 10–12mm long, are carried in dense, terminal clusters. Fruits are oblong, flattened, hairy pods, 15–20mm long. *Flowering:* May–July. *Distribution:* Mainly central Europe; preferring lime-rich soils.

Spanish Broom *Spartium junceum* Up to 300cm An erect, much-branched shrub, similar to Broom, but with smooth, round twigs bearing small, lanceolate leaves. Large, showy, yellow flowers are 20–25mm long, sweetly scented and abundantly produced on the young shoots. *Flowering:* April–June. *Distribution:* Native in Mediterranean region, introduced elsewhere, growing in scrub and on roadsides.

Dwarf Gorse: twig

Common Gorse *Ulex europaeus* 60–200cm A densely branched shrub with green, hairy almost leafless and very spiny twigs, the spines up to 25mm long. Yellow flowers are 15–20mm long, scattered on the younger shoots. Fruits are hairy pods. *Flowering:* All year but mainly in April. *Distribution:* Native in western Europe, planted or naturalised elsewhere; rough grassland and on heaths, usually avoiding lime. **Dwarf Gorse** (*U. minor)* is smaller, often prostrate, with shorter, weaker spines up to 15mm. Flowers are smaller, 10–12mm long. *Flowering:* July–November. *Distribution:* Atlantic Europe from Britain to Portugal, growing on acid heaths. **Western Gorse** (*U. gallii)* is intermediate between the other two species. Flowers are 10–12mm long, differing from Dwarf Gorse in curved wing petals, longer than keel when straightened. *Distribution:* Atlantic Europe from Scotland to north-western Spain.

Broom

Hairy Broom

Dyer's Greenweed

Winged Broom

Spanish Broom

Common Gorse

White Lupin: fruit

Sweet Lupin *Lupinus luteus* 25–80cm An erect, hairy annual with leaves divided into radiating, oblong-obovate leaflets 40–60mm long. Spike-like heads, up to 16cm long, carry fragrant, yellow flowers grouped into regular whorls. Fruits are densely hairy, black pods, 40–50 x 10mm, containing four to six pea-like seeds. *Flowering:* May–July. *Distribution:* Native in western half of Mediterranean region growing on light, acid soils; widely cultivated elsewhere and sometimes naturalised. **White Lupin** (*L. albus*) is often taller, to 120cm, with white or blue flowers in heads up to 100mm long. Pods are larger, 60–100 x 10–20mm, yellow. *Flowering:* April–June. *Distribution:* Native in southern Balkans and Aegean region, widely cultivated elsewhere.

Goat's-rue *Galega officinalis* 40–150cm An erect, more or less hairless perennial with leaves pinnately divided into oblong to lanceolate leaflets each 15–50mm long. Stalked, spike-like flower heads arise from the leaf axils. Flowers are 1–15mm long; calyx with bristle-like teeth; petals white to bluish-purple. Fruits are pods 2–5cm long, rounded in cross-section. *Flowering:* June–September. *Distribution:* Central, eastern and southern Europe, cultivated and naturalised elsewhere; damp ground and in waste areas.

Bladder Senna *Colutea arborescens* Up to 600cm A much-branched, deciduous shrub with leaves pinnately divided, the rounded leaflets up to 30mm long. Showy, bright yellow flowers are 15–20mm long, carried in loose, stalked clusters arising from the leaf axils of young shoots. Fruits are greatly inflated, papery, translucent pods 50–70 x 30mm. *Flowering:* May–August. *Distribution:* Native in central and southern Europe, naturalised further north; open woodland, scrub and waste areas.

Alpine Milk-vetch *Astragalus alpinus* 8–30cm A downy perennial with creeping or ascending stems bearing leaves pinnately divided into small, elliptical leaflets. Flowers are carried in loose, stalked clusters and are whitish or pale violet with bluish-violet keels; standards are 10–14mm. Fruits are oblong, blackish-hairy pods, 10–15mm long. An arctic race has darker flowers and smaller, ovoid pods. *Flowering:* July–August. *Distribution:* Northern Europe, extending southwards in the mountains to the Pyrenees and Alps; grassy, and rocky places up to 3100m.

Pallid Milk-vetch

Wild Lentil *Astragalus cicer* 25–60cm A robust, hairy, ascending perennial with pinnate leaves. Pale yellow flowers are carried in dense, stalked clusters arising from leaf axils; standards are 14–16mm long. Fruits are ovoid to globose pods, 10–15mm long, covered with short black and white hairs. *Flowering:* June–July. *Distribution:* Mainly central Europe, westwards to the Atlantic and eastwards into Russia; scrub and grassy places. **Pallid Milk-vetch** (*A. frigidus*) is hairless and erect, with three to eight pairs of leaflets and loose clusters of yellowish-white flowers; standards 12-14mm. *Flowering:* July–August. *Distribution:* Northern Europe and mountains in central regions; stony and grassy places.

Wild Liquorice *Astragalus glycyphyllos* 30–100cm A robust, more or less hairless perennial with sprawling stems. Leaves are 100–200mm long, pinnately divided into ovate leaflets that taste of liquorice. Cream flowers are carried in small, shortly stalked clusters in the leaf axils; standards are 11–15mm long. Fruits are narrowly oblong pods, slightly flattened and curved, hairless, 30–40mm long. *Flowering:* June–August. *Distribution:* Most of Europe; open woodland, scrub and grassland, preferring lime-rich soils.

Sweet Lupin

Goat's-rue

Bladder Senna

Alpine Milk-vetch

Wild Lentil

Wild Liquorice

Purple Milk-vetch *Astragalus danicus* 8–30cm A slender, sparsely hairy, ascending perennial, the pinnate leaves 40–100mm long; six to 13 pairs of oblong-ovate or oblong leaflets with blunt or notched tips. Purplish or bluish-violet flowers carried in dense clusters; standards 15–18mm. Fruits are ovoid, inflated and white-hairy. *Flowering:* May–July. *Distribution:* Europe from subarctic areas to the Alps; grassy and rocky places.

Mountain Milk-vetch: fruit cluster

Yellow Milk-vetch *Oxytropis campestris* 5–20cm A stemless, tufted, hairy perennial rather similar to Alpine and Purple Milk-vetches. Cream, light yellow or pale violet flowers are carried in dense, ovoid, stalked clusters; standards are 15–20mm long. Fruits are ovoid to oblong-cylindrical, hairy pods, 14–18mm long. *Flowering*: June–September. *Distribution:* Northern Europe, extending to southern Europe in the mountains; grassy and rocky places up to 3000m. **Mountain Milk-vetch** (*O. halleri*) is similar but has blue to purple flowers. *Flowering:* June–August. *Distribution:* Pyrenees, Alps and Carpathians, also in Scotland and Albania; grassy and rocky places.

Pitch-trefoil *Psoralea bituminosa* 20–100cm A hairy perennial with sprawling or erect stems bearing trifoliate leaves which, in warm weather, smell of tar when rubbed. Leaflets are narrowly lanceolate to ovate, 10–60mm long. Blue-violet flowers are 15–20mm long, carried in long-stalked, globose heads. Fruits are flattened, ovoid pods, each with a curved beak up to 15mm. A robust plant, able to continue flowering even in summer-drought conditions. *Flowering:* April–September. *Distribution:* Southern Europe; grassy and waste areas, on roadsides and disturbed ground.

Tufted Vetch *Vicia cracca* 60–200cm A clambering, more or less hairy perennial with pinnately divided leaves ending in branched tendrils. Leaflets are in six to 15 pairs, linear to oblong-ovate, 5–30mm long. Stalked, dense, spike-like flower-clusters are 20–100mm long, arising from leaf axils. Flowers are deep bluish-violet, 8–12mm long, 10 to 30 in each cluster. Fruits are narrow, brown, hairless pods 1–2.5cm long. *Flowering:* June–August. *Distribution:* Almost throughout Europe; scrub and hedges.

Wood Vetch *Vicia sylvatica* 60–200cm A clambering, usually hairless perennial similar to Tufted Vetch. Leaflets are in five to 12 pairs, oblong to slightly ovate, 6–20mm long. Flowers are white with purple veins, 12–20mm long, five to 20 in each rather loose cluster. Fruits are 25–30mm long, black, hairless. *Flowering:* June–August. *Distribution:* Mainly northern, central and eastern Europe; open woodland and sometimes forming sprawling mounds on maritime cliffs and shingle.

Fodder Vetch

Fodder Vetch *Vicia villosa* 30–200cm A variable annual with leaves pinnately divided into four to 12 pairs of linear to elliptical leaflets. Flowers are 10–20mm long, violet, blue or purple, sometimes with the wings yellow or white, carried in clusters usually longer than leaves. Pods are brown, 20–40mm long. *Flowering:* June–November. *Distribution:* Most of Europe, widely cultivated for fodder and often naturalised; bare ground and waste areas. Not native in the north. **Purple Vetch** (*V. benghalensis*) is a similar, hairy annual or short-lived perennial growing up to 80cm, with reddish-purple flowers usually black at tips. Flower clusters are shorter than or equalling leaves. *Flowering:* March–June. *Distribution:* Mediterranean region, growing in similar habitats to Fodder Vetch.

Purple Milk-vetch

Yellow Milk-vetch

Pitch-trefoil

Tufted Vetch

Wood Vetch

Fodder Vetch

Slender Tare

Hairy Tare *Vicia hirsuta* 20–70cm A hairy, sprawling annual with leaves pinnately divided into four to 10 pairs of narrowly oblong leaflets 5–20mm long. Purplish-white flowers are 2–4mm long, in clusters of one to eight. Fruits are oblong, black, hairy pods, 6–11mm long, usually with two seeds. *Flowering:* May–August. *Distribution:* Almost throughout Europe; grassy and waste areas and hedges. **Smooth Tare** (*V. tetrasperma*) is similar but almost hairless, with larger flowers, 4–8mm long, carried singly or in pairs. Pods are longer, 9–16mm, brown, usually hairless, with three to five seeds. *Flowering:* May–August. *Distribution:* Almost throughout Europe; grassland and hedges. **Slender Tare** (*V. tenuissima*) has leaves with two to five pairs of linear leaflets. Flowers are 6–9mm long, in clusters of two to five. Pods are 12–17mm long, brown, hairy or not, with four to six seeds. *Flowering:* June–August. *Distribution:* Western and southern Europe; grassland.

Bush Vetch *Vicia sepium* 30–100cm A clambering, usually hairy perennial with leaves pinnately divided into three to nine pairs of ovate to oblong leaflets 7–30mm long. Dull bluish-purple flowers are 12–15mm long, borne in more or less stalkless clusters of two to six in leaf axils. Fruits are black, hairless pods 20–35mm long. *Flowering:* April–November. *Distribution:* Almost throughout Europe; woodland, scrub and hedges.

Common Vetch *Vicia sativa* Up to 80cm A variable, hairy annual with leaves pinnately divided into three to eight pairs of linear to heart-shaped leaflets 6–30mm long. Purple flowers are 10–30mm long, borne singly or in pairs in the leaf axils. Fruits are yellowish-brown to black pods, hairy or not, 25–70mm long. *Flowering:* April–September. *Distribution:* Throughout Europe; hedges, scrub, grassy and waste areas. Frequently cultivated for fodder.

Yellow Vetch *Vicia lutea* Up to 60cm long A prostrate annual with leaves pinnately divided into three to 10 pairs of linear or oblong leaflets 10–25mm long. Pale yellow, often purple-tinged flowers are 20–35mm long, borne singly or in twos or threes in leaf axils. Fruits are yellowish-brown to black, usually hairy pods 20–40mm long. *Flowering:* June–September. *Distribution:* Mainly western and southern Europe, locally naturalised elsewhere; sparse grass, places, on disturbed ground and maritime shingle.

Yellow Vetchling *Lathyrus aphaca* Up to 100cm A clambering, hairless annual with pairs of broadly arrow-shaped, leaf-like stipules 6–50mm long. Leaves are reduced to tendrils. Yellow flowers are 6–18mm long, usually carried singly on slender stalks to 50mm, arising from axils. Fruits are brown, hairless pods 20–35mm long. *Flowering:* April–August. *Distribution:* Western, central and southern Europe; dry, grassy places and on disturbed ground.

Sea Pea *Lathyrus japonicus* subsp. *maritimus* Up to 90cm long A hairless, rather bluish-green perennial with prostrate stems forming large mats. Leaves are pinnately divided into two to five pairs of elliptical leaflets 2–4cm long. Showy, bright purple flowers are 14–18mm long, in stalked clusters of five to 12; petals become blue with age. Fruits are brown pods 30–50mm long. *Flowering:* June–August. *Distribution:* Coasts of northern and western Europe, growing on maritime shingle; rarely on lake shores inland. Subsp. *japonicus* has flowers 18–22mm long in clusters of two to seven and is restricted to arctic Europe. **Spring Pea** (*L. vernus*) is erect, to 40cm, with leaflets ovate-lanceolate, pointed; tendril absent. *Flowering:* April–June. *Distribution:* Most of Europe, especially in mountains and on lime-rich soils.

Spring Pea

Hairy Tare

Bush Vetch

Common Vetch

Yellow Vetch

Yellow Vetchling

Sea Pea

Marsh Pea

Bitter Vetch *Lathyrus montanus* 15–50cm An erect, more or less hairless perennial with winged stems bearing leaves pinnately divided into two to four pairs of linear leaflets 10–50mm long. Tendrils are absent. Crimson flowers are 10–16mm long, carried in stalked clusters of two to six; petals become bluish with age. Fruits are reddish–brown, hairless pods 25–45mm long. *Flowering:* April–July. *Distribution:* Western, central and southern Europe; woodland, scrub, hedges and on heaths, often on acid soils. **Marsh Pea** (*L. palustris*) clambers up to 120cm, with leaflets 25–80mm long and flowers light purple. *Flowering:* July–August. *Distribution:* Most of Europe but very rare in the Mediterranean region; marshes and fens with lime-rich soil.

Meadow Vetchling *Lathyrus pratensis* 30–120cm A scrambling perennial with leaves divided into a single pair of lanceolate leaflets 10–30mm long and tipped with a tendril. Stipules are like the leaflets. Yellow flowers are 10–16mm long, carried in rather compact, long stalked clusters of five to 12. Fruits are black pods 2–40mm long. *Flowering:* May–August. *Distribution:* Almost throughout Europe; scrub, hedges and moist grassland.

Hairy Vetchling *Lathyrus hirsutus* 20–120cm A clambering, sparsely hairy annual with winged stems. Leaves are divided into a single pair of linear or oblong leaflets 15–80mm long and tipped with tendril. Flowers are 7–15mm long, carried in loose, long-stalked clusters of one to three; standard is reddish-purple; wings pale blue; keel cream. Fruits are brown, densely hairy pods 20–50mm long. *Flowering:* June–August. *Distribution:* Native in central and southern Europe, introduced in Britain but possibly also native in Essex; grassy and bare places.

Grass Vetchling *Lathyrus nissolia* 10–90cm An erect more or less hairless annual barely distinguishable from grass when not in flower. Leaflets and tendrils are absent; instead, each leaf stalk and mid-rib is modified into a linear, grass-like blade up to 130mm long. Crimson to blue flowers are 8–18mm long, carried singly or in pairs on long, slender stalks. Fruits are pale brown pods 30–60mm long. *Flowering:* May–July. *Distribution:* Western, central and southern Europe; grassy places and scrub.

Spiny Restharrow *Ononis spinosa* 10–80cm A hairy, dwarf shrub with erect or ascending branches usually bearing sharp, yellow spines. Leaves are mostly trifoliate; leaflets more pointed than those of Restharrow. Pink or purple flowers are 6–20mm long, carried singly or rarely in pairs in axils on loose, leafy shoots. Fruits are 6–10mm long. *Flowering:* June–September. *Distribution:* Most of Europe; grassland, waste and stony places, often in grazed areas.

Restharrow *Ononis repens* 40–70cm A stickily hairy, fetid-smelling, shrubby perennial with creeping or ascending stems which often root. Leaves are simple to trifoliate, the leaflets usually ovate. Spines may be present, but are normally soft. Pink or purple flowers are 15–20mm long, borne singly or rarely in pairs, in axils of loose, leafy shoots. Fruits are small pods 5–7mm long. *Flowering:* June–September. *Distribution:* Mainly in western and central Europe; dry grassland and on maritime sand and shingle. **O. arvensis** is similar but has erect stems to 100cm, leaves mostly trifoliate and flowers borne in pairs in axils of dense, leafy shoots. Pods are 6–9mm long. *Flowering:* July–August. *Distribution:* Most of Europe except the west.

Ononis arvensis

Bitter Vetch

Meadow Vetchling

Hairy Vetchling

Grass Vetchling

Spiny Restharrow

Restharrow

Large Yellow Restharrow *Ononis natrix* 20–60cm A stickily hairy, fetid-smelling dwarf shrub with trifoliate leaves. Leaflets are variable, linear to ovate, 2–8mm or more long. Yellow flowers are 6–20mm long, carried on loose, leafy shoots; petals often have red or violet veins. Fruits are pods 10–25mm long. *Flowering:* March–August. *Distribution:* Western and southern Europe; dry, open places and on maritime sands.

White Melilot *Melilotus alba* 30–150cm An erect, branching annual or biennial with trifoliate leaves, the toothed leaflets narrow to nearly orbicular. White flowers are 4–5mm long, carried in narrow, spike-like heads; wings and keel are nearly equal, standard is longer. Fruits are obovoid, hairless pods, 3–5mm long, ripening greyish-brown. *Flowering:* June–October. *Distribution:* Most of Europe, doubtfully native in the north; disturbed ground. **Small Melilot** (*M. indica*) is smaller, annual, 15–30cm, with yellow flowers 2–3mm long. Fruits are 1.5–3mm long, almost globose. *Flowering:* June–August. *Distribution:* Native in southern Europe, naturalised in north-western and central Europe; disturbed ground.

Small Melilot: fruit

Tall Melilot: fruits

Ribbed Melilot *Melilotus officinalis* 40–250cm An branching biennial similar to White Melilot. Yellow flowers are 4–7mm long; wings and standard are equal, longer than keel. Fruits are obovoid, hairless pods, 3–5mm long, ripening brown, with style often falling off. *Flowering:* June–September. *Distribution:* Most of Europe, introduced in the north; scrub, disturbed ground, often on clay or saline soils. **Tall Melilot** (*M. altissima*) is very similar but flowers have wings, keel and standard all equal in length. Fruits are hairy, 5–6mm long, ripening black, with persistent style. *Flowering:* June–August. *Distribution:* Most of Europe; hedges and grassland.

Classical Fenugreek *Trigonella foenum-graecum* 10–50cm
A sparsely hairy annual with trifoliate leaves, the toothed leaflets 20–50mm long. Yellowish-white flowers, tinged violet at base, are 12–18mm long, carried singly or in pairs in axils of upper leaves. Fruits are erect or spreading, narrow, slightly curved, hairless pods 80–140mm long including beak. *Flowering:* April–May. *Distribution:* Perhaps native in south-western Asia; cultivated for fodder in central and southern Europe and widely naturalised on disturbed ground. ***Medicago monspeliaca*** is hairier, with leaflets 4–10mm long. Yellow flowers are about 4mm long, carried in clusters of four to 14. Fruits are narrow, drooping, slightly up-curved, hairy pods 7–17mm long. *Flowering:* April–May. *Distribution:* Mainly central and southern Europe.

Medicago monspeliaca: fruit cluster

Black Medick *Medicago lupulina* 5–60cm A hairy annual or short-lived perennial with trifoliate leaves, the leaflets more or less obovate. Small, yellow flowers are 2–3mm long, carried in rounded, stalked clusters arising from leaf axils. Fruits are kidney-shaped, black pods, 1.5–3mm across, the whole head resembling a miniature bunch of grapes. *Flowering:* April–October. *Distribution:* Almost throughout Europe, sometimes cultivated for forage; grassland and disturbed ground.

Lucerne *Medicago sativa* Up to 80cm An ascending perennial with trifoliate leaves, the leaflets obovate to nearly linear. Blue to violet flowers are 7–11mm long, carried in spike-like clusters arising from leaf axils. Fruits are coiled into spirals 4–6mm across, with one-and-a-half to three-and-a-half turns. *Flowering:* April–October. *Distribution:* Cultivated as forage and naturalised almost throughout Europe; grassland and disturbed ground.

Large Yellow Restharrow

White Melilot

Ribbed Melilot

Classical Fenugreek

Black Medick

Lucerne

Sea Medick *Medicago marina* 60cm long A white-hairy, densely leafy, mat-forming perennial with a stout tap-root. Leaves are trifoliate; leaflets obovate. Bright yellow flowers are 6–8mm long, carried in compact clusters of five to 12. Densely white-hairy fruits are coiled into cylindrical spirals 5–7mm across with two to three turns. *Flowering:* March–June. *Distribution:* Shores of the Atlantic from France southwards, Mediterranean and Black Seas; maritime sands.

Toothed Medick *Medicago polymorpha* Up to 40cm An annual with trifoliate leaves, the leaflets obovate to heart-shaped. Yellow flowers are 3–4.5mm long, carried in clusters of one to five in the leaf axils. Fruits are usually spiny, loosely coiled into spirals 4–8mm across, with one-and-a-half to six turns. *Flowering:* April–August. *Distribution:* Native in southern Europe, extending northwards to Britain, introduced elsewhere; dry, sandy ground near sea. **Spotted Medick** (*M. arabica*) has leaflets usually with a dark, central spot and flowers 5–7mm long. *Flowering:* April–August.

Spotted Medick

Alpine Clover *Trifolium alpinum* 5–20cm A densely tufted, hairless perennial with a stout tap-root. Leaves are trifoliate; leaflets 10–40mm long, lanceolate to linear. Pink, purple or cream, strongly scented flowers are 18–25mm long, borne in compact, rounded heads of three to 12, carried on erect, slender stalks above the leaves. *Flowering:* June–August. *Distribution:* Mountains of southern France, northern Spain, Alps and Apennines; meadows and pastures on acid soils, to 2500m.

White Clover *Trifolium repens* 5–20cm A more or less hairless perennial with prostrate stems which branch and root to form extensive mats. Leaves are trifoliate, borne on ascending stalks; leaflets are ovate with white or dark markings, sometimes both. White, yellow or pink, scented flowers are 8–13mm long, carried in long-stalked, globose heads. *Flowering:* April–October. *Distribution:* Almost throughout Europe; grassland.

Reversed Clover: fruiting head

Strawberry Clover *Trifolium fragiferum* Up to 20cm A creeping perennial similar to White Clover but with pale pink flowers 6–7mm long. Globose, pinkish fruiting heads are 10–22mm acrross, resembling strawberries, the upper lip of each calyx tube having inflated and become bladder-like. *Flowering:* April–September. *Distribution:* Almost throughout Europe; grassland, often on damp, heavy soils. **Reversed Clover** (*T. resupinatum*) is a slender annual with pink flowers inverted, bent downwards, making the heads flat-topped. Fruiting heads are inflated. *Flowering:* April–June. *Distribution:* Doubtfully native in southern Europe, introduced in western and central Europe and sometimes cultivated; grassy places, disturbed ground.

Lesser Trefoil: flower head

Hop Trefoil *Trifolium campestre* 10–30cm An annual with erect or ascending stems and obovate leaflets 8–10mm long. Dense, globose flower-heads are 10–15mm across, with 20 to 30 yellow flowers, each 4–5mm long. Broad, flat standards bend downwards over fruits and fade to brown, making heads resemble miniature hops. *Flowering:* April–September. *Distribution:* Almost throughout Europe; dry grassland and disturbed ground. **Lesser Trefoil** (*T. dubium*) is smaller, the flower-heads 5–7mm across with 10 to 20 flowers, each 3–3.5mm long. Standards are folded downwards along mid-line over fruits, turning brown but not giving heads a hop-like appearance. *Flowering:* May–September. *Distribution:* Most of Europe; dry grassland.

Sea Medick

Toothed Medick

Alpine Clover

White Clover

Strawberry Clover

Hop Trefoil

Rough Clover

Crimson Clover:
flower head

Knotted Clover *Trifolium striatum* 4–30cm A softly hairy annual with spreading or ascending stems and obovate to wedge-shaped leaflets 6–16mm long. Ovoid or oblong flower heads are 10–15mm long, unstalked. Pink flowers are 4–5mm long; hairy calyx tube is ovoid, somewhat inflated. *Flowering:* May–July. *Distribution:* Western, central and southern Europe; dry, open ground on light soils. **Rough Clover** (*T. scabrum)* is similar but flowers are whitish, rarely pink; calyx tube is bell-shaped, not inflated, with rigid, sharply pointed teeth. *Flowering:* April–July. *Distribution:* Western and southern Europe; in same habitats as Knotted Clover.

Haresfoot Clover *Trifolium arvense* 4–40cm A normally erect annual or biennial covered with whitish or reddish hairs. Leaflets are 5–20mm long, narrowly oblong. Numerous, densely silky flower heads are ovoid or oblong, up to 20mm long, carried on stalks; corolla about 4mm long, whitish or pink, much shorter than calyx. *Flowering:* April–September. *Distribution:* Almost throughout Europe; dry, open ground on light soils, often avoiding lime.

Red Clover *Trifolium pratense* 5–100cm long A variable, more or less hairy perennial with leaflets elliptical to nearly orbicular, 10–30mm long, often with a pale, crescent-shaped mark. Stipules are triangular, bristle-pointed. Globose or ovoid flowers heads are 20–40mm long, stalkless, often in pairs; flowers are 12–15mm long, normally reddish-purple or pink, rarely cream or white. *Flowering:* May–October. *Distribution:* Native almost throughout Europe and widely cultivated for forage; grassland on moist but well-drained soils. **Crimson Clover** (*T. incarnatum) is* annual with elongated, oblong-ovoid to cylindrical flower-heads and blood-red or rarely pure white flowers. *Flowering:* May–July. *Distribution:* Widely cultivated and naturalised in Europe, but also native on maritime cliff tops in the west and south as subsp. *molinerii* which has flowers yellowish-white or rarely pink, much exceeding calyx.

Sulphur Clover *Trifolium ochroleucon* 20–50cm A perennial similar to Red Clover but with unmarked leaves, stipules which are not bristle-pointed and flowers yellow to yellowish-white or rarely pink. *Flowering:* June–July. *Distribution:* Western, central and southern Europe; woodland margins, hedges, grassland, preferring shady damp conditions with lime-rich soil.

Dorycnium hirsutum 10–80cm An often shrubby perennial with leaves divided into five linear to obovate-oblong leaflets, the lower pair carried close to the stem, appearing stipule-like. Flowers are 3–6mm long, carried in clusters of five to 25 in the leaf axils; standard and wings are white, keel is dark red. Fruits are ovoid to globose pods 3–5mm long. *Flowering:* April–July. *Distribution:*Mediterranean region; rocky and sandy places, field-margins. **D. pentaphyllum** is hairless; flowers are only 3–5mm long, in heads of five to 25; standard and wings are white with dark red keel. Fruits are 3–5mm long. *Flowering:* April–July. *Distribution:* Central and southern Europe.

Greater Bird's-foot-trefoil *Lotus uliginosus* 30–100cm A more or less erect and usually very hairy perennial with leaves divided into five obovate leaflets 8–25mm long, the lower pair close to the stem and stipule-like. Flowers are 10–18mm long, yellow or reddish-tinged, carried in heads of five to 12 in leaf axils; calyx teeth spread in bud, the upper two with an acute angle between them. Fruits are slender pods 15–35mm long. *Flowering:* May–August. *Distribution:* Most of Europe; marshes, fens and wet grassland.

Dorycnium
pentaphyllum

Knotted Clover

Haresfoot Clover

Red Clover

Sulphur Clover

Dorycnium hirsutum

Greater Bird's-foot-trefoil

Narrow-leaved Bird's-foot-trefoil

Bird's-foot-trefoil *Lotus corniculatus* 5–35cm A creeping or ascending, hairy of hairless perennial with leaflets lanceolate to nearly orbicular, 4–18mm long. Flowers are 10–16mm long, yellow or reddish-tinged, in stalked heads of two to seven; calyx teeth are erect in bud, the upper two with an obtuse angle between them. Fruits are slender pods 15–30mm long. *Flowering:* April–September. *Distribution:* Almost throughout Europe; grassy places, maritime shingle.**Narrow-leaved Bird's-foot-trefoil** *(L. tenuis)* is slender with linear to lanceolate leaflets only 1–4mm wide. Flowers are 6–12mm long, in heads of one to four. *Flowering:* June–August. *Distribution:* Most of Europe; grassy places.

Dragon's-teeth *Tetragonolobus maritimus* 10–40cm long A prostrate perennial resembling Bird's-foot Trefoils but with trifoliate leaves with a pair of leaf-like, true stipules at the base. Solitary, pale yellow flowers are 25–30mm long. Fruits are narrow pods 30–60mm long, quadrangular in cross-section with wings about 1mm wide along the angles. *Flowering:* May–September. *Distribution:* Mainly in central and southern Europe, rare in the Mediterranean region, introduced in Britain; grassland on clay or lime-rich, often damp soils, sand-dunes.

Mountain Kidney-vetch *Anthyllis montana* 10–30cm A densely tufted, hairy perennial with woody stems, often forming large clumps. Leaves are pinnately divided into eight to 20 pairs of narrowly elliptical to oblong leaflets. Erect flowering stems terminate in dense, rounded clusters of pink or purple flowers. *Flowering:* June–July. *Distribution:* Alps and mountains of southern Europe; grassy, rocky and stony places, usually on lime-rich soils.

Bladder-vetch *Anthyllis tetraphylla* Up to 40cm long. A prostrate, hairy annual with leaves pinnately divided into three or five leaflets, the terminal much larger than lateral ones. Pale yellow flowers are carried in clusters of one to seven in leaf axils; keel is often red at apex. Fruits are enclosed in inflated, bladder-like calyces up to 12mm wide. *Flowering:* March–July. *Distribution:* Mediterranean region; disturbed ground.

Kidney-vetch *Anthyllis vulneraria* 5–90cm A very variable annual, biennial or perennial with leaves pinnately divided with up to seven pairs of leaflets. Stems terminate in compact heads of numerous flowers, with two deeply-cut, green bracts borne closely below. Flowers may be yellow, red, purple, orange, whitish or a combination of these colours; calyx is inflated and papery. *Flowering:* April–September. *Distribution:* Almost throughout Europe; grassy and rocky places, from coastal areas up to 3000m in the mountains.

Anthyllis hermanniae Up to 50cm A densely branched, dwarf shrub with sharp tips to the twigs. Leaves are simple or trifoliate; leaflets are narrowly oblong and hairy beneath. Small, yellow flowers are carried in clusters of one to three in leaf axils. *Flowering:* April–August. *Distribution:* Mediterranean region; rocky places and cliffs, sometimes on stable sand-dunes. **A. barba-jovis** is a larger shrub, to 90cm, with leaves pinnately divided into six to nine pairs of silvery hairy leaflets. Pale yellow flowers are carried in compact, terminal heads of 10 or more. *Flowering:* April–June. *Distribution:* Mediterranean region, often cultivated for ornament; rocky places and cliffs by the sea.

Anthyllis barba-jovis

Bird's-foot-trefoil

Dragon's-teeth

Mountain Kidney-vetch

Bladder-vetch

Kidney-vetch

Anthyllis hermanniae

Orange Bird's-foot

Scorpion Vetch

Coronilla repanda

Bird's-foot *Ornithopus perpusillus* Up to 30cm long A prostrate, hairy annual with leaves pinnately divided into seven to 13 pairs of elliptical or oblong leaflets. Yellowish-white or pink flowers are 3–5mm long, carried in stalked clusters of three to eight, with pinnate, leaf-like bracts. Fruits are narrow and flattened, 10–18mm long, constricted between each of the four to nine segments. *Flowering:* May–August. *Distribution:* Mainly in western and central Europe; bare and grassy places. **Orange Bird's-foot** (*O. pinnatus*) has yellow to orange flowers 6–8mm long, without obvious bracts. Fruits are 20–35mm long, not constricted between the segments. *Flowering:* April–August. *Distribution:* Western Europe; sandy and grassy places.

Crown-vetch *Securigera varia* 20–120cm A straggling, hairless perennial with leaves divided into seven to 12 pairs of leaflets 6–20mm long. White to purple flowers are 10–15mm long, carried in globose heads of 10 to 20. Fruits are 20–60mm long with three to eight one-seeded segments separating when ripe. *Flowering:* June–August. *Distribution:* Native in central and southern Europe, cultivated and naturalised elsewhere; scrub, grassy and waste areas. **Scorpion Vetch** (*Coronilla coronata*) has leaves with three to six pairs of leaflets 15–30mm long. Yellow flowers are 7–11mm long. *Flowering:* May–July. *Distribution:* Central Europe and western Balkans; dry woods, scrub, grassland on lime-rich soils.

Coronilla scorpioides Up to 40cm A hairless, bluish-green annual with undivided or trifoliate leaves. Terminal leaflet is elliptical to nearly orbicular, up to 40mm long, larger than rounded kidney-shaped laterals. Yellow flowers are 4–8mm long, in heads of two to five. Curved fruits are 20–60mm long with two to 11 segments. *Flowering:* March–June. *Distribution:* Southern Europe; dry, open, often disturbed ground. **C. repanda** is similar but upper leaves are pinnately divided, with two to four pairs of oblanceolate to obovate leaflets 4–15mm long. *Distribution:* Western and central Mediterranean region.

Horseshoe-vetch *Hippocrepis comosa* Up to 40cm A woody-based perennial with leaves divided into three to eight pairs of obovate to linear leaflets 5–15mm long. Yellow flowers are 6–10mm long, carried in long-stalked whorls of five to 12. Fruits are 15–30mm long with horseshoe-shaped segments. *Flowering:* May–July. *Distribution:* Western, central and southern Europe; lime-rich grassland.

Alpine Sainfoin: fruit

Hedysarum coronarium 30–100cm A sparsely hairy perennial with leaves divided into three to five pairs of elliptical to rounded leaflets 15–35mm long. Bright reddish-purple flowers are 12–15mm long, carried in dense, oblong, stalked heads of 10 to 35. Fruits are flattened with two to four hairless, prickly segments. *Flowering:* April–May. *Distribution:* Mediterranean region, native in the west and centre but also cultivated for fodder and more widely naturalised. **Alpine Sainfoin** (*H. hedysaroides*) has up to 10 pairs of leaflets. Reddish-violet, rarely white, flowers are 13–25mm long. Fruits have no prickles. *Flowering:* July–August. *Distribution:* Mountains of central Europe, arctic Russia and the Ural mountains; grassy and stony places, screes.

Onobrychis arenaria 10–80cm. A perennial similar to Hedysarum with leaves divided into three to 12 pairs of narrow leaflets. Flowers are pink with purple veins, carried in stalked, spike-like heads. Fruits are 4–6mm long, hairy, normally toothed on the sides and margin. *Flowering:* June–September. *Distribution:* Mainly central, eastern and south-eastern Europe.

Bird's-foot

Crown-vetch

Coronilla Scorpioides

Horseshoe-vetch

Hedysarum coronarium

Onobrychis arenaria

Wood Crane's-bill

Meadow Crane's-bill *Geranium pratense* Up to 80cm A branched, hairy perennial, with leaves divided into five to seven, ovate, deeply cut lobes. Cup-shaped flowers are 30–40mm across, several in a compact cluster, drooping after flowering. Petals are obovate, not notched at the tip, blue-violet. *Flowering:* June–September. *Distribution:* Throughout most of Europe, rare in the Mediterranean and much of the north; grassland, usually on chalky soils. **Wood Crane's-bill** (*G. sylvaticum*) up to 60cm, is similar, but has leaves with less deeply cut, ovate, toothed, lobes. Flowers are 12–35mm across, erect after flowering. *Flowering:* June–September. *Distribution:* Most of Europe, but restricted to mountains in the south; in damp woods, and on mountain meadows.

Pencilled Crane's-bill *Geranium versicolor* Up to 80cm A hairy perennial, with five long-stalked basal leaves, each one divided into five lobes. Flowers are 25mm across in a loose inflorescence; spreading petals pale pink or white, with violet veins, each deeply notched at the tip. *Flowering:* June–August. *Distribution:* Southern Balkan Peninsula, central and southern Italy and Sicily, a garden escape elsewhere; mountain woodland.

Dusky Crane's-bill *Geranium phaeum* Up to 70cm An upright perennial, with both glandular and non-glandular hairs. Leaves are similar to those of Pencilled Cranesbill, but less deeply cut, with five to seven lobes. Flower clusters open, at the tips of stems, or in leaf axils. Flowers are 15–20mm across; spreading petals rounded or with a point at the tip, slightly bent back, purple, maroon, or almost black. *Flowering:* June–August. *Distribution:* Central Europe, to the Pyrenees, Italy and western Russia, often a garden escape; woodlands and damp, shady places.

Bloody Crane's-bill *Geranium sanguineum* Up to 40cm A clump-forming, hairy perennial. Leaves are divided, the five to seven lobes with pointed oblong segments. Flowers are 25–30mm across, on long stalks; notched, spreading petals bright crimson-purple, rarely pinkish. *Flowering:* June–August. *Distribution:* Most of Europe; well-drained soils.

Cut-leaved Crane's-bill

Long-stalked Crane's-bill *Geranium columbinum* Up to 60cm An erect or ascending, hairy annual, sometimes reddish. Lower leaves are alternate, the uppermost opposite, all deeply divided into five to seven linear lobes. Flowers are 14–20mm across, on long stalks; spreading petals pinkish-purple. *Flowering:* May–September. *Distribution:* Throughout Europe, except for the far north; dry grassy places. **Cut-leaved Crane's-bill** (*G. dissectum*) is similar, but has flowers up to 10mm across, on short stalks. Petals notched at the tip. *Flowering:* May–September. *Distribution:* Most of Europe, except the north-east; hedgebanks and cultivated land.

Hedgerow Crane's-bill

Dove's-foot Crane's-bill *Geranium molle* Up to 40cm A downy-hairy, usually grey-green annual, the stems branched, prostrate or ascending and covered in long soft white hairs, with short glands. Basal leaves are divided into five to seven lobes; stem leaves more deeply cut. Flowers 10mm across, pinkish purple, with deeply notched, spreading petals. *Flowering:* April–September. *Distribution:* All Europe, except the far north; bare grassy places. **Hedgerow Crane's-bill** (*G. pyrenaicum*) up to 70cm, is a larger, less hairy, perennial. Flowers are 15mm across; petals lilac to pinkish-purple. *Flowering:* May–September. *Distribution:* Southern and western Europe, often naturalised elsewhere; woods and grassy areas.

Meadow Crane's-bill

Pencilled Crane's-bill

Dusky Crane's-bill

Bloody Crane's-bill

Long-stalked Crane's-bill

Dove's-foot Crane's-bill

Little-Robin: fruit

Musk Stork's-bill:
flower cluster

Pale Flax: fruit

Allseed

Herb-Robert *Geranium robertianum* Up to 50cm A strong-smelling annual or biennial, often tinged deep red, the leaves with three to five deeply divided lobes and long stalks with both glandular and non-glandular hairs. Flowers are 20mm across; sepals lanceolate; petals pink, rounded or slightly notched at the tip, narrowed into a stalk-like base; pollen orange. *Flowering:* April–November. *Distribution:* All Europe, except the far north; shady areas, on rocks and as a weed. **Little-Robin** (*G. purpureum*) is similar, but with smaller flowers 10–15mm across, ovate sepals and yellow pollen. *Flowering:* April–October. *Distribution:* Southern and western Europe.

Common Stork's-bill *Erodium cicutarium* Up to 100cm Usually an annual, the pinnate leaves up to 150mm, with deeply divided lobes. Flowers are about 20mm across, white, lilac or pinkish-purple, up to twelve together in an cluster with brown, leaf-like bracts at the base. *Flowering:* June–September. *Distribution:* Throughout Europe, introduced in many areas; dry and sandy grassy areas, disturbed ground. **Musk Stork's-bill** (*E. moschatum*) up to 50cm, is annual or biennial, smelling of musk. Leaves reach 200mm, with ovate, toothed or divided leaflets. White or purple flowers up to 30mm across. *Flowering:* June–September. *Distribution:* Southern and western Europe, naturalised elsewhere; waste and arable land.

Fagonia cretica Up to 40cm A prostrate, spiny perennial, with branched, angled stems. Opposite leaves are twice cut into three groups of three, rather leathery, asymmetrical leaflets each 5–15mm. Solitary flowers are about 10mm; both sepals and purplish petals deciduous. Fruit is sharply angled. *Flowering:* January–May. *Distribution:* Southern parts of the Mediterranean.

Small Caltrops *Tribulus terrestris* Up to 60cm A downy-hairy, prostrate, creeping annual with opposite leaves, those of a pair often unequal in size, each with five to eight pairs of elliptical or oblong-lanceolate leaflets. Flowers are 4–5mm; petals yellow. Star-shaped fruit is made up of five hard carpels, spiny on the sides. *Flowering:* May–October. *Distribution:* Southern Europe, locally to north-western France, and east-central Russia.

Perennial Flax *Linum perenne* Up to 60cm A greyish-green perennial, stems often woody-based, prostrate, ascending or upright. Leaves are linear or linear-lanceolate, those in the middle of the stem one- to three-veined, the remainder one-veined. Flowers are 25mm, in clusters, usually bright blue, but sometimes paler; flower stalks erect. *Flowering:* May–August. *Distribution:* Central and eastern Europe, westwards to Britain and the Pyrenees; dry grassland, on lime-rich soils. **Pale Flax** (*L. bienne*) is similar, but may also be biennial or annual. Flowers are 15mm, pale blue-lilac, the petals soon falling. *Flowering:* May–August. *Distribution:* Western and southern Europe.

Fairy Flax *Linum catharticum* Up to 15cm Generally resembling Perennial Flax, but much smaller in all its parts and usually annual, with lanceolate, one-veined leaves. Flowers are white, up to 6mm across, on long slender stalks, drooping in bud. *Flowering:* May–September. *Distribution:* Most of Europe, mountains only in the south; grassland, especially on lime-rich soils. **Allseed** (*Radiola linoides*) is rarely more than 10cm high, with thread-like stems and elliptical leaves. Flowers are only 1mm across, white, four-petalled, many in tight cluster. *Flowering:* July–August. *Distribution:* Most of Europe, absent from the north-east and far north; bare, sandy, usually seasonally wet ground.

Herb-Robert

Common Stork's-bill

Fagonia cretica

Small Caltrops

Perennial Flax

Fairy Flax

Upright Yellow Sorrel

Dog's Mercury:
♀ flowers

Wood Sorrel *Oxalis acetosella* Up to 10cm A low, creeping downy perennial, with a rosette of trifoliate leaves, each leaflet rounded and notched at the tip. Flowers are 8–15mm, solitary on long stalks, white with lilac-purple veins, occasionally pale purple or violet. *Flowering:* April–May. *Distribution:* Most of Europe, rare in the south; woodlands and shaded areas.

Procumbent Yellow Sorrel *Oxalis corniculata* Up to 50cm
A creeping, downy-hairy prostrate perennial, rooting at the nodes. Leaves are trifoliate, often tinged purple, the leaflets deeply notched at the tip. Flowers are 4–7mm, yellow, in clusters of one to seven. *Flowering:* May–October. *Distribution:* Southern Europe, northwards to France, Hungary and the Ukraine, often naturalised elsewhere; dry places, especially on cultivated ground. **Upright Yellow Sorrel** (*O. stricta*) is similar but has erect, non-rooting stems, and flowers 5–9mm. *Flowering:* May–October. *Distribution:* An American and eastern Asian species, naturalised throughout Europe.

Bermuda-buttercup *Oxalis pes-caprae* Up to 20cm A perennial with a buried bulb, and a rosette of trifoliate basal leaves, with the lobes deeply notched at the tip. Flowers are 20–25mm, yellow, in a cluster of up to ten. *Flowering:* March–June. *Distribution:* A South African plant, introduced and widely naturalised in the Mediterranean and western Europe; cultivated and waste land.

Annual Mercury *Mercurialis annua* Up to 50cm An almost hairless branched annual, the opposite leaves ovate to elliptical-lanceolate and toothed. Small, greenish flowers are unisexual; sepals three; petals absent; male flowers borne in clusters on long, erect spikes; females flowers on different plants, in few-flowered, stalkless clusters. *Flowering:* May–November. *Distribution:* Most of Europe, but introduced in much of the north and west; a weed of cultivated ground. **Dog's Mercury** (*M. perennis*) is perennial, with leaves more crowded into the upper part of the stem. Flowers are 4–5mm, larger than those of Annual Mercury. *Flowering:* May–October. *Distribution:* Most of Europe; beech or oak woodland.

Castor-oil-plant *Ricinus communis* Up to 400cm A soft-wooded or large, sometimes annual, herb. Leaves up to 60cm have five to nine lanceolate or ovate-lanceolate, pointed, irregularly toothed lobes. Flowers are unisexual, in stout spikes, the clusters of greenish males borne below prickly looking, globular clusters of reddish females. Globular fruits are 10–20mm, often spiky; seeds smooth, shiny, black or reddish, marked with white, grey or brown. *Flowering:* February–December. *Distribution:* Native to the tropics, cultivated for oil and as an ornamental, and naturalised in south and central Europe; waste areas and arable land.

Tree Spurge *Euphorbia dendroides* Up to 200cm A summer-deciduous shrub, with regularly-forked branches. Stem leaves are oblong-lanceolate, blunt, with a small point; leaves around the base of the inflorescence are shorter and wider, those below the flowers are broad, diamond-shaped and yellowish. Flowers small, with hemispherical, lobed glands on the rim. *Flowering:* April–June. *Distribution:* Mediterranean; on rocks near the sea.

Wood Sorrel

Procumbent Yellow Sorrel

Bermuda-buttercup

Annual Mercury: ♂ flowers

Castor-oil-plant: ♂ and ♀ flowers

Tree Spurge

Large Mediterranean Spurge *Euphorbia characias* Up to 180cm

A large, greyish-green, tufted perennial, often densely hairy, occasionally with stems that survive for two years only. Leaves are linear, lanceolate or ovate, wider towards the tip, those below the flowers hemispherical or triangular and usually joined in pairs. Flowers are small, the glands on the rim either reddish-brown with short horns, or yellowish and long-horned. *Flowering:* July–September. *Distribution:* Mediterranean and Portugal; dry open ground.

Euphorbia chamaesyce: cyathium

Purple Spurge *Euphorbia peplis* Up to 40cm

A prostrate, usually four-branched, fleshy, hairless annual with red-purple stems. Leaves are opposite, oblong, blunt, greyish, and short-stalked. Flowers are small, in axils of leaves; glands on the rim semi-circular, reddish-brown, with pale horns. *Flowering:* July–September. *Distribution:* Coasts of southern and western Europe, as far north as Britain; sandy shores or rarely inland. **E. chamaesyce** is similar, but has asymmetrical, ovate to oblong leaves, flowers with hemispherical glands and small whitish horns. *Flowering:* July–September. *Distribution:* Southern Europe, northwards to Russia; open areas.

Petty Spurge: fruit

Sun Spurge *Euphorbia helioscopia* Up to 50cm

An upright, hairless annual, with a single, reddish stem. Leaves are obovate and finely toothed. Small flowers with green oval glands on the rim form a broad umbel; fruits smooth. *Flowering:* April–November. *Distribution:* Throughout Europe, but only casual in the far north; arable and waste land. **Petty Spurge** (*E. peplus)* is branched from the base. Leaves are ovate, untoothed. Fruits have wavy edges. *Flowering:* April–November. *Distribution:* Most of Europe, except the far north; weed or arable and disturbed ground.

Sea Spurge *Euphorbia paralias* Up to 70cm

A fleshy, grey-green perennial, branched from the base. Stem leaves are fleshy, overlapping, ovate; leaves below the inflorescence diamond-shaped. Flowers are small, with horned glands on the rim. *Flowering:* April–August. *Distribution:* Western and southern Europe; sandy or shingly coasts.

Leafy Spurge: inflorescence

Cypress Spurge *Euphorbia cyparissias* Up to 70cm

A perennial, sometimes branched. Leaves are linear-lanceolate to elliptical-oblong, those below the flowers diamond-shaped or rounded, becoming bright red. Flowers in a regularly once- or twice-branched umbel are small; glands on rim have two long slender horns. *Flowering:* May–August. *Distribution:* Most of Europe, but only as an introduction in much of the north; dry grassy places. **Leafy Spurge** (*E. esula*) up to 120cm, is a larger perennial, with non-flowering branches arising in leaf axils. Leaves are longer and wider than those of Cypress Spurge, with leaves below the umbel shorter and wider, and those below flowers diamond-shaped. Glands have two horns. *Flowering:* May–September. *Distribution:* Most of Europe, but introduced in the north; dry areas.

Ruta chalepensis

Rue *Ruta graveolens* Up to 45cm

A grey-green, aromatic shrub. Leaves are pinnately divided, the smallest leaflets 2–9mm wide, lanceolate or narrowly oblong. Yellow flowers are 20mm, the four petals incurved, hooded and minutely toothed at the tips. *Flowering:* June–September. *Distribution:* Native to the Balkan Peninsula and the Crimea, and possibly southern Mediterranean areas; widely naturalised. **R. chalepensis** up to 75cm, is similar but larger, with triangular-ovate sepals and fringed petals. *Flowering:* June–September. *Distribution:* Southern Europe; in dry shady places.

Large Mediterranean Spurge

Purple Spurge

Sun Spurge

Sea Spurge

Cypress Spurge

Rue

Burning-bush *Dictamnus albus* 40–80cm A bushy perennial herb often woody at the base, the whole plant gland-dotted and smelling of lemon when crushed. Dark green, pinnate leaves have three to six pairs of leathery, lanceolate to ovate leaflets. Flowers are showy, borne in terminal spikes; five petals 20–25mm, white, pink or bluish, dotted and streaked with purple; ten up-curved stamens prominent. *Flowering:* May–June. *Distribution:* Southern and parts of central Europe as far north as eastern Russia; stony scrub.

Common Milkwort *Polygala vulgaris* 7–35cm An ascending to erect perennial with alternate leaves, the lower obovate to elliptical, the upper narrower. Dense flower spike with ten to 40 blue, white or pink flowers; elongates in fruit. Two petal-like inner sepals are 4–7mm, persistent; corolla has a prominent fringed crest. *Flowering:* June–September. *Distribution:* Most of Europe; grasslands. Similar **Heath Milkwort** (*P. serpyllifolia*) has opposite lower leaves and three to ten flowers. *Flowering:* June–August. *Distribution:* Western and central Europe.

Heath Milkwort

Shrubby Milkwort *Polygala chamaebuxus* 5–15cm A spreading, very dwarfed shrub with leathery leaves 15–30mm, ovate to linear-lanceolate. Flowers are solitary or paired in leaf axils. Two inner petal-like sepals are white, yellow or purplish-pink, deciduous; corolla coloured like inner sepals but lower petal bright yellow becoming purple or reddish, with a very small, lobed crest. *Flowering:* May–August. *Distribution:* Alps and mountains of west-central Europe; woods, grassy and rocky areas.

Indian Balsam *Impatiens glandulifera* 100–200cm A stout annual with leaves opposite or in whorls of three, 5–18cm, lanceolate to elliptic, the margins sharply toothed. Flowers are 25–40mm purplish-pink or rarely white; three sepals coloured like the petals, the lowest sac-like and extended backwards into a straight spur. Petals five, the lower four united into two pairs. Fruit is an explosive capsule 15–30mm. *Flowering:* July–October. *Distribution:* Native to the Himalayas, naturalised in many parts of Europe; waste ground, river banks.

Touch-me-not Balsam *Impatiens noli-tangere* 20–180cm An annual with alternate leaves 1.5–10cm, narrowly ovate or oblong and toothed. Flowers are 20–35mm, yellow with brown spots. Lowest of the three sepals sac-like, extending backwards into a curved spur. Petals five, the lower four united into two pairs. Fruit is a linear capsule, exploding when ripe. *Flowering:* June–August. *Distribution:* Most of Europe; shady, damp places. Similar **Small Balsam** (*I. parviflora*) has larger leaves 4–20cm but smaller, yellow flowers 6–18mm with a straight or slightly curved spur. *Flowering:* July–November. *Distribution:* Native of central Asia naturalised in much of Europe.

Small Balsam

Rough Marsh-mallow

Marsh-mallow *Althaea officinalis* Up to 200cm A perennial densely clothed with stellate grey hairs. Large leaves are triangular-ovate, toothed and either undivided or palmately lobed up to half-way to the base. Flowers are usually lilac-pink; six to nine epicalyx segments narrow, united at the base; sepals ovate and curving over the hairy fruit; petals 15–20mm, sometimes shallowly notched; anthers purplish. *Flowering:* June–September. *Distribution:* Most of Europe except Scandinavia; damp places. **Rough Marsh-mallow** (*A. hirsutus*) is an annual up to 60cm, the upper leaves palmate with narrow lobes. Sepals are erect around the hairless fruit. *Flowering:* May–July. *Distribution:* Mainly southern Europe; dry soils.

Burning-bush

Common Milkwort

Shrubby Milkwort

Indian Balsam

Touch-me-not Balsam

Marsh-mallow

Greater Musk Mallow

Dwarf Mallow: fruit

Hyeres Tree-mallow

Musk Mallow *Malva moschata* 30–125cm An erect, hairy-stemmed perennial with upper leaves palmately five- to seven-lobed, each lobe twice-pinnately lobed. Flowers have three at most sparsely hairy epicalyx segments; bright pink petals 20–30mm, twice as long as sepals. Circular fruit of many segments is clothed with long white hairs. *Flowering:* July–August. *Distribution:* Most of Europe but only naturalised in Scandinavia; mainly grassy places. Very similar **Greater Musk Mallow** (*M. alcea*) has broadly ovate, densely hairy epicalyx segments. *Flowering:* June–September. *Distribution:* Similar to Musk Mallow but rare in the Mediterranean.

Common Mallow *Malva sylvestris* Up to 150cm An erect or spreading perennial, very variable in many characters. Rounded to kidney-shaped leaves are palmately cut into three to seven shallow, blunt and toothed lobes. Flowers have three oblong-lanceolate to elliptical epicalyx segments; petals 12–30mm, pink to purple often with darker veins and a beard of short hairs near the base. *Flowering:* June–September. *Distribution:* Throughout Europe except for the far north; waste places. Similar **Dwarf Mallow** (*M. neglecta*) is annual, with narrower epicalyx segments and lilac to whitish petals only 9–13mm. *Flowering:* June–September. *Distribution:* Most of Europe.

Tree-mallow *Lavatera arborea* Up to 300cm A large, bushy biennial with stems woody at the base. Young growth is stellately hairy. Orbicular leaves, folded like a fan, reach 200mm, the five to seven shallow lobes toothed. Flowers have three rounded to ovate-oblong epicalyx segments united towards the base, much longer than sepals and enlarged in fruit; petals 15–20mm, pinkish-purple, much darker on veins and at the base. *Flowering:* July–September. *Distribution:* Coasts of the Mediterranean and western Europe northwards to Ireland; rocks, also naturalised in hedges and waste areas. **Hyeres Tree-mallow** (*L. olbia*) is shrubby with three- to five-lobed leaves broader than long, epicalyx as long as sepals and purple petals 15–30mm. *Flowering:* April–June. *Distribution:* Western Mediterranean.

Smaller Tree-mallow *Lavatera cretica* 50–150cm An often spreading, stellately hairy annual or biennial with leaves similar to those of Tree Mallow. Flowers have three ovate epicalyx segments united only at the base and slightly shorter than the sepals; petals 10–20mm, lilac. Often mistaken for Common Mallow which has narrower and free epicalyx segments. *Flowering:* June–July. *Distribution:* Mediterranean and western Europe northwards to Britain, usually near the sea.

Bladder Ketmia *Hibiscus trionum* A roughly hairy annual. Upper leaves are cut almost to the base into three pinnately lobed segments. Flowers have six to 13 linear epicalyx segments; purple-veined sepals united, becoming membranous and inflated, enclosing the fruit; petals about 20mm, pale yellow with a dark violet basal patch. *Flowering:* June–September. *Distribution:* Native to south-eastern and south-central Europe, naturalised in the Mediterranean and sometimes further north; cultivated and waste ground.

Fleshy-leaved Thymelaea *Thymelaea hirsuta* 40–100cm A much-branched, rather sprawling evergreen shrub, the white-woolly twigs densely clothed with fleshy overlapping leaves only 3–8mm long. Upper leaf surface is white-hairy, lower surface shiny and more or less smooth. Unisexual or hermaphrodite flowers are yellowish, with a densely hairy tube and four tiny sepals. *Flowering:* October–May. *Distribution:* Mediterranean region.

Musk Mallow

Common Mallow

Tree-mallow

Smaller Tree-mallow

Bladder Ketmia

Fleshy-leaved Thymelaea

Garland-flower

Spurge-laurel *Daphne laureola* Up to 100cm An evergreen shrub with greenish, hairless twigs with leaves clustered towards their tips. Shining, leathery leaves are 30–120mm, obovate-oblanceolate. Yellowish-green flowers borne in short, dense spikes in axils of previous year's leaves; four sepals petal-like, petals absent. Ripe fruit is black. **Garland-flower** (*D. cneorum*) is sprawling, with greyish, hairy young twigs and evenly distributed, narrower leaves only 10–18mm long. Fragrant pink flowers, white-hairy on the outside, borne in stalkless clusters. Fruit brownish-yellow. *Flowering:* February–April. *Distribution:* Central Europe and parts of the Mediterranean; woods, usually on lime-rich soils.

Mezereon *Daphne mezereum* Up to 200cm Bushy, deciduous shrub flowering before the leaves fully appear. Erect twigs are grey-brown, with oblong-lanceolate leaves rather crowded towards the tips. Fragrant flowers pinkish-purple, hairy on the outside, borne in clusters of two to four in axils where previous year's leaves have fallen; four sepals petal-like, petals absent. Ripe fruit is bright red. *Flowering:* February–April. *Distribution:* Most of Europe but not the far north, west or south; woods, preferring lime-rich soils.

Tutsan *Hypericum androsaemum* 30–70cm A dwarf deciduous shrub, the spreading stems with two raised lines. Opposite leaves are broadly ovate to ovate-oblong, stalkless and sometimes clasp the stem. Flowers are yellow, in few-flowered terminal clusters. Sepals are 8–12mm, unequal, enlarging in fruit; petals slightly shorter than sepals; numerous stamens in five bundles, with yellowish anthers. Fruit is a black berry. *Flowering:* June–August. *Distribution:* Mainly western Europe, scattered in the south; shady places.

Square-stalked
St John's-wort

Perforate St John's-wort *Hypericum perforatum* 10–100cm A perennial with tiny black glands on all parts. Stems have two raised lines along their length. Opposite leaves are ovate to linear, more or less stalkless and with numerous large translucent dots. Yellow flowers borne in large clusters; petals and stamens persistent. Fruit is a capsule. *Flowering:* June–September. *Distribution:* Throughout most of Europe; woods, grassland. **Imperforate St John's-wort** (*H. maculatum*) has four-lined stems, leaves with a few large translucent dots. *Flowering:* June–August. *Distribution:* Most of Europe; damp woods and hedges. **Square-stalked St John's-wort** (*H. tetrapterum*) has narrowly four-winged stems. *Flowering:* June–September. *Distribution:* Much of Europe; damp, open places.

Slender St John's-
wort

Hairy St John's-wort *Hypericum hirsutum* A perennial herb with black glands confined to the sepals. Stems lack raised lines. Roughly hairy leaves are opposite, oblong to lanceolate. Yellow flowers form a loose, cylindrical inflorescence. Sepals have fine black glandular teeth; petals twice as long, sometimes red-veined. *Flowering:* July–August. *Distribution:* Most of Europe but not the north-east and far south; damp woods and grassy areas. Similar **Slender St John's-wort** (*H. pulchrum*) has hairless, ovate leaves half-clasping the stem. *Flowering:* June–August. *Distribution:* Mainly north-western Europe; dry areas.

Marsh St John's-wort *Hypericum elodes* 10–30cm A perennial covered with short, white, cottony hairs. Stems are creeping and rooting below, erect above. Opposite leaves are 5–30mm, rounded to broadly elliptical. Both sepals and yellow petals are persistent; sepals have fine red glandular teeth. *Flowering:* June–September. *Distribution:* Western Europe east to Germany and Italy; wet places.

Spurge-laurel

Mezereon

Tutsan

Perforate St John's -wort

Hairy St John's-wort

Marsh St John's-wort

Viola alba: leaf and stipules

Early Dog Violet: leaf and stipules

Sweet Violet *Viola odorata* Up to 15cm A creeping downy perennial, with a rosette of kidney-shaped leaves and long rooting stolons; stipules ovate. Fragrant, long-stalked flowers are 15mm; sepals ovate; unequal petals dark violet or white, the lowest with a spur about 6mm long. *Flowering:* March–May & June–September. *Distribution:* Europe, except parts of the Mediterranean and the far south; woods and hedges. **V. alba** produces non-rooting stolons, a rosette of triangular-ovate dark-green leaves, and has linear-lanceolate stipules. Flowers white or violet. *Flowering:* March–May. *Distribution:* Central and southern Europe; shady places and grassland.

Common Dog Violet *Viola riviniana* Up to 15cm An almost hairless perennial. Leaves are small, up to 40mm, heart-shaped, blunt-tipped; stipules ovate or lanceolate, toothed. Flowers are 10–13mm; sepals short, pointed; unequal petals broad, blue-violet, the lower with a light purple spur 3–5mm. *Flowering:* March–May & July–September. *Distribution:* Throughout Europe, except the south–east; woods and grassland. **Early Dog Violet** (*V. reichenbachiana*) has thinner leaves, with narrowly lanceolate, fringed stipules. Flowers have sharp sepals, narrow violet petals often darker at the base and a deep blue spur 3–6mm. *Flowering:* March–May. *Distribution:* Mainly south-western and central Europe; shady places.

Heath Dog Violet *Viola canina* Up to 40cm A perennial plant with prostrate or ascending stems, lacking a basal rosette. Leaves are ovate or lanceolate, usually heart-shaped at the base, blunt-tipped; stipules toothed, shorter than the leaf stalk. Flowers are 15–25mm, blue or white, petals unequal, the lower with a white or greenish spur. *Flowering:* April–June. *Distribution:* Most of Europe but rare in the south; heaths and open woods.

Fen Violet *Viola persicifolia* Up to 25cm A mostly hairless perennial, with no basal rosette. Leaves are 20–40mm, triangular-lanceolate, the base heart-shaped or cut straight across; stipules 10mm, often fringed. Flowers are 10–15mm, white with violet veins; petals barely longer than wide; spur greenish. *Flowering:* April–July. *Distribution:* Most of Europe, absent from far north, south-east and the Mediterranean; fens and marshes.

Mountain Pansy

Dwarf Pansy

Wild Pansy *Viola tricolor* Up to 40cm A hairless or downy-hairy annual, biennial or perennial, with branched stems. Lower leaves are heart-shaped or ovate, the upper ovate or lanceolate, with a wedge-shaped base and bluntly toothed margins; stipules deeply divided. Flowers are 10–50mm; unequal petals yellow, violet or bi-coloured, longer than the sepals, the lower with a spur up to 6.5mm. *Flowering:* April–November. *Distribution:* Most of Europe, but only on mountains in the south; grassland and open places. **Mountain Pansy** (*V. lutea*) is similar, but perennial, with ovate, oblong or lanceolate leaves. Flowers are 15–30mm, the lower petal densely veined. *Flowering:* May–August. *Distribution:* Western and central Europe.

Field Pansy *Viola arvensis* Up to 40cm A branched, more or less erect annual, with ovate lower leaves, and oblong upper leaves; stipules deeply divided. Flowers are 10–15mm; sepals equalling or longer than petals; unequal petals creamy to blue-violet, the lower spurred, creamy-yellow. *Flowering:* April–November. *Distribution:* Throughout Europe; open or arable land. **Dwarf Pansy** (*V. kitaibeliana*) up to 20cm, is smaller, downy, with flowers only 4–8mm, creamy-white to yellow, with a yellow centre. *Flowering:* April–July. *Distribution:* Southern and central Europe; dry bare habitats.

Sweet Violet

Common Dog Violet

Heath Dog Violet

Fen Violet

Wild Pansy

Field Pansy

Grey-leaved Cistus

Narrow-leaved Cistus

Halimium umbellatum:
leafy stem tip

Large Pink Cistus *Cistus incanus* Up to 100cm A spreading or erect evergreen shrub with ovate or elliptical, wavy and densely hairy, short-stalked leaves. Flowers are 40–60mm, in one- to seven-flowered inflorescences; five sepals equal; pinkish-purple petals rather crumpled. *Flowering:* June–August. *Distribution:* Southern Europe, most common in the east; in scrub. Similar **Grey-leaved Cistus** (*C. albidus*) has oblong, densely greyish-white, stalkless leaves. *Flowering:* June–August. *Distribution:* South-western Europe, eastwards to Italy.

Gum Cistus *Cistus ladanifer* Up to 250cm A tall, very sticky evergreen shrub. Opposite leaves are linear-lanceolate, green and hairless above, densely white-felted beneath, shortly stalked. Solitary flowers are 70–100mm; sepals three; rather crumpled petals white, occasionally with a crimson blotch at the base. *Flowering:* June–August. *Distribution:* Southwestern Europe; open maquis-style vegetation. **Narrow-leaved Cistus** (*C. monspeliensis*) is shorter-up to 100cm-with leaves sparsely hairy above. Flowers are 20–30mm, white, two to eight together; sepals five. *Flowering*: June–August. *Distribution:* south Europe.

Sage-leaved Cistus *Cistus salvifolius* Up to 100cm A prostrate or spreading shrub, with opposite, ovate or elliptical, shortly stalked leaves, rough above, rounded or wedge-shaped at the base. Flowers are 30–50cm, solitary or up to four together; sepals five; rather crumpled petals white. *Flowering:* June–August. *Distribution:* Southern Europe; open ground.

Halimium halimifolium Up to 100cm A much branched upright shrub, with opposite elliptical or broad lanceolate leaves, white-felted on both sides when the leaves are young, green or grey above on mature leaves. Flowers are 20–30mm; two outer sepals smaller than three inner, all covered in stalked scales; petals yellow, often with a dark basal spot. *Flowering:* June–October. *Distribution:* South-western Europe to Italy; open scrubland, usually near the coast. **H. umbellatum** has ascending, twisted branches, densely white-felted. Leaves are narrow, dark green above, white-felted beneath, with inrolled margins, crowded at the tips of branches. Flowers are white, in terminal inflorescences of three to six. *Distribution:* France, northern Spain and northern Portugal; open scrub.

Spotted Rock-rose *Tuberaria guttata* Up to 30cm An annual with downy-hairy leaves. Leaves are mostly basal, elliptical or obovate, the few stem leaves narrower. Flowers are 10–20mm, on long stalks, in short terminal inflorescences; outer two sepals much smaller than inner three; yellow petals have a dark purplish spot at the base. *Flowering:* May–August. *Distribution:* Southern and western Europe, north to Britain and Germany; dry open places, often on limy soil.

Common Rock-rose *Helianthemum nummularium* Up to 50cm A prostrate or ascending evergreen undershrub, with branched wiry stems. Opposite leaves are oblong, lanceolate, ovate or round, hairless or downy-hairy above, white-felted beneath, the margins often rolled under; stipules lanceolate, longer than the leaf stalks. Flowers are in a one-sided, one- to twelve-flowered inflorescence; outer two sepals smaller than inner three; petals 6–18mm, bright yellow, rarely paler or white, orange or pink. *Flowering*: May–September. *Distribution:* Most of Europe, except the far north; grassland and on rocks, usually on lime-rich soil.

Large Pink Cistus

Gum Cistus

Sage-leaved Cistus

Halimium halimifolium

Spotted Rock-rose

Common Rock-rose

Helianthemum oelandicum

Hoary Rock-rose *Helianthemum canum* Up to 30cm A prostrate or upright evergreen perennial, often forming small mats. Opposite leaves are elliptical to ovate-lanceolate or linear, densely grey-hairy beneath, similar or green above. Yellow flowers are 10–15mm; outer two sepals smaller than inner three. *Flowering:* May–June. *Distribution:* Central and southern Europe, Britain, Ireland and Sweden; on rocks. **H. oelandicum** up to 20cm, is often more tufted, with elliptical or linear-lanceolate leaves, green on both sides. Flowers are 6–20mm, yellow, up to 20 together. *Flowering:* May–July. *Distribution:* Much of Europe, absent from parts of the north.

White Rock-rose *Helianthemum apenninum* Up to 50cm Resembles Common Rock-rose, but has narrower leaves with margins rolled over, green above or grey-white and densely hairy on both sides. Flowers are 20–25cm, white with a yellow centre; outer two sepals smaller than inner three. *Flowering:* June–September. *Distribution:* Southern and western Europe, extending to southern England and Germany; usually on lime-rich soils.

Fumana thymifolia Up to 20cm A small evergreen shrub, ascending or with upright stems and short axillary branches. Leaves are linear to narrowly elliptical, opposite, short, either blunt or with a fine point, hairless or glandular-hairy, with margins rolled over. Flowers are 10–15mm, yellow; two outer sepals smaller than three inner. *Flowering:* May–June. *Distribution:* Mediterranean and Portugal; bare, dry, open areas.

Frankenia laevis

Sea-heath *Frankenia laevis* Up to 40cm A branched, mat-forming prostrate perennial, often woody at the base, usually downy. Leaves are 2–5mm, narrow, the margins tightly rolled under. Flowers are 8–12mm, in small clusters or solitary, on the upper parts of the stems and branches; petals four to six, purple or white. *Flowering:* July–August. *Distribution:* Western Europe, northwards to southern England, eastwards to south-eastern Italy; sandy soil by the sea. **F. hirsuta** is very similar, with slightly longer leaves, sometimes not rolled up. Flowers are in dense clusters at the ends of the stems and branches. *Flowering:* July–August. *Distribution:* South-eastern Europe and Mediterranean; sand or shingle on coasts.

Squirting Cucumber *Ecballium elaterium* Up to 60cm A roughly hairy perennial. Fleshy leaves are long-stalked, heart-shaped or triangular, toothed or shallowly lobed, wavy. Flowers are 18–20mm, different sexes on the same plants; males yellowish, several in a group in leaf axils; females solitary. Fruits 50 x 25mm, ovoid, roughly hairy, propelled from the plant when ripe by a jet of seeds and liquid contents. *Flowering:* July–September. *Distribution:* Southern Europe, sporadic elsewhere; sandy and stony ground.

Bryonia alba

White Bryony *Bryonia dioica* Up to 400cm A far-scrambling perennial, climbing by spring-like tendrils. Leaves are deeply divided into five lobes, all about the same length. Flowers in axillary inflorescences are 10–18mm, males and females on separate plants, greenish-white, with conspicuous darker veins. Fruit is a red berry, 6–10mm diameter. *Flowering:* May–September. *Distribution:* Southern, south-central and south-western Europe, northwards to Britain, often naturalised; in hedges and scrubland. Similar **B. alba** has the central leaf-lobe much larger than the others. Flowers with sexes on different or the same plants. Fruit a black berry, 7–8mm. *Flowering:* May–September. *Distribution:* Southern, central and eastern Europe, often naturalised; in hedges and scrubland.

Hoary Rock-rose

White Rock-rose

Fumana thymifolia

Sea-heath

Squirting Cucumber

White Bryony: ♂ flowers

Barberry Fig *Opuntia ficus-barbarica* Up to 500cm An erect, branched cactus with flattened stems made up of oblong segments, up to 500 x 200cm. Leaves are 3mm, usually falling early. Each segment has a number of whitish cushion-like structures, the areoles, usually spineless, but with small spiny bristles. Flowers are 70–100mm, bright yellow, with numerous sepals, petals and stamens. Fruit oval, fleshy and edible. *Flowering:* June–September. *Distribution:* Widely naturalised in the Mediterranean; open ground.

Grass-poly *Lythrum hyssopifolia* Up to 25cm A hairless annual with erect or ascending branches. Alternate, upwardly pointing leaves are linear to oblong. Pink flowers of 2–3mm with five to six petals are numerous in leaf axils. *Flowering:* July–September. *Distribution:* Throughout Europe, but sporadic in the north; on ground that is seasonally flooded, or disturbed.

False Grass-poly

Purple-loosestrife *Lythrum salicaria* Up to 150cm An erect perennial, varying in its downy hairiness. Stem is occasionally branched, with four raised lines. Leaves are either opposite or in whorls of three, ovate to lanceolate, pointed, stalkless. Flowers are 10–15mm, in whorls forming a long spike; petals reddish-purple, stamens twelve. *Flowering:* June–August. *Distribution:* Throughout Europe, except the far north; by rivers, lakes and ponds, and in damp areas. Similar **False Grass-poly** (*L. virgatum)* is more slender, hairless, with linear-oblong leaves that have wedge-shaped bases. Flowers are 6–10mm, red-purple. *Flowering:* June–August. *Distribution:* Most of Europe; marshlands and wet places, sometimes naturalised.

Water-chestnut *Trapa natans* Up to 200cm An aquatic annual rooting in bottom mud. Submerged leaves are linear, stalkless, usually falling early. Floating leaves are triangular on long stalks, toothed, hairless above, slightly downy beneath, the base wedge-shaped. Flowers are 15mm, in axils of floating leaves; petals white, falling quickly; distinctive fruit has several horn-like spines. *Flowering:* June–July. *Distribution:* Southern and central Europe, northwards to France, and Russia; in waters rich with nutrients.

Myrtle *Myrtus communis* Up to 500cm A medium sized, much branched evergreen shrub, with glandular hairs on young shoots. Leathery opposite leaves are ovate-lanceolate, pointed, extremely aromatic when crushed. Fragrant flowers are to 30mm across, on long stalks, white with numerous stamens, fragrant. Fruit is a blue-black berry, 10x8mm. *Flowering:* June–August. *Distribution:* Mediterranean and south-west Europe; scrub on lime-free soils.

Alpine Enchanter's-nightshade: leaf and fruit

Enchanter's-nightshade *Circaea lutetiana* Up to 60cm A creeping, downy perennial with opposite, ovate, pointed leaves, the bases heart-shaped or flat. White flowers are 4–8mm, two-petalled, in a long leafless spike which elongates after flowering; dry, rounded fruit covered with hooked bristles. *Flowering:* June–September. *Distribution:* Most of Europe, except the north-east; woods and shady areas. **Alpine Enchanter's-nightshade** (*C. alpina*) up to 30cm, is smaller, less downy, with more heart-shaped, deeply toothed leaves. Flowers are 1–2.5mm, the spike not lengthening until all flowers have fallen; fruits often with straight bristles. *Flowering:* June–August. *Distribution:* Northern Europe to the Pyrenees, Apennines and Yugoslavia; mountain woods. The hybrid between these two species, **Upland Enchanter's-nightshade** (*C. x intermedia*) has shallowly heart-shaped, mostly hairless leaves. Flowers are sterile.

Barbary Fig: fruiting plant

Grass-poly

Purple-loosestrife

Water-chestnut

Myrtlc

Enchanter's-nightshade

Large-flowered
Evening-primrose

Common Evening-primrose *Oenothera biennis* Up to 150cm

An upright biennial with alternate, lanceolate stem leaves, their margins finely toothed. Flowers are 45–60mm, yellow, fragrant at night; sepals four, reddish, bent back when in flower; petals four; stamens eight, in two whorls of four; stigma four-lobed. *Flowering:* June–September. *Distribution:* A North American plant, naturalised in Europe, except for the far north and parts of the south; waste ground. Similar **Large-flowered Evening-primrose** (*O. glazioviana*) is downy-hairy, with red spots on the stem. Flowers are 80–100mm, yellow; sepals red or red-striped. *Flowering:* June–September. *Distribution:* A plant of temperate North America, naturalised in central Europe; waste ground.

Fragrant Evening-primrose *Oenothera stricta* Up to 100cm

A hairy annual or perennial with linear basal leaves; stem leaves alternate, narrowly lanceolate, wavy, toothed. Flowers are 40–90mm, yellow, fragrant in the evening; sepals red tinged. *Flowering:* June–September. *Distribution:* A plant of temperate South America, naturalised in western and central Europe; waste areas.

Hampshire-purslane *Ludwigia palustris* Up to 50cm

A purplish perennial, the prostrate, creeping, stems with opposite, stalked, ovate-elliptic leaves. Flowers are 2–5mm, solitary in leaf axils; sepals and stamens four; petals absent. *Flowering:* June–July. *Distribution:* Western, central and southern Europe; in wet areas, often floating in water.

Rosebay Willowherb *Chamerion angustifolium* Up to 250cm

A large, patch-forming perennial with long, showy flower spikes and alternate, lanceolate leaves. Flowers are 20–30mm, pinkish-purple; four petals slightly unequal; stigma four-lobed. Small seeds have a long plume of silky white hairs. *Flowering:* June–August. *Distribution:* Throughout Europe, but rare in the south; woods, heathland and mountains, and waste places.

Hoary Willowherb

Great Willowherb *Epilobium hirsutum* Up to 200cm

A creeping, hairy or downy perennial forming large clumps. Leaves are stalkless, opposite, oblong to lanceolate, toothed, the bases clasping the stem. Flowers are 15–25mm, one to three together, bright pinkish-purple; petals four, equal, notched at the tip; stigma four-lobed. *Flowering:* June–August. *Distribution:* Throughout Europe, except for the far north; wet areas. Similar but smaller **Hoary Willowherb** (*E. parviflorum*) grows up to 75 cm, with flowers 6–9mm. *Flowering:* June–August. *Distribution:* Throughout Europe, except the far north; wet or damp areas. **Broad-leaved Willowherb** (*E. montanum*) up to 80cm, has ovate to broadly lanceolate, short-stalked, toothed leaves. Flowers are 5–9mm; petals deeply notched; stigma four-lobed. *Flowering:* June–August. *Distribution:* Most of Europe; waste and shady places.

Spear-leaved Willowherb *Epilobium lanceolatum* Up to 60cm

A perennial with four-angled stems. Leaves are alternate, oblong, blunt, wedge-shaped at the base, toothed, with short stalks. Flowers are 5–10mm; four petals white, becoming pink as they age; stigma four-lobed. *Flowering:* June–August. *Distribution:* West, central and southern Europe; a weed of waste places.

Common Evening-primrose

Fragrant Evening-primrose

Hampshire Purslane

Rosebay Willowherb

Great Willowherb

Spear-leaved Willowherb

Marsh Willowherb

Alpine Willowherb

Whorled Water-milfoil

Square-stalked Willowherb *Epilobium tetragonum* Up to 110cm

A perennial, with four raised lines on the stem. Leaves are oblong to oblong-lanceolate, toothed, stalkless. Flowers are 9–15mm in a loose, downy inflorescence, pale purplish-pink; four petals slightly notched; stigma not lobed. *Flowering:* June–August. *Distribution:* Throughout Europe, except for the far north; hedgerows, woods, waste and cultivated land. **Marsh Willowherb** (*E. palustre*) up to 70cm, has untoothed leaves. Flowers are 4–8mm, pale pink or white. *Flowering:* June–August. *Distribution:* Throughout Europe, except parts of the Mediteranean; wet or marshy ground.

Chickweed Willowherb *Epilobium alsinifolium* Up to 30cm

A creeping perennial, with sparsely hairy, occasionally glandular stems. Leaves are alternate, ovate-lanceolate to lanceolate, with a short stalk. Flowers are 10–15mm, purplish-pink; four petals notched; stigma not lobed. *Flowering:* July–August. *Distribution:* Most of European mountains, and at low levels in Arctic regions; mountain streams and springs. **Alpine Willowherb** (*E. anagallidifolium)* is also creeping, forming patches, with opposite, small ovate or elliptical leaves. Nodding flowers are 4–5mm, reddish-pink. *Flowering:* July–August. *Distribution:* Northern Europe, southwards to the mountains of Yugoslavia and Corsica; stream sides and mountain springs.

Spiked Water-milfoil *Myriophyllum spicatum* Up to 300cm

An aquatic perennial, rooting in the bottom mud, the leaves in whorls of three, four or five, pinnately cut into fine linear segments, upper leaf-like bracts entire. Tiny unisexual flowers are four-petalled, borne in whorls of four forming a spike, reddish males in the upper part of spike, greenish females in the lower part. *Flowering:* June–September. Distribution: Throughout most of Europe; still and slow water, either fresh or brackish. **Whorled Water-milfoil** (*M. verticillatum*) is similar, but has pinnately divided bracts; all flowers greenish-yellow, a few are hermaphrodite. *Flowering:* July–August. *Distribution:* Almost all Europe; still or flowing fresh water.

Mare's-tail *Hippuris vulgaris* Up to 150cm An creeping aquatic

perennial with upright aerial shoots. Whorled leaves are ovate to linear-lanceolate, their size and shape varying with the speed of flow of the water. Flowers are small, without petals, either male, female, hermaphrodite or sterile, borne in the axils of the fairly rigid aerial leaves. *Flowering:* June–July. *Distribution:* Most of Europe, but uncommon in the south-west and far south; still or flowing water.

Dogwood *Cornus sanguinea* Up to 400cm A much-branched deciduous

shrub with dark red twigs. Opposite leaves are elliptical or ovate, pointed, pale green, downy-hairy, with three to five pairs of conspicuous veins. Flowers are 8–14mm, with four dirty-white petals, in a crowded, flat-topped cluster 40–50mm across. Berries purple-black. *Flowering:* June–August. *Distribution:* Most of Europe; scrub and woodland margins.

Dwarf Cornel *Cornus suecica* Up to 25cm A creeping perennial herb

with a short upright stem. The unstalked leaves are more or less rounded, or ovate to elliptical, blunt-tipped. Dark purplish flowers are 2mm, several together in a tight cluster surrounded by four large white bracts 30mm across, the whole giving the appearance of a single flower. Fruit is a red berry. Flowering: June–August. Distribution: Northern Europe, southwards to the Netherlands; on heathland, mountains and moors, avoiding lime.

Square-stalked Willowherb

Chickweed Willowherb

Spiked Water-milfoil

Mare's-tail

Dogwood

Dwarf Cornel

Ivy *Hedera helix* Up to 30m A vigorous, evergreen-climber or creeper, the stems with clinging, hair-like aerial roots. Leaves are glossy green, three- to five-lobed on non-flowering shoots, ovate and pointed on flowering shoots. Greenish flowers are 6–10mm, in a many-flowered umbel; petals five, at first erect, later bent back; fruit a black berry. *Flowering:* September–November. *Distribution:* Western, central and southern Europe, northwards to Norway, eastwards to Latvia and the Ukraine; climbing on trees, or over rocks.

Marsh Pennywort *Hydrocotyle vulgaris* Up to 30cm A mat-forming, creeping perennial. Almost circular leaves are shallowly lobed; long stalks are attached to the middle of the leaf blade. Flowers are small, pinkish-green, in an umbel at the base of the leaves. Fruits are 2mm, rounded, ridged. *Flowering:* June–August. *Distribution:* Western, central and southern Europe, to Scandinavia and Russia; in damp places and shallow water.

Sanicle *Sanicula europea* Up to 60mm A perennial with long-stalked, shiny basal leaves, which are palmately divided into three to five lobes. Flowers are small, petals pink or white, in tight umbels at the ends of branched flowering stems. Fruit 4–5mm, covered with small hooked bristles. *Flowering:* May–July. *Distribution:* Most of Europe, except the far north and east, on mountains only in southern Europe; woodlands.

Astrantia *Astrantia major* Up to 100cm A usually unbranched perennial, with long-stalked leaves, divided into three to seven, obovate to lanceolate, toothed lobes. Small white flowers form a dense umbel 20–30mm across, surrounded by a ring of pointed, petal-like bracteoles, joined for most of their length. Cylindrical fruits are 6–8mm. *Flowering:* June–September. *Distribution:* Central Europe to northern Spain, central Italy, Bulgaria and Russia; woods and mountain meadows. **A. minor** up to 40cm, is similar, but more slender and branched. Flowers in an umbel 10–15mm across, the sepal-like bracts not joined. *Flowering:* July–August. *Distribution:* Pyrenees, south-western Alps, northern Apennines; alpine meadows and rocks, often on acid soils.

Astrantia minor

Field Eryngo *Eryngium campestre* Up to 70cm A perennial with leathery, spiny, basal leaves divided into spiny, pinnate segments; stem leaves lobed, spiny. Flowers are small, greenish, in a dense round umbel, about 10mm across, several in each inflorescence. Bracts beneath umbel are narrow and spiny. Fruits have dense overlapping scales. *Flowering:* June–September. *Distribution:* Central and southern Europe to southern England; dry places. **E. amethystinum,** up to 45cm, is similar but has a broadly winged leaf-stalk, a bluish inflorescence and an umbel 20mm across; bracts have one to four pairs of spines. *Flowering:* June–September. *Distribution:* Balkans, Aegean, Italy and Sicily; dry places.

Eryngium amethystinum

Sea-holly *Eryngium maritimum* Up to 60cm A very spiny, bluish-green perennial, the leathery, ovate, stalked basal leaves with very sharp, tough spines; stem leaves stalkless but equally spiny. Flowers are small, light blue, in a dense round umbel, 20mm across, with spiny, stalkless bracts underneath; fruits densely scaly. *Flowering:* June–September. *Distribution:* All of Europe, but not in the north; on sand or shingle, by the sea. **E. alpinum** up to 70cm, is similar, but with less vicious spines on the basal leaves. Flowers small, more steely blue, in a conical umbel, surrounded by many violet, pinnately divided bracts, with soft spines. *Flowering:* July–September. *Distribution:* Alps, the Jura, western and central Yugoslav mountains.

Eryngium alpinum: umbel

Ivy

Marsh Pennywort: young fruits

Sanicle

Astrantia

Field Eryngo

Sea-holly

Rough Chervil *Chaerophyllum temulentum* Up to 100cm An upright, roughly hairy biennial with purple or purple-spotted stems. Basal leaves two- or three-pinnate, often purple, the final lobes blunt. Flowers are white, in six to twelve long-stalked, simple umbels in a compound umbel. Fruit 4–7mm, narrowed at the tip. *Flowering:* May–July. *Distribution:* Most of Europe, but sporadic in much of the north and the Mediterranean; shady places.

Bur Chervil: fruit

Cow Parsley *Anthriscus sylvestris* Up to 150cm A downy perennial, with a purple stem, and three-pinnate basal leaves. Flowers are white, clustered on six to twelve umbels with lanceolate, often pink bracteoles, in a compound umbel; fruits 7–10mm, oblong, black. *Flowering:* April–June. *Distribution:* Most of Europe, but rare in the Mediterranean; wood margins, hedgebanks and shady places. **Bur Chervil** (*A. caucalis*) up to 100cm, is annual, with wiry stems, flowers in two to six umbels in a compound umbel; fruit usually covered in hooked spines. *Flowering:* May–June. *Distribution:* Western, central and southern Europe to southern Sweden; dry sandy places.

Scandix australis: fruits

Shepherd's-needle *Scandix pecten-veneris* Up to 50cm A nearly hairless annual, with two- to three-pinnate leaves, the lobes linear. Flowers are white, usually in a simple umbel with broad, toothed bracteoles, opposite a leaf; petals towards rim of umbel often larger than the central ones; fruits 15–80mm, with a long beak flat on the upper side. *Flowering:* May–August. *Distribution:* Western, central and southern Europe, northwards to Scandinavia; waste and arable land, becoming scarce. **S. australis** is similar, but the fruits are only up to 40mm long, and flattened on both sides. *Flowering:* May–August. *Distribution:* Southern Europe.

Sweet Cicely *Myrrhis odorata* Up to 200cm A softly hairy perennial, smelling strongly of aniseed when crushed. Leaves are two- to three-pinnate, with oblong-lanceolate, toothed, white-blotched lobes. Flowers are in four to twenty simple umbels in a compound umbel, some with male flowers only; bracteoles present beneath the simple umbels; fruits 15–25mm, ridged, dark shiny brown when ripe. *Flowering:* May–July. *Distribution:* Alps, Pyrenees, Apennines and the mountains of the western Balkans; cultivated for culinary purposes and fodder; mountain meadows, widely naturalised.

Coriander *Coriandrum sativum* Up to 50cm A hairless annual, with a characteristic spicy smell. Leaves are one- to three-pinnate, the lower segments ovate to wedge-shaped. Flowers are white, on three to ten simple umbels in a compound umbel; bracteoles under the simple umbels usually linear; petals on the outer flowers longer than the rest; fruits up to 6mm, ovoid, ridged. *Flowering:* June–August. *Distribution:* A plant of North Africa and Western Asia, widely cultivated for culinary purposes, and often naturalised in dry areas.

Perfoliate Alexanders

Alexanders *Smyrnium olusatrum* Up to 150cm A hollow-stemmed, hairless, strong-smelling biennial. Dark green, shiny, leaves are divided into three, the terminal segment also three-lobed. Flowers are yellow, on three to eighteen simple umbels in a compound umbel. Fruits are 7–8mm, black. *Flowering:* April–June. *Distribution:* Southern Europe, northwards to north-western France, often naturalised elsewhere; by or near the sea, in bare places. **Perfoliate Alexanders** (*S. perfoliatum*) has angled, winged stems, yellow-green leaves and simple umbels. *Flowering:* April–June. *Distribution:* Southern Europe, north to Czechoslovakia; in woods and on rocks.

Rough Chervil

Cow Parsley

Shepherd's -needle

Sweet Cicely

Coriander

Alexanders

Bunium alpinum

Great Pignut *Bunium bulbocastanum* Up to 100cm An upright perennial, with two- to three-pinnate basal leaves, the lobes linear-lanceolate. Flowers are white, three to ten simple umbels in a compound umbel. Beneath the umbels are five to ten lanceolate, pointed bracts. Narrowly-ridged fruits are 3–5 mm, elliptical-oblong. *Flowering:* June–August. *Distribution:* Southern England and the Balearics northwards to central Germany and Yugoslavia; downland, especially on lime-rich soil. **B. alpinum** up to 75cm, is similar, but has up to sixteen simple umbels, and only one to five bracts. *Flowering:* June–August. *Distribution:* Mountains of southern Europe; in meadows.

Pignut *Conopodium majus* Up to 50cm A nearly hairless perennial, with two- to three-pinnate leaves, often withering by flowering time; stem leaves with linear lobes. Flowers are white, in six to twelve, small, simple umbels in a compound umbel with up to two bracts beneath it, and two or more under each simple umbel. Fruits are 3–4mm, oblong, faintly ridged. *Flowering:* May–July. *Distribution:* Western Europe, eastwards to Italy; in grassland or woods.

Greater Burnet-saxifrage: compound umbel

Burnet-saxifrage *Pimpinella saxifraga* Up to 60cm A variably downy perennial with solid stems. Pinnate leaves with three to seven pairs of ovate or linear lobes. Flowers are white or rarely, pinkish, in six to twenty-five simple umbels in a compound umbel, usually without bracts; fruits 2–2.5mm, ovoid, with faint ridges. *Flowering:* May–September. *Distribution:* Most of Europe, but absent from the far south; grassland, especially on lime-rich soils. **Greater Burnet-saxifrage** (*P. major*) is taller, hairless, with a hollow stem. Leaves are larger, with only one pair of lobes. Flowers are white or deep pink; fruits 2.5–3.5mm, with prominent ridges. *Flowering:* May–September. *Distribution:* Europe, except for the far north and south; shady grassland.

Ground-elder *Aegopodium podograria* Up to 100cm A far-creeping, invasive perennial with basal leaves cut into three segments, each segment with three lanceolate to ovate, toothed lobes. Flowers are white, in ten to twenty simple umbels in a compound umbel; fruits 3–4mm, ovoid, ridged. *Flowering:* June–August. *Distribution:* Throughout most of Europe, rare in the south; hedges and woods, also a pernicious weed of cultivation.

Lesser Water-parsnip: fruits

Greater Water-parsnip *Sium latifolium* Up to 200cm A robust aquatic plant, with two- to three-pinnate submerged leaves, and three- to eight-pinnate aerial leaves, the lobes toothed. Flowers are white, in 20 to 30 simple umbels in a round compound umbel, the bracts two to six, leaf-like, the bracteoles lanceolate. Flattened ovoid fruits are 2.5–4mm, ridged. *Flowering:* June–September. *Distribution:* Europe, except for parts of the west, and much of the Mediterranean; ditches, and shallow water. **Lesser Water-parsnip** (*Berula erecta*) is smaller, with ten to 20 simple umbels in a compound umbel opposite a leaf; numerous bracts leaf-like; fruits 1.5–2mm. *Flowering:* July–September. *Distribution:* Europe, except the far north.

Rock Samphire *Crithmum maritimum* Up to 50cm A fleshy, hairless perennial, woody at the base. Leaves one- to two-pinnate, with linear, fleshy lobes. Flowers are greenish-yellow, in eight to thirty-six simple, thick-stalked umbels; bracts and bracteoles triangular to linear-lancolate, downwardly directed; fruits 5–6mm, yellowish or purple, with thick ridges. *Flowering:* July–October. *Distribution:* Atlantic, Mediterranean and Black Sea coasts, northwards to Scotland; rocks, cliffs, rarely sand or shingle.

Great Pignut

Pignut

Burnet-saxifrage

Ground-elder

Greater Water-parsnip

Rock Samphire

Seseli annuum:
compound umbel

Moon Carrot *Seseli libanotis* Up to 120cm. A biennial or perennial dying after flowering. The basal leaves are narrow, one- to three-pinnate. Flowers are white or pink, in 10 to 60 simple umbels each with eight to 15 bracts beneath and forming a tight compound umbel. Fruits are ovoid, hairless or downy, with blunt ridges. *Flowering:* July–September. *Distribution:* Most of Europe, except the far north, west and south; dry grassland, especially on lime-rich soils. Despite its name, **S. annuum** is also biennial or perennial, but has only 12 to 20 simple umbels with stalks finely hairy on the inner side. *Flowering:* June–September. *Distribution:* France and Russia to northern Spain and Bulgaria; dry grassland.

Tubular Water-dropwort *Oenanthe fistulosa* Up to 80cm An upright, creeping perennial, with hollow, minutely grooved, thin-walled, grey-green stems. Lower leaves are one- to two-pinnate; upper leaves pinnate, often with an bladdery stalk. Flowers are white, in two to four simple umbels in a compound umbel; fruits 3–4mm, more or less cylindrical; styles as long as the fruit. *Flowering:* June–September. *Distribution:* Western, central and southern Europe, to south Sweden and Russia; fresh shallow water, and wet areas.

Hemlock Water-dropwort *Oenanthe crocata* Up to 150cm
A branched, hairless perennial, with hollow, grooved stems, smelling of parsley, and very poisonous. Basal leaves are three- to four-pinnate, the lobes broad, wedge-shaped; stems leaves two- to three-pinnate, the lobes ovate to linear. Flowers are white, in 10 to 40 simple umbels in a terminal compound umbel; fruits 4–6mm, cylindrical; styles half as long as the fruit. *Flowering:* June–August. *Distribution:* Western Europe and the western Mediterranean; ditches and wet grassy areas.

Narrow-leaved Water-
dropwort: fruit

Corky-fruited Water-dropwort *Oenanthe pimpinelloides* Up to 100cm An upright perennial, with a solid, grooved stem. Basal leaves are two-pinnate, the lobes wedge-shaped; stems leaves one- or two-pinnate, the lobes linear to linear-lanceolate. Flowers are white, in six to 15 simple umbels forming a compound umbel; fruits 3mm, cylindrical, on thickened stalks; styles more than two thirds as long as fruit. *Flowering:* June–September. *Distribution:* Western and southern Europe; ditches or damp grassland. **Narrow-Leaved Water-dropwort** (*O. silaifolia*) has a hollow stem and narrower leaf lobes. Flowers in four to 10 simple umbels; style half as long as fruit. *Flowering:* June–September. *Distribution:* Western and southern Europe; wet places, especially in meadows.

Fool's Parsley *Aethusa cynapium* Up to 200cm A variable sized annual or occasional biennial, very poisonous, the leaves two- to three-pinnate, with lanceolate or ovate lobes. Flowers are white, in four to 20 simple umbels with downward-pointing bracteoles on outer edge of umbel, in a compound umbel; fruits 3–4mm, ovoid, ridged. *Flowering:* June–October. *Distribution:* Most of Europe, rare in the Mediterranean; mostly a weed of cultivation.

Fennel *Foeniculum vulgare* Up to 250cm A greyish-green, hairless perennial with vertically grooved stems, smelling strongly of aniseed when crushed. Leaves are three- to four-pinnate, the lobes thread-like and feathery in appearance. Flowers are yellow, in four to 30 simple umbels in a compound umbel; fruits 10mm, ovoid-oblong, ridged. *Flowering:* July–September. *Distribution:* Most of Europe except the north; probably only native in the south, cultivated and naturalised; bare ground, coasts.

Moon Carrot

Tubular Water-dropwort

Hemlock Water-dropwort

Corky-fruited Water-dropwort

Fool's Parsley

Fennel

Bladderseed: fruit

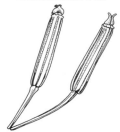
Kundemannia sicula:
fruits

Bupleurum lancifolium

Bladderseed *Physospermum cornubiense* Up to 120cm A hairless perennial with grooved, solid stems. Long-stalked basal leaves are divided into three segments, each segment itself three lobed, the lobes 10–30mm long and pinnately-cut. Flowers are white, in six to 20 simple umbels in a compound umbel; bracts and bracteoles lanceolate; fruits 3–4mm, ovoid-heart-shaped, the two lobes finely ridged. *Flowering:* July–August. *Distribution:* Southern Europe to England, Hungary and Russia; woods.

Pepper-saxifrage *Silaum silaus* Up to 100cm A hairless perennial, with solid stems. Basal leaves are one- to four-pinnate, the finely toothed lobes lanceolate to linear; stem leaves one-pinnate or reduced to an inflated leaf stalk. Flowers are yellow in five to 15 simple umbels in a compound umbel, the stalks sharply-angled; bracts up to three; bracteoles several, linear-lanceolate. Fruits are 4–5mm, ovoid. *Flowering:* June–September. *Distribution:* Western, central and eastern Europe; grassland.
Kundemannia sicula has leaves with ovate, sharply-toothed lobes, a compound umbel of five to 30 simple ones, and nearly cylindrical fruits. *Flowering:* April–June. *Distribution:* Mediterranean and southern Portugal.

Spignel *Meum athamanticum* Up to 60cm A strongly aromatic perennial, the stem base surrounded by remains of old leaf-stalks. Leaves are three- to four-pinnate, the final lobes stiff and thread-like. Flowers are white or purplish, in three to 15 simple umbels with small bracteoles in a compound umbel; bracts up to two. Fruits 4–10mm, oblong to ovoid, ridged. *Flowering:* June–August. *Distribution:* Mountains of western and central Europe.

Hemlock *Conium maculatum* Up to 250cm A hairless biennial or occasionally annual, all parts very poisonous; stems are hollow, grooved, often purple-spotted. Leaves are two- to four-pinnate, soft, oblong-lanceolate to triangular, toothed. Flowers are white, in six to 20 simple umbels in a compound umbel; bracts up to six, triangular to ovate; bracteoles three to six, wider at the base, only on outer edge of simple umbels. Globular fruits are 2.5–3.5mm. *Flowering:* June–August. *Distribution:* Throughout Europe except for the far north; in damp areas, or dry bare ground.

Thorow-wax *Bupleurum rotundifolium* Up to 75cm A grey-green upright annual, with undivided, elliptical to round leaves, the upper encircling the stem. Flowers are yellow, in three to 10 simple umbels in a compound umbel; bracteoles four to six, obovate and joined. Fruits are 3–3.25mm, elliptical, blackish brown, with narrow ridges. *Flowering:* June–July. *Distribution:* Central and southern Europe and Russia southwards; a weed of arable land, becoming rarer. ***B. lancifolium*** is similar, but has ovate or oblong-lanceolate leaves with two to five simple umbels; upper bracts more rounded. *Flowering:* June–August. *Distribution:* Southern Europe; open habitats, often mistaken for Thorow-wax.

Honewort *Trinia glauca* Up to 50cm A grey-green, hairless perennial, with the base covered in remains of old leaves; stems much-branched, angled, the lower branches often as long as the main stem. Lower are leaves two- to three-pinnate, with up to five narrow lobes. Flowers white, males and females on separate plants, in five to 30 simple umbels in a compound umbel, the stalks usually longer on female plants. Ridged fruits are 2–3mm, ovoid. *Flowering:* May–June. *Distribution:* Central and southern Europe, northwards to southern England; grassland, particularly on lime-rich soils.

Bladderseed

Pepper-saxifrage

Spignel

Hemlock

Thorow-wax

Honewort

Wild Celery *Apium graveolens* Up to 100cm A yellowish-green biennial, with a charateristic celery smell; stems stout, solid. Leaves one- to two-pinnate, with triangular to lanceolate segments, toothed or lobed. Flowers are white, in four to 12 simple umbels in a compound umbel which is often opposite a leaf. Ovoid fruits are 1.5–2mm. *Flowering:* June–August. *Distribution:* Coasts of Europe; ditches and other damp places near the sea.

Fool's Water-cress *Apium nodiflorum* Up to 100cm A prostrate or upright perennial, with hollow stems that root at lower nodes. Leaves are pinnate, the toothed or lobed segments lanceolate to ovate. Flowers are white in three to 12 short-stalked simple umbels in a compound umbel, opposite a leaf; bracts one or two; bracteoles five to seven, white-margined. Ovoid, ridged fruits are 1.5–2mm. *Flowering:* June–September. *Distribution:* Most of Europe; wet areas.

Cowbane *Cicuta virosa* Up to 120cm A stout perennial with two to three-times pinnate leaves up to 300mm long, the lobes 50–100mm, linear-lanceolate to linear and deeply toothed; bases of leaflets asymmetric. Flowers are white or pink, in 10 to 20 simple umbels in a compound umbel; bracts absent; bracteoles narrow. Globular fruit up to 2mm across has broad, flattened ridges. *Flowering:* June–August. *Distribution:* Most of Europe but rare in the south and absent from most islands; wet places and in shallow water. **Stone Parsley** (*Sison amomum*) is a purplish biennial with an unpleasant, petrol-like smell when crushed, ovate, toothed and often lobed leaflets and three to six simple umbels on slender stalks of different lengths. Fruits have slender ridges. *Flowering:* June–September. *Distribution:* Southern and western Europe northwards to Britain; hedge banks and grassy areas.

Stone Parsley:
compound umbel

Longleaf *Falcaria vulgaris* Up to 90cm A grey-green often patch-forming annual, biennial or perennial; stems solid, branched, angled. Large leaves are divided into threes with linear to lanceolate, pointed, toothed segments. Flowers are white, in 12 to 18 simple umbels in a compound umbel. Oblong, ridged fruits are 3–4mm. *Flowering:* July–September. *Distribution:* Northern France and central Russia southwards, occasionally introduced elsewhere.

Whorled Caraway *Carum verticillatum* Up to 120cm An upright, little-branched perennial, the basal leaves in whorls and divided into many thread-like segments. Flowers are white, in up to 12 simple umbels in a compound umbel; bracts up to ten, linear; bracteoles many, narrow, down-turned. Ovoid, ridged fruits are 2.5–4mm. *Flowering:* July–August. *Distribution:* Western Europe, northwards to Scotland and the Netherlands; marshy places.

Wild Angelica *Angelica sylvestris* Up to 200cm A vigorous, upright, nearly hairless perennial, the stem usually purple-tinged. Leaves are large, two- to three-pinnate, with oblong-ovate toothed lobes, the leaf stalks forming a sheath. Flowers are white to pinkish; each compound umbel with numerous simple umbels; bracts few or none; bracteoles thread-like. Ovoid fruits of 4–5mm are winged. *Flowering:* July–September. *Distribution:* Most of Europe; damp places. **Garden Angelica** (*A. archangelica*) the source of culinary Angelica, has usually green stems, and aromatic leaf stalks . Flowers are greenish-white or cream; fruits have thick corky wings. *Flowering:* July–September. *Distribution:* Northern and eastern Europe, often cultivated; damp places, often on the coast.

Garden Angelica: fruit

Wild Celery

Fool's Water-cress

Cowbane

Longleaf

Whorled Caraway

Wild Angelica

Ferula tingitana

Hog's Fennel: fruit

Giant Fennel *Ferula communis* Up to 250cm A very vigorous perennial, with three- to four-pinnate leaves, the lobes up to 50mm long; leaf stalks sheathing the stem. Flowers are yellow, in 20 to 40 simple umbels in each compound umbel; bracteoles linear-lanceolate, falling as the flowers age. Fruits are 15mm, strongly compressed, elliptical. *Flowering:* June–August. *Distribution:* Mediterranean; dry areas. **F. tingitana** is similar, but has leaf lobes up to 10mm long, with rolled-under margins. *Flowering:* June–August. *Distribution:* Southern and south-eastern Spain, Portugal; dry places.

Masterwort *Peucedanum ostruthium* Up to 100cm An almost hairless perennial, with angled, hollow stems. Basal leaves are divided into three ovate to lanceolate, pointed, toothed lobes; stalks of stem leaves bladdery. Flowers are white or pinkish, in 30 to 60 simple umbels in a compound umbel. Round, winged fruits are 4–5mm. *Flowering:* June–July. *Distribution:* Central Europe south to Spain and Italy, naturalised in the north; hilly, grassy places.

Milk-parsley *Peucedanum palustre* Up to 160cm A biennial or short-lived perennial, with a hollow, often purplish stem. Lower leaves are two- to four-pinnate, the stalks channelled; stem leaves with linear lobes, the leaf bases forming inflated sheaths. Flowers are white, in 20 to 40 simple umbels in a compound umbel; bracts and bracteoles lanceolate, larger on the outer edge of umbels, down-turned. Ovoid fruits are 4–5mm, flattened and winged. *Flowering:* July–September. *Distribution:* Throughout Europe, except the southwest and far south; marshland or damp grass. **Hog's Fennel** (*P. officinale*) is a dark green, hairless, solid-stemmed perennial, the leaves many-lobed. Flowers are yellow; bracts thread-like. Ridged fruits are 5–10mm. *Flowering:* July–September. *Distribution:* Central and southern Europe to south-eastern England; near the sea.

Wild Parsnip *Pastinaca sativa* Up to 100cm A strong-smelling, downy-hairy biennial, with hollow or solid, usually angled stems. Basal leaves are pinnate, with broad toothed segments. Flowers are yellow, in five to 20 simple umbels with angled stalks; bracts and bracteoles up to two, usually falling early. Ovoid, winged fruits are 5–7mm. The whole plant contains a blistering agent. *Flowering:* July–September. *Distribution:* Most of Europe, except the Arctic, only as an escape in parts of the north; grassland and waste places.

Hogweed *Heracleum sphondylium* Up to 250cm An robust roughly hairy or hairless biennial or perennial, with very stout stems. Leaves vary from palmately lobed to pinnate, with up to nine toothed segments, downy on the veins. Flowers are white, in 15 to 45 simple umbels in compound umbels up to 200mm across; bracteoles usually present, bracts sometimes absent. Fruits are 5–12mm, elliptical, flattened. The plant contains a blistering agent in its sap. *Flowering:* April–November. *Distribution:* Throughout Europe, except the far north and much of the Mediterranean; grassy or rough areas.

Giant Hogweed *Heracleum mantegazzianum* Up to 500cm Like a huge version of Hogweed, this species has a purple-blotched stem up to 100mm across, and huge, three-lobed or pinnate basal leaves. Flowers are white, 12mm, the outer larger than the inner, in 50 to 150 simple umbels in a compound umbel up to 500mm across. Fruits are 7–11mm, sometimes hairy. *Flowering:* June–August. *Distribution:* Widely naturalised throughout Europe, a native of south-western Asia; waste areas, especially by water. Like Hogweed, it contains a photo-sensitive blistering agent.

Giant Fennel

Masterwort

Milk-parsley

Wild Parsnip

Hogweed

Giant Hogweed

Hartwort

Knotted Hedge-parsley

Ivory-fruited Hartwort *Tordylium apulum* Up to 50cm A stout annual with solid, ridged stems, densely hairy at the base. Leaves are pinnate, the lower with ovate, toothed segments, the upper with linear segments. Flowers are whitish, in three to eight simple umbels in a compound umbel; the outer flowers have one petal longer than the rest; bracts and bracteoles narrow, pointed. Winged fruits of 5–8mm have thickened margins. *Flowering:* May–August. *Distribution:* Mediterranean; dry grassland. **Hartwort** (*T. maximum*) up to 130cm, has leaves with heart-shaped segments and white flowers in five to 15 simple umbels, the outer flowers with two to three petals larger. Fruits are rounded and ridged. *Flowering:* May–August. *Distribution:* Southern Europe; rough grassland.

Spreading Hedge-parsley *Torilis arvensis* Up to 100cm A usually upright annual, with leaves varying from two-pinnate to three-lobed, the lobes at least 2mm, toothed. Flowers are white or pinkish, in two to 12 simple umbels in a compound umbel; bracts occasionally one; bracteoles numerous. Fruits are 3–6mm, with straight bristles. *Flowering:* July–September. *Distribution:* Europe, except the north and east; waste places. **Knotted Hedge-parsley** (*T. nodosa*) up to 50cm, is usually prostrate and roughly hairy, leaves one- to two-pinnate; small compound umbel, always opposite a leaf. *Flowering:* May–July. *Distribution:* Southern and western Europe, naturalised in central Europe; dry or grassy places.

Upright Hedge-parsley *Torilis japonica* Up to 125cm An upright annual or biennial, with one- to three-pinnate leaves, the lobes narrowly ovate. Flowers are white, in five to 12 simple umbels in a compound umbel; outer flowers have longer petals; bracts four to 12. Fruits are 3–4mm, with hooked bristles. *Flowering:* July–September. *Distribution:* All Europe, except the far north and much of the Mediterranean; hedges and woodland edges.

Orlaya grandiflora Up to 40cm An annual, with occasionally branched stems that are hairy at the base. Leaves are two- to three-pinnate, the final segments oblong. Flowers are white or pinkish, in five to 12 simple umbels; flowers around the rim have petals up to eight times longer than the others; bracteoles two to three. Ridged, spiny fruits to 8mm are ovoid. *Flowering:* July–September. *Distribution:* Southern, central and western Europe north to Belgium; dry places.

Wild Carrot *Daucus carota* subsp. *carota* Up to 150cm A very variable annual or biennial, with hairless or roughly hairy stems. Leaves are two to three-pinnate, the lobes linear or lanceolate, hairy or hairless. Flowers are white, in many small, simple umbels, making a large, flat-topped compound umbel, usually with a single deep purple central flower; bracts three-forked or pinnate; bracteoles on outside of umbels divided into three, those on the inside smaller, undivided. Fruits are 2–4mm, flattened, often with hooked bristles. The compound umbel becomes bowl-shaped in fruit. *Flowering:* June–September. *Distribution:* Throughout Europe; grassland, often near sea.

Pseudorlaya pumila Up to 20cm A densely hairy annual, branched from the base, with two- to three-pinnate, ovately-lobed leaves. Flowers are white or purplish, in two to five simple umbels on stalks of unequal length, in a compound umbel; bracts two to five, linear, pointed, sometimes divided into three; bracteoles linear-lanceolate. Ovoid fruits are 7–10mm, ridged and spiny. *Flowering:* May–August. *Distribution:* Mediterranean; on sand near the coast.

Ivory-fruited Hartwort: ripe fruits

Spreading Hedge-parsley

Upright Hedge-parsley

Orlaya grandiflora

Wild Carrot

Pseudorlaya pumila

Diapensia *Diapensia lapponica* Up to 6cm A densely tufted evergreen perennial with crowded, leathery leaves 5–10mm. Solitary flowers borne on long erect stalks which have a single bract in the lower part and two small ones close beneath the flower. Leathery calyx is deeply five-cleft; white petals up to 10mm are joined at base; stamens with broad, flattened stalks. Fruit is an ovoid capsule. *Flowering:* May–June. *Distribution:* Arctic regions and mountains south to Scotland and Norway; rocky places.

Common Wintergreen *Pyrola minor* 5–20cm A hairless perennial with a loose basal rosette of elliptical, finely toothed leaves 25–60mm long, their stalks shorter than the blades; leaves on erect flowering stem reduced to scales. Globose flowers 5–7mm across are borne in long spikes; calyx lobes 1.5–2mm; petals whitish to pinkish-lilac; short style is straight, without a disc at the tip. *Flowering:* June–August. *Distribution:* Most of Europe but rare in the south; moors, woods, sometimes on sand-dunes. **Round-leaved Wintergreen** (*P. rotundifolia*) has broad leaves with stalks longer than blades, calyx lobes 2–4.5mm, petals nearly always white and a curved style with a disc at the tip. *Flowering:* June–July. *Distribution:* Europe south to Spain, Italy and Bulgaria; wet places in woods, moors and sand-dunes.

Round-leaved
Wintergreen

One-flowered Wintergreen *Moneses uniflora* 5–15cm A perennial resembling Common Wintergreen but with light green, opposite leaves in a basal rosette; stem bears a single scale-leaf. Solitary flower is 13–20mm across, white, the petals spreading; straight style protrudes. *Flowering:* May–June. *Distribution:* Most of Europe except the far south and some islands; conifer woods, sometimes moorland.

Yellow Bird's-nest *Monotropa hypopitys* 5–25cm A perennial completely lacking chlorophyll, the whole plant pale cream-coloured or yellow, sometimes tinged with pink or brown. Scale-like leaves are 5–13mm, sometimes with fringed margins. Flowers in a spike which is down-curved at first, later erect; five petals 6–13mm, each with an expanded, sac-like base and backwardly curved tip. *Flowering:* June–August. *Distribution:* Most of Europe but rare in the far south; mainly damp .beech and conifer woods.

Cross-leaved
Heath

Bell Heather *Erica cinerea* 15–75cm A small, hairless, evergreen shrub with leaves of 4–5mm in whorls of three. Leafmargins are rolled under, completely covering lower surface and giving leaf a needle-like appearance. Flowering stems have many short, leafy shoots beneath the terminal flower cluster. Reddish- purple corolla is 4–7mm, urn-shaped with very short lobes. *Flowering:* July–September. *Distribution:* Western Europe, eastwards to Norway, Germany and Italy; heaths, moors and woods, always on acid soils. **Cross-leaved Heath** (*E. tetralix*) is more straggling, with hairy leaves in whorls of four and pale pink flowers. *Flowering:* July–September. *Distribution:* Western and northern Europe eastwards to Latvia and Finland; in wetter places than Bell Heather.

Cornish Heath *Erica vagans* Up to 80cm A low and sprawling evergreen shrub with needle-like, bright green leaves in whorls of four to five. Leafmargins are rolled under to conceal the lower leaf surface. Clusters of flowers in leaf axils are grouped into large cylindrical inflorescences. Pinkish or white corolla is 2.5–3.5mm, bell-shaped with erect lobes; purple anthers protrude beyond corolla. *Flowering:* July–August. *Distribution:* Western Europe, from Spain to Britain; heaths on acid soils.

Diapensia

Common Wintergreen

One-flowered Wintergreen

Yellow Bird's-nest

Bell Heather

Cornish Heath

Heather *Calluna vulgaris* Up to 150cm A small, much-branched evergreen shrub with tiny scale-like leaves 2.5–3.5mm, arrow-head shaped, pressed against and clasping the stem. Narrow spikes of flowers are often crowded to form large branched inflorescences. Flowers have four pinkish-purple, petal-like sepals 3–4mm and a deeply four-lobed corolla, similar to but shorter than sepals. There are six to eight small bracts below each flower, the upper four also resembling sepals. *Flowering:* July–September. *Distribution:* Most of Europe but rare in the Mediterranean region; often dominant on heaths and moors, also woods, sand-dunes.

Cassiope hypnoides 5–15cm A dwarf evergreen shrub, the spreading stems mat-forming. Alternate leaves are 2–4mm, very narrow and somewhat overlapping. Flowers are nodding on slender stalks at tips of shoots; crimson sepals 2mm; white corolla 4–5mm, broadly bell-shaped to hemispherical and cut about halfway to the base into five lobes; stamens ten. *Flowering:* June–August. *Distribution:* Arctic Europe, extending to Iceland and mountains of Scandinavia; snow patches and wet places.

Yellow Azalea

Alpenrose *Rhododendron ferrugineum* 50–120cm A twiggy evergreen shrub, the young shoots and undersides of leaves covered with rusty-coloured scales. Short- stalked leaves are alternate, 20–40mm, elliptic-oblong. Pink flowers about 15mm long in clusters of six to ten have a funnel-shaped corolla lobed to about the middle; stamens ten. *Flowering:* May–August. *Distribution:* Pyrenees, Alps and northern Apennines, extending into Yugoslavia; open woods, meadows and rocky places, usually on acid soils. **Yellow Azalea** (*R. luteum*) is deciduous and reaches 400cm. Yellow flowers have five stamens. *Flowering:* May. *Distribution:* Native to eastern Europe, naturalised in Britain; damp peaty soils and conifer woods.

Trailing Azalea *Loiseluria procumbens* A creeping evergeen shrub with stems branching and rooting to form large mats. Opposite leaves are 4–7mm, oblong, blunt, the margins rolled under. Terminal flowers are solitary or in small clusters; sepals red; pink corolla 4mm, bell- to cup-shaped, with five spreading lobes; stamens five. *Flowering:* May–July. *Distribution:* Northern Europe and mountains south to Pyrenees and Alps; dry, exposed places.

Bog-rosemary *Andromeda polifolia* 15–35cm A dwarf, spreading evergreen shrub. Alternate leaves are 10–40mm, narrow and pointed, with rolled under margins; upper surface dark green, lower silvery-bluish. Slender-stalked flowers are nodding, in terminal clusters of two to eight; reddish calyx has short triangular lobes; corolla 5–8mm, urn-shaped with short, curved lobes, pink but fading to white. *Flowering:* May–September. *Distribution:* Northern Europe, scattered southwards to Alps and Carpathians; bogs.

Alpine Bearberry

Bearberry *Arctostaphyllos uva-ursi* Up to 150cm long A spreading dwarf evergreen shrub, the rooting stems forming dense mats. Leathery alternate leaves are 12–30mm, obovate, untoothed, paler on the underside. Flowers in terminal clusters have two small bracts at base of each flower stalk. Reddish calyx has rounded lobes; urn-shaped corolla 5–6mm, greenish-white to pink; stamens ten. Fruit is a bright red berry 10mm across. *Flowering:* May–July. *Distribution:* Most of Europe except the far south; heaths, moors and open woods. **Alpine Bearberry** (*A. alpinus*) has toothed leaves which wither, but persist until spring, and black berries. *Flowering:* May–August. *Distribution:* Northern Europe and mountains in the south.

Heather

Cassiope hypnoides

Alpenrose

Trailing Azalea

Bog-rosemary

Bearberry: fruits

Small Cranberry: fruit

Bog Bilberry: fruit

Northern Androsace

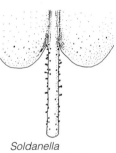

Soldanella hungarica: leaf base

Cranberry *Vaccinium oxycoccos* Up to 80cm A dwarf, spreading evergreen shrub. Ovate to oblong leaves of 6–10mm are dark, shiny green above and whitish below; margins inrolled beneath. Flowers are borne on erect, minutely hairy, thread- like stalks; pinkish-red corolla is divided almost to the base into four recurved lobes. Edible berry, 8–10mm, is globose or pear-shaped, red when ripe. *Flowering*: June–August. *Distribution:* Northern and central Europe south to France and northern Italy; peat bogs, wet heaths. Very similar **Small Cranberry** (*V. microcarpum*) is smaller in all its parts and has triangular-ovate leaves.

Bilberry *Vaccinium myrtillus* Up to 60cm An erect, much-branched deciduous shrub, the twigs green and three-angled. Ovate, toothed leaves are 10–30mm, bright green with flat margins. Flowers are usually solitary; globose corolla 4–6mm, with very short, recurved lobes, green or pink-tinged. Edible berry is 6–10mm, globose and blue-black with a whitish bloom when ripe. *Flowering*: April–June. *Distribution:* Most of Europe, only on mountains in the south; heaths, moors, woods, on acid soils. Similar **Bog Bilberry** (*V. uliginosum*) is deciduous, with blue-green leaves and brown, cylindrical twigs. *Flowering:* May–June. *Distribution:* Similar to Bilberry.

Cowberry *Vaccinium vitis-idaea* Up to 30cm A small evergreen shrub with a creeping rhizome and erect or arching aerial stems. Elliptical to obovate leaves are untoothed, leathery, dark green above but paler and with inrolled margins beneath. Flowers borne in short, crowded spikes; white or pink, bell-shaped corolla has four or five lobes. Globose red berry is 5–10mm, acid but edible when ripe. *Flowering*: June–August. *Distribution:* Northern and central Europe south to Italy and Bulgaria; moors and woods on acid soils.

Androsace maxima 3–15cm An annual with a basal rosette of ovate to obovate, toothed leaves 6–30mm. One to several leafless stems each bear a terminal cluster of white to pink flowers; leafy bracts equalling the flower stalks are partially joined in a ring beneath the cluster; flower stalks elongate in fruit. Bell-shaped, densely hairy calyx is 8–10mm but enlarges in fruit; corolla shorter. *Flowering*: April–May. *Distribution:* Europe north to France, Germany and Russia; dry, open places, often on lime-rich soils. Similar **Northern Androsace** (*A. septentrionalis*) reaches 30cm in height and has small bracts much shorter than flower stalks. *Flowering*: May–July. *Distribution:* Northern and central Europe south to the Alps; grassy places**.**

Alpine-bells *Cortusa matthioli* 20-40cm A rusty-hairy perennial with very long-stalked basal leaves, the blades 10–25cm, rounded to kidney-shaped and shallowly cut into five to seven coarsely toothed lobes. Nodding flowers borne in loose terminal clusters on leafless stems; bell- to funnel-shaped corolla about 10mm, deeply lobed, purplish-violet. *Flowering*: June–July. *Distribution*: Mountains of southern Europe westwards to the Alps; woods, damp lime-rich soils.

Alpine Snowbell *Soldanella alpina* 5-15cm A hairless, mat-forming perennial with a basal rosette of long-stalked, leathery evergreen leaves. Leafless stems bear two to four flowers and may double their height in fruit. Nodding violet or bluish flowers have a funnel-shaped corolla divided to more than halfway, giving a distinctive fringe. *Flowering:* April–August. *Distribution:* Mountains from the Pyrenees, southern Italy and Yugoslavia north to Germany. Similar **S. hungarica** differs in being covered with glandular hairs. *Distribution:* East-central Europe and the Balkans, southern Italy.

Cranberry

Bilberry

Cowberry

Androsace maxima

Alpine-bells

Alpine Snowbell

Auricula *Primula auricula* Up to 16cm A perennial with loose rosettes of orbicular to lanceolate, smooth, fleshy leaves 15–120mm long, often dusted with white, mealy powder. Deep yellow flowers are 15–25mm across, funnel-shaped with a white-mealy throat, carried in stalked clusters of two to 30. *Flowering*: May–July. *Distribution*: Alps, Carpathians and Apennines up to 2900m; rock-crevices or wet, grassy places.

Primrose *Primula vulgaris* Up to 10cm A clump-forming, hairy perennial with loose rosettes of oblanceolate to obovate, wrinkled leaves 50–250mm long. Flowers are usually pale yellow, but white in the Balearics, purple or red in the Balkans, 20–40mm across, carried singly on long, slender stalks. Fruit is a capsule enclosed within the persistent calyx. *Flowering*: March–June. *Distribution:* Most of Europe; woodland, scrub, hedges.

Oxlip

Cowslip *Primula veris* 10–30cm A hairy perennial with leaf-rosettes similar to those of Primrose. Lobes of calyx are acute at apex. Bright yellow flowers are funnel-shaped, 8–28mm across, with orange spots at base of each lobe, all drooping to one side in a cluster of ten to 30 on a long naked stalk. Ripe capsule is shorter than calyx, containing dry seeds. *Flowering*: April–June. *Distribution:* Most of Europe except the far north and south; open woodland, scrub and grassland on lime-rich soils. **Oxlip** (*P. elatior*) is similar but lobes of calyx are drawn out to a fine point. Ripe capsule is at least as long as calyx. *Flowering:* March–August. *Distribution*: Western, central and southern Europe; woodland, scrub and grassland.

Scottish Primrose

Bird's-eye Primrose *Primula farinosa* 3–30cm A short-lived perennial with loose rosettes of oblanceolate to elliptical leaves 10–100mm long, usually densely white-mealy beneath. Flowers are normally lilac-pink with a yellow throat, 8–16mm across, carried in a cluster of two to many on a long naked stalk. *Flowering:* May–August. *Distribution:* Mainly northern and central Europe; marshes and damp grassland. **Scottish Primrose** (*P. scotica*) is smaller, to 6cm, with leaves 10–50mm long. Dark purple flowers are 5–8mm across with a yellow throat. *Flowering*: May–September. *Distribution:* North Scotland; moist, coastal grassland and dunes.

Water-violet *Hottonia palustris* 30–90cm. An aquatic perennial with both submerged and floating stems bearing leaves 20–130mm long, pinnately divided into linear segments. Erect, leafless flowering stems projecting above the water carry three to nine whorls of flowers each 20–25mm across, lilac-pink with a yellow throat. Fruits are capsules 3–6mm long. *Flowering:* May–July. *Distribution*: Mainly western and central Europe; shallow, still, fresh water.

Cyclamen

Sowbread *Cyclamen hederifolium* Up to 15cm A tuberous, hairless perennial flowering before the leaves develop. Leaves are heart-shaped and angled, resembling those of Ivy, often with pale, marbled patterns above and reddish beneath. Pink flowers are carried singly on slender, reddish, leafless stalks which coil down to soil-surface as fruit develops; lobes are strongly reflexed, united at base into a five-angled rim. *Flowering*: July–November. *Distribution:* Native in southern Europe, naturalised in western Europe including Britain; woodland and scrub. **Cyclamen** (*Cyclamen purpurascens*) is similar but flowers are reddish-pink or purplish, appearing with the leaves; lobes not forming an angular, basal rim. *Flowering*: June–October. *Distribution:* Alps, Carpathians and Yugoslavia; woodland.

Auricula

Primrose

Cowslip

Bird's-eye Primrose

Water-violet

Sowbread

Chickweed Wintergreen *Trientalis europaea* 5–30cm A slender, hairless perennial with erect stems growing from an underground rhizome. Leaves are obovate to lanceolate, up to 90mm long, mostly in a single whorl at top of the stem. White or pink-tinged flowers are 11–19mm across, bowl-shaped, on slender stalks arising from leaf axils. *Flowering:* May–August. *Distribution:* Northern and central Europe; woods and moors on acid soils.

Creeping-Jenny

Yellow Pimpernel *Lysimachia nemorum* 10–45cm long A creeping, hairless perennial with opposite, ovate leaves 15–30mm long. Yellow flowers are about 12mm across with five spreading corolla lobes, carried singly on wiry stalks arising from leaf axils. Fruits are globose capsules about 3mm across. *Flowering:* May–September. *Distribution:* Mainly western and central Europe; woodland, hedges and other damp, shady places. **Creeping-Jenny** (*L. nummularia*) is similar but has broader leaves and cup-shaped flowers dotted with black glands. *Flowering:* June–August. *Distribution:* Most of Europe; damp woodland, grassland, other moist places.

Dotted Loosestrife

Yellow Loosestrife *Lysimachia vulgaris* 50–160cm A hairy perennial with erect stems growing from a creeping rhizome. Leaves are opposite or in whorls of three to four, ovate to lanceolate, 55–90mm long. Yellow flowers are 15–20mm across, carried in terminal, branched, open, spike-like heads. *Flowering:* July–August. *Distribution:* Most of Europe; wet woodland, fens, lake shores and river banks. **Dotted Loosestrife** (*L. punctata*) is similar but has flowers up to 35mm across, carried in the leaf axils, usually in pairs. *Flowering:* July–October. *Distribution:* Native in central and south-eastern Europe, naturalised further north and west; marshes, other wet places.

Tufted Loosestrife *Lysimachia thyrsiflora.* 30–70cm A usually hairless perennial with erect stems. Opposite or rarely whorled leaves are 70–95mm long, lanceolate, dotted with many black glands; bases stalkless and half clasping the stem. Yellow flowers carried in two to three dense spikes in each leaf axil in middle part of stem; petals seven, 4–6mm long. *Flowering:* June–July. *Distribution:* From France and Romania northwards; marshes.

Blue Pimpernel

Scarlet Pimpernel *Anagallis arvensis* subsp. *arvensis* 6–50cm long An almost hairless, prostrate annual with slender, branching stems bearing opposite, ovate to lanceolate leavs 8–18mm long. Flowers which close by early afternnoon or in dull weather are red, blue or various paler shades, 10–15mm across, carried singly on wiry stalks arising from leaf axils; corolla lobes usually have numerous, marginal hairs. Fruits are globose capsules 4–6mm across. *Flowering:* March–October. *Distribution:* Almost throughout Europe; disturbed ground. **Blue Pimpernel** (*A. arvensis* subsp.*coerulea*) always has blue flowers; corolla lobes bear few or no marginal hairs. *Distribution:* Most of Europe, but not native in much of the north.

Chaffweed

Bog Pimpernel *Anagallis tenella* 5–15cm long A delicate, creeping, rooting, hairless perennial with usually opposite, nearly orbicular leaves 4–9mm long. Funnel-shaped flowers are up to 14mm across, opening in sunshine, solitary on wiry stalks in leaf axils; corolla lobes are white with reddish veins. *Flowering:* May–September. *Distribution:* Mainly western Europe; fens, bogs and damp places. **Chaffweed** (*A. minima*) is a tiny, erect annual to about 4cm with alternate, ovate leaves. Minute, white or pink, almost stalkless flowers are borne in leaf axils. Pink, globose capsules 1.5mm. *Flowering:* June–August. *Distribution:* Most of Europe; damp, open, often sandy ground.

Chickweed Wintergreen

Yellow Pimpernel

Yellow Loosestrife

Tufted Loosestrife

Scarlet Pimpernel

Bog Pimpernel

Sea-milkwort *Glaux maritima* 5–30cm long A fleshy perennial with erect or creeping and rooting stems bearing elliptical leaves 4–15mm long. Almost stalkless flowers are 3–6mm across, carried in the leaf axils; calyx is white to purple with five petal-like lobes; corolla is absent . *Flowering*: May–September. *Distribution*: Coastal Europe and saline places inland.

Brookweed *Samolus valerandi* 5–60cm A hairless perennial forming a basal rosette of glossy, obovate to spoon-shaped leaves 10–90mm long. Erect, leafy stems terminate in loose, sometimes branched, spike-like heads of white, bell-shaped flowers 2–3mm across. Fruits are globose capsules 2–3mm across containing numerous, reddish-brown seeds. *Flowering*: April–August. *Distribution:* Most of Europe; wet places, especially coastal.

Coris monspeliensis 10–30cm A woody-based biennial or perennial with ascending to erect, much-branched stems bearing alternate, linear leaves 2–20mm long. Pink, purple or blue flowers are carried in dense, spike-like, terminal heads; each flower is 9–12mm long with five unequal corolla lobes forked at the tips. Fruits are globular capsules 0.5–2mm across. *Flowering*: April–July. *Distribution:* Mediterranean region; dry places, especially coastal.

Jersey Thrift

Thrift *Armeria maritima* 5–60cm A cushion-forming perennial with a branched, woody base producing rosettes of numerous, grass-like leaves up to 150 x 4mm. Slender, erect, leafless stalks terminate in dense, globular flower heads 10–30mm across, below which extends a membranous, sleeve-like sheath, 10–20mm long. Papery calyces and pink, purplish, red or white corollas are funnel-shaped, persistent. *Flowering:* April–October. *Distribution:* Most of Europe; salt-marshes, coastal cliffs, grassland, rocky places in mountains to 3100m. **Jersey Thrift** (*A. arenaria*) has rosettes with fewer, broader leaves up to 14mm wide, and sheath 20–60mm long. *Flowering*: May–September. *Distribution:* Mainly western Europe; dry grassland and rocky places, mostly in the mountains to 3000m.

Limoniastrum
monopetalum

Common Sea-lavender *Limonium vulgare* 15–70cm A hairless perennial with a woody, branched base bearing sparse rosettes of usually erect, long-stalked, oblanceolate to spathulate leaves 100–150 x 15–40mm. Erect, branching flowering stems bear numerous, spreading spikes 10–20mm long, densely packed with lilac flowers 6–8mm long. *Flowering*: July–September. *Distribution:* Western and southern Europe; muddy salt-marshes. **Limoniastrum monopetalum** is a branched, leafy shrub to 120cm, with fleshy, bluish-green leaves 20–30 x 5mm, clasping stem. Flower-spikes are 50–100mm long, loosely packed with pink flowers 10–20mm across. *Distribution:* Mediterranean region; maritime sands and salt-marshes.

Wild Jasmine *Jasminum fruticans* Up to 300cm An evergreen or semi-evergreen shrub with four-angled stems bearing alternate, glossy, dark green, usually trifoliate leaves with oblong leaflets 7–20mm long. Yellow flowers are 12–15mm across, carried in clusters of one to five on short, lateral branches; corolla consists of a tube with five, spreading, oblong lobes. Fruits are juicy, black, globose berries 7–9mm across. *Flowering:* April–June. *Distribution:* Southern Europe; woodland margins and scrub.**Common Jasmine** (*J. officinale*) is a climbing shrub to 10m with opposite, pinnate leaves and white flowers, sometimes purplish outside. *Flowering*: May–September. *Distribution:* Native to south-western Asia; cultivated for ornament and widely naturalised in southern Europe.

Common Jasmine

Sea-milkwort

Brookweed

Coris monspeliensis

Thrift

Common Sea-lavender

Wild Jasmine

Guernsey Centaury

Yellow Centaury *Cicendia filiformis* 3–14cm A slender annual with linear leaves 2–6mm long. Stems are simple or branched, terminating in small, solitary, yellow, star-shaped flowers which open only in full sun. Calyx has four short, triangular lobes. Fruit is an ovoid capsule 4–5mm long. *Flowering*: June–October. *Distribution:* Western and southern Europe; open, damp, sandy or peaty ground. **Guernsey Centaury** (*Exaculum pusillum)* is similar but calyx is deeply divided into linear lobes; flowers are pink or cream. *Flowering*: June–October. *Distribution:* South-western Europe.

Yellow-wort *Blackstonia perfoliata* 10–60cm A greyish-green annual with a basal rosette from which arises an erect stem bearing pairs of ovate to triangular leaves, their bases usually united. Yellow flowers are carried in a loose, forking, terminal cluster; each flower is 8–35mm across with six to 12 spreading, corolla lobes. *Flowering:* March–October. *Distribution*: Western, central and southern Europe; grassland, bare ground and maritime sands.

Seaside Centaury

Common Centaury *Centaurium erythraea* 10–50cm A slender, erect biennial with a basal rosette of obovate to elliptical, three- to seven-veined leaves 10–50 x 8–20mm. Pink to deep pinkish-purple flowers are 5–20mm across, with a five-lobed corolla carried in loose, branched clusters. *Flowering:* April–September. *Distribution:* Almost throughout Europe; dry grassland, bare, stony places, scrub. **Seaside Centaury** (*C. littorale*) is often shorter, to 25cm, with narrower, three- veined, basal leaves only 3–5mm wide. Stems are several with flowers solitary or in dense clusters. *Flowering*: June–August. *Distribution:* Northern and central Europe; grassy and sandy places near the sea and inland, saline habitats.

Centaurium maritimum 10–20cm A slender annual or biennial with a basal leaf- rosette and sometimes branched stem with elliptic-oblong leaves 6–20mm, the upper ones longest. The few flowers are 20–25mm across with elliptical corolla lobes, yellow, rarely tinged with purple. *Flowering:* April–August. *Distribution:* Western and southern Europe; usually coastal sandy or grassy places.

Slender Centaury

Lesser Centaury *Centaurium pulchellum* 2–20cm Similar to Common Centaury but smaller, more slender and annual, lacking a basal leaf-rosette. Stems usually fork from below middle, with spreading to ascending branches. Pinkish-purple flowers are 4–8mm across, carried at the tips and in the forks of the branches. *Flowering:* April–September. *Distribution*: Almost throughout Europe; bare or grassy, often damp ground, especially near the sea. **Slender Centaury** (*C. tenuiflorum*) is similar but has erect branches and more densely clustered flowers. *Flowering*: July–October. *Distribution:* Western and southern Europe; bare or grassy, damp ground near the sea.

Spotted Gentian

Great Yellow Gentian *Gentiana lutea* 50–120cm A stout, erect perennial with basal rosettes of bluish-green, lanceolate to ovate, ribbed leaves up to 300mm long. Unbranched flowering stems bear opposite, clasping leaves below dense whorls of star-shaped, yellow or rarely brick-red flowers; corolla five- to nine-lobed. *Flowering:* June–August. *Distribution:* Mountains of central and southern Europe; grassy or rocky places and marshes. **Spotted Gentian** (*G. punctata*) is smaller, to 60cm, with pale greenish-yellow, purple-spotted, erect, bell-shaped flowers 14–35mm long. *Flowering:* July– September. *Distribution:* Mountains of central Europe, southwards to northern Greece; open woodland, grassy and rocky places.

Yellow Centaury

Yellow-wort

Common Centaury

Centaurium maritimum

Lesser Centaury

Great Yellow Gentian

Willow Gentian: leaf and seed

Marsh Gentian *Gentiana pneumonanthe* 5–40cm A perennial with ascending to erect stems bearing linear to oblong or ovate-lanceolate, one-veined leaves 20–40mm long. Trumpet-shaped, blue flowers are 25–50mm long, greenish outside, carried singly at the stem tips and sometimes in the axils of the upper leaves. Seeds are not winged. *Flowering:* July–September. *Distribution:* Most of Europe; bogs and wet heaths, avoiding lime-rich soils. **Willow Gentian** (*G. asclepiadea*) is taller, to 60cm, with lanceolate to ovate, three- to five-veined leaves. Blue flowers are 35–50mm long, paler outside but not greenish, carried in clusters of one to three in the leaf axils. Seeds are winged. *Flowering:* August–October. *Distribution:* Mainly in the mountains of central Europe; damp or shady places, to 2200m.

Alpine Gentian *Gentiana nivalis* 1–15cm A slender, erect annual with simple or branched stems and ovate to elliptical leaves. Intense blue flowers are 8mm across, solitary at the stem tips, each with a long corolla tube and five spreading, pointed lobes. *Flowering:* June–August. *Distribution:* Northern Europe and mountainous areas as far south as Bulgaria; grassy places, arctic heaths, marshes and stony places, to 3100m.

Spring Gentian *Gentiana verna* 2–20cm A perennial forming compact clumps of basal rosettes of elliptical to broadly ovate leaves 5–15mm long. Erect stems bear solitary, bright blue flowers 15–20mm across; corolla tube is greenish-blue outside with five longitudinal, white lines; lobes are oval and spreading. *Flowering:* March–August. *Distribution:* Western Ireland, Northern England, Arctic Russia, central Europe and in the mountains of southern Europe; short grass, rocky and moist places, to 3000m.

Trumpet Gentian *Gentiana acaulis* Up to 10cm A perennial, sometimes forming mats, with elliptical or lanceolate leaves crowded towards the base of the erect stem. Large, solitary, trumpet-shaped, deep blue flowers are 40–70mm long; corolla has green spots inside the throat; lobes are spreading and pointed. *Flowering:* May–August. *Distribution:* Central and parts of southern Europe, in the mountains; grassy, stony and boggy places, avoiding lime-rich soils. There are six other, very similar and closely related species scattered on lime-rich soils in the mountains of Europe.

Dune Gentian

Autumn Gentian *Gentianella amarella* 5–30cm An erect biennial with opposite, elliptical to lanceolate leaves 10–20mm long. Dull purple, bell-shaped flowers are 12–22mm long, carried at the stem tips and in the upper leaf axils; calyx lobes are equal, erect; corolla has four to five spreading, triangular lobes and a ring of long, white hairs in the top of the tube. *Flowering:* July–September. *Distribution:* Northern and central Europe; grassland and sand-dunes. **Dune Gentian** (*G. uliginosa*) is smaller, to 15cm, the length from the flower to the penultimate pair of leaves forming at least half the height of the plant (at most a sixth for Autumn Gentian). Calyx lobes are unequal, spreading. *Flowering:* August–November. *Distribution:* Northern and north-central Europe; dune-slacks and damp grassland.

Field Gentian *Gentianella campestris* 2–35cm Resembles Autumn Gentian but flowers are bluish-lilac or white, 15–30mm long, with the corolla always four-lobed. The calyx has two broadly ovate outer lobes much larger and overlapping the two narrowly lanceolate inner ones. *Flowering:* July–October. *Distribution:* Northern and central Europe, southwards to Spain and Italy; grassland, heaths and sand-dunes.

Marsh Gentian

Alpine Gentian

Spring Gentian

Trumpet Gentian

Autumn Gentian

Field Gentian

Slender Gentian

Fringed Gentian *Gentianella ciliata* 5–30cm A slender biennial with spoon-shaped to narrowly lanceolate leaves 10–30mm long. Blue flowers are 40–50mm across, in clusters in the axils of the upper leaves; the four spreading, ovate corolla lobes with prominently fringed margins. *Flowering:* August–October. *Distribution:* Mainly central and southern Europe; dry, grassy and rocky places. **Slender Gentian** (*G. tenella*) is smaller, annual or biennial, to 10cm, with leaves 5–12mm long. Normally sky-blue or dirty violet flowers are 12–25mm across, not fringed at the margins. *Flowering:* July–August. *Distribution:* Northern Europe and mountains of central Europe.

Bogbean *Menyanthes trifoliata* 12–35cm A hairless, creeping perennial of wet places, sometimes forming large, floating mats. Leaves are trifolate, held on erect stalks, with obovate leaflets up to 100mm long. Star-shaped flowers are about 15mm across, carried in spike-like heads of ten to 20; five densely fringed corolla lobes pink beneath but paler to white above. Fruit is a globular capsule. *Flowering:* April–July. *Distribution:* Most of Europe but rare in the Mediterranean region; wet bogs and fens or other shallow, fresh water.

Fringed Water-lily *Nymphoides peltata* Up to 160cm long A hairless, aquatic perennial with long stems and long-stalked, floating, almost circular leaves 30–100mm across. Yellow flowers are 30–40mm across with five spreading, fringed corolla lobes; they are solitary and carried above the water on long stalks which arise in clusters of two to five from the leaf axils. *Flowering:* June–September. *Distribution:* Most of Europe; in still and slow-moving, fresh water.

Oleander *Nerium oleander* Up to 400cm A robust, extremely poisonous, evergreen shrub with straight, erect, greyish branches bearing linear-lanceolate, leathery, dark green leaves 60–120mm long. Showy, usually pink flowers, with five spreading corolla lobes, are 30–40mm across, clustered at the stem tips. Fruits are erect, narrow, reddish-brown pods 80–160mm long. *Flowering:* April–September. *Distribution:* Mediterranean region; native along watercourses and by springs, widely planted for ornament.

Greater Periwinkle

Lesser Periwinkle *Vinca minor* 30–60cm long An evergreen, more or less prostrate dwarf shrub with opposite, lanceolate to ovate, glossy dark green, leathery leaves 15–45mm long. Blue-violet flowers are 25–30mm across; corolla tube short, with five large spreading lobes. Fruits are narrow, forked pods. *Flowering:* February–May. *Distribution:* Western, central and southern Europe, not native in much of the north; woodland, hedges and rocky places. **Greater Periwinkle** (*V. major*) has stems up to 100cm long, ovate leaves 25–90mm long and flowers 30–50mm across. *Flowering:* April–May. *Distribution:* Native in western and central Mediterranean region, cultivated and naturalised elsewhere, northwards to Britain.

Cionura erecta

Swallow-wort *Vincetoxicum hirundinaria* Up to 120cm An erect perennial with opposite, ovate to lanceolate, pointed leaves 60–100mm long on short stalks. White or yellow flowers are 3–10mm across, in stalked clusters of six to eight from the leaf axils. Fruits are narrow, forked, pointed pods about 60mm long. *Flowering:* June–September. *Distribution:* Most of Europe; scrub, grassy and rocky places. ***Cionura erecta*** has sprawling, woody-based stems, long-stalked, heart-shaped leaves and dense clusters of creamy flowers. *Flowering:* May–July. *Distribution:* South-eastern Balkan peninsula and Aegean region; rocky places and maritime sands.

Fringed Gentian

Bogbean

Fringed Water-lily

Oleander

Lesser Periwinkle

Swallow-wort

Field Madder *Sherardia arvensis* Up to 40cm long A more or less prostrate, hairy, branching annual with oblanceolate leaves 5–20mm long, carried in whorls of four to six. Small, lilac-pink, funnel-shaped flowers are 2–3mm across, carried in dense, terminal heads of four to ten, above a ruff of united leaves. Fruits are dry and bristly, 2–7mm long, with persistent, enlarged calyx. *Flowering:* April–October. *Distribution:* Almost throughout Europe; dry grassland and disturbed ground.

Dyer's Woodruff

Squinancywort *Asperula cynanchica* 10–50cm An ascending to erect, tufted perennial with branched, four-angled stems bearing narrowly lanceolate to linear leaves 20–35mm long, arranged in whorls of four. Funnel-shaped flowers are 3–4mm across with four lobes, pink outside, white inside, carried in loose, terminal clusters. *Flowering:* June–September. *Distribution:* Most of Europe; dry, lime-rich grassland and sand-dunes. **Dyer's Woodruff** (*A. tinctoria*) resembles Squinancywort but leaves are arranged in whorls of six towards base of the stem and four higher up. Flowers have three lobes. *Flowering:* June–August. *Distribution:* Mainly central Europe; open woodland.

Woodruff *Galium odoratum* 15–25cm An almost hairless perennial with erect, unbranched stems growing from a creeping rhizome, which spreads to carpet the ground. Leaves are elliptical, 20–50mm long, in whorls of six to nine, smelling of vanilla when crushed; margins have tiny, forward-pointing prickles. White flowers are funnel-shaped with four lobes, 4–7mm across, in long-stalked, terminal heads. *Flowering:* April–June. *Distribution:* Most of Europe but rare in the Mediterranean region; woodland.

Common Marsh Bedstraw *Galium palustre* 15–70cm A slender perennial with erect flowering stems bearing broadly oblanceolate leaves 5–20mm long, arranged in whorls of four to six. Leaf margins have backward-pointing bristles. White flowers are 2–3mm across, carried in stalked clusters at the tops of the stems. *Flowering:* June–August. *Distribution:* Almost throughout Europe; marshes, fens and other wet places. **Great Marsh-bedstraw** (*G. palustre* subsp. *elongatum*) is taller, with stems 50–100cm; leaves are 20–35mm long; flowers are 3–4mm across. *Distribution:* Most of Europe; wet places. **Fen Bedstraw** (*G. uliginosum*) has usually narrowly lanceolate leaves 10–20mm long, ending in a minute point, arranged in whorls of six to eight. White flowers are 2.5–3mm across. *Flowering:* June–August. *Distribution:* Most of Europe; fens and other wet places.

Fen Bedstraw

Lady's Bedstraw *Galium verum* 50–120cm A sprawling perennial with numerous stems bearing linear leaves 15–30mm long, in whorls of eight to 12. Bright yellow flowers are 2–3mm across, carried in large numbers in branching, terminal heads. *Flowering:* June–September. *Distribution:* Most of Europe; open woodland, hedges, grassland and sand-dunes.

Hedge Bedstraw *Galium mollugo* 30–150cm A sprawling to erect, scrambling perennial with oblong to broadly oblanceolate leaves 10–25mm long, arranged in whorls of six to eight. Leaf margins have forward-pointing bristles. White flowers are 2–3mm across, in loose, much branched, ovoid, terminal heads. *Flowering:* June–September. *Distribution:* Most of Europe; open woodland, hedges and grassland. **Upright Hedge-bedstraw** (*G. mollugo* subsp. *erectum*) is similar but with leaves 10–40mm long. White or yellowish flowers are 3–5mm across, carried in rather dense heads. *Distribution:* Most of Europe; open habitats.

Upright Hedge-bedstraw

Field Madder

Squinancywort

Woodruff

Common Marsh Bedstraw

Lady's Bedstraw

Hedge Bedstraw

Slender Bedstraw:
leaf and fruit

Corn Cleavers: fruit

Madder

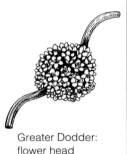

Greater Dodder:
flower head

Heath Bedstraw *Galium saxatile* 15–35cm A mat-forming perennial with ascending stems bearing obovate to oblanceolate leaves 4–11mm long, in whorls of six to seven. Leaf margins have forward-pointing bristles. White flowers are 2.5–4mm across, in branched, cylindrical heads at stem tips. Fruits covered with pointed warts. *Flowering:* June–August. *Distribution:* Mainly western and west-central Europe; acid grassland, heaths and scrub. **Slender Bedstraw** (*G. pumilum*) has narrowly oblanceolate leaves 10–16mm long; margins have backward-pointing bristles. Fruits are smooth or with rounded warts. *Flowering:* June–July. *Distribution:* Western and central Europe; open woodland, grassland, rocky places.

Cleavers *Galium aparine* 80–180cm A vigorous annual with sprawling stems bearing backward-pointing bristles. Leaves are oblanceolate, 30–60mm long, in whorls of six to nine. Whitish flowers are 1.5–1.7mm across, carried in stalked clusters arising from leaf axils. Fruits consist of two globular sections side by side, densely covered with hooked hairs. *Flowering:* May–September. *Distribution:* All Europe; woodland, hedges and disturbed ground. **Corn Cleavers** (*G. tricornutum*) has hairless, warty fruits carried on strongly downcurved stalks. *Flowering:* June–September. *Distribution:* Western, central and southern Europe.

Crosswort *Cruciata laevipes* 20–60cm A slender, hairy, ascending perennial with broadly lanceolate to ovate, yellowish-green leaves 12–20mm long, arranged in whorls of four. Yellow, honey-scented flowers are 2–3mm across, carried in compact clusters in the leaf axils. *Flowering:* April–June. *Distribution:* Western, central and southern Europe; open woodland, scrub, hedges and grassland, preferring lime-rich soils.

Wild Madder *Rubia peregrina* 30–120cm A scrambling, evergreen, woody-based perennial with linear to broadly ovate, leathery leaves 15–60mm long, in whorls of four to eight. Yellowish-green flowers are 4–6mm across with five spreading, pointed lobes, carried in loose clusters. Fruits are juicy, black berries 4–6mm across. *Flowering:* June–August. *Distribution:* Western and southern Europe; woodland, scrub and rocky places. **Madder** (*R. tinctorum*) has thicker stems, stained orange-red at and below ground-level; leaves are 20–100mm long. *Distribution*: Perhaps native in the eastern Mediterranean region, naturalised in central and southern Europe.

Jacob's-ladder *Polemonium caeruleum* 30–90cm A clump-forming perennial with erect, unbranched stems bearing alternate, pinnate leaves up to 400mm long, with usually ten to 12 pairs of leaflets. Drooping, blue flowers are 20–30mm across, in loose, terminal heads; corolla with five spreading lobes; yellow stamens protrude. *Flowering:* May–August. *Distribution:* Mainly northern and central Europe; rocky places and damp meadows, mainly in the mountains, to 2300m.

Dodder *Cuscuta epithymum* Up to 150cm A rootless, twining, parasitic annual, lacking chlorophyll. Yellow to red, smooth, thread-like stems smother the host plant. Leaves are reduced to scales. Pink, bell-shaped flowers are 3–4mm across, carried in globular clusters 5–10mm across. *Flowering:* April–October. *Distribution:* Almost throughout Europe; mainly on plants of the Mint and Pea families. **Greater Dodder** (*C. europaea*) is larger, with flower heads 10–15mm across. *Flowering:* August–September. *Distribution:* Most of Europe; usually on Stinging Nettle.

Heath Bedstraw

Cleavers: fruits

Crosswort

Wild Madder

Jacob's-ladder

Dodder

Hedge Bindweed *Calystegia sepium* Up to 300cm or more A twining perennial with many slender stems growing from an underground rhizome. Alternate leaves are heart- to arrow-shaped, up to 150mm long. Showy, trumpet-shaped, white or pink flowers are 30–40mm across, carried singly on slender stalks arising from the leaf axils; calyx is partly concealed by two leaf-like bracteoles. *Flowering:* June–September. *Distribution:* Almost throughout Europe; woodland margins, scrub, hedges, fens and waste areas.

Large Bindweed *Calystegia silvatica* Up to 300cm or more Resembles Hedge Bindweed but has larger flowers.The two large overlapping bracteoles are 14–50mm wide, completely concealing the calyx; funnel-shaped corolla is 60–75mm across, pure white or with five pale pink stripes. *Flowering:* July–September. *Distribution:* Native in southern Europe, naturalised from gardens elsewhere; scrub, hedges and waste areas. **Hairy Bindweed** (*C.pulchra*) has shortly-hairy stems, leaf and flower stalks, the latter narrowly winged; flowers pink with white stripes. *Flowering:* July–August. *Distribution:* Of uncertain origin, naturalised in northern and central Europe.

Hairy Bindweed

Ipomoea sagittata

Sea Bindweed *Calystegia soldanella* Up to 50cm long A creeping or trailing, non-twining perennial with stems largely buried in sand. Leaves are fleshy, kidney-shaped, broader than long, heart-shaped at base. Trumpet-shaped flowers are 25–40mm across, pink with five equidistant white stripes radiating from the throat. *Flowering:* June–September. *Distribution:* Coasts of western and southern Europe; maritime sands. **Ipomoea sagittata** has trailing or twining stems bearing narrowly arrow-shaped leaves 3–8cm long, with three linear lobes, two pointing backwards and one forwards. Flowers are pink to purple. *Flowering:* July–September. *Distribution:* Mediterranean region; brackish marshes and lagoons near the sea.

Mallow-leaved Bindweed *Convolvulus althaeoides* Up to 100cm long A hairy perennial with trailing or twining stems. Toothed leaves are 10–80mm long, the lower triangular ovate, those further up the stems becoming progressively more deeply cut into several linear lobes. Pinkish-purple, funnel-shaped flowers are 30–40mm across; leaf-like bracteoles are absent. *Flowering:* March–May. *Distribution:* Southern Europe; dry and rocky places. **C. siculus** is an annual or short-lived perennial with lanceolate to ovate leaves and blue flowers 7–10mm across. *Flowering:* March–May. *Distribution:* Mediterranean region.

Field Bindweed *Convolvulus arvensis* Up to 200cm long A creeping or twining perennial with slender stems branched from the base, growing from pale, fleshy, underground rhizomes. Ovate-oblong to linear leaves are 20–50mm long, with backward-pointing or spreading, basal lobes. White, pink or longitudinally striped, funnel-shaped flowers, up to 30mm across, are carried in stalked clusters of one to two from the leaf axils. *Flowering:* June–September. *Distribution:* Almost throughout Europe; disturbed ground, roadsides and coastal grassland; a troublesome weed of cultivation.

Dwarf Convolvulus *Convolvulus tricolor* Up to 60cm A branching, hairy annual or short-lived perennial with sprawling or ascending, non-twining stems. Oblanceolate leaves are stalkless, 10–30mm long. Flowers are solitary; hairy sepals have differently shaped upper and lower sections; corolla is 20–50mm across, very showy, with concentric bands of yellow, white and blue. *Flowering:* March–May. *Distribution:* Mediterranean region; dry fields.

Hedge Bindweed

Large Bindweed

Sea Bindweed

Mallow-leaved Bindweed

Field Bindweed

Dwarf Convolvulus

Heliotrope *Heliotropium europaeum* 10–50cm An erect or ascending, greyish-hairy annual with forking stems bearing ovate to elliptical leaves up to 55mm long. White or lilac flowers are 3–4mm across, carried in dense, coiled, clusters which straighten as the flowers open. *Flowering:* May–September. *Distribution:* Western, central and southern Europe; disturbed ground.

Common Gromwell *Lithospermum officinale* 20–100cm A hairy perennial with one to several erect stems, much-branched above. Leaves are lanceolate, pointed, up to 100mm long. Cream or greenish-white flowers are 3–4mm across, with five spreading lobes, in leafy sprays. Fruits are hard, white, shiny, ovoid nutlets 2.7–4mm long. *Flowering:* May–July. *Distribution:* Almost throughout Europe; woodland margins, scrub and hedges on lime-rich soils. **Field Gromwell** (*L. arvense*) is annual, to 50cm, with little-branched stems and blunt leaves, the lower stalked. Flowers are white, rarely blue or purplish. Fruits are conical, greyish-brown and warty. *Flowering:* April–September. *Distribution:* Almost throughout Europe; disturbed ground and dry, open places.

Field Gromwell: leaf and fruiting calyx

Honeywort *Cerinthe major* 15–60cm An erect, almost hairless annual with usually white-spotted leaves, the lower obovate-spoon-shaped, the upper ovate-lanceolate. Drooping, tubular flowers are 15–30mm long, carried with leaf-like bracts in arching, curling, terminal sprays; yellow corolla has small, recurved, ovate lobes at tip and sometimes a reddish-brown ring in throat. When corolla is entirely dark red so are the bracts. *Flowering:* March–June. *Distribution:* Mediterranean region; disturbed ground. **Lesser Honeywort** (*C. minor*) has yellow flowers 10–12mm long, with straight, lanceolate lobes, almost as long as the tube. *Flowering:* April–July. *Distribution:* Central and eastern Europe; disturbed ground.

Lesser Honeywort

Dyer's Alkanet *Alkanna tinctoria* 10–30cm A whitish-bristly, woody-based perennial with creeping or ascending stems. Basal leaves are linear-lanceolate, 60–150mm long; lower stem-leaves are linear-oblong. Blue flowers are 6–7mm across, carried together with longer, leaf-like bracts in spreading sprays. *Flowering:* March–June. *Distribution:* Mainly southern Europe; sandy and rocky places.

Purple Viper's-bugloss

Viper's-bugloss *Echium vulgare* 20–90cm A biennial with a basal leaf-rosette and erect flowering stems covered with red-based bristles. Hairy leaves are elliptical to narrowly lanceolate, 50–150mm long. Funnel-shaped flowers are 10– 19mm long, pink in bud, blue when open, in erect spires of short, downcurved, axillary sprays. *Flowering:* May–September. *Distribution:* Almost throughout Europe; bare ground, maritime sand and shingle. **Purple Viper's-bugloss** (*E. plantagineum*) is softly hairy with ovate rosette leaves. Flowers are larger, 18–30mm long. *Flowering:* March–August. *Distribution:* Western and southern Europe; disturbed ground, maritime sands.

Lungwort *Pulmonaria officinalis* 20–30cm A hairy perennial with clumps of long- stalked, oval, pointed leaves greatly enlarging to up to 160mm long after flowering. The blades white-spotted. Pink and blue, funnel-shaped flowers are 10mm across, with five rounded lobes, carried in terminal clusters on leafy stems. *Flowering:* March–May. *Distribution:* Mainly in central and southern Europe, northwards to southern Sweden, naturalised in Britain; woodland and hedges.

Heliotrope

Common Gromwell

Honeywort

Dyer's Alkanet

Viper's-bugloss

Lungwort

Russian Comfrey

Bugloss

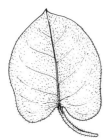

Abraham-Isaac-and Jacob

Common Comfrey *Symphytum officinale* 50–120cm An erect, bristly perennial with ovate-lanceolate basal leaves 150–250mm long. Upper leaf bases often extend down stems as wings. Tubular to bell-shaped flowers are 12–18mm long, in coiled, terminal sprays; calyx has teeth at least equalling tube; corolla is purple-violet, pinkish or white. *Flowering* May–June. *Distribution:* Most of Europe; fens, damp grassland, river banks. **Russian Comfrey** (*S. x uplandicum*) is a hybrid up to 200cm, with leaf bases only shortly extended. Flowers are violet, or open pink and turn blue. *Flowering:* June–August. *Distribution:* Widely naturalised in northern Europe.

Tuberous Comfrey *Symphytum tuberosum* 15–40cm Similar to Common Comfrey but with creeping, tuberous rhizomes. Basal leaves wither at flowering; stem leaves are lanceolate, the upper shortly extended at base. Pale yellow flowers are 13–19mm long. *Flowering:* May–July. *Distribution:* Western, central and southern Europe; damp, shady places.

Alkanet *Anchusa officinalis* 20–80cm A hairy, erect, branching perennial with lanceolate leaves 50–120mm long. Violet or reddish, funnel-shaped flowers are 7–15mm across, carried in dense, coiled, terminal sprays. *Flowering:* June–August. *Distribution:* Mainly central and southern Europe; grassy places and waste areas. **Bugloss** (*A. arvensis*) is a bristly annual with wavy-edged, lanceolate leaves. Blue flowers are 4–6mm across, the dense clusters later elongating. *Flowering:* April–September. *Distribution:* Most of Europe; bare and disturbed ground.

Borage *Borago officinalis* 15–70cm An erect, bristly annual with stalked, ovate to lanceolate, basal leaves 50–200mm long, and stalkless, clasping upper leaves. Blue flowers are 20–25mm across carried in loose, arching sprays; corolla has five spreading, lanceolate, pointed lobes; stamens and stigma form a central cone. *Flowering:* April–September. *Distribution:* Native in southern Europe, cultivated and widely naturalised further north; disturbed ground. **Abraham-Isaac-and-Jacob** (*Trachystemon orientalis*) is perennial with heart-shaped, long- stalked, basal leaves 150–500mm long. Flowers are bluish-violet, 9–12mm across. *Flowering:* April–May. *Distribution:* Native to Bulgaria and Turkey, naturalised in Britain; woodland and shady places.

Oysterplant *Mertensia maritima* Up to 60cm long A bluish-grey, hairless, fleshy perennial with usually trailing, leafy stems. Leaves are 5–60mm long, spoon-shaped, obovate or lanceolate, the lower stalked, the upper stalkless. Bell-shaped flowers are 6mm across, opening pink, becoming pale blue, carried in branching, terminal sprays. *Flowering:* June–August. *Distribution:* Coasts of northern Europe; sand and shingle.

Field Forget-me-not *Myosotis arvensis* Up to 60cm An erect, slender, branching, hairy biennial with oblanceolate leaves up to 80mm long. Small, blue flowers with a central yellow eye are about 3mm across, arranged in gradually uncoiling sprays. Calyx teeth remain closed over shiny, dark, ovoid nutlet. *Flowering:* April–October. *Distribution:* Almost throughout Europe; bare and disturbed ground.**Changing Forget-me-not** (*M. discolor*) has flowers about 1.3mm across, opening pale yellow, becoming pink, violet or blue. *Flowering:* May–June. *Distribution:* Most of Europe except the east; dry places. **Early Forget-me-not** (*M. ramosissima*) is a small annual, 2–40cm,with flowers to 3mm across. Fruiting calyces have teeth half open. *Flowering:* April–June. *Distribution:* Almost throughout Europe; dry, bare places.

Early Forget-me-not: fruiting calyx

Common Comfrey

Tuberous Comfrey

Alkanet

Borage

Oysterplant

Field Forget-me-not

Myosotis nemorosa

Water Forget-me-not *Myosotis scorpioides* Up to 100cm A perennial with a creeping rhizome and runners. Ascending or erect stems bear oblong to oblong-lanceolate leaves up to 100mm long. Blue flowers up to 8mm across have a central yellow eye. *Flowering:* May–September. *Distribution:* Northern and central Europe; by fresh water, often partly submerged. **M. nemorosa** is similar but biennial, usually without runners. Stems are shorter, shining, to 50cm. Flowers are not more than 6mm across. *Flowering:* May–August. *Distribution:* Most of Europe; woodland and wet meadows. **Tufted Forget-me-not** (*M. laxa* subsp. *caespitosa*) is annual or biennial, to 50cm, with no runners. Flowers are smaller, to 5mm across. *Flowering:* May–August. *Distribution:* Most of Europe; wet places.

Wood Forget-me-not *Myosotis sylvatica* Up to 50cm A leafy, much-branched biennial or perennial, similar to Water Forget-me-not but without runners. Leaves are broadly ovate to elliptical, up to 80mm long. Blue flowers with central yellow eye are up to 8mm across, but often smaller. *Flowering:* April–August. *Distribution:* Most of Europe; woodland and grassy places.

Green Hound's-tongue: fruiting calyx

Hound's-tongue *Cynoglossum officinale* 30–60cm An erect, greyish-hairy biennial with oblong to lanceolate leaves to 250mm long. Dull purple, broadly funnel- shaped flowers are up to 10mm across, carried in arching, terminal sprays. Fruits consist of four ovoid nutlets in the persistent calyx, each 5–8mm across, with a thickened margin and covered with hooked bristles. *Flowering:* May–August. *Distribution:* Most of Europe; dry, grassy places and maritime sands. **Green Hound's-tongue** (*C. germanicum*) has glossy, dark green leaves. Flowers only 5–6mm. Fruits lack thickened margin. *Flowering:* May–July. *Distribution*: Mainly western and central Europe; woodland, preferring lime-rich soils.

Vervain *Verbena officinalis* 30–60cm An erect, hairy perennial with slender, tough, four-angled stems bearing opposite, pinnately lobed, roughly diamond-shaped leaves 40–60mm long. Upper leaves are smaller and less deeply lobed. Flowers are carried in long, slender spikes at the branch tips. Slightly two-lipped corollas are pale pink, about 4mm across, with five lobes. *Flowering:* April–October. *Distribution:* Most of Europe; scrub, waste areas.

Common Water-starwort *Callitriche stagnalis* Up to 60cm An aquatic perennial with slender, branching stems forming dense, submerged or floating mats, or sometimes creeping over wet mud. Small, submerged leaves are opposite, narrowly elliptical; floating leaves are broadly elliptical to almost round, in flat rosettes on the water surface. Tiny, unisexual flowers, carried in the leaf axils lack petals and sepals. Fruits are about 1.75mm long, with four winged lobes. *Flowering:* May–September. *Distribution:* Most of Europe except the east; still or slow-moving fresh water, or on wet mud.

Blue Bugle

Bugle *Ajuga reptans* 10–40cm A creeping perennial with long, leafy runners and basal rosettes of ovate leaves, 25–90mm long. Erect flowering stems are four-angled, hairy on two opposite faces, alternating at each joint. Blue flowers are 14–17mm long, in spikes with leaf-like bracts often blue-tinged; corolla has one five-lobed lip. *Flowering:* April–June. *Distribution:* Most of Europe; damp woodland, scrub and grassland. **Blue Bugle** (*A. genevensis*) lacks runners. Stems are usually hairy on all sides. Basal leaves are usually withered when flowers open. *Flowering:* May–July. *Distribution:* Mainly central and south-eastern Europe; grassy and rocky places.

Water Forget-me-not

Wood Forget-me-not

Hound's-tongue

Vervain

Common Water-starwort

Bugle

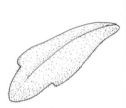

Ajuga iva

Water Germander

Ground-pine *Ajuga chamaepitys* 5–30cm A usually hairy annual or short-lived perennial. Leaves and bracts are divided into three linear segments 0.5–3mm wide, which may be three-lobed at tips. Yellow flowers are 7–25mm long, red- or purple-spotted, two to four at each joint; corolla with a single five-lobed lip. *Flowering:* March–September. *Distribution:* Most of Europe except the north; bare and stony ground. **A. iva** is a tufted, very hairy, woody-based perennial with linear leaves 14–35mm long, sometimes with two to six short lobes. Flowers are purple, pink or yellow. *Flowering:* March–September. *Distribution:* Southern Europe; bare and stony places.

Tree Germander *Teucrium fruticans* Up to 250cm A evergreen shrub with four- angled, densely white-hairy twigs. Leaves are lanceolate to ovate, flat, 20–40mm long, white- or reddish-hairy beneath, usually becoming smooth and shiny above. Blue or lilac flowers are 15–25mm long, paired in the axils of leaf-like bracts; corolla has one five-lobed lip; stamens protrude. *Flowering:* February–June. *Distribution:* Western and central Mediterranean region; dry, sunny, rocky places.

Wall Germander *Teucrium chamaedrys* 5–50cm A hairy, dwarf-shrubby perennial with annual flowering stems. Leaves are oblong-obovate, up to 20mm long, shiny and green above, hairy beneath. Pale to deep purple flowers are 9–16mm long, whorled along with leaf-like bracts in spikes. Corolla has a single five-lobed lip. *Flowering:* May–September. *Distribution:* Mainly central and southern Europe; lime-rich grassland, bare and rocky places. **Water Germander** (*T. scordium*) resembles a Mint, with creeping runners and leaves softly hairy on both sides, smelling unpleasantly of garlic if crushed. Pink flowers 7–10mm long, in small, axillary groups. *Flowering:* June–October. *Distribution:* Most of Europe; wet places. **Cut-leaved Germander** (*T. botrys*) is a hairy annual with leaves 10–25mm long, one to two times pinnately cut into oblong lobes. Purplish-pink flowers 15–20mm long, in small, axillary groups. *Flowering:* June–October. *Distribution:* Western, central and southern Europe; bare, stony ground.

Wood Sage *Teucrium scorodonia* 15–50cm A hairy, rhizomatous perennial with erect, branching stems bearing triangular-ovate, wrinkled, sage-scented leaves. Pale greenish-yellow flowers are about 9mm long, carried in erect spires up to 150mm long. Corolla has a single five-lobed lip. *Flowering:* July–September. *Distribution:* Western, central and southern Europe; dry woodland, scrub, heaths, stable sand-dunes and screes.

Felty Sage *Teucrium capitatum* 6–45cm A dwarf shrub usually densely covered with short, white, greenish or golden hairs. Leaves are 7–27mm long, narrowly obovate or oblong, often with the round-toothed margins rolled underneath. Small, white or reddish flowers are carried together with bracts in dense, ovoid or globular, terminal heads; corolla has a single five-lobed lip. *Flowering:* May–August. *Distribution:* Southern Europe; dry, open places.

Alpine Skullcap *Scutellaria alpina* 25–35cm An ascending, slightly hairy perennial with simple or branched stems. Leaves are ovate, toothed, 15–30mm long. Flowers are 20–25mm long, erect, in dense, terminal heads. Calyx has a distinctive, shield-shaped flap on the upper side. Corolla has a long, purplish tube and arched, upper lip; lower lip is spreading, often white. *Flowering:* June-August. *Distribution:* Mountains of southern and south-central Europe; lime-rich rocks, screes and grassy slopes, to 2500m.

Ground-pine

Tree Germander

Wall Germander

Wood Sage

Felty Sage

Alpine Skullcap

Lesser Skullcap

Marrubium
peregrinum: calyx

Tuberous Jerusalem
Sage

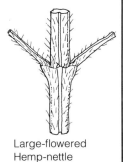

Large-flowered
Hemp-nettle

Skullcap *Scutellaria galericulata* 7–70cm A more or less erect perennial with ovate-elliptical to oblong-lanceolate, shallowly toothed leaves 10–50mm long. Violet-blue, rarely pink flowers are 10–18mm long, carried in axillary pairs with leaf-like bracts; calyx has a shield-shaped flap on upper side; two-lipped corolla has a curved tube. *Flowering:* June– September. *Distribution:* Almost throughout Europe; wet places. **Lesser Skullcap** (*S. minor*) is smaller, 10–20cm, with usually untoothed leaves 8–20mm long. Pink flowers are 6–10mm long; corolla tube is almost straight. *Flowering:* July–October. *Distribution:* Mainly western Europe; damp, heathy places.

Prasium majus Up to 100cm A small shrub with ovate to ovate-lanceolate, bluntly toothed leaves 20–50mm long. White or lilac flowers are 17–20mm long, in axillary pairs towards the branch- tips; upper lip of corolla oblong, hooded; lower lip three-lobed. Fruits are fleshy berry-like nutlets, 3–4mm across, enclosed in enlarged, persistent calyx. *Flowering:* February–June. *Distribution:* Mediterranean region; bushy and rocky places.

White Horehound *Marrubium vulgare* 30–60cm An erect, white-felty perennial with opposite, circular to broadly ovate, wrinkled leaves 15–40mm long, bluntly toothed at the margins; upper surface is greyish and less hairy than lower. White flowers are 15mm long, borne in dense whorls in the axils of paired, leaf-like bracts; calyx tube has ten tiny, hooked teeth at the rim. *Flowering:* April–October. *Distribution:* Most of Europe; dry ground, waste areas. **M. peregrinum** is whitish- or yellowish-hairy with oblong or obovate leaves. Calyx tube has only five teeth. *Flowering:* June–August. *Distribution:* Mainly east-central and south-eastern Europe; dry, open places.

Bastard Balm *Melittis melissophyllum* 20–70cm An erect, strong-smelling perennial with hairy stems bearing opposite, oblong to ovate, toothed leaves 20–150mm long. White, pink, purple or parti-coloured flowers are 25–40mm long, carried in whorls of two to six in the axils of leaf-like bracts; upper lip of corolla is weakly hooded; lower lip is three-lobed . *Flowering:* May–July. *Distribution:* Western, central and southern Europe; open woodland, hedges and shady, rocky places.

Jerusalem Sage *Phlomis fruticosa* Up to 130cm A whitish- to yellowish-hairy, sage-like shrub with opposite elliptical to lanceolate-ovate leaves 30–90mm long. Very showy, bright yellow flowers are 23–35mm long, carried in dense whorls of up to 36 towards the stem tips; upper lip of corolla is markedly hooded. *Flowering:* March–June. *Distribution:* Mediterranean region from Sardinia eastwards; rocky and bushy places. **Tuberous Jerusalem Sage** (*P. tuberosa*) is a herbaceous perennial reaching 150cm. Flowers are purple or pink. *Flowering:* May–July. *Distribution:* Central and south-eastern Europe; in herbaceous vegetation.

Downy Hemp-nettle *Galeopsis segetum* Up to 50cm A softly hairy, branching annual with opposite, lanceolate to ovate, toothed leaves. Pale yellow or rarely lilac, purple-blotched two-lipped flowers are 25–30mm long, carried in whorls. *Flowering:* July–September. *Distribution:* Central Europe and parts of western Europe; disturbed ground, avoiding lime-rich soils. **Large-flowered Hemp-nettle** (*G. speciosa*) is taller, to 100cm, with stems swollen at nodes. Corolla normally has a large, purple blotch on lower lip. *Flowering:* July–September. *Distribution:* Most of Europe except much of the south; disturbed ground.

Skullcap

Prasium majus

White Horehound

Bastard Balm

Jerusalem Sage

Downy Hemp-nettle

Red Hemp-nettle

Large Red Dead-
nettle

Spotted Dead-nettle

Hen-bit Dead-nettle

Common Hemp-nettle *Galeopsis tetrahit* Up to 50cm A roughly hairy, branching annual with stems swollen at nodes, bearing opposite lanceolate to broadly ovate, toothed leaves. Whorled flowers are two-lipped, 15–20mm long, pink, rarely white or pale yellow, with darker markings. *Flowering:* July–September. *Distribution:* Most of Europe; open woodland, heaths, fens and disturbed ground. **Red Hemp-nettle** (*G. angustifolia*) is softly hairy, with stems barely swollen at nodes. Leaves are narrow. Deep reddish-pink flowers have a yellow-blotched lower lip. *Flowering:* July–October. *Distribution:* Western, central and southern Europe; disturbed ground.

Lamium garganicum Up to 50cm A perennial with opposite, heart-shaped, hairy, toothed leaves up to 70 x 40mm. Pink to purple, often striped and mottled flowers are 25–40mm long, carried in loose whorls; slender corolla tube 15–25mm; upper and lower lips 10–15mm; anthers are hairy. *Flowering:* April–June. *Distribution:* Mountains of southern Europe; rocky places. **Large Red Dead-nettle** (*L. orvala*) is larger, to 100cm, with triangular-ovate leaves 40–150mm long. Flowers are pink to dark purple; anthers are hairless. *Flowering:* April–July. *Distribution:* South- central and adjacent southern Europe; scrub.

White Dead-nettle *Lamium album* 20–80cm A hairy, slightly aromatic perennial with creeping, underground stems and erect, flowering shoots. Opposite leaves are ovate or ovate-oblong, toothed, 25–120mm long. White flowers are 20–25mm long, with hooded upper lip, carried in rather dense whorls. *Flowering:* March–December. *Distribution:* Most of Europe but rare in the south; hedges, roadsides, waste areas. **Spotted Dead-nettle** (*L. maculatum*) is strongly aromatic and leaves often have pale central zone. Flowers are usually pinkish-purple. *Flowering:* April–October. *Distribution:* Mainly central and southern Europe; open woodland, waste areas.

Red Dead-nettle *Lamium purpureum* Up to 40cm A softly hairy, branching annual, often tinged with purple. Opposite leaves and bracts are ovate or ovate- orbicular, 10–50mm long, toothed at margins and carried on distinct stalks. Whorled, pinkish-purple flowers are 10–18mm long; upper lip 4–6mm. Flowering: All year. Distribution: Almost throughout Europe; disturbed ground. **Cut-leaved Dead-nettle** (*L. hybridum*) has leaves and bracts irregularly and more deeply toothed. *Flowering:* March–October. *Distribution:* Most of Europe except the south-east. **Henbit Dead-nettle** (*L. amplexicaule*) has bracts wider than long, to 30 x 40mm, usually stalkless and often clasping the stem, forming a ruff below each whorl of flowers. *Flowering:* March–October. *Distribution:* Almost throughout Europe.

Yellow Archangel *Lamiastrum galeobdolon* 15–60cm A hairy perennial with long, leafy, creeping runners and erect, flowering stems. Opposite leaves are ovate to almost circular, coarsely toothed, 30–80mm long. Whorled, bright yellow flowers are 14–25mm long; upper lip hooded; lower lip with brownish markings. *Flowering:* May–June. *Distribution:* Most of Europe; woodland and other shady places.

Motherwort *Leonurus cardiaca* 30–200cm An erect, strongly scented perennial opposite, with stalked leaves 3–12cm, cut into three to seven, radiating, toothed lobes. White, pale pink, or purple-spotted flowers are 8–12mm long, carried in compact whorls; back of upper lip densely hairy. *Flowering:* July–September. *Distribution:* Most of Europe; hedges, waste areas.

Common Hemp-nettle

Lamium garganicum

White Dead-nettle

Red Dead-nettle

Yellow Archangel

Motherwort

Black Horehound *Ballota nigra* Up to 130cm A hairy, straggling perennial with strong, unpleasant odour when handled. Opposite leaves are ovate or ovate-oblong, bluntly toothed, up to 80 x 60mm. Two-lipped, lilac, pink or white flowers are 7–13mm long, carried in whorls. *Flowering:* June–September. *Distribution:* Most of Europe; hedges, waste areas.

Hedge Woundwort *Stachys sylvatica* 30–120cm A hairy, strong-smelling perennial. Opposite leaves are heart-shaped, pointed, 40–140mm long, toothed at margins. Dull reddish-purple flowers are carried in whorls grouped into spikes; corollas are 13–18mm long with white markings. *Flowering:* June–October. *Distribution:* Most of Europe but rare in the Mediterranean region; woodland, hedges and other shady places. **Marsh Woundwort** (*S. palustris*) is nearly odourless, with oblong shortly stalked or stalkless leaves. Flowers are pale pinkish-purple. *Flowering:* July–September. *Distribution:* as Hedge Woundwort; damp places.

Marsh Woundwort

Field Woundwort *Stachys arvensis* 10–40cm An erect or sprawling, hairy annual with opposite heart-shaped, bluntly toothed leaves 10–40mm long. White, pale pink or purple flowers are 6–8mm long, carried in whorls in the axils of leaf-like bracts towards the stem tips. *Flowering:* April–November. *Distribution:* Western, central and southern Europe; disturbed, often sandy ground, avoiding lime-rich soils. **Annual Woundwort** (*S. annua*) has lanceolate, pointed leaves and white or pale yellow flowers 10–16mm long; corolla sometimes has red spots. *Flowering:* June–October. *Distribution:* Most of Europe except the north; disturbed ground.

Annual Woundwort

Ground-ivy *Glechoma hederacea* Up to 50cm A creeping, rooting, hairy, often purplish-tinged perennial with opposite, stalked, nearly orbicular to kidney- shaped leaves up to 35 x 40mm. Ascending shoots bear usually pairs of pale violet flowers in the axils of leaf-like bracts; corollas are 15–22mm long, with purple spots on lower lip. *Flowering:* March–June. *Distribution:* Almost throughout Europe; woodland, hedges, and sparse grassland. **G. hirsuta** is more hairy, with leaves 25–50 x 25–60mm. Flowers are 20–30mm long, pale blue with white spots on lower lip. *Flowering:* April–May. *Distribution:* East-central and south-eastern Europe; woodland and scrub.

Glechoma hirsuta: calyx

Selfheal *Prunella vulgaris* Up to 50cm A creeping, mat-forming perennial with upright, flowering stems. Opposite leaves are ovate to rhombic, sometimes bluntly toothed, up to 5cm long. Deep violet-blue, two-lipped flowers are 13–15mm long, carried together with purplish bracts in dense, shortly cylindrical, terminal heads with a a pair of leaves directly below. *Flowering:* March–November. *Distribution:* Almost throughout Europe; woodland, grassland, waste areas. **Large Selfheal** (*P. grandiflora*) has flower heads without a pair of leaves directly below. Flowers are larger, 25–30mm long; corolla tube is whitish; lips are deep violet. *Flowering:* June–September. *Distribution:* Central and southern Europe.

Large Selfheal

Cut-leaved Selfheal *Prunella laciniata* Up to 30cm A creeping, hairy perennial with ascending flowering stems, similar to Selfheal but with upper leaves deeply pinnately lobed. Yellowish-white flowers are 15–17mm long, carried in dense, terminal heads. Plants with purplish flowers are hybrids with Selfheal and occur where the two grow in proximity. *Flowering:* April–October. *Distribution:* Western, central and southern Europe, naturalised in Britain; grassy and bare places, often on lime-rich soils.

Black Horehound

Hedge Woundwort

Field Woundwort

Ground-ivy

Selfheal

Cut-leaved Selfheal

Basil Thyme *Acinos arvensis* Up to 40cm A sprawling, hairy, faintly aromatic or odourless annual. Opposite leaves are lanceolate to ovate, 8–15mm long, sometimes slightly toothed. Violet, two-lipped flowers are 7–10mm long, with white markings on the lower lip, in whorls of three to eight towards the stem tips. Curved calyx tube is swollen at base. *Flowering:* May–September. *Distribution:* Most of Europe; grassy places, bare ground and rocks, preferring lime-rich conditions.

Wild Basil *Clinopodium vulgare* 30–80cm A softly hairy, faintly scented, erect perennial with opposite, ovate-lanceolate or ovate, shallowly toothed leaves 20–65mm long. Pinkish-purple flowers are 12–22mm long, crowded with bristle-like bracteoles into dense whorls towards the stem tips. *Flowering:* May–September. *Distribution:* Almost all Europe; scrub, grassy places, preferring lime-rich soils. **Wood Calamint** (*Calamintha sylvatica* subsp. *sylvatica*) is mint-scented, with coarsely toothed leaves and loosely whorled, lilac flowers. *Flowering:* August–September. *Distribution:* Western and south-central Europe; scrub, hedges. **Common Calamint** (*C. sylvatica* subsp. *ascendens*) has shallowly toothed leaves 20–40mm long. Flowers are 10–16mm long, pale pink, with fine purple dots. *Flowering:* July–September. *Distribution:* Western, south-central and southern Europe.

Winter Savory

Hyssop *Hyssopus officinalis* 20–60cm An almost hairless, aromatic perennial with erect stems woody at base and bearing opposite linear to oblong, blunt leaves 10–50mm. Sparsely whorled, two–lipped, blue or violet flowers are 7–12mm, carried in slender, spikes at the stem tips. *Flowering:* July–September. *Distribution:* South-central, eastern and southern Europe; dry places. **Winter Savory** (*Satureja montana*) is a semi-evergreen dwarf shrub with pointed, rather leathery leaves 5–30mm, hairy at margins. Pale pink or white flowers are 6–12mm, carried in spike-like heads. *Flowering:* July–October. *Distribution:* Southern Europe; dry places.

Marjoram *Origanum vulgare* Up to 90cm An erect, hairy, woody-based perennial with opposite, ovate leaves 10–40mm long. Two-lipped, white or purplish-pink flowers are 4–7mm long, densely crowded with the bracts into terminal, flat-topped clusters. *Flowering:* April–September. *Distribution:* Most of Europe; scrub, grassland and rocky places, on lime-rich soils.

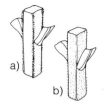

a) Large Thyme
b) Breckland Thyme

Wild Thyme *Thymus polytrichus* Up to 10cm An aromatic, creeping, mat-forming perennial with small, opposite, obovate to nearly circular leaves. Flowering shoots are bluntly four-angled, hairy all round or on two opposite faces. Small, two-lipped, purple flowers are crowded into dense, terminal heads. *Flowering:* April–August. *Distribution:* Western, central and southern Europe; dry grassland, heaths, sand-dunes and rocks. **Breckland Thyme** (*T. serpyllum*) has flowering stems almost circular in cross-section, hairy all round. Leaves are linear to elliptical. *Flowering:* July–August. *Distribution:* Mainly northern and central Europe. **Large Thyme** (*T. pulegioides*) is larger and taller, to 25cm, not creeping. Flowering stems are hairy on the angles only. *Flowering:* July–August. *Distribution:* Most of Europe.

Gipsywort *Lycopus europaeus* 20–120cm An erect, hairy perennial with opposite, ovate-lanceolate or elliptical, deeply pinnately lobed, leaves 30–100mm long. Small, white, purple-spotted flowers, about 4mm long, are carried in whorls; corolla has a short tube and four lobes, the uppermost broadest. *Flowering:* June–September. *Distribution:* Most of Europe; wet places.

Basil Thyme

Wild Basil

Hyssop

Marjoram

Wild Thyme

Gipsywort

Whorled Mint

Peppermint

Round-leaved Mint

Corn Mint *Mentha arvensis* Up to 60cm An ascending to erect, hairy perennial with a rather acrid, sickly scent when bruised. Opposite leaves are elliptic-lanceolate to broadly ovate, 20–50mm long. Flowering stems usually tipped with leaves. Lilac or white flowers in dense, axillary whorls; calyces are 1.5–2.5mm long, with short, triangular teeth; stamens protrude noticeably from four-lobed corollas. *Flowering:* May–October. *Distribution:* Most of Europe; disturbed, damp ground. **Whorled Mint** (*M. x verticillata*) is the hybrid with Water Mint, differing in its longer calyx teeth and stamens not protruding. *Flowering:* July–September. *Distribution:* Most of Europe.

Water Mint *Mentha aquatica* 20–90cm An erect, strongly aromatic perennial with creeping underground stems. Opposite leaves are ovate to ovate-lanceolate, 30–90mm long, often purplish. Lilac flowers are densely crowded into terminal heads up to 20mm across, sometimes separated into distinct whorls below; stamens protrude from four-lobed corollas. *Flowering:* July–October. *Distribution:* Almost throughout Europe; wet places. **Peppermint** (*M. x piperita*) is the hybrid with Spear Mint, differing in its more pungent scent, narrower leaves and usually longer, more pointed flower heads with no protruding stamens. *Flowering:* July–September. *Distribution:* Widespread in Europe, mostly as a garden escape; wet places.

Horse Mint *Mentha longifolia* 40–120cm An erect, pale-hairy perennial with a musty scent. Opposite leaves are usually oblong-elliptical, pointed, toothed, 50– 90mm long. Whorls of lilac or white flowers are crowded into terminal, pointed spikes 40–100mm long. *Flowering:* August–September. *Distribution:* Most of Europe; wet places. **Spear Mint** (*M. spicata*) usually has a strong, sweet scent. Leaves are lanceolate to lanceolate-ovate, sometimes hairless. *Flowering:* July–October. *Distribution:* Naturalised from cultivation in much of Europe; wet places. **Round-leaved Mint** (*M. suaveolens*) is apple-scented, with ovate-oblong to nearly circular, wrinkled leaves, hairy on upper surface, densely white-woolly underneath. *Flowering:* July–September. *Distribution:* Western and southern Europe; wet places.

Pennyroyal *Mentha pulegium* 10–40cm A creeping, mat-forming to ascending perennial with a pungent Peppermint-like scent. Opposite leaves are elliptical, hairy or almost hairless, 8–30mm long. Lilac flowers are 4.5–6mm long, in dense whorls; corolla four-lobed. *Flowering:* June–October. *Distribution:* Western, central and southern Europe; damp, bare ground.

Common Lavender *Lavandula angustifolia* Up to 100cm A much-branched, aromatic, evergreen shrub with twigs densely clad with lanceolate, oblong or linear leaves 20–40mm long, initially white-hairy, later becoming green. Lavender-blue or purplish two-lipped flowers are 10–12mm long, crowded into dense, narrowly cylindrical spikes 20–80mm long, at the tips of long, slender, almost leafless stems. *Flowering:* June–September. *Distribution:* Mediterranean region; dry, stony hillsides.

French Lavender *Lavandula stoechas* Up to 100cm A greyish, evergreen shrub similar to Common Lavender but with a rich, eucalyptus-like scent and distinctive, quadrangular flower spikes 20–30mm long, at tips of leafy twigs. Bracts are tightly overlapping, those at tips of spikes very long, showy, purple and petal-like. Dark purple flowers are 6–8mm long, emerging along the four angles of the heads. *Flowering:* February–June. *Distribution:* Mediterranean region; garigue and maquis scrub, avoiding lime-rich soils.

Corn Mint

Water Mint

Horse Mint

Pennyroyal

Common Lavender

French Lavender

Rosemary *Rosmarinus officinalis* Up to 200cm A much-branched, aromatic, evergreen shrub with opposite, linear, leathery leaves 15–40mm long, dark green on upper surface and white-hairy beneath. Pale blue flowers are 10–12mm long, carried in spike-like, axillary clusters; upper lip of corolla very concave; stamens two. *Flowering:* All year. *Distribution:* Native in the Mediterranean region; planted elsewhere in southern Europe for ornament and its aromatic oil; dry scrub.

Meadow Clary *Salvia pratensis* Up to 100cm An erect, branching, hairy perennial with opposite, long-stalked, ovate or ovate-oblong, wrinkled, doubly toothed basal leaves 70–150cm long. Upper leaves are smaller and stalkless. Violet-blue flowers are 20–30mm long, carried in whorls of four to six in narrow, rather lax, terminal spires; corolla has sickle-shaped, hooded upper lip and spreading lower lip; stamens two. *Flowering:* June–July. *Distribution:* Most of Europe; hedges and grassland on lime-rich soils.

Wild Clary *Salvia verbenaca* 10–80cm Resembles Meadow Clary but is smaller, with basal leaves 40–120mm long, deeply cut into toothed lobes. Blue, lilac or violet flowers are 6–10mm long. *Flowering:* April–September. *Distribution:* Western and southern Europe; grassland, disturbed ground.

Chinese Teaplant *Lycium chinense* Up to 350cm A deciduous shrub with arching grey-white stems bearing lanceolate to ovate leaves 10–140mm long, usually widest below middle. Purple and yellow, broadly funnel-shaped flowers are 10–15mm long; corolla-lobes 5–8mm long. Berries ripen red. *Flowering:* August–October. *Distribution:* Native to China, planted for hedges and locally naturalised in Europe. **Duke of Argyll's Teaplant** (*L. barbarum*) is similar but somewhat spiny; leaves are very narrowly elliptical to narrowly lanceolate, usually widest at middle. Lilac-purple flowers are about 9mm long, becoming brownish; corolla lobes about 4mm long. *Flowering:* May–August. *Distribution:* Native to China, planted for hedges and widely naturalised in Europe.

Duke of Argyll's Teaplant

Deadly Nightshade *Atropa bella-donna* 50–150cm A stout, erect, herbaceous but shrubby-looking perennial with stems much branched in upper part. Leaves are .ovate, pointed, up to 200mm long. Brownish-violet or greenish, bell-shaped flowers are 25–30mm long, carried singly on short stalks in the upper axils; corolla lobes are spreading or slightly recurved. Shiny, black, juicy berries 15–20mm across, backed by spreading, triangular, persistent calyx lobes. Whole plant is extremely poisonous. *Flowering:* June–October. *Distribution:* Western, central and southern Europe; woods, scrub, rocky places, mainly in mountains, preferring lime-rich soils; also naturalised as a relic of cultivation for medicinal use.

White Henbane *Hyoscyamus albus* 30–90cm A stickily hairy annual, biennial or perennial with erect, branching stems. Leaves are orbicular-ovate, all stalked, 40–100mm long, deeply incised with broad, rounded teeth. Yellowish-white flowers are 30mm long, tubular-bell-shaped with a greenish or purplish throat, carried in dense sprays. Fruits are capsules, dry when ripe. *Flowering:* March–July. *Distribution:* Southern Europe; waste ground with soil unusually rich in nutrients. **Henbane** (*H. niger*) is similar but leaves are larger, 150–200cm long, those on the stems stalkless and clasping. Pale yellow flowers usually have purple veins and throat. *Flowering:* May–September. *Distribution:* Almost all Europe; in similar habitats to White Henbane.

Henbane

Rosemary

Meadow Clary

Wild Clary

Chinese Teaplant

Deadly Nightshade

White Henbane

Withania somnifera 60–120cm An erect, shrubby, branching, greyish-hairy perennial. Stalked leaves are ovate to obovate or oblong, 30–100mm long. Yellowish-green, bell-shaped flowers are about 5mm long, carried in axillary clusters of four to six. Shining berries 5–8mm across, ripen red, each surrounded by the inflated, persistent calyx. *Flowering:* April–May. *Distribution:* Mediterranean region; roadsides, scrub and waste areas.

Bittersweet *Solanum dulcamara* 30–200cm A scrambling, branching perennial with stems becoming woody. Leaves are ovate, heart- or arrow-shaped, pointed, 50–90mm long, sometimes pinnately cut into a few lobes at base. Dark purple flowers are 10–15mm across, carried in loose, branching sprays of ten to 25; corollas have five recurved, lanceolate lobes; yellow anthers form a conical, central column. Shiny, juicy, ovoid berries 10–15mm long, ripen red. *Flowering:* May–September. *Distribution:* Most of Europe; damp woodland, hedges, maritime shingle and waste areas.

Black Nightshade *Solanum nigrum* Up to 70cm A branching annual with ovate-rhombic to lanceolate leaves 25–70mm long. White flowers are similar in form to those of Bittersweet, carried in sprays of five to ten; corollas are 10–14mm across; yellow anthers form a cone. Globose berries 6–10mm across, ripen dull black. *Flowering:* January–October. *Distribution:* Almost throughout Europe; disturbed ground. **Hairy Nightshade** (*Solanum villosum*) is very similar but has flowers in sprays of three to five. Fruits ripen red, orange or yellow. *Flowering:* February–June. *Distribution:* Most of Europe, but only naturalised in the north; disturbed ground.

Hairy Nightshade

Solanum linnaeanum 50–300cm A stout, erect, much-branched shrub bearing many yellowish prickles on stems and leaf veins. Leaves are 50–130mm long, deeply pinnately cut into rounded, wavy-edged lobes. Pale violet, rounded and weakly five-angled corollas are 25–30mm across; anthers form cone. Tomato-like, globose berries are 20–30mm across, green with paler marbling, ripening yellow. *Flowering:* May–August. *Distribution:* Native to Africa, naturalised in southern Europe; waste areas, maritime sands.

Mandrake *Mandragora autumnalis* Up to 15cm A rosette-forming perennial with a stout tap-root producing dark green, wrinkled, lanceolate leaves up to 300mm long, held flat against the ground. Pale violet, bell-shaped flowers are 25–40mm long, with broadly triangular lobes, carried singly on slender stalks from centre of rosette. Fruits are tomato-like, ellipsoid berries up to 30mm long, ripening yellow. *Flowering:* October–April. *Distribution:* Mediterranean region; deep soil- pockets in rocky places. ***M. officinarum*** is similar but has greenish-white flowers up to 25mm long with narrowly triangular lobes. Fruits are globose. *Distribution:* Endemic to northern Italy and western Yugoslavia; rocky places.

Mandrake officinarum

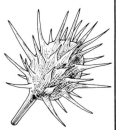

Thorn-apple *Datura stramonium* 50–200cm A stout, erect annual with ovate to elliptical, pointed, coarsely toothed leaves 50–180mm long. White or purple, trumpet-shaped flowers are 50–100mm long; calyx teeth are 5–10mm long, unequal. Fruits are ovoid capsules 35–70mm long, usually covered with slender, equal spines up to 15mm long. *Flowering:* July–October. *Distribution:* Native in America, naturalised through most of Europe; disturbed ground. **Angels'-trumpets** (*D. ferox*) has calyx-teeth 3–5mm long, almost equal. Capsules have stout, conical, unequal spines 10–30mm long. *Distribution:* Native in eastern Asia; naturalised from cultivation in Mediterranean region.

Angels'-trumpets: fruit

Withania somnifera

Bittersweet

Black Nightshade

Solanum linnaeanum

Mandrake

Thorn-apple

Musk

Dense-flowered
Mullein

Monkeyflower *Mimulus guttatus* Up to 50cm A creeping perennial, with ascending or upright, hollow stems. Opposite leaves are ovate, blunt-tipped, toothed, the lowest stalked. Flowers are 40 x 30mm, two-lipped with small red spots in the throat, on stalks in a three- to seven-flowered spike. *Flowering:* June–September. *Distribution:* A plant of western North America, naturalised in most of Europe; by streams and water. **Musk** (*M. moschatus*), up to 35cm, is smaller, stickily hairy, musky scented; flowers 20 x 10mm, pale yellow sometimes with red stripes at the throat. *Flowering:* June–September. *Distribution:* From western North America, locally naturalised in all but eastern Europe, and as an escape from cultivation; damp, shady places.

Purple Mullein *Verbascum phoeniceum* Up to 100cm A perennial, stickily hairy on upper parts of stems. Basal leaves are ovate, wavy-edged; stems leaves small, few. Flowers are 20–30mm across, purple; stamens with violet hairs on the filaments; flowering spike usually unbranched. *Flowering:* June–August. *Distribution:* South-eastern and east-central Europe, northwards to central Russia, westwards to Germany; waste places, often naturalised from cultivation.

Orange Mullein *Verbascum phlomoides* Up to 120cm A biennial plant covered in grey or white down; basal leaves elliptical; stem leaves ovate to lanceolate, toothed; bracts 9–15mm. Flowers are 20–55mm, yellow- or orange-yellow in crowded, branched spikes; upper three stamens with white or yellow hairs on the filaments. *Flowering:* June–August. *Distribution:* Most of Europe, apart from the north; dry, grassy or waste places. **Dense-flowered Mullein** (*V. densiflorum*) is very similar, with yellow-grey down; stem leaves have stalks running down on to the stems; bracts 15–40mm, the bases also running down the stems. *Flowering:* June–August. *Distribution:* Most of Europe, northwards to the Netherlands, southern Sweden and central Russia, rarer in the west; dry, grassy or bare areas.

Great Mullein *Verbascum thapsus* Up to 200cm A biennial, covered in dense white or greyish down. Basal leaves are up to 500mm, elliptical; stem leaves have stalks running down on to the winged stems. Flowers are 12–35mm across, yellow, more or less flat, in a crowded unbranched spike; three upper stamens with white hairs on filaments. *Flowering:* June–August. *Distribution:* Most of Europe, except the far north and much of the Balkans; open scrub and dry bare places.

White Mullein *Verbascum lychnitis* Up to 150cm. A downy-grey biennial with ovate to oblong-lanceolate toothed basal leaves, their bases wedge-shaped basally, green above, downy underneath. Flowers are 12–20mm across, white, in a branched spike, with linear or lanceolate bracts 8–15 mm long; stamens all with yellow or white hairs on filaments. *Flowering:* June–September. *Distribution:* Europe southwards from England and central Russia, rare in the Mediterranean; dry, bare or grassy areas.

Dark Mullein *Verbascum nigrum* Up to 100cm A sparsely hairy perennial, with ridged stems; basal leaves dark green, ovate to oblong, heart-shaped at the base, wavy-edged. Flowers are 18–25mm across, yellow, in a short-branched spike, with linear bracts, 4–15 mm long; stamens all with filaments covered in violet hairs. *Flowering:* June–September. *Distribution:* England, Scandanavia and northern Russia, southwards to northern Spain, Italy and Greece, and the Ukraine; dry grassy places.

Monkeyflower

Purple Mullein

Orange Mullein

Great Mullein

White Mullein

Dark Mullein

Scrophularia peregrina Up to 90cm A more or less hairless annual with a square stem. Leaves are 100 x 60mm, ovate, toothed, blunt-tipped, usually heart-shaped at the base. Two-lipped flowers are 6–9mm across, dark red or purple-brown, in a branched spike with leaf-like bracts. *Flowering:* April–June. *Distribution:* Native to the Mediterranean and Portugal, a casual further north; scrubland, cultivated and waste ground.

Common Figwort *Scrophularia nodosa* Up to 150cm An unpleasant smelling, hairless perennial, with a square and sometimes winged stem. Opposite leaves are up to 120 x 70mm, ovate to ovate-lanceolate, pointed, doubly toothed, usually heart-shaped at the base. Two-lipped flowers are 7–10mm across, green with purple-brown upper lips, in branched spikes with leaf-like bracts; calyx lobes with narrow, papery margins. *Flowering:* June–September. *Distribution:* Most of Europe; woods, damp shady places.

Water Figwort *Scrophularia auriculata* Up to 100cm An occasionally downy perennial with winged stems. Opposite leaves are 50–250 mm long, ovate to elliptical, with two small, toothed lobes at the base. Two-lipped flowers are 5–9mm across, greenish with purple-brown upper lips, in branched spikes; bracts linear; toothed calyx lobes with broad, papery margins. *Flowering:* June–September. *Distribution:* Western Europe, eastwards to Germany, Italy and Crete; river banks, damp places. **Green Figwort** (*S. umbrosa*) is very similar, but has more broadly-winged stems, and leaves lacking the basal lobes; flowers olive-brown; bracts leaf-like. *Flowering:* June–September. *Distribution:* Scotland, Denmark and Latvia southwards, but absent from parts of western Europe.

Green Figwort

Scrophularia ramosissima

French Figwort *Scrophularia canina* Up to 60cm A hairless, branched perennial, with opposite, toothed, pinnately-lobed leaves 10–18mm long. Two-lipped flowers 4–9mm across, dark purplish-red, in clusters of up to 25 in a loose spike, with small bracts; flower stalks glandular-hairy. *Flowering:* June–August. *Distribution:* Southern and south-central Europe; dry, bare and waste places. **S. ramosissima** is similar, but has numerous stiff branches, and flowers about 4mm with persistent, spiny stalks. *Flowering:* May–August. *Distribution:* Northern Mediterranean; maritime sand and other dry areas.

Hedge–hyssop *Gratiola officinalis* Up to 50cm A perennial with hollow stems, creeping and rooting at the base, erect and four-angled above. Opposite leaves are 20–50mm long, narrow, toothed and half clasping the stem. Flowers are solitary in leaf axils; corolla somewhat two-lipped, white with purplish veins. *Flowering:* June–August. *Distribution:* Europe north to Holland, Estonia and the southern Urals; wet, grassy places, ditches.

Daisy-leaved Toadflax *Anarrhinum bellidifolium* Up to 80cm A hairless biennial or perennial. Basal leaves are 80 x 30 mm, obovate to elliptic-lanceolate, coarsely toothed, blunt-tipped and tapering to the stalk; stem-leaves alternate, divided into three to five narrow segments. Two-lipped flowers are 4–5mm, lilac to blue with a slender, curved spur; calyx lobes narrowly triangular. *Flowering:* March–August. *Distribution:* South-western Europe to France, Germany and Italy; rocks, walls and bare places. **A. duriminium** is glandular-downy, with smaller, basal leaves; stem leaves divided into three; flowers 6mm, pale yellow or cream, in dense, often branched spikes; calyx lobes linear-lanceolate, pointed. *Flowering:* March–July. *Distribution:* Iberian Peninsula; dry places.

Anarrhinum duriminium

Scrophularia peregrina

Common Figwort

Water Figwort

French Figwort

Hedge-hyssop

Daisy-leaved Toadflax

Snapdragon *Antirrhinum majus* Up to 30–80cm An upright or straggling perennial, woody at the base and becoming tattered with age. Leaves are opposite below, alternate above, linear to ovate, up to 12 times as long as wide, wedge-shaped at the base. Two-lipped flowers are 25–45 mm, usually red, purple or pink in a terminal spike, with ovate bracts. *Flowering:* May–October. *Distribution:* South-western Europe, eastwards to Sicily, widely grown in gardens and extensively naturalised; dry areas, rocks and walls.

Trailing Snapdragon *Asarina procumbens* Up to 60 cm A stickily hairy, prostrate perennial, woody at the base; Leaves are up to 50 x 60cm, ovate or heart-shaped, toothed, sometimes palmately-lobed. Two-lipped flowers are 30–35mm, the tube whitish, often purple-veined, the lips yellow, solitary in the leaf axils, on stalks up to 20mm long; calyx deeply divided, the lobes lanceolate and unequal. *Flowering:* April–September. *Distribution:* Southern France and north-eastern Spain; shady and stony places, usually in mountains.

Misopates calycinum

Lesser Snapdragon *Misopates orontium* Up to 50cm Resembling a smaller and annual Snapdragon but with linear to oblong-elliptical, opposite or alternate leaves. Flowers are 10–15mm, usually pink, in a loose, downy spike, with leaf- like bracts decreasing in size towards the top of the stem; calyx lobes linear. *Flowering:* July–October. *Distribution:* South-western and central Europe, probably introduced in much of central Europe and naturalised further north; cultivated and bare areas. **M. calycinum** is similar, but usually hairless, with white flowers 18–25 mm, in a dense spike which elongates in fruit. *Flowering:* May–August. *Distribution:* Western Mediterranean to Portugal; on cultivated land and other dry open habitats.

Chaenorhinum rubrifolium: fruit

Small Toadflax *Chaenorhinum minus* Up to 40cm A downy, greyish, slender annual. Leaves are 5–35mm, linear or oblong-lanceolate, blunt-tipped, at least the lower opposite. Two-lipped flowers are 5–9mm, solitary in axils of alternate leaves, pale purple with a short blunt spur. *Flowering:* May–October. *Distribution:* Most of Europe, but a doubtful native in much of the north; a weed of cultivated land and bare areas. **C. rubrifolium** has ovate leaves, the lowest red on the undersides and usually in a basal rosette, the upper green on both sides; flowers up to 20mm, yellow, blue, violet or lilac, the inside of the lower lip usually yellow. *Flowering:* April–October. *Distribution:* Mediterranean, mainly in the west; dry areas.

Pale Toadflax *Linaria repens* Up to 120cm A greyish, hairless, upright perennial, usually branched. Whorled leaves are crowded on the stems, linear to linear-lanceolate, pointed. Branched spikes bear two-lipped flowers are 8–15mm, pale lilac or white, with violet veins and a straight spur 3–5mm long; calyx lobes 2–3mm. *Flowering:* June–September. *Distribution:* Northern Spain and Italy to north-west Germany, often naturalised in north-west and central Europe; dry, grassy or bare areas.

Jersey Toadflax *Linaria pelisseriana* Up to 50cm An annual with usually unbranched stems and linear, alternate or whorled leaves. Flowers in dense spikes are two-lipped, 15–20mm, purple-violet, whitish on the inside, with a 7–9mm spur; upper lip very long, with parallel lobes; calyx lobes 4–5mm, linear-lanceolate, more or less equal. *Flowering:* June–August. *Distribution:* Mediterranean and western Europe, northwards to the Channel Islands; cultivated, bare or waste ground.

Snapdragon

Trailing Snapdragon

Lesser Snapdragon

Small Toadflax

Pale Toadflax

Jersey Toadflax

Linaria angustissima

Common Toadflax *Linaria vulgaris* Up to 90cm A greyish, more or less hairless perennial, occasionally branched. Alternate leaves are linear, elliptical or linear-lanceolate, crowded. Flowering spike dense, branched, the flowers two- lipped, 25–35mm, pale or bright yellow, the lower lip orange-spotted; stout spur 10–13mm. *Flowering:* June–October. *Distribution:* Most of Europe apart from the far north and much of the Mediterranean; bare areas and waste ground. **L. angustissima** is similar, but with narrower leaves; flowers 15–20mm, with a spur up to 10mm. *Flowering:* June–October. *Distribution:* Southern and east-central Europe, but absent from much of the Mediterranean; bare areas and dry ground.

Purple Toadflax *Linaria purpurea* Up to 90cm Like a large, perennial Jersey Toadflax with linear, pointed, whorled or alternate leaves. Two-lipped flowers are 9–12 mm, purple-violet, with a curved spur 5 mm long. *Flowering:* June–August. *Distribution:* Central and southern Italy and Sicily, frequently naturalised elsewhere; dry, bare or waste ground, and walls.

Alpine Toadflax *Linaria alpina* Up to 25cm A sprawling, grey-green annual, with whorled, linear or oblong-lanceolate leaves. Flowering spike with three to 15 two-lipped flowers each 13–22mm, violet or occasionally yellow, white or pink, yellow inside, with an 8–10mm spur; calyx lobes blunt. *Flowering:* May–August. *Distribution:* Mountains of central and southern Europe; on scree, rocks and river gravel, from 1500–3800m.

Ivy-leaved Toadflax *Cymbalaria muralis* Up to 60 cm A trailing perennial, with ivy-like, five- to nine-lobed leaves, the lobes triangular. Two-lipped flowers are 9–15mm, lilac or violet with a yellow spot and a 1.5–3mm spur, solitary on long stalks in the leaf axils. *Flowering:* April–October. *Distribution:* Native among shady rocks and woods in the southern Alps, western Yugoslavia, Italy and Sicily, but widely naturalised throughout much of Europe on walls or bare places.

Sharp-leaved Fluellen

Round-leaved Fluellen *Kickxia spuria* Up to 50cm A downy-hairy, sprawling annual, with broadly ovate lower leaves, and ovate-lanceolate or heart-shaped upper leaves. Two-lipped flowers are solitary on hairy stalks in the leaf axils, each 10–15mm, yellow, with a purple upper lip and a curved spur. *Flowering:* July–October. *Distribution:* Southern, central and western Europe to Poland, the Netherlands and England, naturalised further north; cultivated or bare land. **Sharp-leaved Fluellen** (*K. elatine*) has usually arrow-shaped leaves, yellowish or bluish flowers 7–15mm, with violet upper lip and straight spur; flower stalk hairless. *Flowering:* July–October. *Distribution:* Southern, central and western Europe, northwards to England, eastwards to Moldavia and the Crimea, and naturalised elsewhere; arable fields and bare land.

Green-flowered Foxglove

Small Yellow Foxglove *Digitalis lutea* Up to 100cm A nearly hairless perennial, with oblong-lanceolate toothed leaves. Flowers are 9–25mm, pale yellow or whitish, in a many-flowered, one-sided spike; tubular corolla is weakly two-lipped with short, pointed lobes. *Flowering:* June–September. *Distribution:* Western and west-central Europe, southwards to southern Italy, occasionally naturalised; woods and hillsides, mainly on limestone. **Green-flowered Foxglove** (*D. viridiflora*), up to 80cm, is downy-hairy, with oblong-lanceolate to elliptical leaves; flowers greenish-yellow with distinct veins. *Flowering:* June–September. *Distribution:* Balkan Peninsula; woodland.

Common Toadflax

Purple Toadflax

Alpine Toadflax

Ivy-leaved Toadflax

Round-leaved Fluellen

Small Yellow Foxglove

Grecian Foxglove: fruit

Rusty Foxglove *Digitalis ferruginea* Up to 120cm A biennial or perennial with oblong-lanceolate to lanceolate leaves, sometimes downy beneath. Flowers are 15–35mm, tubular-globose with a long-projecting lower lip, red-brown or yellowish, netted with darker veins, in a long, dense spike; calyx lobes ovate or oblong- elliptical, blunt-tipped, with papery margins. *Flowering:* June–September. *Distribution:* Southern Europe from Italy eastwards; woodland and scrub. Similar **Grecian Foxglove** (*D. lanata*) often has reddish stems, flowers white or yellowish and calyx lobes lacking papery margins. *Flowering:* June–September. *Distribution:* Balkans, southern Hungary and Romania; woodlands and scrub.

Foxglove *Digitalis purpurea* Up to 180cm A downy-hairy biennial or perennial, with long-stalked, ovate or lanceolate, softly hairy basal leaves. Flowers are 40–55mm, bell-shaped and weakly two-lipped, purple, pale pink or white, usually black spotted on the inside, in a long, many-flowered spike. *Flowering:* June–September. *Distribution:* Western Europe, also grown as ornamental and medicinal plant; in woodland, scrub, heath and mountains.

Fairy Foxglove *Erinus alpinus* Up to 30cm A stickily hairy perennial, usually forming a loose cushion. Leaves are 5–20mm, oblanceolate, wedge-shaped, usually toothed at the tip. Flowers in a loose spike are 6–9mm across, pinkish-purple corolla is tubular with five lobes, the upper two narrower than the lower three. *Flowering:* May–October. *Distribution:* Southern to south-central Europe, introduced in the British Isles; mountain rocks, grassland.

Rock Speedwell *Veronica fruticans* Up to 15cm A sprawling perennial, with stems woody at the base. Opposite leaves are hairless or downy, obovate to oblong, occasionally toothed, on a short stalk. Flowers are 11–15mm across, deep blue with a red centre; calyx and corolla lobes four; stamens two. *Flowering:* July–September. *Distribution:* North-western Europe, mountains of central and southern Europe; rocks and stony grassland.

Heath Speedwell *Veronica officinalis* Up to 50cm A creeping, hairy perennial, with opposite ovate to elliptical, softly hairy, toothed leaves, on 2–6mm stalks. Flowers are 8mm across, lilac-blue, veined, in a dense terminal spike; calyx lobes four, equal, corolla lobes four, unequal. *Flowering:* May–August. *Distribution:* Most of Europe; woodlands and dry heathy areas. **Wood Speedwell** (*V. montana*) is similar, but has broadly ovate leaves, often purple beneath, on 7–15mm stalks; flowers 8–10mm across, pale lilac, in a loose spike. *Flowering:* May–June. *Distribution:* Western, central and southern Europe, northwards to Denmark, eastwards to Latvia and western Ukraine; damp woodland.

Wood Speedwell

Pink Water Speedwell

Blue Water Speedwell *Veronica anagallis-aquatica* Up to 100cm A usually hairless perennial, often branched at the base. Opposite leaves are 20–100cm, light green, ovate to ovate-lanceolate, the lower often stalked, the upper stalkless. Flowers are 5–10mm across, with blue usually four-lobed corolla veined with violet, in stalked spikes in the axils of upper leaves. *Flowering:* June–August. *Distribution:* Throughout Europe except the far north; river and stream sides. Two other common species occur in wet places. **Brooklime** (*V. beccabunga*), up to 40cm, has leaves thick, round to oblong, stalked; flowers pale or dark blue. *Flowering:* May-September. **Pink Water Speedwell** (*V. catentata*) has dark green, linear to linear-lanceolate leaves; flowers 3–5mm across, pink with red veins. *Flowering:* June–August.

Rusty Foxglove

Foxglove

Fairy Foxglove

Rock Speedwell

Health Speedwell

Blue Water Speedwell

Wall Speedwell *Veronica arvensis* Up to 40cm An upright, occasionally branched, downy-hairy annual. Opposite leaves are 2–15mm, triangular-ovate, heart-shaped at the base, toothed, the lower short-stalked, the upper stalkless. Flowers are 2–3 mm across, blue, in dense spikes, with leafy bracts longer than the flower stalks; corolla usually four-lobed. *Flowering:* March–October. *Distribution:* Throughout Europe; cultivated ground, walls and other dry habitats.

Grey Field Speedwell *Veronica polita* Up to 30cm A downy, sprawling, greyish annual. Opposite leaves are 5–15mm, ovate, the lower wider than long, regularly toothed. Flowers are 4–8mm across, blue, solitary, in leaf axils; corolla unequally four-lobed. Capsule with both long and short hairs. *Flowering:* March–November. *Distribution:* Most of Europe, except the Arctic, but probably only introduced in the north-east; cultivated ground.
Green Field Speedwell (*V. agrestis*) is similar, but green, the leaves longer than wide, irregularly toothed; flowers whitish, upper lobe of corolla blue or pink. Capsule has sparse long hairs only. *Flowering:* March–November. *Distribution:* Most of Europe except parts of the south-east and the far north; cultivated ground.

Green Field
Speedwell

Common Field Speedwell *Veronica persica* Up to 50cm Larger than the previous two species, with broad, ovate, short-stalked, pale green leaves. Flowers are 8–12mm across, bright blue, solitary, on stalks 5–30 mm long, in the leaf axils; corolla unequally four-lobed. Capsule has prominent ridges on outer edges. *Flowering:* All year. *Distribution:* Native of south-western Asia, naturalised throughout Europe; cultivated ground.

Ivy-leaved Speedwell *Veronica hederifolia* Up to 60cm A sprawling, downy annual with slender stems. Opposite leaves are stalked, 5–15mm, five- to seven- lobed, the end lobe largest. Flowers are 4–9mm across, blue or lilac, solitary in leaf axils, the stalks about as long as the leaves; calyx lobes hairy; corolla unequally four-lobed. *Flowering:* March–August. *Distribution:* Most of Europe, except the Arctic, probably introduced in the north; cultivated ground. Similar **V. cymbalaria** has white flowers and hairy, not hairless, capsules. *Flowering:* March–May. Distribution: Southern Europe.

Veronica cymbalaria:
fruit

Spiked Speedwell *Veronica spicata* Up to 60cm An upright, unbranched, hairy annual, with opposite leaves 20–80mm, linear to lanceolate-ovate, short-stalked, toothed. Flowers are 4–8mm across, blue, in a long, leafless spike; corolla unequally four-lobed. *Flowering:* July–October. *Distribution:* Most of Europe, but rare in the west; rocks and dry grassland, usually on lime-rich soils. **Garden Speedwell** (*V. longifolia*), up to 120cm, is hairless with slightly longer, more toothed leaves; flowers lilac or pale blue, in a dense spike, usually with one or more branches. *Flowering:* July–August. *Distribution:* Northern, central and eastern Europe westwards to Belgium, southwards to Bulgaria; damp places, woods and river banks.

Garden Speedwell

Cornish Moneywort *Sibthorpia europaea* Up to 40cm A prostrate perennial, creeping and rooting at the nodes forming large mats. The long-stalked alternate leaves are round with up to 13 very shallow lobes. Flowers are solitary on long stalks in the leaf axils, 1.5–2.5mm across, with slightly unequal corolla lobes, white or cream, often pinkish on the lower lobes, *Flowering:* June–October. *Distribution:* Western Europe, northwards to Britain, and on mountains in Greece and Crete; damp shady places.

Wall Speedwell

Grey Field Speedwell

Common Field Speedwell

Ivy-leaved Speedwell

Spiked Speedwell

Cornish Moneywort

Crested Cow-wheat

Small Cow-wheat

Field Cow-wheat *Melampyrum arvense* Up to 50cm A hemiparasitic annual with opposite, linear or lanceolate, untoothed leaves. Two-lipped flowers are 20–25mm, purple, the lower lip and throat yellow, in a cylindrical spike, with long, slender-toothed, ovate-lanceolate bracts which are green, white or reddish pink; calyx lobes 9–12mm, equal. *Flowering:* June–September. *Distribution:* From Finland and Britain, southwards to Spain, Italy and Turkey; arable land. **Crested Cow-wheat** (*M. cristatum*) has occasionally toothed leaves; flowers 12–16mm, yellow but purple tinged at least on the lower lip, in a four-angled, more dense spike; bracts ovate to heart-shaped, purple. *Flowering:* June–September. *Distribution:* Most of Europe, except parts of the north and south; wood margins and dry places.

Common Cow-wheat *Melampyrum pratense* Up to 60cm An upright hemiparasitic annual, with opposite, linear to ovate leaves. Two-lipped flowers are 10–18mm, pale to bright yellow, in a loose, one-sided spike, paired at the base of green, ovate to linear-lanceolate, toothed or entire bracts; calyx lobes 4–5mm, linear. *Flowering:* May–September. *Distribution:* Most of Europe; woods, grasslands and heaths. **Small Cow-wheat** (*M. sylvaticum*) is more slender, the leaves lanceolate to elliptic-lanceolate; flowers usually deep yellow, the throat open, the lower lip often purple-spotted; calyx lobes lanceolate. *Flowering:* June–August. *Distribution:* Northern Europe, southwards in mountains to Pyrenees, central Italy and southern Bulgaria; woods.

Eyebright *Euphrasia nemorosa* Up to 40cm An upright, hemiparasitic annual, with up to nine pairs of ascending branches. Mostly opposite leaves are ovate, deeply veined, toothed. Two-lipped flowers are 5–8.5mm, white to lilac, in terminal spikes; capsule 4–6mm, oblong to elliptical, more than twice as long as wide, slightly shorter than calyx. *Flowering:* June–October. *Distribution:* Northern and central Europe, southwards to north-eastern Spain; grassland.

Euphrasia pectinata Up to 35cm Hemiparasitic annual resembling Eyebright but with three or fewer pairs of branches. Lower stem leaves are 3–13mm, variable in shape, toothed; upper leaves 5–13mm, often very broad. Flowers are 6.5–9mm, usually white; capsule 5–7mm, three to five times as long as wide. *Flowering:* June–October. *Distribution:* Widespread in southern Europe; open woods, grassland.

Odontites lutea

Red Bartsia *Odontites verna* Up to 50cm A downy-hairy, often purple-tinged, hemiparasitic annual, with lanceolate, toothed, opposite leaves. Two-lipped flowers are 8–10mm, reddish-pink, almost stalkless in a loose one-sided spike. *Flowering:* June–September. *Distribution:* Most of Europe; waste ground, roadsides and fields. **O. lutea** has linear, untoothed leaves, and bright yellow flowers 5–8mm. *Flowering:* June–September. *Distribution:* Southern and central Europe; dry grassy areas and scrubland.

Alpine Bartsia *Bartsia alpina* Up to 40cm A downy, upright, hemiparasitic perennial, with opposite, ovate, toothed leaves, 10–25 x 6–15mm. Two-lipped flowers are 15–20mm, dark purple, the throat open, the upper lip longer than the three-lobed lower lip, in a short spike; bracts leaf-like, dull purple. *Flowering:* July–August. *Distribution:* Northern Europe, southwards in mountain ranges to Pyrenees, southern Alps and Bulgaria; damp areas, usually on chalky soils.

Field Cow-wheat

Common Cow-wheat

Eyebright

Euphrasia pectinata

Red Bartsia

Alpine Bartsia

Bellardia trixago

Southern Red Bartsia

Lousewort

Rhinanthus alectorolophus

Bellardia trixago Up to 70cm. An erect, unbranched and glandular-hairy, hemiparasitic annual with opposite, linear to linear-lanceolate, blunt-toothed leaves 15–90mm long. Two-lipped flowers and leafy bracts in a terminal spike; corolla 20–25mm, purple and white, purple and yellow or sometimes entirely white, the upper lip much shorter than the three-lobed lower lip. *Flowering:* June–August. *Distribution:* Southern Europe; rocky, stony or grassy places.

Yellow Bartsia *Parentucellia viscosa* Up to 70cm A stickily hairy hemiparasitic, upright annual, with oblong to lanceolate, pointed, roughly toothed leaves. Two-lipped flowers are 16–24mm, yellow, the lower lip three-lobed, in a loose-flowered spike; bracts leaf-like; calyx lobes linear-lanceolate, almost as long as flower tube. *Flowering:* June–September. *Distribution:* Southern and western Europe, northwards to Scotland, casual further north; damp, sandy and grassy places. **Southern Red Bartsia** (*P. latifolia*) has triangular-lanceolate, deeply toothed leaves; flowers 8–10mm, red-purple, rarely white; calyx lobes about half as long as the tube. *Flowering:* June–September. *Distribution:* Southern Europe; dry, sandy and stony places.

Moor-king *Pedicularis sceptrum-carolinum* Up to 100cm An upright, hairless, often reddish hemiparasitic perennial. Basal leaves lanceolate, pinnately lobed, the lobes ovate, blunt, toothed, in a basal rosette; stem leaves few or none. Two-lipped flowers are up to 32mm, pale yellow, the lower lip with a red margin, alternate or in whorls of three, in a long, loose spike; calyx lobes toothed. *Flowering:* July–August. *Distribution:* Scandinavia and northern and central Russia, locally in central Europe, southern Germany and central Romania; wet woods, damp grassland and scrub.

Marsh Lousewort *Pedicularis palustris* Up to 70cm A more or less hairless, hemiparasitic branched annual or biennial, with usually alternate, triangular, lanceolate or linear, pinnately-lobed leaves, the lobes oblong, toothed. Two- lipped flowers are 15–25mm, reddish-pink, in a loose spike; bracts leaf-like; calyx ovate, without obvious lobes, inflated in fruit. *Flowering:* May–September. *Distribution:* Europe, southwards to the Pyrenees, northern Italy, southern Bulgaria and southern Urals; damp meadows and marshy areas. Similar **Lousewort** (*P. sylvatica*) up to 25cm, is often perennial; flowers pink or red; calyx slightly two-lipped, lobes unequal. *Flowering:* April–July. *Distribution:* Western and central Europe to Sweden, Lithuania and Ukraine; wet heaths and bogs.

Greater Yellow-rattle *Rhinanthus angustifolius* Up to 60cm A hemiparasitic, often branched, hairy or hairless, black-streaked annual. Leaves are opposite, linear to ovate, toothed. Two-lipped flowers are 16–20mm, the tube 2–3mm wide, slightly curved; bracts longer than calyx which inflates in fruit. *Flowering:* May–September. *Distribution:* Europe, except the Mediterranean and the south-west; grassland. **R. alectorolophus** is larger, hairy, without black streaks; calyx with long white hairs. *Flowering:* May–September. *Distribution:* Northern France, Netherlands and west-central Russia, to northern Italy and Yugoslavia.

Yellow-rattle *Rhinanthus minor* Up to 50cm Resembles Greater Yellow Rattle but smaller. Flowers 13–15mm, with straight corolla tube; bracts longer or slightly shorter than the usually hairless calyx. *Flowering:* May–September. *Distribution:* Most of Europe, rare in the Mediterranean; rough, grassy places.

Bellardia trixago

Yellow Bartsia

Moor-king

Marsh Lousewort

Greater Yellow-rattle

Yellow-rattle

Purple Toothwort:
flower

Toothwort *Lathraea squamaria* Up to 30cm A creamy-white, pink-tinged perennial without chlorophyll, parasitic on tree-roots. Stems stout, with leaves reduced to alternate, triangular scales, clasping the stem. Two-lipped flowers are 14–20mm, pinkish tinged, two-lipped, in a dense one-sided spike; bracts thin, like the leaves; calyx about 10mm. *Flowering:* April–May. *Distribution:* Much of Europe, but absent in parts of the north and south; woods and hedges. **Purple Toothwort** (*L. clandestina*), to 5cm, has kidney-shaped scale-leaves; flowers 40–50mm, violet, lower lip reddish-purple, in a short four- to eight-flowered spike; calyx 18–20mm. *Flowering:* April–May. *Distribution:* Western Europe from Belgium to northern Spain and southern Italy.

Shrubby Globularia *Globularia alypum* Up to 100cm A small evergreen shrub, the young twigs and leaves with abundant chalky secretions. Alternate leaves are oblanceolate to ovate, pointed or three-lobed, very leathery, short-stalked, regularly arranged on the main stem, in tight bundles on non-flowering side branches. Small blue flowers are two-lipped, in a round terminal head 1–2.5cm across, occasionally with stalkless axillary flower heads below; broadly ovate bracts form a ring beneath the head. *Flowering:* June–August. *Distribution:* Mediterranean region; scrubland.

Common Globularia *Globularia punctata* Up to 30cm A tufted, evergreen perennial, with a rosette of stalked, obovate, prominently veined basal leaves. Stem leaves are lanceolate to oblong, stalkless. Two-lipped blue flowers are small, numerous, in a round head 15mm across with a ring of numerous, lanceolate bracts beneath. *Flowering:* May–June. *Distribution:* Northern France and Czechoslovakia southwards to northern Spain, southern Italy and north-eastern Greece; grassland, rocks and woods, often on chalk.

Pyrenean Violet *Ramonda myconi* Up to 12cm A hairy perennial, with a flat rosette of deep green, ovate, blunt, toothed leaves, each tapering to a short stalk. Flowers are 30–40mm across, one to six together on glandular-hairy stalks 6–12mm long; corolla blue to violet with a yellow centre, with usually five spreading lobes; anthers forming a yellow cone around the projecting style. *Flowering:* June–August. *Distribution:* Pyrenees and mountains of north-eastern Spain; shaded areas on limestone rocks.

Bear's-breeches *Acanthus mollis* Up to 150cm A stout, usually hairless, dark-green perennial. Large leaves are pinnately lobed, the lobes sharply toothed but not spiny. Flowers are 3.5–5cm, in a dense terminal spike, each with a spiny bract. Dull purple calyx is two-lipped, the large slightly hooded upper lip projecting. White corolla has a three-lobed lower lip, upper lip is absent. *Flowering:* June–September. *Distribution:* Western and central Mediterranean and Portugal; roadsides and shady places, often cultivated and naturalised. Similar **Spiny Bear's-breeches** (*A. spinosus*) has spine-toothed basal leaves. *Flowering:* July–August. *Distribution:* Eastern Mediterranean west to south-east Italy.

Spiny Bear's-
breeches

Hemp Broomrape *Orobanche ramosa* Up to 40cm A parasitic plant, lacking chlorophyll, the often branched stems yellow. Leaves are scale-like, 3–10mm long, ovate or lanceolate, pointed. Tubular, two-lipped flowers 10–22mm, white at the base, blue or violet at the tip, in a loose or dense spike; bracts 6–10mm, ovate-lanceolate; bracteoles linear-lanceolate. *Flowering:* June–September. *Distribution:* Southern and south-central Europe; often parasitic on cultivated plants.

Toothwort

Shrubby Globularia

Common Globularia

Pyrenean Violet

Bear's-breeches

Hemp Broomrape

Thyme Broomrape *Orobanche alba* Up to 40cm A stout, unbranched parasite with stems usually purple-red, glandular-hairy and swollen at the base. Scale-like leaves are 12–20mm, lanceolate. Two-lipped flowers are 15–25mm, reddish-purple, yellow or white, glandular-hairy, scented; corolla tube straight, lower lip three-lobed, the central lobe largest; bracts 12–25mm, lanceolate, pointed. *Flowering:* June–August. *Distribution:* Europe northwards to Scotland, Belgium and central Russia; parasitic on Thyme and other Mints. **Thistle Broomrape** (*O. reticulata*) is similar, but taller and stouter, stems yellow to purple-tinged, the lobes of lower lip equal in size. *Flowering:* June–August. *Distribution:* Europe northwards to England, and Estonia; parasite of thistles.

Ivy Broomrape

Knapweed Broomrape *Orobanche elatior* Up to 70cm Parasite with an unbranched, usually glandular-hairy stem. Scale-like leaves are 10–20mm, triangular-lanceolate. Two-lipped flowers in a dense spike are 12–25mm; corolla yellow often tinged pink, curved, upper lip often two-lobed, lower with three equal lobes; bracts 15–25mm, lanceolate. *Flowering:* June–August. *Distribution:* England and Estonia southwards to eastern Spain, northern Italy, Bulgaria; parasitic on members of the Daisy family. **Ivy Broomrape** (*O. hederae*) has a yellowish-purple stem; leaves oblong to lanceolate; flowers in a loose spike cream, tinged with red-purple, corolla tube straight, upper lip entire, lower lip with middle lobe largest. *Flowering:* June–August. *Distribution:* Western, southern and south-central Europe; parasitic on Ivy.

Greater Broomrape *Orobanche rapum-genistae* Up to 80cm A stout parasite with pale-yellow, sometimes purple-tinged stems. Scale-like leaves are 15–60mm, ovate to linear-lanceolate. Two-lipped flowers in a dense spike are 20–25mm, yellow, with unpleasant smell; bracts linear-lanceolate. *Flowering:* June–July. *Distribution:* Western Europe to Scotland, eastwards to Germany and Italy; parasitic on shrubs of the Pea family.

Pale Butterwort

Alpine Butterwort *Pinguicula alpina* Up to 15cm An insectivorous perennial, with a flat rosette of pale yellow-green leaves, the sticky upper surfaces trapping insects which are covered by the leaf rolling up. Two-lipped flowers are 10–16mm, white with yellowish spots, and a yellowish spur. *Flowering:* June–August. *Distribution:* Arctic Europe, mountains in south to central Europe and Pyrenees; bogs, damp rocks. **Pale Butterwort** (*P. lusitanica*) is smaller with greyish leaves; flowers pinkish to lilac. *Flowering:* June–October. *Distribution:* Western Europe; heaths and bogs.

Large-flowered Butterwort

Common Butterwort *Pinguicula vulgaris* Up to 250cm Insectivorous perennial with a rosette of yellow-green leaves sticky on the upper surface. Two-lipped flowers are 15–22mm, violet, white at the throat, with a straight spur 3–10mm. *Flowering:* May–July. *Distribution:* Northern, western and central Europe; wet rocks, bogs and heathland. Similar **Large-flowered Butterwort** (*P. grandiflora*) has violet to lilac flowers 25–40mm. *Flowering:* April–July. *Distribution:* South-west Ireland, mountains of Europe from Spain to Switzerland; bogs and wet rocks.

Greater Bladderwort *Utricularia vulgaris* Up to 100cm An aquatic insectivorous perennial, with leaves pinnately divided into narrow segments bearing small bladders which engulf and digest small water creatures. Bright yellow flowers are 12–18mm, two-lipped with a conical spur, in a leafless spike. *Flowering:* June–August. *Distribution:* Most of Europe; deep, fresh water.

Thyme Broomrape

Knapweed Broomrape

Great Broomrape

Alpine Butterwort

Common Butterwort

Greater Bladderwort

Sea Plantain: leaf

Greater Plantain

Plantago altissima

Branched Plantain

Buck's-horn Plantain *Plantago coronopus* Up to 20cm A perennial producing basal rosettes of pinnately-lobed, toothed, usually hairy leaves. Flowers are very small, densely packed on several terminal, leafless, ascending stems. *Flowering* May–October. *Distribution:* Mostly on coasts eastwards to Poland and the Crimea, northwards to the Faeroes and southern Sweden; also inland in western Europe and the Mediterranean; dry bare or sandy patches. **Sea Plantain** (*P. maritima*) has several rosettes of linear, fleshy, sometimes slightly toothed leaves and flowers in looser spikes. *Flowering:* June–September. *Distribution:* Most of Europe; salt-marshes and coastal habitats, rarely on mountains inland.

Hoary Plantain *Plantago media* Up to 30cm A perennial with a basal rosette of elliptical to ovate elliptical leaves 50–150mm long, greyish-downy and narrowing into a stalk less than half length of blade. Small, fragrant, whitish flowers are crowded into a dense terminal spike 20–60mm long, at tip of a naked stem. *Flowering:* May–August. *Distribution:* Throughout Europe, but possibly not native in the north; dry grassland, especially on lime-rich soils. **Greater Plantain** (*P. major*) has hairless, usually ovate leaves with stalks equalling blades, and greenish-yellow, flowers in a spike twice as long as leaves. *Flowering:* June–October. *Distribution:* Most of Europe; waste ground, and in turf.

Ribwort Plantain *Plantago lanceolata* Up to 60cm A perennial, often producing several rosettes of linear-lanceolate, three- to seven-veined, hairless or downy leaves 20–300mm long. Flowers are small, brownish, in a short, dense, terminal spike on a long, deeply furrowed stalk. *Flowering:* April–October. *Distribution:* Throughout Europe, except the far north; waste places and grassland. **P. altissima** is similar, but larger in all parts, the leaves mostly hairless; flowers in a longer spike. *Flowering:* April–October. *Distribution:* East-central Europe and the Balkans; grassy places.

Plantago lagopus Up to 20cm Resembles Ribwort Plantain but is often annual, with only a single basal rosette of leaves. Flowers have densely hairy sepals, making the whole flower spike appear tufted. *Flowering:* May–August. *Distribution:* Southern Europe; dry, sandy or stony ground.

Glandular Plantain *Plantago afra* Up to 50cm A branched, glandular-downy, upright annual with linear or linear-lanceolate leaves opposite or up to four at each node. Flowers are small, brownish, in short, ovoid spikes, on long stalks up the stem. *Flowering:* May–August. *Distribution:* Southern Europe; dry habitats. **Branched Plantain** (*P. arenaria*) is similar, but hairs are not glandular; bracts beneath flower heads are leaf-like. *Flowering:* May–August. *Distribution:* Southern, central and eastern Europe, frequently naturalised in the north; bare dry places.

Shoreweed *Littorella uniflora* Up to 25cm An aquatic perennial, creeping and rooting to form a turf of rosettes of linear leaves semi-circular in cross-section. Whitish, four-petalled male flowers are 5–6mm, solitary on short, naked stems; stalkless female flowers of 4–5mm and with two or four petals form a cluster of two to eight at the base of the male flower stem. *Flowering:* June–August. *Distribution:* Western and central Europe to northern Italy, much of Scandinavia and north-western Russia and Romania; lake shores, often well submerged.

Buck's-horn Plantain

Hoary Plantain

Ribwort Plantain

Plantago lagopus

Glandular Plantain

Shoreweed

Dwarf Elder *Sambucus ebulus* Up to 200cm A patch-forming perennial, with several upright, normally unbranched stems. Leaves are pinnate, with five to thirteen oblong to oblong-lanceolate, pointed, toothed leaflets. Small, strongly-scented flowers are white or pink-tinged, usually five-lobed, in a large umbel-like head 50–160 mm across. Ripe berries black. *Flowering:* July–August. *Distribution:* From Holland and north Ukraine southwards, once grown as a medicinal plant and naturalised in other areas; scrub, waysides.

Twinflower *Linnaea borealis* Up to 50 cm A mat-forming, evergreen, dwarf shrub with slender stems. Leaves are ovate, toothed. Flowers are 5–9mm, pinkish-white, hairy inside, in pairs on a single glandular-hairy stalk 45–80mm long. *Flowering:* June–August. *Distribution:* Northern Europe, scattered in mountains southwards to the Alps, eastern Carpathians and southern Urals; woods, especially conifer, heathland and tundra.

Blue Honeysuckle

Fly Honeysuckle *Lonicera xylosteum* Up to 300cm An upright, deciduous shrub, with opposite, round, elliptical-ovate leaves usually downy-hairy beneath. Yellowish-white, two-lipped flowers are 8–12mm, in pairs on a single stalk in axils of upper leaves. *Flowering:* May–June. *Distribution:* Europe, except the far north and parts of the far south; woods, hedgerows and scrub. **Blue Honeysuckle** (*L. caerulea)* is smaller and less hairy; flowers 12–16mm, the corolla with five equal lobes; fruit a black double berry. *Flowering:* May–July. *Distribution:* North-eastern Europe, Pyrenees to Bulgaria and south-western Czechoslovakia; mountain woods, scrub, 1350 –2500m.

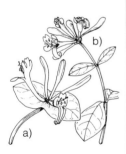

a) Perfoliate Honeysuckle
b) *Lonicera etrusca*

Honeysuckle *Lonicera periclymenum* Up to 600cm A vigorous, woody, deciduous climber. Leaves are oblong to elliptical, dark green above, greyish green below. Fragrant flowers in long-stalked terminal heads. Corolla is 35–55mm, yellow or creamy-white, often red-tinged, with a long tube and two lips. *Flowering:* June–October. *Distribution:* Western, central and southern Europe, north-eastwards to southern Sweden; woodland and hedges. **L. etrusca** has leaves greyish- or whitish- green above, woolly-hairy beneath; flowers yellow, often purple-tinged, flower head solitary or two to three together at the tips of branches. *Flowering:* May–July. *Distribution:* Southern Europe; woods and scrub. **Perfoliate Honeysuckle** (*L. caprifolium)* has upper leaves joined at the base to encircle the stem; flowers in stalkless heads. *Flowering:* May–July. *Distribution:* Eastern, central and southern Europe, westwards to Italy, often naturalised; woods and scrub.

Moschatel *Adoxa moschatellina* Up to 10cm A delicate, hairless perennial, with basal leaves divided into three lobes, each lobe further divided; opposite stem leaves also three–lobed. Five small, green flowers form a cubical head 6–10mm across. Four lateral flowers have three-lobed calyx, five-lobed corolla; top flower has two-lobed calyx, four-lobed corolla. *Flowering:* March–May. *Distribution:* Most of Europe to France, southern Italy and Bulgaria but only on mountains in the south; woods and shady habitats.

Common Cornsalad

Narrow-fruited Cornsalad *Valerianella dentata* Up to 40cm An upright, much-branched annual, with opposite, ovate leaves, the lower spoon-shaped. Flowers are small, bluish or pink, in terminal heads with a ruff of bracts with toothed, papery margins. *Flowering:* April–August. *Distribution:* Most of Europe; bare cultivated ground. **Common Cornsalad** (*V. locusta*) is similar, but with spoon-shaped bracts, and pinkish flowers. *Flowering:* April-August. *Distribution:* Most of Europe; bare ground, walls.

Dwarf Elder

Twinflower

Fly Honeysuckle

Honeysuckle

Moschatel

Narrow-fruited Cornsalad

Marsh Valerian

Common Valerian *Valeriana officinalis* Up to 200cm A usually unbranched, often downy perennial. Leaves are opposite, pinnate or pinnately-lobed, the 3–25 leaflets lanceolate, toothed, the lower ones stalked. Hermaphrodite flowers are 2.5–5mm, funnel-shaped, unequally five-lobed, pale pink, in a compound head made up of several smaller, dense heads. *Flowering:* June–August. *Distribution:* Most of Europe, rare in the far south; woods and grassy places. **Marsh Valerian** V. *dioica*, is similar, but shorter, with basal leaves on long stalks; male and female flowers on different plants. *Flowering:* May–June. *Distribution:* Europe, northwards to Norway, eastwards to Macedonia and western Russia; marshes.

Annual Valerian *Centranthus calcitrapae* Up to 40cm A single-stemmed or branched, upright annual, with opposite, deeply pinnately-lobed leaves, the lobes entire or toothed. Flowers are 2–3mm, pink or white, the tube five-lobed and with a short spur, in clusters forming a head. *Flowering:* May–August. *Distribution:* Southern Europe; waste places.

Red Valerian *Centranthus ruber* Up to 80cm A hairless, grey-green, usually branched and upright perennial, with opposite, ovate to lanceolate, pointed leaves, the upper irregularly toothed and clasping the stem. Tubular, five-lobed flowers are 5–10mm, pink, white or red, with a 2–12mm long spur, in several oblong clusters together forming a terminal head. *Flowering:* May–September. *Distribution:* Mediterranean; walls and rocky places.

Cut-leaved Teasel: stem leaves

Teasel *Dipsacus fullonum* Up to 200cm A hairless biennial, with stout stems, prickly on the angles. Basal leaves are elliptical or oblong–lanceolate, rough, untoothed; stem leaves narrower, often joined around the stem, entire or toothed. Flowers are small, pale purple, in a globular, spiny head 30–90mm across, with two or three rows of upcurved, linear bracts at the base, the longest as long as the head; flowers often opening only two or three rows at a time. *Flowering:* July–August. *Distribution;* Southern, western and central Europe to north-eastern Ukraine; waste areas, woods and streamsides. Similar **Cut-leaved Teasel** (*D. laciniatus*) has stems with slender prickles, pinnately-lobed stem leaves and pale pink flowers. *Flowering:* July–August. *Distribution:* Europe, northwards to central France, Germany and the Ukraine; meadows, by streams and in waste places.

Devil's-bit Scabious *Succisa pratensis* Up to 100cm A more or less downy, upright perennial, with narrowly obovate or elliptical, sometimes slightly toothed basal leaves. Flowers are 4–7mm, purple, pinkish or white, in a dense round head 15–30mm across; male and female flowers in separate heads, the female smaller. *Flowering:* June–October. *Distribution:* Europe, apart from the far north and parts of the Mediterranean; damp grassland.

Pterocephalus papposus: fruit

Field Scabious *Knautia arvensis* Up to 100cm A hairy perennial, often with several stems. Basal leaves in rosettes are either entire or pinnately-lobed; stem-leaves are pinnate, with up to 16 narrow lobes and a broader terminal lobe. Flowers small, lilac, pink or purple, in flat heads which are either hermaphrodite and 25–40mm across, or female and 15–30mm across; petals of outer flowers larger than the inner. *Flowering:* June–October. *Distribution:* Most of Europe, absent from parts of the Mediterranean; dry grassland and open woods. **Pterocephalus papposus** is annual, covered in long hairs; pink or purplish flowers in hemispherical heads. *Flowering:* April-July. *Distribution:* Eastern Mediterranean; dry, bare places.

Common Valerian

Annual Valerian

Red Valerian

Teasel

Devil's-bit Scabious

Field Scabious

Small Scabious *Scabiosa columbaria* Up to 70cm A branched, downy perennial, with basal rosettes of entire or pinnately–lobed leaves; stem-leaves pinnately- lobed, the lobes often also pinnate, roughly hairy. Flowers are bluish-lilac, in a head 15–25mm across with a ruff of green bracts beneath. *Flowering* June–October. *Distribution:* From southern Scotland and Estonia southwards; dry grassland, on limestone. Similar **S. triandra** has lyre-shaped basal leaves, blue-violet flowers and lacks black bristles in the flower head. *Distribution:* Southern and south-central Europe; dry grassland.

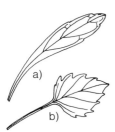

Spreading Bellflower

Rampion Bellflower *Campanula rapunculus* Up to 100cm A biennial, with milky sap. Basal leaves are obovate, stalked; stem leaves linear-lanceolate. Flowers are 10–20mm, pale blue or white, bell-shaped, in a branched spike; calyx teeth very long, hairlike. *Flowering:* June–July. *Distribution:* Southwards from the Netherlands and south-central Russia; wood edges, waste places and grassland. **Spreading Bellflower** (*C. patula*) has flowers 17–35mm in a spreading head; calyx teeth sharply pointed. *Flowering:* June–July. *Distribution:* Most of Europe.

Bearded Bellflower *Campanula barbata* Up to 30cm A creeping perennial, with mainly basal, oblong-lanceolate leaves narrowed at the base and roughly hairy; stem-leaves few. Flowers are 20–30mm, pale blue, white-hairy inside, usually drooping, in a few-flowered head; calyx teeth pointed, half as long as the corolla. *Flowering:* June–August. *Distribution:* Alps, east Sudeten mountains and Norway; open woods, meadows and rocks. **Alpine Bellflower** (*C. alpina*) has woolly leaves; flowers 15–20mm, lilac to lavender, sometimes solitary. *Distribution:* Eastern Alps, Carpathians and Balkan peninsula; rocks. **Fairy's Thimble** (*C. cochleariifolia*) is creeping, with rounded, toothed basal leaves; flowers violet, few or solitary. *Distribution:* Pyrenees, Alps and Carpathians to central Apennines and southern Bulgaria; rocky places.

a) Alpine Bellflower
b) Fairy's Thimble

Clustered Bellflower *Campanula glomerata* Up to 80cm A downy or roughly hairy perennial with angled, reddish stems. Lower leaves are ovate-lanceolate to heart-shaped, bluntly toothed, long-stalked. Flowers up to 35mm, deep violet, in a dense head; calyx teeth lanceolate, pointed. *Flowering:* June–October. *Distribution:* Most of Europe; grassland, particularly chalky soils. **C. cervicaria** is biennial, flowers up to 16mm, pale blue; calyx teeth ovate, blunt. *Distribution:* Most of Europe, rare in the Mediterranean.

Campanula cervicaria

Nettle-leaved Bellflower *Campanula trachelium* Up to 100cm A hairy perennial, with angled stems. Leaves are ovate-heart-shaped, pointed, toothed, the lower stalked. Flowers are 15–50mm, pale blue or violet, in a leafy spike; calyx teeth triangular, pointed. *Flowering:* July–September. *Distribution:* Europe, northwards to Sweden; woodland and scrub. **Giant Bellflower** (*C. latifolia*) is stouter, with more regularly toothed leaves; flowers pale blue or white, solitary in leaf axils. *Distribution:* Most of Europe but absent from the north, south-west and most of the Mediterranean; more hilly areas.

Giant Bellflower

Harebell *Campanula rotundifolia* Up to 70cm. A perennial with creeping stems abruptly becoming erect and with downy, round basal leaves. Nodding flowers are 10-30mm, blue, solitary or in a loose spike; calyx teeth linear to narrowly triangular. *Flowering:* June–October. *Distribution:* Much of Europe, rare in south; dry heath, dunes, rocks.

Small Scabious

Rampion Bellflower

Bearded Bellflower

Clustered Bellflower

Nettle-leaved Bellflower

Harebell

Venus's-looking-glass

Large Venus's-looking-glass *Legousia speculum-veneris* Up to 40cm A downy-hairy, much branched annual, with obovate leaves, the lower sometimes stalked. Flowers are up to 20mm across, violet, several often in large clusters; calyx teeth linear, pointed, as long as the cylindrical ovary beneath. *Flowering:* May–July. *Distribution:* South-western and south-central Europe, northwards to the Netherlands; cultivated and bare or waste ground. **Venus's-looking-glass** (*L. hybrida)* is smaller and roughly hairy; flowers reddish-purple in small clusters. *Flowering:* May–August. *Distribution:* Mainly western and southern Europe; bare or stony places, arable land.

Round-headed Rampion *Phyteuma orbiculare* Up to 50cm An upright, unbranched perennial, the basal leaves linear-lanceolate or elliptical, toothed, stalked. Flowers are small, blue or blue-violet, up to 30 in a dense, globular head 10–25mm across with a ring of ovate-lanceolate, pointed bracts beneath. *Flowering:* June–August. *Distribution:* Southern England and Latvia southwards to southern Spain and Albania; dry grassland, on chalky soil.

Betony-leaved Rampion

Spiked Rampion *Phyteuma spicatum* Up to 100cm An upright perennial, with ovate, blunt, long-stalked lower leaves, heart-shaped at the base; upper leaves narrow. Flowers are small, yellowish or pale blue, in a cylindrical spike up to 200mm long. *Flowering:* May–July. *Distribution:* Southern Norway and Estonia southwards to northern Spain and Yugoslavia; meadows and woodland, up to 2000m. **Betony-leaved Rampion** (*P. betonicifolium)* has deep blue flowers in a spike up to 40mm long. *Distribution:* Alps, and mountains of northern Italy; meadows and woods.

Ivy-leaved Bellflower *Wahlenbergia hederacea* Up to 30cm A slender, creeping perennial, with shallowly lobed, ivy-like leaves. Bell-shaped flowers are 6–10mm, pale blue, solitary in leaf axils. *Flowering:* July–August. *Distribution:* Western Europe, northwards to Scotland; damp places, woods, streamsides and moorland. Rare **W. nutabunda** is taller, branched, with winged leaf stalks; flowers pale blue, pink or white in large spikes. *Flowering:* May–July. *Distribution:* Western Mediterranean; dry places.

Wahlenbergia nutabunda

Sheep's-bit *Jasione montana* Up to 50cm An upright, slightly hairy annual or biennial, with wavy-edged, linear-oblong to lanceolate leaves. Flowers are small, blue, in globular heads, with a ruff of bracts beneath. *Flowering:* May–September. *Distribution:* Most of Europe, northwards to Finland; dry grassland, heath and shingle, on lime-free soils. **J. laevis** is a larger perennial, with non-flowering shoots; leaves without wavy edges. *Distribution:* Western and west-central Europe, northwards to Luxembourg; dry meadows.

Jasione laevis: flower head

Heath Lobelia *Lobelia urens* 20–60cm An erect perennial with solid, leafy stems and linear-lanceolate to oblong, toothed leaves. Blue or purple-blue flowers are carried in a loose spike; calyx teeth triangular; corolla 10–15mm long, two-lipped, the upper lip two-lipped. the lower with three larger lobes, in a loose spike. *Flowering:* August–September. *Distribution:* Western Europe, northwards to southern England and Belgium; acid heaths and woodland. **Water Lobelia** (*L. dortmanna)* is an aquatic plant with a hollow stem and stalkless leaves in a basal rosette; flowers pale lilac. *Flowering:* July–August. *Distribution:* Northern and north-central Europe, scattered to south-western France and Russia; still or slow-moving, usually acid water.

Water Lobelia

Large Venus's-looking-glass

Round-headed Rampion

Spiked Rampion

Ivy-leaved Bellflower

Sheep's-bit

Heath Lobelia

Hemp-agrimony *Eupatorium cannabinum* Up to 175cm An upright, often reddish, downy perennial, with three- to five-lobed leaves, the lobes ovate to lanceolate, pointed, toothed. Florets are small, in pinkish clusters 2–5mm across gathered together in a terminal head; outer involucral bracts shorter than the inner; seeds with a parachute of white hairs. *Flowering:* July–September. *Distribution:* Most of Europe; damp places, by fresh water, and on waste ground.

Canadian Goldenrod

Goldenrod *Solidago virgaurea* Up to 100cm A mostly downy perennial, with oblanceolate to obovate leaves, downy underneath. Flower heads are yellow, in branched spikes; disc florets 10 to 30, surrounded by six to 12 ray florets; seeds with 5mm long parachute of hairs. *Flowering:* June–September. *Distribution:* Most of Europe; woods, heaths, grassy places and rocks. **Canadian Goldenrod** (*S. canadensis*) has lanceolate leaves, and flower heads in one-sided sprays; seed parachute 2–2.5mm. *Distribution:* A Canadian native, widely naturalised in Europe; roadsides, waste places. **Early Goldenrod** (*S. gigantea*) is shorter, greyish-green; leaves deeply toothed; flower heads with longer ray florets. *Distribution:* A North American plant, much naturalised; roadsides, waste places.

Annual Daisy *Bellis annua* Up to 20cm A roughly hairy, upright annual, with oblanceolate or broadly obovate, spoon-shaped, toothed or entire leaves, the lower stalked. Flower heads are 5–20mm across, solitary on slender stalks; inner disc florets yellow, ray florets white, tinged with pink; involucral bracts bluntly pointed; seeds hairless. *Flowering:* April–August. *Distribution:* Mediterranean, Portugal, Bulgaria; damp, shady places.

Bellis sylvestris

Daisy *Bellis perennis* Up to 25cm A spreading perennial, with oblanceolate to obovate, spoon-shaped, slightly toothed leaves narrowing abruptly to the stalk, in a flat rosette. Flower heads are 15–30mm across, solitary on a slender stalk; disc florets yellow, white ray florets sometimes reddish on the back; involucral bracts oblong, usually blunt; seeds hairless. *Flowering:* Most of the year. *Distribution:* Most of Europe, naturalised further north; meadows, roadsides and grassy places. **B. sylvestris** is similar, but has dark green, three-veined leaves, narrowing gradually to a short stalk; involucral bracts pointed. *Distribution:* Europe; grassland.

European
Michaelmas Daisy

Alpine Aster *Aster alpinus* Up to 50cm An upright, hairy perennial with spoon-shaped, elliptical, broadly-stalked basal and lower leaves; upper leaves oblong to linear-lanceolate, stalkless. Flower heads are 35–45mm, solitary at the tips of stems; disc florets yellow; ray florets violet-blue, rarely pink or white. *Flowering:* July–September. *Distribution:* Mountains from central Germany southwards, also at lower altitudes in eastern Russia; rocky and stony places, dry woodland to 3200m. **European Michaelmas Daisy** (*A. amellus*) has lanceolate, obovate or oblong leaves; flower heads 20–30mm in branched clusters; ray florets blue, rarely red or white. *Distribution:* North-central France and Lithuania southwards to northern Italy and Macedonia; scrub, open woods and rocky areas.

Sea Aster *Aster tripolium* Up to 100cm An upright annual or biennial, with branched, often reddish stems. Fleshy leaves are linear to lanceolate, the lower stalked. Flower heads are usually composed of yellow disc florets only, rarely with 20 to 30 blue or lilac ray florets. *Flowering:* July–October. *Distribution:* Most of Europe; coastal salt-marshes, cliffs and salt water inland.

Hemp Agrimony

Goldenrod

Annual Daisy

Daisy

Alpine Aster

Sea Aster

Tall Fleabane

Broad-leaved Cudweed: flower head

Marsh Cudweed: flower head

Helichrysum italicum: flower heads

Carpathian Cat's-foot

Blue Fleabane *Erigeron acer* Up to 100cm A densely hairy annual, biennial or perennial, with elliptical to obovate, stalked basal leaves. Flower heads are 10–15mm, up to 70 in a terminal cluster; disc florets yellow; ray florets lilac, erect. *Flowering:* July–September. *Distribution:* Most of Europe; dry, stony or sandy, bare places. **Tall Fleabane** (*E. annuus*) is taller, with broadly ovate leaves; flower heads 15–25mm across in a branched flowering stem; ray florets white or pale blue. *Distribution:* A North American native, widely naturalised, mainly in central Europe; waste or disturbed areas.

Red-tipped Cudweed *Filago lutescens* Up to 25cm An irregularly branched annual, with dense yellowish hairs and oblong-lanceolate or spoon-shaped leaves. Flower heads of disc florets only are 5 x 2.5mm, yellowish-white, in clusters of 10 to 25, with one or two leaves overtopping the cluster; involucral bracts red-tipped. *Flowering:* July–August. *Distribution:* South-eastern England and southern Sweden south to central Spain, Sicily and Bulgaria; heathland, sandy areas. **Broad-leaved Cudweed** (*F. pyramidata*) has silvery-hairy leaves, and five to 20, five-angled flower heads; involucral bracts slightly bent back in fruit, not reddish. *Distribution:* Southern and western Europe; damp, sandy places.

Jersey Cudweed *Gnaphalium luteoalbum* Up to 50cm An upright annual, covered in dense white down. Leaves are oblong to linear. Flower heads of disc florets only are small, yellow, reddish above, in dense clusters. *Flowering:* July–September. *Distribution:* Europe northwards to southern England, and Sweden; damp, sandy places. **Marsh Cudweed** (*G. uliginosa*) is much branched, silvery-hairy, with yellow flower heads, in clusters of three to ten. *Distribution:* Most of Europe; bare, damp areas.

Stinking Everlasting *Helichrysum stoechas* Up to 100cm A strongly aromatic, slightly woody, branched perennial, with narrowly linear, white-downy leaves, sometimes hairless above. Flower heads of disc florets only are 4–6mm across, yellow, in terminal clusters up to 60mm across; involucral bracts papery. *Flowering:* June–September. *Distribution:* Southern and western Europe, northwards to France; dry, bare places. **H. italicum** is smaller, with greenish leaves, flower heads 2–4mm across; involucral bracts glandular. *Distribution:* Southern Europe; dry, bare places.

Mountain Everlasting *Antennaria dioica* Up to 30cm A mat-forming, densely-hairy perennial, woody at the base, with several rosettes of obovate to spoon- shaped, blunt leaves, dark green and hairless above, densely white-hairy beneath; upper stem leaves shortly pointed. Flower heads are small, pinkish or red, two to 12 in a cluster, of disc florets only; male and female heads on different plants. *Flowering:* June–July. *Distribution:* Most of Europe, but only on mountains in the south; grassland, heaths and rocky areas, to 3000m. **Carpathian Cat's-foot** (*A. carpatica*) is more downy, with oblanceolate to linear, pointed leaves; flower heads brown or blackish, in tight clusters; male florets cream. *Distribution:* Pyrenees, Alps, Carpathians; damp grassland, rocks, 1500–3100m.

Edelweiss *Leontopodium alpinum* Up to 30cm An upright, densely white-hairy perennial, with obovate to oblong leaves. Flower heads of yellowish-white disc florets are small, mostly globular, in dense clusters, with whorl of leaves beneath; involucral bracts densely hairy. *Flowering:* July–September. *Distribution:* Mountains; usually on limestone.

Blue Fleablane

Red-tipped Cudweed

Jersey Cudweed

Stinking Everlasting

Mountain Everlasting

Edelweiss

Elecampane

Small Fleabane

Astericus aquaticus:
flower head

Trifid Bur-marigold

Ploughman's-spikenard *Inula conyza* Up to 120cm An upright, slightly hairy perennial, branched at the top. Lower leaves are elliptical to oblong-lanceolate, toothed, the upper stalkless, with a wedge-shaped base. Flower heads are up to 2mm across, in a loosely branched cluster; disc and ray florets dull yellow, the rays 7–9mm long. *Flowering:* July–September. *Distribution:* Western, central and southern Europe to Denmark and the Ukraine; grassy and rocky areas, open woodland and scrub.

Golden-samphire *Inula crithmoides* Up to 100cm A hairless perennial, often woody at the base, with fleshy, linear to linear-lanceolate leaves, usually three-toothed at the apex. Flower heads are up to 25mm across; florets all yellow, ray florets 14 to 25, longer than bracts. *Flowering:* July–October. *Distribution:* Coastal in southern and western Europe, found inland in eastern Spain; shingle, salt-marshes and cliffs. **Elecampane** (*I. helenium*) is larger, to 250cm, downy-hairy, with ovate-elliptical leaves, the upper heart-shaped, clasping the stem; flower heads 60–80mm. *Distribution:* Cultivated and widely naturalised, probably native in south-eastern Europe; woods and grassy areas.

Common Fleabane *Pulicaria dysenterica* Up to 60 cm A branched, woolly-hairy perennial. Leaves oblong-lanceolate, wavy-edged, green above, greyish-woolly beneath. Short-stalked flower heads are 15–30mm across, in loose clusters; both disc and ray florets yellow; involucral bracts linear or pointed. *Flowering:* July–September. *Distribution:* Southern, western and central Europe, northwards to Denmark; damp places. **Small Fleabane** (*P. vulgaris*) is smaller, annual, with lanceolate upper leaves; flower heads 8–10mm; ray florets smaller. *Distribution:* Most of Europe, from southern England, southern Sweden and central Russia southwards.

Pallenis spinosa Up to 60cm An annual or biennial, downy-hairy, with branched stems woody at the base. Leaves are lanceolate to elliptical, with a minute point; upper leaves stalkless, clasping the stem. Flower heads are 15–25mm, yellow, at the tips of branches, with disc florets and two outer rows of three-toothed ray florets; involucral bracts long, spiny. *Flowering:* June–August. *Distribution:* Southern Europe; bare areas.

Astericus maritimus Up to 20cm A roughly hairy perennial, with branched, upright stems, and oblong or spoon-shaped, stalked leaves. Flower heads 15–20mm, yellow, at tips of branches; ray florets as long as involucral bracts; outer bracts 10mm, leathery below, with a blunt, spoon-shaped apex. *Flowering:* May–July. *Distribution:* Mediterranean, southern Portugal and Greece; seaside rocks. **A. aquaticus** is annual, with oblanceolate leaves, and yellow flower heads; ray florets much shorter than the bracts which have a leaf-like apex. *Distribution:* Mediterranean to Portugal and southern Bulgaria; damp sandy places.

Nodding Bur-marigold *Bidens cernua* Up to 90cm A downy-hairy annual, with linear-lanceolate to lanceolate, pointed, toothed, stalkless leaves. Flower heads are 15–25mm across, yellow, solitary, nodding, of either disc florets only, or with disc and ray florets; involucral bracts leaf-like. *Flowering:* July–October. *Distribution:* Most of Europe, except the far north and much of the Mediterranean; damp places. **Trifid Bur-marigold** (*B. tripartita*) is almost hairless; leaves three-lobed, with winged stalks; flower heads upright, always of disc florets only. *Distribution:* Most of Europe, rare in the far north and south; damp areas, often by fresh water.

Ploughman's-spikenard

Golden-samphire

Common Fleabane

Pallenis spinosa

Astericus maritimus

Nodding Bur-marigold

Jerusalem Artichoke

Shaggy Soldier

Stinking Chamomile

Sunflower *Helianthus annuus* Up to 300cm A stout, roughly hairy and usually unbranched annual with broadly ovate, toothed leaves 100–400 x 50–350mm, the lower ones heart-shaped at the base. Solitary, usually nodding flower head reaches 300mm across; disc florets brownish; ray florets 25mm or more long, yellow .*Flowering:* August–October. *Distribution:* Native to N. America, grown as a field crop in Europe and naturalised in many scattered places. **Jerusalem Artichoke** *(H. tuberosus)* is a tuberous perennial with smaller leaves white-hairy beneath; erect flower heads 40–80mm across, the disc florets yellow. *Flowering:* September–November. *Distribution:* Also N. American, cultivated for it's edible tubers; naturalised in many areas.

Gallant Soldier *Galinsoga parviflora* Up to 80cm A branched, sparsely hairy annual with ovate, pointed, toothed leaves, the stalk shorter than the leaf- blade. Flower heads are about 10mm across, in loose clusters; disc florets yellow; ray florets white, four to five around the disc. *Flowering:* June–October. *Distribution:* A South American plant, widely naturalised; waste places, cultivated ground. **Shaggy Soldier** (*G. quadriradiata)* is similar, but with hairy stems, and glandular-hairy flower stalks. *Distribution:* Native to Central and South America, widely naturalised; waste and cultivated areas.

Corn Chamomile *Anthemis arvensis* Up to 80cm A usually branched, greyish, downy-hairy annual or biennial. Leaves are much divided into linear segments, each with a bristle-like point. Flower heads are 15–40mm across, solitary at the tips of branches; disc florets yellow, ray florets white; involucral bracts hairy, oblong or oblong-obovate, with brown papery margins. *Flowering:* April–October. *Distribution:* Most of Europe; weed of cultivation. **Stinking Chamomile** (*A. cotula)* is similar but more upright, with wider leaf lobes and a strong, unpleasant smell; flowers 12–30mm across. *Distribution:* Most of Europe, northwards to England and southern Finland; waste and disturbed areas.

Yellow Chamomile *Anthemis tinctoria* Up to 50cm A grey-downy, upright perennial, with twice-pinnately-lobed leaves, the lobes oblong to linear. Flower heads are 25–40mm across; both disc and ray florets yellow. *Flowering:* July–August. *Distribution:* Most of Europe, except for much of the west and north, introduced elsewhere; dry, waste or bare places.

Yarrow *Achillea millefolium* Up to 60cm An upright, aromatic, downy perennial, with much-divided dark green leaves, the final segments ovate to lanceolate, or linear. Flower heads are up to 10mm across, in flat-topped clusters; disc florets creamy-white; ray florets white or pinkish, short, usually five. *Flowering:* June–November. *Distribution:* Most of Europe, rare in the Mediterranean; waste places, grassland, especially as turf weed.

Sneezewort *Achillea ptarmica* Up to 150cm A branched, downy perennial, with lanceolate, pointed, regularly toothed leaves, the bases clasping the stem. Flower heads are 12–20mm across, up to 15 together in a loose cluster; disc florets creamy; outer ray florets white, short. *Flowering:* July–September. *Distribution:* Southwards to northern Spain, northern Italy, south-western Romania and south-central Russia; damp grassland, on acid soils.

Sunflower

Gallant Soldier

Corn Chamomile

Yellow Chamomile

Yarrow

Sneezewort

Scentless Mayweed

Anacyclus clavatus

Sea Mayweed *Tripleurospermum maritimum* Up to 80cm A prostrate or upright, branched perennial. Leaves are much divided, the segments short and fleshy, either blunt or with a bristle-like point. Flower heads are 30–50mm across, solitary, up to 50 on a plant; disc florets yellow, ray florets white. Flowering: April–October. Distribution: Coastal areas of western and northern Europe; bare areas near the sea. **Scentless Mayweed** (*T. inodorum*) is annual, with the leaf segments not fleshy. *Distribution:* Most of Europe; bare or waste ground, or on salty soils.

Scented Mayweed *Matricaria recutita* Up to 60cm A strongly aromatic, hairless annual, with much divided leaves, the segments pointed. Flower heads are 10–25mm, solitary; disc florets yellow; ray florets white, turned down; involucral bracts with pale margins. *Flowering:* April–October. *Distribution:* Most of Europe but probably native only in the south and east; fields, waste places and saline soils, often grown as a medicinal plant. Very similar **Anacyclus clavatus** has stalks of flower heads becoming thickened and club-shaped after flowering; ray florets sometimes so short as to appear absent. *Distribution:* Mediterranean region and Iberia; disturbed ground.

Pineappleweed *Matricaria discoidea* 8–45cm A pineapple-scented perennial with rather fleshy stems branching above. Leaves are two- to three-times divided into narrow, flattened segments. Flower heads are 5–12mm but enlarge as they mature; disc florets greenish-yellow, ray florets absent; involucral bracts have a colourless margin. *Flowering:* June–July. *Distribution:* A weed of Asia and North America, widespread throughout Europe, but absent from much of south; bare and waste places, roadsides.

Cottonweed *Otanthus maritimus* Up to 50 cm A densely white-woolly perennial, with upright, woody stems. Leaves oblong to oblong lanceolate, shallowly toothed, stalkless. Flower heads of disc florets only are 6–9mm across, yellow, in small clusters at the tips of stems; involucral bracts ovate, the outer white-woolly. *Flowering:* August–November. *Distribution:* South-western Europe, northwards to south-eastern Ireland; coastal sand and shingle.

Crown Daisy *Chrysanthemum coronarium* Up to 80cm An ascending or upright, usually hairless annual. Leaves usually pinnately-lobed, the lobes divided into oblong or lanceolate, toothed segments. Flower heads are 30–50mm across, solitary on the tips of stalks; disc and ray florets yellow, the rays occasionally white at the tips; involucral bracts ovate, with a brown band and white papery margin and papery appendages. *Flowering:* April–July. *Distribution:* Central and southern Portugal, Mediterranean, occasionally naturalised; waste places and cultivated ground.

Corn Marigold *Chrysanthemum segetum* Up to 80cm A bluish-green, rather fleshy, annual. Leaves are oblong or obovate-oblong, the middle and lower stem leaves deeply toothed, the upper mostly entire and clasping the stem. Flower heads are 35–55mm across, bright golden-yellow, solitary at the tips of stems with both disc and ray florets; outer involucral bracts blunt, yellow-green, with pale brown bands at the margins, the apex papery. *Flowering:* June–October. *Distribution:* Extensively naturalised in western and parts of northern Europe, and locally elsewhere, probably native only in the Aegean region; cultivated fields and waste land, fluctuating greatly in numbers, usually on lime-free soil.

Sea Mayweed

Scented Mayweed

Pineappleweed

Cottonweed

Crown Daisy

Corn Marigold

Feverfew

Tansy *Tanacetum vulgare* Up to 150cm. A strongly aromatic perennial, branched towards the top. Leaves are glandular, pinnately lobed, the segments further lobed or divided; lower leaves stalked. Flower heads are 5–10mm across, yellow, up to 100 in a dense, flat-topped cluster; only disc florets present. *Flowering:* July–October. *Distribution:* Most of Europe, often as an escape from cultivation; grassland and waste places. **Feverfew** (*T. parthenium)* is usually yellowish-green, the flower heads 10–25mm, disc florets yellow, ray florets white. *Distribution:* Balkan Peninsula, but cultivated medicinally, and naturalised widely; hedgerows, walls and waste places.

Oxeye Daisy *Leucanthemum vulgare* Up to 100cm A perennial, little if at all branched. Leaves are dark grey-green, the basal obovate or spoon-shaped to oblong-obovate, long-stalked, gently toothed; stem leaves stalkless, deeply lobed. Flower heads 20–90mm across, usually solitary; disc florets yellow, ray florets white; involucral bracts ovate-oblong to lanceolate, with a dark, papery margin. *Flowering:* May–September. *Distribution:* Mainland Europe; hedgerows, walls, meadows and waste places.

Field Wormwood

Mugwort *Artemisia vulgaris* Up to 150cm An aromatic, tufted perennial, stems often red- or purple-tinged. Leaves are stalkless, pinnately lobed, the segments occasionally also deeply lobed, dark green and hairless above, densely woolly-hairy beneath. Yellowish flower heads are 1.5–3.5mm across, ovoid, numerous in branched spikes; florets all disc; involucral bracts greyish, downy-hairy. *Flowering:* July–September. *Distribution:* Most of Europe, rare in far north and south; roadsides, waste places. **Wormwood** (*A. absinthium)* is smaller, woody, and much more aromatic; leaves white, silky-hairy, two- or three-times lobed. *Distribution:* Most of Europe. **Field Wormwood** (*A. campestris)* is non-aromatic; leaves three-pinnately lobed. *Distribution:* Most of Europe, except much of north; dry sandy places.

Sea Wormwood *Seriphidium maritimum* Up to 60cm A strongly aromatic perennial, densely grey or white hairy, often woody at the base. Leaves are two- to three-pinnate, withering early; stem leaves stalkless, undivided or few-lobed. Flower heads 1.5–3.5mm, in nodding, or upright, branched spikes; disc florets only present. *Flowering:* August–October. *Distribution:* Coasts of western and northern Europe; salt-marshes, salty soils.

Colt's-foot *Tussilago farfara* Up to 15cm A perennial, flowering before the large, round, shallowly-lobed and toothed leaves emerge; leaves green above, white-woolly beneath, up to 300mm when mature. Flower heads are 15–35mm across, solitary, on a stem with many purplish scales; both disc and narrow ray florets bright yellow. Fruiting head nodding. *Flowering:* February–April. *Distribution:* Most of Europe; damp waste places.

White Butterbur

Butterbur *Petasites hybridus* Up to 30cm A distinctive perennial, flowering before the leaves emerge; leaves up to 100cm across, heart-shaped, downy-grey beneath, margins with irregular, blunt teeth. Flower heads unisexual, lilac or yellowish, 60 to 130 heads on each purplish-scaled stem, those of male plants 60–85mm across, of female plants 30–65mm. *Flowering:* March–May. *Distribution:* Europe northwards to Britain, Germany and central Russia, naturalised in some areas; damp places, streamsides and roadsides. **White Butterbur** (*P. albus),* has yellowish-white, fragrant flowers and smaller leaves, white-hairy beneath; *Distribution:* Norway southwards to France, Italy and Bulgaria; damp shade.

Tansy

Oxeye Daisy

Mugwort

Sea Wormwood

Colt's-foot

Butterbur

Alpine Adenostyles

Common Adenostyles *Adenostyles alliaria* Up to 200cm A downy
perennial with lower leaves up to 500mm across, triangular, heart- or kidney-
shaped, irregularly toothed, upper leaves clasping the stem. Flower heads
are 6–8mm long, reddish-purple, narrow, composed of only three to four disc
florets. *Flowering:* July–August. *Distribution:* Mountains from the Vosges and
Carpathians southwards to central Spain, Corsica and northern Greece;
woods, by streams and on damp rocks, to 2700m. **Alpine Adenostyles**
(*A. alpina*) is shorter, the lower leaves up to 150mm wide, kidney-shaped,
regularly toothed, hairless. *Distribution:* Alps, Apennines, the Jura, Corsica.

Arnica *Arnica montana* Up to 60cm A glandular-hairy, aromatic
perennial, with obovate, elliptical or oblanceolate leaves 60–170mm long.
Flower heads are 45–60mm across, up to seven in a branched cluster, their
stalks with two linear- lanceolate bracts; disc and ray florets yellow.
Flowering: May–August. *Distribution:* Southern Norway and Latvia,
southwards to Carpathians, Apennines and southern Portugal; alpine
meadows and open woods, to 2850m.

Austrian Leopard's-
bane

Large-flowered Leopard's-bane *Doronicum grandiflorum* Up to
35cm A downy perennial, with ovate, toothed basal leaves, narrowed to a
long stalk; upper leaves lanceolate, clasping the stem. Flower heads are
35–65mm across, solitary on densely glandular–downy stalks; both disc and
long ray florets yellow. *Flowering:* July–August. *Distribution:* Alps, southwards
to northern Spain, Corsica and Albania; rocks and scree, usually on
limestone. **Austrian Leopard's-bane** (*D. austriacum*) is taller; flower
heads five to 15 together in branched clusters. *Distribution:* Mountains of
central and southern Europe; meadows, stream sides and in woods.

Broad-leaved
Ragwort

Wood Ragwort *Senecio ovatus* Up to 200cm An upright, densely leafy
perennial, branched at the top. Leaves are elliptical to lanceolate, toothed,
often hairy beneath. Flower heads are 20–35mm across, in a branched, flat-
topped cluster; all florets yellow, the five to eight ray florets 12–15mm long.
Flowering: July–September. *Distribution:* Most of Europe but absent from
much of Scandinavia, the Mediterranean and the southeast; damp meadows,
and woods. **Broad-leaved Ragwort** (*S. fluviatilis*) has slightly broader,
hairless leaves, and ray florets 8–12mm long. *Distribution:* Central and
eastern Europe, naturalised in north-western Europe; damp meadows,
woods.

Hoary Ragwort

Common Ragwort *Senecio jacobaea* Up to 150cm A stout, often hairless
biennial or perennial, branched at the top. Leaves are pinnately lobed, the
terminal lobe blunt; stem leaves clasping the stem, sparsely downy beneath,
the lower stalked. Flower heads are 15–20mm across, yellow, numerous in
dense clusters; ray florets 12 to 15. *Flowering:* June–November. *Distribution:*
Most of Europe, but rare in the far north; dry grassy and waste places.
Hoary Ragwort (*S. erucifolius*) is downy-grey, with a more pointed terminal
leaf lobe and flower heads in a narrow cluster. *Distribution:* Most of Europe.

Oxford Ragwort *Senecio squalidus* Up to 60cm An annual or short-lived
perennial, with branching, upright stems. Leaves are mostly hairless, the lower
deeply pinnately lobed, with a winged stalk. Flower heads are 15-25mm
across, yellow, few or many in loose clusters. *Flowering:* April–November.
Distribution: Central and southern Europe, mainly in mountains, naturalised in
Britain and elsewhere; woods, scrub, rocks and walls, and waste ground.

Common Adenostyles

Arnica

Large-flowered Leopard's-bane

Wood Ragwort

Common Ragwort

Oxford Ragwort

Groundsel *Senecio vulgaris* Up to 40cm A sparsely downy, fleshy annual, with weak, unequally branched stems. Leaves are pinnately lobed, the lobes toothed; lower leaves stalked, upper stalkless, clasping the stem. Flower heads are 4–5mm across, yellow, in open clusters; usually with disc florets only, rarely ray florets also present. *Flowering:* All year. *Distribution:* Most of Europe; dry, disturbed sandy ground, wood edges.

Field Marigold *Calendula arvensis* Up to 30cm A more or less upright annual, often cottony-hairy, usually much-branched. Downy-hairy or sparsely felted leaves are oblong to narrowly obovate, the margins sometimes faintly toothed. Flower heads are 10–35mm across, solitary at tips of stems; disc florets yellow, orange or occasionally brown or violet, ray florets orange or yellow. *Flowering:* May–October. *Distribution:* Central and south-central Europe, naturalised further north; arable land, especially vineyards, and waste places.

Acanthus-leaved Carline Thistle *Carlina acanthifolia* Up to 30cm across A stemless perennial, dying after flowering. Leaves are pinnately-lobed, velvety-white beneath, the margins spiny-toothed. Flower heads are 30–70mm across, lilac, of disc florets only; inner involucral bracts yellowish, long, narrow, wide-spreading. *Flowering:* July–September. *Distribution:* From central France and southern Poland to the Pyrenees, Italy and northern Greece; meadows and on rocks, usually on limestone. **Stemless Carline Thistle** (*C. acaulis*) has stalkless flower heads; florets white to purple-brown; involucral bracts white or pale pink, purple-brown beneath. *Flowering:* July–September. *Distribution:* Central France and Russia, southwards to central Spain and Greece; meadows, rocks and woods.

Stemless Carline Thistle: floret

Carline Thistle *Carlina vulgaris* Up to 70cm An upright, hairless or downy biennial. Leaves are linear-oblong to ovate, spiny-toothed. Flower heads are 15–30mm across, yellowish-brown, solitary or in groups of two or three; disc florets only; outer involucral bracts linear-oblong to lanceolate, spiny, the inner long-linear, yellowish. *Flowering:* July–September. *Distribution:* Most of Europe; woodland, stony and grassy places.

Globe-thistle *Echinops ritro* Up to 60cm A stout white woolly and often glandular perennial. Leaves are pinnately-lobed, spiny, mostly hairless above, densely white-hairy beneath, the margins rolled over. Globular flower heads are 35–45mm across, blue, composed of five-lobed disc florets. *Flowering:* June–September. *Distribution:* Southern and eastern Europe, northwards to eastern Russia; dry, often rocky areas. Similar **Glandular Globe-thistle** (*E. sphaerocephalus*) is up to 200cm; leaves larger, clasping stem; flower heads white or greyish. *Distribution:* Southern and central Europe, often naturalised further north; habitat as for Globe-thistle.

Glandular Globe-thistle

Lesser Burdock *Arctium minus* Up to 150cm A downy biennial, with broadly ovate basal leaves, heart-shaped at the base, the leaf stalk hollow. Flower heads are 15–30 mm across, ovoid, solitary or in short stalked clusters, of purple disc florets only; outer involucral bracts end in long, hooked spines. *Flowering:* July–September. *Distribution:* Throughout Europe, except the Arctic; waste places, often in shade. **Greater Burdock** (*A. lappa*), is similar, but has solid basal leaf-stalks, larger, globular flower heads; involucral bracts become spreading in fruit. *Distribution:* Most of Europe, except the far north; habitat as for Lesser Burdock.

Greater Burdock: fruiting head

Groundsel

Field Marigold

Acanthus-leaved Carline Thistle

Carline Acanthus

Globe-thistle

Lesser Burdock

Heart-leaved
Saussurea

Alpine Saw–wort *Saussurea alpina* Up to 50cm An upright perennial, with ovate to linear-lanceolate, usually toothed lower leaves, downy-grey beneath, rounded or wedge-shaped at the base; stalk winged. Flower heads are 15–20mm across, ovoid, in clusters at the tips of stems, of purple disc florets only. *Flowering:* July–September. *Distribution:* Europe, southwards to the southern Carpathians, Alps and Pyrenees; grassland, screes and rocks, 500–3000m. **Heart-leaved Saussurea** *(S. discolor)* has triangular-lanceolate lower leaves, heart- or wedge-shaped at the base; stalks wingless; flower heads in compact clusters, scented; florets bluish-violet. *Distribution:* Alps, Carpathians, Apennines and Bulgaria.

Musk Thistle *Carduus nutans* Up to 150cm A perennial, with white, cottony, winged stems, the wings with spiny triangular lobes. Leaves with six to ten pairs of spine-tipped lobes. Flower heads are 20–45mm across, usually solitary, nodding on long stalks; of reddish-purple disc florets only; involucral bracts spine-tipped, the uppermost bent back. *Flowering:* June–September. *Distribution:* Western and central Europe, northwards to Scotland, southwards to Sicily, Yugoslavia and Ukraine; bare or grassy areas.

Melancholy Thistle *Cirsium heterophyllum* Up to 150cm A perennial, unbranched or branched only at the top. Leaves are lanceolate to oblong, white-woolly beneath, pinnately lobed, toothed or entire, softly spiny, clasping the stem. Flower heads are 35–50mm wide, solitary on long stalks; of purple disc florets only; involucral bracts upright, with weak spines. *Flowering:* June–August. *Distribution:* Northern Europe and in mountains southwards to Pyrenees and Romania; roadsides, meadows, woods and scrub.

Woolly Thistle

Spear Thistle *Cirsium vulgare* Up to 300cm A downy biennial, with winged, spiny stems. Leaves are pinnately lobed, spiny, sparsely cottony-hairy or downy underneath; leaf-bases run down onto stem. Flower heads 20–40mm across; purple florets all disc; involucral bracts narrowing into sharp spines. *Flowering:* July–September. *Distribution:* Throughout Europe; waste places, bare ground. **Woolly Thistle** *(C. eriophorum)* is white-woolly, very spiny, with a wingless stem; flower heads 40–70mm across, densely cottony-hairy; involucral bracts unarmed or with short, weak spines. *Distribution:* Western and central Europe, Italy and Balkans.

Marsh Thistle: spiny-winged stem

Creeping Thistle *Cirsium arvense* Up to 120cm A far-creeping perennial, with spineless stems. Leaves usually clasping the stem, often cottony beneath, lanceolate to oblong, entire or pinnately lobed, the lobes triangular with often stout spines. Flower heads 15–25mm across, scented, one to five at the ends of stems; lilac-purple florets all disc; involucral bracts purple-tinged, with weak spines. *Flowering:* June–September. *Distribution:* Most of Europe; cultivated or waste places, grassland. **Marsh Thistle** *(C. palustre)* is biennial, not creeping, the stem spiny-winged; florets purple. *Distribution:* Most of Europe; woods, damp meadows and marshy areas.

Dwarf Thistle *Cirsium acaule* Up to 35cm A perennial, usually stemless with wavy-edged leaves are in a wavy-edged basal rosette, oblong-lanceolate, pinnately lobed, the lobes ovate or semi-circular in cross-section, toothed, spiny. Flower heads 20-50mm across, solitary; purple florets all disc; involucral bracts with spiny tips. *Flowering:* June-September. *Distribution:* England and Estonia to Spain, Yugoslavia and south-eastern Russia; short grassland, usually on lime.

Alpine Saw-wort

Musk Thistle

Melancholy Thistle

Spear Thistle

Creeping Thistle

Dwarf Thistle

Syrian Thistle *Notobasis syriaca* Up to 150cm A usually branched, spiny annual, bluish above. Basal leaves are white-veined above, cottony-hairy beneath, toothed or lobed, and spiny; stem leaves leathery, oblong-lanceolate to lanceolate, pinnately lobed, spiny, the uppermost reduced to strong spines surrounding flower heads. Flower heads are 15–25mm across, solitary or in clusters; florets all disc, purple, rarely white. *Flowering:* May-August. *Distribution:* Mediterranean region; cultivated ground, dry places.

Galactites tomentosa Up to 100cm An annual, with leaves white-veined above, downy-white beneath; stalked basal leaves are oblanceolate, toothed, soon withering; stalkless stem leaves pinnately lobed, spiny, the margins running onto the stem. Flower heads are 10–15mm across; purple florets all disc, the outer enlarged, sterile. *Flowering:* May–August. *Distribution:* Mediterranean and south-western Europe; dry, bare places.

Onopordum illyricum

Cotton Thistle *Onopordum acanthium* Up to 300cm A tall, very spiny biennial, covered with white, cottony down, the stems with broad, lobed, spiny wings. Leaves are oblong-ovate to broadly lanceolate, greyish-green, margins wavy or spiny toothed. Flower heads are 25–60mm across, solitary or in clusters of up to five; florets purple, all disc; involucral bracts gradually tapering into spines. *Flowering:* July–September. *Distribution:* Europe northwards to France and Russia, naturalised in the north; bare and waste ground. **O. illyricum** is smaller, with yellowish, hairy stems, pinnately lobed leaves, and cottony-hairy flower heads with down-curving spines. *Distribution:* Mediterranean, Portugal and southern Bulgaria; dry or waste areas.

Globe Artichoke

Cardoon *Cynara cardunculus* Up to 100cm A vigorous, woolly-downy perennial. Leaves are up to 500 x 350mm, bright green, downy above, densely woolly below, the ovate to linear-lanceolate lobes with stout yellow spines at the tip and clustered at the base. Flower heads are 45–60mm across, solitary; florets blue, lilac or white; involucral bracts with a strong spine. *Flowering:* June–August. *Distribution:* Southern and western Mediterranean; waste and stony ground, dry grassland, often relic of cultivation. Similar but larger **Globe Artichoke** (*C. scolymus*) has flower heads up to 80mm across; involucral bracts fleshy. *Distribution:* Grown for flower heads, unknown in the wild but naturalised in places.

Milk Thistle *Silybum marianum* Up to 150 cm A spiny, hairless or cottony-hairy annual or biennial. Stalked basal leaves are pinnately lobed, spiny, with white veins; stem leaves stalkless, clasping the stem, with yellowish-white spines. Flower heads 25–40mm across, solitary on long stalks; florets purple, all disc; outer involucral bracts with triangular apical appendages narrowing into spines of 20–50mm. *Flowering:* June–August. *Distribution:* Mediterranean and south- western Europe, naturalised elsewhere; roadsides, waste places.

Single-flowered Saw-wort

Saw–wort *Serratula tinctoria* Up to 100cm An upright, downy or hairless perennial, with ovate-lanceolate, irregularly toothed or pinnately lobed leaves, the lobes saw-toothed. Flower heads are 15–20mm across, in branched clusters; florets purple, all disc; involucral bracts greenish or purple-tinged. *Flowering:* July–October. *Distribution:* Most of Europe, except Scandinavia and much of the Mediterranean; damp grassland. **Single-flowered Saw-wort** (*S. lycopifolia*) has solitary flower heads 20- 30mm across. *Distribution:* East-central Europe; meadows and scrubland.

Syrian Thistle

Galactites tomentosa

Cotton Thistle

Cardoon

Milk Thistle

Saw-wort

Red Star-thistle *Centaurea calcitrapa* Up to 100cm An ascending or upright perennial, much branched from the base. Leaves are grey-woolly when young, becoming greenish and downy, the lower pinnately lobed and usually withering early; upper with linear-lanceolate, spiny lobes. Flower heads are 8–10mm across, stalkless, surrounded by upper leaves; florets all disc, pale purple; involucral bracts ending in a long yellow spine, with shorter spines at base. *Flowering:* July–September. *Distribution:* Southern and south-central Europe, naturalised in western and central Europe; dry waste places.

Brown Knapweed *Centaurea jacea* Up to 120cm A perennial with up to five ascending or erect, little-branched stems. Leaves have rough margins, the basal ovate to broad-lanceolate, entire, toothed or pinnately lobed; stem leaves stalkless, oblong-lanceolate, entire or toothed. Flower heads are 10–20mm across; florets purple, rarely white, all disc florets but the outer ring larger and resembling ray florets; involucral bracts brownish. *Flowering:* June–September. *Distribution:* Most of Europe; grassy places.

Greater Knapweed

Common Knapweed *Centaurea nigra* Up to 100cm An erect or ascending, branched perennial. Leaves are green to grey cottony-hairy, the lower lanceolate to ovate, toothed or lobed, upper lanceolate, entire. Flower heads 20–40mm across, solitary or in clusters at the tips of branches; florets purple, all disc; involucral bracts with black or blackish-brown apical appendages. *Flowering:* June–September. *Distribution:* Europe east to Sweden and Italy, one area in Yugoslavia; grassland. **Greater Knapweed** (*C. scabiosa*) is taller with pinnately lobed lower leaves; flower heads solitary. *Distribution:* Europe, from central Spain, central Italy and Bulgaria northwards; grassy areas, usually on limestone.

Perennial Cornflower *Centaurea montana* Up to 80cm A creeping perennial, with upright, winged stems. Leaves are lanceolate, entire, toothed or lobed, sparsely to densely downy-hairy beneath, the lower shortly stalked. Flower heads are 60–80mm across, solitary at the tips of stems; florets all disc, outer blue, larger than violet inner; involucral bracts with short, dark-brown apical appendages. *Flowering:* May–July. *Distribution:* From the Ardennes and Carpathians to the Pyrenees, central Italy and central Yugoslavia; meadows and open woodland, often on limestone.

Downy Safflower

Safflower *Carthamus tinctorius* Up to 60cm An annual with ovate to lanceolate-ovate, sometimes pinnately lobed leaves, often spiny-toothed. Flower heads are broadly ovoid; florets all disc, yellow, orange or reddish; involucral bracts are spiny, the outer leaf-like. *Flowering:* June–September. *Distribution:* A West Asian plant, grown for its flowers in southern and central Europe, and often naturalised; dry and bare places. **Downy Safflower** (*C. lanatus*) is glandular-hairy with pinnately lobed leaves with strong terminal spines; florets yellow or rarely white. *Flowering:* June–September. *Distribution:* Southern Europe, northwards to France and Czechoslovakia.

Carduncellus caeruleus

Carduncellus mitissimus Less than 10cm A stemless, cobweb-hairy perennial with pinnately lobed leaves, the lobes spine-tipped and sometimes also spiny-toothed. Flower heads are 15–20mm across; florets all disc, blue-purple; involucral bracts with spiny teeth and apex, the outer ones leaf-like. *Flowering:* May–July. *Distribution:* Endemic to France and north-east Spain. **C. caeruleus** is very similar but has a stem up to 60cm high. *Flowering:* June–August. *Distribution:* Western Mediterranean; dry, open habitats.

Red Star-thistle

Brown Knapweed

Common Knapweed

Perennial Cornflower

Safflower

Carduncellus mitissimus

Scolymus maculatus

Endive: flower heads

Golden-thistle *Scolymus hispanicus* Up to 80cm A more or less hairy perennial, with spiny-winged stems. Long-stalked basal leaves are oblanceolate, pinnately lobed, with strong, rigid spines; stem leaves stiff, lobed, spiny. Flower heads are 15–25mm, in a narrow cluster, composed of yellow ray florets; involucral bracts lanceolate, with a spiny apex. *Flowering:* June–September. *Distribution:* Southern Europe to north-western France; dry, open habitats. **S. maculatus** is annual, the leaves with strongly thickened white margins; flower heads 15–20mm, with ovate-lanceolate, spiny involucral bracts. *Distribution:* Southern Europe, naturalised elsewhere; dry, bare places.

Chicory *Cichorium intybus* Up to 120cm A branched, hairless or slightly hairy perennial, with milky sap. Basal leaves are pinnately lobed, pointed; stem leaves lobed or entire, clasping the stem. Flower heads are 25–40mm across, several together in leafy spikes, composed of bright blue ray florets only; seeds 2–3mm long. *Flowering:* June–September. *Distribution:* Most of Europe, doubtfully native in the north; grassland, roadsides and waste areas, often a relic of cultivation. **Endive** (*C. endivia*) is annual or biennial, with the stalks of the flower heads strongly thickened, and larger seeds. *Distribution:* Southern Europe, widely cultivated elsewhere; similar habitats to Chicory.

Spotted Cat's-Ear *Hypochoeris maculata* Up to 80cm A sometimes sparingly branched perennial. Basal leaves are 40–300mm, elliptical to ovate, slightly to deeply toothed, hairy, usually with dark purple blotches; stem leaves few or none. Flower heads 45–60mm across, composed of pale yellow ray florets only; involucral bracts in several rows, margins often downy. *Flowering:* June–August. *Distribution:* Europe, except the Arctic and most of the Mediterranean; meadows and open woodlands, especially on lime-rich soils.

Common Cat's-ear *Hypochoeris radicata* Up to 100cm A usually branched, hairless or roughly hairy perennial. Leaves are all basal, oblong to elliptical or oblanceolate, toothed or pinnately lobed. Flower heads are 20–40mm across, of bright yellow ray florets only, solitary at the ends of stems which are usually thickened below the head; involucral bracts in several rows, hairless. *Flowering:* June–September. *Distribution:* Europe northwards to south-eastern Norway, eastwards to Latvia, western Ukraine and the Aegean; dry, grassy places.

Autumn Hawkbit *Leontodon autumnalis* Up to 60cm A perennial, often with several, usually branched stems, hairless or sometimes with a few hairs. Leaves are stalked, narrowly oblanceolate, pointed, wavy-edged, toothed to deeply pinnately lobed, the lobes narrowly lanceolate or linear. Flower heads are 10–35mm across in a loosed-branched cluster, composed of up to seven deep yellow ray florets only, the outermost with a red stripe on the outer surface; involucral bracts small, scale-like. *Flowering:* July–October. *Distribution*: Most of Europe, but rarer in the south; dry, grassy places.

Rough Hawkbit *Leontodon hispidus* Up to 70cm A perennial, often with several branches. Leaves are oblanceolate, obtuse to acute, toothed to pinnately lobed with a large terminal lobe, hairless or with trifid hairs. Flower heads are 25–40mm across, solitary at the ends of stems; ray florets only, bright yellow, the outermost orange, reddish or rarely, dull violet. *Flowering:* June–October. *Distribution:* Most of Europe; dry grassland, often on lime-rich soils.

Golden-thistle

Chicory

Spotted Cat's-ear

Common Cat's-ear

Autumn Hawkbit

Rough Hawkbit

Hawkweed Oxtongue

Bristly Oxtongue *Picris echioides* Up to 90cm A much branched annual or biennial, covered with rough, raised hairs and sometimes also with slender spines. Basal leaves are elliptical or oblong, blunt or sharp-pointed, wavy to toothed, with a winged stalk; lower stem leaves are similar, but with the stalk clasping the stem; upper lanceolate or ovate, stalkless, clasping the stem. Flower heads are 20–25mm across, many in a cluster, composed of yellow ray florets only; outer involucral bracts triangular. *Flowering:* June–November. *Distribution:* Southern Europe, widely naturalised further north; rough, grassy places. **Hawkweed Oxtongue** (*P. hieracioides*) is similar, but spineless, without raised hairs; flower heads fewer; involucral bracts lanceolate to narrowly elliptical. *Distribution:* Most of Europe; grassland or waste places.

Viper's-grass *Scorzonera humilis* Up to 120cm A mostly hairless, usually unbranched perennial. Basal leaves linear to ovate-elliptical, pointed, narrowed into a stalk; flowering stems with up to seven leaves, the upper scale-like. Flower heads are 20–30mm, composed of yellow ray florets which are sometimes brownish outside, longer than the involucral bracts. *Flowering:* May–July. *Distribution:* Much of Europe, except the northern, southern and eastern margins; damp grassland.

Goat's-beard *Tragopogon pratensis* Up to 70cm A more or less hairless, few- branched annual or perennial, with linear-lanceolate leaves clasping the stem. Flower heads are 15–25mm across, yellow, solitary at the tips of stems, opening only on sunny mornings; outer involucral bracts either slightly longer or slightly shorter than the florets. *Flowering:* May–August. *Distribution:* Most of Europe; dry grassland, roadsides and in waste places.

Salsify *Tragopogon porrifolius* Up to 125cm Resembling Goatsbeard, but with broadly linear leaves, widened at the base. Flower heads are up to 50mm across, solitary on inflated stalks; florets dull purple; involucral bracts about the same size as florets. *Flowering:* April–June. *Distribution:* Mediterranean, to eastern Romania, widely cultivated and often naturalised in northern, western and central Europe; grassland, waste places and old cultivated ground.

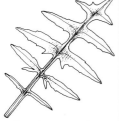

Sonchus tenerrimus

Prickly Sow-thistle *Sonchus asper* Up to 200cm An often branched annual or biennial, hairless except for the upper part of the stem and leaf stalks. Leaves are very spiny, entire or pinnately lobed, the lobes linear or triangular; upper leaves clasp the stem. Flower heads are 20–30mm across, in a loose cluster, composed of pale yellow ray florets. *Flowering:* May–November. *Distribution:* Most of Europe; waste places and cultivated ground. **S. tenerrimus** is often perennial, the leaves white-downy when young; flower heads with white, downy- hairy base and stalk. *Distribution:* Southern Europe; dry areas.

Smooth Sow-thistle *Sonchus oleraceus* Up to 140cm An often branched, greyish annual or biennial. Leaves are hairless, the lower undivided, with a winged stalk; upper larger, pinnately lobed, clasping the stem, softly spiny along the margins, often downy-white at the base of the flower heads and the upper part of the flower stalk. Flower heads 20–35mm, in a loose cluster, composed of pale yellow ray florets. *Flowering:* May–November. *Distribution:* Throughout most of Europe; waste ground, and as a weed of cultivation.

Bristly Oxtongue

Viper's-grass

Goat's-beard

Salsify

Prickly Sow-thistle

Smooth Sow-thistle

Marsh Sow-thistle

Great Lettuce: leaf, underside

Purple Lettuce

Perennial Sow-thistle *Sonchus arvensis* Up to 150cm A creeping, often branched perennial. Leaves are hairless, greyish beneath, the lower pinnately lobed, the upper less deeply lobed and clasping the stem; leaf margins softly spiny. Flower heads are 40–50mm across in terminal clusters, of golden yellow ray florets only. *Flowering:* July–September. *Distribution:* Throughout Europe, except for parts of south-west; dry, bare and cultivated areas. **Marsh Sow-thistle** (*S. palustris*) is up to 400cm; lower leaves clasping the stem, with lanceolate lobes on either side of stem; flower heads in tight clusters. *Distribution:* England, Scandinavia and north-central Russia southwards to France, northern Italy and Bulgaria; marshes, wet areas.

Prickly Lettuce *Lactuca serriola* Up to 180 cm An upright, rigid-stemmed, branched, often pungent annual or biennial. Leaves are rigid, spiny on margins and midrib beneath; basal leaves usually deeply pinnately lobed; stem leaves all held vertically in a north-south plane. Flower heads of seven to 35 yellow ray florets are 11–15mm across, in a long, crowded spike. *Flowering:* July–September. *Distribution:* Most of Europe; bare and waste ground. Similar **Great Lettuce** (*L. virosa*) is larger, with upper leaves held horizontally; flower heads in a long, pyramidal spike. *Distribution:* Southern, western and central Europe; stony or sandy places. **Least Lettuce** (*L. saligna*) is smaller, spineless, whitish; leaves clasp stem with two narrow lobes. *Distribution:* Europe northwards to southern England, central Germany, south-central Russia; bare, grassy places, often by sea.

Alpine Blue-sow-thistle *Cicerbita alpina* Up to 250cm A perennial, the upper parts with dense, reddish, glandular hairs. Leaves are hairless, grey-green beneath, the lower pinnately lobed with a winged stalk, the upper smaller and less divided. Flower heads 20mm across, in leafy spikes; of pale blue ray florets only. *Flowering:* July–September. *Distribution:* Scandinavia, and mountains of Europe; grassy and rocky places, and open woodland to 2200m. **Purple Lettuce** (*Prenanthes purpurea*) has leaves not or less deeply lobed; florets purple, few. *Distribution:* Central France and Poland southwards to northern Spain, Italy and Greece; woods and shady places.

Wall Lettuce *Mycelis muralis* Up to 100cm A hairless, often purple-tinged perennial with pinnately lobed leaves, the terminal lobe triangular; leaf stalk winged; leaves become smaller and less divided up the stem. Flower heads 7–10mm across, of loose branched clusters; each composed of five, yellow ray florets only. *Flowering:* June–September. *Distribution:* Most of Europe, naturalised in Ireland; shady places, woods, on walls and rocks.

Common Dandelion *Taraxacum officinale* Up to 50cm A very variable perennial, with a rosette of basal leaves ranging from almost entire to deeply pinnately lobed, on often winged stalks. Flower heads are 35–50mm, solitary at tips of stout, hollow stalks; composed of yellow ray florets only. *Flowering:* All year, but at best April–June. *Distribution:* Throughout Europe; grassland, waste ground and cultivated land.

Nipplewort *Lapsana communis* Up to 125cm A hairy annual, with ovate, toothed leaves, pinnately lobed towards the base, the terminal lobe larger. Flower heads are 10–20mm across, nipple-shaped in bud, carried in branched clusters, of yellow ray florets only, not opening on dull days. *Flowering:* June–October. *Distribution:* Throughout Europe; shady, bare or waste land, often a garden weed.

Perennial Sow-thistle

Prickly Lettuce

Alpine Blue-sow-thistle

Wall Lettuce

Common Dandelion

Nipplewort

Smooth Hawk's-beard *Crepis capillaris* Up to 100cm An annual or biennial, often many-stemmed and branched from the base. Leaves are hairless or sparsely hairy, pinnately lobed, the lobes triangular; stem leaves clasp the stem. Flower heads are 10–15mm across, in loose clusters, of yellow ray florets only, the outer often red-tinged; outer involucral bracts spreading. *Flowering:* June–November. *Distribution:* Western, central and southern Europe; naturalised in parts of north and east; grassland and waste areas.

Beaked Hawk's-beard *Crepis vesicaria* Up to 150cm A usually branched annual or perennial. Leaves are hairless or downy, the basal and lower stem leaves oblanceolate or ovate, blunt-tipped, toothed or pinnately lobed, narrowed at the base; upper lanceolate, clasping the stem. Flower heads are 15–25mm across, upright in bud, in a loose cluster; ray florets only, yellow, the outer orange beneath. *Flowering:* May–July. *Distribution:* Southern, central and western Europe, northwards to the Netherlands and western Austria, naturalised in Britain and Ireland; grassland and waste places. **Stinking Hawk's-beard** (*C. foetida*) is smaller, the leaves stiffly hairy, smelling of bitter almonds when crushed; flower heads fewer, smaller, drooping in bud. *Distribution:* Most of Europe, except from the north.

Stinking Hawk's-beard

Mouse-ear Hawkweed *Hieraceum pilosella* Up to 50cm A perennial, with long, leafy stolons, and a basal rosette of leaves. Leaves are oblanceolate, spoon-shaped or elliptical, blunt-tipped, with long hairs on both sides. Flower heads are 20–30mm across, solitary at the tips of leafless stems; of lemon-yellow ray florets only. *Flowering:* May–October. *Distribution:* Most of Europe; grassland.

Yellow Fox-and-cubs

Fox-and-cubs *Hieraceum aurantiaca* Up to 65cm A perennial, with leafy stolons above or below the ground, and a rosette of few, pale green or greenish-grey, ovate-lanceolate leaves, narrowed at the base. Blackish-hairy stems have few leaves. Flower heads are 15–20mm, up to ten together at the tips of stems; of orange-brown or brick-red ray florets only. *Flowering:* June–August. *Distribution:* Northern and central Europe, mainly in mountain areas, southwards to south-central France and Bulgaria, widely cultivated and naturalised elsewhere; meadows and waste areas, up to 2600m. Very similar **Yellow Fox-and-cubs** (*H. caespitosum*) differs in having yellow florets. *Distribution:* Northern and eastern Europe.

Alpine Hawkweed *Hieracium alpinum* Up to 35cm A perennial, with dark, stellate hairs and simple glandular and non-glandular hairs on the stems. Leaves are mostly in a basal rosette, more or less obovate and densely hairy; stem leaves few, small. Flower heads are 25–35mm across, usually solitary on a few-leaved stem; of yellow ray florets only. *Flowering:* July–August. *Distribution:* Northern and central Europe; grassland and rocky areas, on mountains.

Leafy Hawkweed *Hieracium umbellatum* Up to 150c A downy-hairy perennial, sometimes becoming hairless with age. Leaves are on stems only, crowded, linear, lanceolate or oblong-lanceolate, pointed, wedge-shaped or narrowed at the base, entire or toothed. Flower heads are 20–30mm across, many together in clusters, on stalks with leafy bracts; of yellow ray florets only. *Flowering:* June–November. *Distribution:* Most of Europe; grassland and heathland.

Smooth Hawk's-beard

Beaked Hawk's-beard

Mouse-ear Hawkweed

Fox-and-cubs

Alpine Hawkweed

Leafy Hawkweed

Lesser Water-plantain

Narrow-leaved Water-plantain

Arrowhead *Sagittaria sagittifolia* 30–90cm An aquatic perennial. Long-stalked aerial leaves are arrowhead-shaped; if present, floating leaves are lanceolate to ovate, lacking basal lobes of aerial leaves, submerged leaves narrower, transluscent. Unisexual flowers in whorls in a usually unbranched spike have parts in threes; petals 10–15mm, white with a purple basal patch; purple stamens numerous. *Flowering:* July–August. *Distribution:* Throughout Europe but rare in the far north and south; shallow, still or slow-moving water, marshy ground. **Lesser Water-plantain** (*Baldellia ranunculoides*) has elliptical to lanceolate leaves in a basal rosette and white or pale pink hermaphrodite flowers borne in an umbel or one to two whorls; stamens six.

Water-plantain *Alisma plantago-aquatica* 20–100cm A stout aquatic perennial. Leaves are usually all aerial, the first ones reduced to a narrow-bladed stalk, later leaves with an ovate blade rounded or heart-shaped at the base. Flowers borne in a much branched cluster, their parts in threes; petals 3.5–6.5mm, usually pale lilac, sometimes white. Flowers open from early afternoon to early evening. *Flowering:* June–August. *Distribution:* All Europe except for a few islands; still and slow-moving water and marshy places. Very similar **Narrow-leaved Water-plantain** (*A. lanceolatum*) has leaf blades which narrow gradually into the stalk. *Distribution:* As for Water-plantain.

Starfruit *Damasonium alisma* Up to 30cm, sometimes more An aquatic perennial with floating and sometimes submerged and aerial leaves, all basal and long- stalked. Floating leaves are up to 8cm, ovate to oblong with a heart-shaped base; aerial leaves narrower with a wedge-shaped base. Flowers are about 6mm across, parts in threes. White petals have a yellow basal spot. Pod-like fruits usually six, spreading to form a distinctive star shape. *Flowering:* June–August. *Distribution:* Western and southern Europe, north to England; ponds and ditches.

Flowering-rush *Butomus umbellatus* Up to 150cm A usually aquatic perennial spreading and forming clumps by means of a creeping rhizome. Narrow, emergent leaves are all basal, about as long as stems, triangular in cross-section. Cylindrical stem bears a terminal umbel of flowers with unequal stalks. Flower parts in threes; perianth segments 10–15mm, all petal-like, pink with darker veins, the outer three segments greenish on the outer midrib. *Flowering:* July–September. *Distribution:* Most of Europe; still and slow-moving water, wet mud.

Frogbit *Hydrocharis morsus-ranae* A free-floating aquatic plant with stolons bearing clusters of leaves and roots at the nodes. Leaves are about 30mm across, round to kidney-shaped, floating on the water. Unisexual flowers, borne above the water, have three crumpled white petals, each with a yellow basal spot. Male flowers in clusters of one to four, female flowers solitary. Fruit is fleshy. *Flowering:* July–August. *Distribution:* Most of Europe, though rare in the Mediterranean; still and slow-moving water.

Water-soldier *Stratiotes aloides* An aquatic plant, submerged for most of the year but rising to the surface to flower. Short stems bear stolons and large basal rosettes of narrow, brittle, spiny-toothed leaves up to 50cm long. White flowers have three thick petals 15–25mm long; males several in a cluster, females solitary, on different plants. *Flowering:* June–August. *Distribution:* Most of Europe, rare in the south and west; still and slow-moving chalky waters.

Arrowhead

Water-plantain

Starfruit

Flowering-rush

Frogbit

Water-soldier

Various-leaved
Pondweed:
submerged leaves

Broad-leaved Pondweed *Potamogeton natans* Up to 100cm, rarely 500cm in deep water An aquatic perennial with a creeping rhizome and both floating and submerged leaves. Floating leaves up to 12.5cm are ovate to elliptical, the joint between the stalk and blade flexible and discoloured; submerged leaves very narrow, up to 300 x 1–3mm. Flowers forming a dense cylindrical spike held above the water; four perianth-segments greenish. *Flowering:* May–September. *Distribution:* Almost all of Europe; usually shallow, organically rich water. **Various-leaved Pondweed** (*P. gramineus*) has elliptical to oblong submerged leaves up to 80 x 30mm and few if any floating leaves. *Flowering:* June–September. *Distribution:* Throughout but rare in the Mediterranean region.

Fennel Pondweed *Potamogeton pectinatus* 40–200cm A much-branched submerged aquatic perennial with only the flowers appearing above the water surface. Very fine leaves 50–200mm long and less than 2mm wide consist of two parallel tubes; sheathing bases have white margins. Inconspicuous greenish flowers carried in a short, aerial spike; perianth segments four. *Flowering:* May–September. *Distribution:* Throughout Europe; still or slow-moving water; tolerant of salty and mildly polluted water.

Bog Asphodel *Narthecium ossifragum* 5–45cm A rhizomatous perennial with rigid, curved basal leaves of 30–200mm arranged in a flat fan; stem leaves much smaller, clasping. Terminal spike with six to 20 bright yellow flowers which, with the stem, turn orange after pollination. Six spreading perianth segments all petal-like, 6–9mm long; stamens woolly. *Flowering:* July–September. *Distribution:* Northwest Europe, east to Sweden and Czechoslovakia, south to Portugal; acid bogs and heaths.

Black False-
helleborine

White False-helleborine *Veratrum album* 50–175cm A robust, rhizomatous perennial with hollow, leafy stems. Leaves are alternate, the lower 100–250mm, elliptical, finely hairy beneath and with a long sheathing base. Much branched inflorescence contains numerous flowers each 15–25mm across. Six perianth segments are wide-spreading, greenish or yellowish, or whitish on the the inside. *Flowering:* July–August. *Distribution:* Much of Europe except the islands, the north-west and parts of the north-east; damp mountain pastures. **Black False-helleborine** (*V. nigrum*) differs in having completely hairless leaves and reddish- brown flowers 9–15mm across. *Flowering:* June–August. *Distribution:* Central and southern Europe west to Italy; mountain meadows and woods.

White Asphodel *Asphodelus albus* 30–150cm A rhizomatous perennial with a solid stem and flat leaves 150–600 x 10–20mm, all basal. White, star-shaped flowers in a dense terminal spike have six narrow, spreading perianth segments 15–20mm long. *Flowering:* May–July. *Distribution:* Southern Europe northwards to France, Switzerland and Hungary; heaths, woods and grassy places.

Hollow-stemmed Asphodel *Asphodelus fistulosus* 15–70cm
A slender annual or perennial with hollow, cylindrical stems and leaves. Leaves are 30–350 x 4mm, all basal. Flowers borne in dense, sometimes branched spikes. Six somewhat spreading perianth segments are 5–12mm, oblong and blunt, joined at the base, pinkish-white with a darker central stripe. *Flowering:* April–May. *Distribution:* Mediterranean and south-western Europe; dry, sandy soils, often cultivated fields and roadsides.

Broad-leaved Pondweed

Fennel Pondweed

Bog Asphodel

White False-helleborine

White Asphodel

Hollow-stemmed Asphodel

Asphodeline liburnica

Yellow Asphodel *Asphodeline lutea* 40–80cm A fleshy-rooted perennial with a stout stem completely covered with sheathing, papery leaf bases. Alternate, linear leaves reach 300 x 15–30mm, the lower curved outwards. Dense, terminal flower spike is 100–200mm long, one to three greenish-yellow flowers in axil of each papery bract; bracts 20–30 x 8–12mm, the tip drawn out. Perianth has a short tube and six narrow, spreading lobes 20–25mm long. *Flowering:* April–May. *Distribution:* Mediterranean, from Italy and Sicily eastwards; dry grassy and rocky areas. Similar **A. liburnica** has the stem leafy in the lower half only; bracts up to 15 x 3mm. *Flowering:* June–July. *Distribution:* Southern Italy, Balkan peninsula, Crete.

St Bernard's Lily *Anthericum liliago* 20–70mm A hairless perennial, the flat, grass-like leaves 120–400 x 3–7mm, all basal and with papery sheathing bases. Spike is unbranched or with a few short basal branches, with six to ten white, star-shaped flowers. Perianth segments are joined at the very base, the six narrow segments 16–22mm and considerably longer than the stamens. *Flowering:* May–July. *Distribution:* From Belgium and Sweden south to Portugal, Italy and Greece; dry, grassy or rocky areas, open woods.

St Bruno's Lily *Paradisea liliastrum* 30–50cm Resembles St Bernard's Lily but has as many as 20 flowers in a loose, one-sided spike. Flowers are trumpet-shaped, 30–50mm long, the perianth segments joined towards the base but flaring towards their tips; stamens and style curved upwards. *Flowering:* June–August. *Distribution:* Pyrenees, Alps, the Jura and Apennines; mountain meadows.

Merendera filifolia

Meadow Saffron *Colchicum autumnale* An autumn-flowering perennial. Erect, broadly lanceolate leaves 150–350mm long develop in spring as the fruit ripens and are absent when flowers appear. One to three flowers are goblet-shaped, with pale purple perianth lobes 30–45mm long and a paler tube 50–200mm long; stamens six. Flowers appear from below ground but the stalk elongates later so ripe fruit is borne above soil level. *Flowering:* August–November. *Distribution:* South west and central Europe; damp meadows. **Merendera filifolia** has leaves only 1.5–2.5mm wide and perianth segments pressed together, not fused. *Flowering:* October–February. *Distribution:* Balearics and southern France, Spain and Portugal.

Bulbocodium vernum 5–20cm Stemless perennial with spreading, grass-like leaves 150 x 15mm. Usually solitary, pink or sometimes white flowers appear with the leaves; perianth is 40–85mm long, tubular below, with six strap-shaped lobes initially hooked together but later wide-spreading. *Flowering:* February–May. *Distribution:* Pyrenees, south-west and west-central Alps. **B. versicolor** has flowers only 25–30mm long. *Flowering:* February–April. *Distribution:* Eastern Europe westwards to Hungary and Italy.

Drooping Star-of-Bethlehem

Star-of-Bethlehem *Ornithogallum umbellatum.* 20–30cm Bulbous perennial often surrounded by clusters of leaves produced by offsets. Grass-like leaves are all basal, 2–5mm wide with a white central stripe on the upper side. Eight to 20 flowers are borne in a cluster at tip of a naked stem. Six perianth segments are 15–22mm long, all white with a broad green stripe on the back. *Flowering:* April–June. *Distribution:* Native to southern and south-central Europe but widely naturalised as far north as Finland. Similar **Drooping Star-of-Bethlehem** (*O. nutans*) has flowers in a one-sided spike. *Distribution:* Native to the south-east Balkan peninsula but cultivated in most of Europe.

Yellow Asphodel

St Bernard's Lily

St Bruno's Lily

Meadow Saffron

Bulbocodium vernum

Star-of-Bethlehem

Wild Tulip *Tulipa sylvestris* 8–45cm Bulbous perennial sometimes also producing creeping, rooting stems. Erect flowering stem has two to three narrow leaves 30cm long, with incurved margins forming a channel. One or rarely two yellow or sometimes cream flowers droop in bud. Three inner perianth segments are 21–70 x 6–26mm, outer three slighty shorter and narrower, sometimes tinged green, pink or crimson on the outside. *Flowering:* April–June. *Distribution:* Southern Europe north to France and central Russia, naturalised elsewhere; mainly grassy and rocky areas.

Tulipa orphanidea 8–27cm An eastern species generally resembling Wild Tulip. Three to seven leaves deep, dull green on upper side, reach 320mm long. Flowers, which do not droop, are bright sometimes reddish orange with a darker basal blotch on the inside; perianth segments are smaller, the inner 30–47 x 10–19mm. *Flowering:* April–May. *Distribution:* Eastern Balkan Peninsula and the Aegean; dry, stony soils.

Fritillaria tubiformis

Fritillary *Fritillaria meleagris* 12–50cm A slender perennial with a small bulb and solitary, drooping flower. Four to eight alternate, linear leaves up to 200mm are bluish green. Six perianth segments form a bell-shaped flower 30–45mm long, purple, pink or white, the outside usually with a chequerboard pattern of alternate light and dark purple squares. *Flowering:* April–May. *Distribution:* From southern England and central Russia south to the southern Alps and central Yugoslavia, also naturalised elsewhere; damp grassland.Very similar **F. tubiformis** has perianth segments chequered on the inner surface and rounded, not pointed at the tips. *Flowering:* May–July. *Distribution:* Mountain meadows in the south-western Alps.

Orange Lily *Lilium bulbiferum* 40–150cm A bulbous perennial sometimes with bulbils in the leaf axils. Numerous whorled leaves 70–150mm long are hairy on the lower surface. One to three flowers at tip of stem are erect; six spreading perianth segments orange or red, black spotted on inner side. *Flowering:* June–July. *Distribution:* Central Europe south to Spain, Italy and Yugoslavia; mountain meadows and woods.

Lilium carniolicum: leaf, underside

Martagon Lily *Lilium martagon* 30–100cm Tall, bulbous perennial with whorls of oblanceolate leaves up to 160mm long. Large flowers hang down on curved stalks. Six pink to purplish-red, often spotted, perianth segments up to 35mm are strongly recurved, revealing prominent stamens. *Flowering:* June–September. *Distribution:* From France and the Baltic south to central Spain and Greece, naturalised elsewhere; woods and scrub. Two similar species found in mountain pastures and woods or scrub have alternate leaves and yellow, orange or red, purplish-spotted flowers with segments 50––65mm long. **L. carniolicum**, from the Pyrenean region and naturalised in Britain, has leaves hairy on the veins beneath; **Pyrenean Lily** (*L. pyrenaicum*), from the Alps and Balkans to Greece and Romania, is hairless. *Flowering:* June–July for both.

Sea-squill *Urginea maritima* 50–150cm A perennial with a bulb 50–150mm in diameter. Leaves are 30–100 x 3–10cm, in a basal rosette appearing after the flowers and persisting until the following autumn. Leafless spike emerging from bare ground is long and dense, containing 50 or more star-shaped flowers. Six oblong perianth segments are 6–8mm long, white with a green or purple stripe. *Flowering:* August–October. *Distribution:* Mediterranean region and Portugal; maritime sands, dry and rocky places.

Wild Tulip

Tulipa orphanidea

Fritillary

Orange Lily: flower and bulbils

Martagon Lily

Sea-squill

Spring Squill

Siberian Squill

Spanish Bluebell

Bellevalia romana

Compact Grape-
hyacinth: fertile flower

Autumn Squill *Scilla autumnalis* 4–25cm A bulbous perennial with linear leaves 40–150 x 1–2mm, all basal and produced in late summer or autumn after flowering. Terminal spike contains six to 20 flowers with ascending stalks; bracts absent. Six perianth segments are 3–5mm, all petal-like, purplish to lilac. *Flowering:* July–September. *Distribution:* Southern and western Europe as far north as England and Hungary. **Spring Squill** (*S. verna*) has violet-blue flowers and bluish bracts forming a dense head produced after the leaves in summer. *Flowering:* April–June. *Distribution:* Western Europe; dry grassy places usually near the sea.

Alpine Squill *Scilla bifolia* 5–20cm A bulbous perennial with flowers appearing in spring with the leaves. Leaves usually two, linear, the lower half sheathing the stem. One to ten erect flowers form a somewhat one-sided spike. Six spreading perianth segments are 5–10mm, all bright blue to pale lilac, sometimes white at the base. *Flowering:* March–June. *Distribution:* Central and southern Europe; meadows and woodland. **Siberian Squill** (*S. sibirica*) has drooping, cup- to funnel-shaped blue flowers. *Flowering:* April. *Distribution:* A Russian native widely cultivated and naturalised in Europe.

Bluebell *Hyacinthoides non-scripta* 20–50cm A perennial with three to six leaves are about as long a the stem, all basal. Flower-spike is one-sided and drooping at the tip, with four to 16 fragrant, hanging flowers. Cylindrical blue perianth 14–20mm long has six segments joined at the base, their tips curving outwards; anthers cream. *Flowering:* April–June. *Distribution:* Native to western Europe, also naturalised in central Europe; woods, hedgerows and heaths. It hybridises with the similar **Spanish Bluebell** (*H. hispanica*) which has erect spikes with scentless flowers on all sides. Perianth is bell-shaped, the segments not curved at the tips; anthers blue. *Flowering:* May. *Distribution:* Native to Iberia, naturalised in southern and western Europe.

Dipcadi serotinum 10–40cm A bulbous perennial with few linear leaves. Loose, one-sided flower spike has three to 20 brownish, orange-red .or greenish flowers. Tubular perianth is 12–15mm long, outer three segments with tips curving outwards, inner three angled inwards. *Flowering:* April–June. *Distribution:* Southwest Europe, from Portugal to France and Italy; dry, sandy and rocky areas. **Bellevalia romana** has 20 to 30 top-shaped flowers each 8–10mm long. Whitish at first, they turn brownish later. *Flowering:* April–May. *Distribution:* Western Mediterranean, eastwards to France; fields.

Grape-hyacinth *Muscari neglecta* 4–30cm A bulbous perennial with three to six semi-cylindrical leaves 60–400 x 1–8mm. Dense spike has sterile upper flowers smaller and paler than the fertile lower flowers. Perianth of fertile flowers is dark blue, 3–7.5mm long, ovoid to urn-shaped, with six small, whitish, recurved lobes. *Flowering:* April–May. *Distribution:* Most of Europe from France and southern Russia southwards, naturalised in Britain; dry, grassy places. **Compact Grape-hyacinth** (*M. botryoides*) has shorter, bluish leaves and bright blue fertile flowers. *Flowering:* March–May. *Distribution:* Central and south-east Europe.

Tassel Hyacinth *Muscari comosum* 15–50cm Resembles Grape-hyacinth but has leaves 5–17mm wide and loose flower spikes. Fertile flowers on spreading stalks are 5–9.5mm long, more oblong and pale brown; violet sterile flowers on fleshy, ascending stalks form a terminal tuft. *Flowering:* April–July. *Distribution:* As Grape-hyacinth but only introduced in the north.

barlotto

"The Goodly King"

Barbara Baraldi

Carlo Lucarelli

C. J. Sansom

Your next appointment is on …………… at …… 11.55

44 ⁰·2·

Flu vac
Tues 21st Dec   at

4 x 70 = 280 =   at   11·4

4 x 2
2 + 1   at   4·4

          2/17+1

Autumn Squill

Alpine Squill

Bluebell

Dipcadi serotinum

Grape-hyacinth

Tassel Hyacinth

Chives *Allium schoenoprasum* 5-50cm A tuft–forming perennial with very narrowly conical bulbs clustered on a short rhizome and cylindrical, hollow stems and leaves. Dense terminal umbel 15–50mm across is protected by two or three papery, sheaths which persist after flowers open. Bell-shaped flowers have six narrow, spreading, petal-like perianth segments each 7–15mm long, pale purple, lilac or white. *Flowering:* June–July. *Distribution:* Most of Europe but confined to mountains in the south; damp places.

Rosy Garlic *Allium roseum* 10–65cm A perennial with bulbs producing numerous bulblets. The two to four leaves are 120–350mm long, linear and flat but sheathing the base of the stem. Terminal umbel with five to 30 flowers and up to 70mm across has two to four papery sheaths. Sometimes most flowers are replaced by bulbils. Bell- to cup-shaped flowers have pink or white perianth segments 7–12mm long, the outer three obovate, inner three narrowly elliptical. *Flowering:* June. *Distribution:* Southern Europe; naturalised in Britain; dry, open ground.

Few-flowered Leek: flower head with bulbils

Three-cornered Leek *Allium triquetrum* 10–45cm Bulbous perennial with both stems and leaves triangular in cross-section; stems limp after flowering. One-sided umbel contains three to 15 drooping, bell-shaped flowers on stalks up to 25mm long. Lanceolate perianth segments are 10–18cm, white with a green central stripe. *Flowering:* April–June. *Distribution:* Western Mediterranean but naturalised in Britain; shady and waste places. **Few-flowered Leek** (*A. paradoxum*) is a brighter green and the umbel has one to four flowers and numerous bulbils. *Flowering:* April–May. *Distribution:* Native to the Caucasus but naturalised in central and north-west Europe.

Ramsons *Allium ursinum* 10–50cm Perennial with a solitary, very narrow bulb and sharply-angled stem. The two bright green leaves have a narrowly elliptical to narrowly ovate blade 60–250mm long and a strongly curved stalk 50–200mm long. Loose, flat-topped umbel 25–60mm across has six to 20 white flowers and two papery sheaths beneath. Six lanceolate perianth segments are 7–12mm long. *Flowering:* April–June. *Distribution:* Most of Europe except parts of the north-east and rare in the Mediterranean; woods.

Keeled Garlic *Allium carinatum* 30–60cm Bulbous perennial with cylindrical stems and two to four, sheathing leaves with flat blades only 2mm wide. Loose umbel has two papery sheaths unequal in size. Cup-shaped, purple flowers have long stalks, the outer ones downcurved; six blunt perianth segments are 4–6mm long; stamens protrude from flower. Some or all of the flowers may be replaced by bulbils. *Flowering:* August. *Distribution:* Southern and central Europe, naturalised in the north-west; heaths, scrub and grassy places. Similar **Field Garlic** (*A. oleraceum*) has semi-circular leaves up to 4mm wide and pinkish, greenish or brownish flowers, their stamens not protruding. *Flowering:* July–August. *Distribution:* Much of Europe, rare in the south; arable, waste and rocky ground.

Field Garlic: cross section of leaf

Wild Onion *Allium vineale* 30–120cm Perennial with ovoid bulbs and yellowish bulblets. Two to four cylindrical, hollow leaves are 150–600 x 1.5–4mm. Roughly globose to hemispherical umbel is 20–50mm across; protective papery sheath soon falls. Bell-shaped flowers are orange from pink to dark red or greenish-white. Some, more frequently all, flowers may be replaced by bulbils. *Flowering:* June–July. *Distribution:* Throughout Europe except the far north and parts of Russia; dry pastures and waste ground.

Chives

Rosy Garlic

Three-cornered Leek

Ramsons

Keeled Garlic

Wild Onion: bulbils

Lily-of-the-valley *Convallaria majalis* Up to 37cm A perennial with leaves arising directly from a creeping rhizome, their sheathing bases forming the 'stem'; ovate to elliptical leaf blades are 10–240mm long. Fragrant, drooping flowers are borne in an erect, one-sided spike. White or pink perianth is globose bell-shaped with six lobes reaching one third to the base. *Flowering:* May–June. *Distribution:* Most of Europe but for the far north and some areas in the south; dry woods on lime-rich soils.

Angular Solomon's-seal *Polygonatum odoratum* 15–65cm
A hairless perennial with arching, angled stems. Alternate leaves are 150–650mm, ovate, stalkless, in two rows. One to two greenish-white, fragrant flowers hang from leaf axils. Tubular perianth is 12–30mm, with six short lobes. *Flowering:* June–July. *Distribution:* Most of Europe except the far north and most islands; woods and rocky places, preferring lime-rich soils. Similar **P. latifolium** has smaller, short-stalked leaves hairy on veins beneath; scentless flowers smaller, up to five in a cluster. *Flowering:* May. *Distribution:* East-central and south-east Europe. **Solomon's-seal** (*P. multiflorum*) has cylindrical stems; scentless flowers in clusters of two to five, perianth somewhat pinched in at the middle. *Flowering:* May–June. *Distribution:* Most of Europe except parts of south-west, east and many islands.

Solomon's-seal

Whorled Solomon's-seal *Polygonatum verticillatum* 20–80cm
A perennial with angled stems with whorls of three to eight leaves 40–150 x 3–25mm. Greenish-white flowers hanging from leaf axils are solitary or paired on a single stalk. Bell-shaped perianth is 5–10mm, pinched in at the middle and with six short lobes. *Flowering:* June–July. *Distribution:* From northern Spain, central Italy and Bulgaria northwards; woods, scrub.

Herb-Paris *Paris quadrifolia* 10–40cm A perennial with a creeping rhizome and erect stems with a single whorl of four to eight, obovate, stalkless leaves 50–160mm long at the tip. Solitary flower on a stalk 20–80mm long is greenish with four to six lanceolate sepals and four to six extremely narrow petals, all 20–35mm long. *Flowering:* June–August. *Distribution:* Most of Europe, rare in the Mediterranean; damp woods on lime-rich soils.

Asparagus *Asparagus officinalis* Up to 150cm Perennial with erect or, in coastal forms spreading, much-branched stems. True leaves reduced to thin, whitish scales bearing in their axils clusters of four to 15 cladodes(green, needle-like side-shoots) 10–30mm long. One to two flowers in axils are unisexual, males and females on different plants. Bell-shaped perianth is 4.5–6.5mm long with six greenish-yellow segments. Ripe berries red. *Flowering:* April–June. *Distribution:* Most of Europe north to the British Isles and Denmark; waste ground, dunes and cliffs. **A. maritimus** has erect, ridged stems and green side-shoots in clusters of 10 to 30. *Flowering:* May–June. *Distribution:* Mediterranean, south-east Europe; sandy, coastal soils.

Asparagus maritimus: stem

Large Butcher's-broom

Butcher's-broom *Ruscus aculeata* 10–100cm A stiff, evergreen shrub, the leaves replaced by leaf-like cladodes (green flattened stems) 10–40mm long, ovate to lanceolate and spiny at the tips. Small, unisexual flowers are dull green, borne in centre of cladodes. Berry bright red. *Flowering:* January–April. *Distribution:* Western and southern Europe north to England and Hungary; woods, scrub. **Large Butcher's-broom** (*R. hypoglossum*) has an unbranched stem and cladodes 30–100mm long. *Flowering:* December–April. *Distribution:* South-eastern and south-central Europe.

Lily-of-the-valley

Angular Solomon's-seal

Whorled Solomon's-seal

Herb-Paris

Asparagus

Butcher's-broom

Sarsaparilla *Smilax aspera* Up to 15m A scrambling or climbing perennial with angled stems woody towards the base and often armed with stiff prickles. Leathery leaves up to 110mm long are usually narrowly heart- or arrowhead-shaped, the margins, main veins and stalk with prickles. Flowers borne in clusters of five to 30, males and females on different plants; six, white or greenish perianth segments 2–4mm long. Ripe berry is black or red. *Flowering:* August–October. *Distribution:* Southern Europe; dry scrub, walls.

Black Bryony *Tamus communis* Up to 400cm A climbing perennial with large tubers producing annual, twining stems. Long-stalked, alternate leaves are 80–150 x 40–110mm, heart-shaped and dark glossy green. Greenish-yellow flowers 3–6mm across are borne in clusters in leaf axils, males and females on different plants; perianth six-lobed. Berry red or sometimes yellowish when ripe. *Flowering:* May–July. *Distribution:* Southern and western Europe northwards to England and introduced in Ireland.

Slender Sternbergia

Common Sternbergia *Sternbergia lutea* 4–10cm Autumn-flowering bulbous perennial similar in appearance to a crocus. Stem visible at flowering, elongating in fruit. Linear leaves are 40–100 x 2–15mm, all basal, appearing with the flowers. Yellow flowers have a tube 5–8mm long and six narrow perianth segments 30–40 x 4–15mm, initially forming a broad bell, later spreading; stamens six. *Flowering:* September–October. *Distribution:* Mediterranean; dry, stony soils. Similar **Slender Sternbergia** (*S. colchiflora*) has a mostly underground stem and leaves appearing after the flowers, narrower perianth segments and a tube 25–30mm long. Sometimes flowers in spring. *Distribution:* Southern Europe, absent from most islands.

Spring Snowflake

Summer Snowflake *Leucojum aestivum* Up to 60cm Bulbous perennial with broadly linear leaves up to 300 x 5–20mm, all basal. Hollow flowering stem is flattened and two-winged, with a terminal umbel of two to five flowers enclosed in bud by a papery sheath. Bell-shaped flowers hang from stalks of unequal length. Six perianth segments are 14–18mm, white with a green spot at the thickened tip. *Flowering:* April–June. *Distribution:* South of a line from Ireland, England, Holland and Czechoslovakia to Sardinia and Greece; wet meadows, marshy ground. **Spring Snowflake** (*L. vernum*) has solitary flowers with segments 20–25mm. *Flowering:* February–April. *Distribution:* Hills from France, Belgium and Germany to the Pyrenees, northern Italy and Yugoslavia; naturalised further north.

Snowdrop *Galanthus nivalis* Up to 25cm Early flowering bulbous perennial with a single pair of bluish, linear leaves 50–130 x 2–7mm. Pendulous flowers solitary, initially enclosed by a papery sheath. Perianth segments all petal-like, outer three 12–35mm, white, inner three shorter, 6–11mm, white with a green patch at the tip. *Flowering:* February–March. *Distribution:* From France and Russia south to Pyrenees, Sicily and Greece, introduced further north; damp, deciduous woods.

Sea Daffodil *Pancratium maritimum* Up to 50cm Bulbous perennial with flat, bluish-green leaves up to 500 x 20mm, all basal and withered by the time the flowers open. Stout, flattened flowering stem bears a terminal umbel of three to 15 white, fragrant flowers initially enclosed by two papery sheaths. Six narrow perianth segments 30–50mm, merging into a long slender tube below; central trumpet-shaped corona has a toothed rim. *Flowering:* July–September. *Distribution:* Southern Europe; hot, dry, maritime sands.

Sarsaparilla: fruits

Black Bryony

Common Sternbergia

Summer Snowflake

Snowdrop

Sea Daffodil

Wild Daffodil *Narcissus pseudonarcissus* Up to 50cm Spring-flowering bulb with usually bluish-green strap-shaped leaves 80–500 x 5–15mm. Solitary flower initially enclosed in a papery sheath. Six perianth segments 18–40mm, more or less spreading, white to deep yellow; central trumpet-shaped corona 15–45mm, the same colour or darker than the perianth. *Flowering:* February–April. *Distribution:* Western Europe from Portugal to England, naturalised elsewhere; damp grassland and open woods.

Autumn Narcissus *Narcissus serotinus* 10–25cm Autumn-flowering bulb with one or two narrow, thread-like, blue-green leaves 100–200 x 1mm appearing in the following spring. Fragrant flowers are solitary or two at the stem tip, held erect; sheath membranous. Six white perianth segments 10–16mm, wide-spreading; short central corona only 1–1.5 x 3–4mm, orange, six-lobed. *Flowering:* September–October. *Distribution:* Mediterranean and southern Portugal; dry, stony hillsides.

Pheasant's-eye Daffodil *Narcissus poeticus* 20–50cm Bulb flowering in early summer. Flat, bluish-green leaves are 200–400 x 5–13mm. Flowers solitary, on a flattened stalk, with a papery sheath. Six oblong perianth segments 15–30mm, spreading, white or cream; cup-shaped corona 1–2.5 x 8–14mm, yellow but with a minutely-toothed red rim. *Flowering:* April–May. *Distribution:* Native from central France and Spain to southern Italy and north-west Greece; naturalised in Britain and elsewhere; mountain meadows.
Bunch-flowered Daffodil (*N. tazetta*) is spring- or sometimes autumn-flowering, with a terminal umbel of three to 15 fragrant flowers on stalks of unequal length. Perianth segments are 8–22mm, broad and usually overlapping; corona 3–6 x 6–11mm, yellow or orange. *Flowering:* November–April. *Distribution:* Mediterranean and southern Portugal.

Bunch-flowered
Daffodil

Variegated Iris: outer
perianth segment and
petaloid style

Iris aphylla 15–30cm Slender rhizomatous perennial with stems branching below the middle or from the base. Leaves are 150–400 x 6-22mm, the lower curved. Three to five short-stalked flowers are violet to purple; three inner perianth segments 40–65 x 22–30mm, erect; outer three 40–65 x 20–25mm, down-turned, each partly overlain by a petal-like stigma. *Flowering:* April–May. *Distribution:* East-central Europe, scattered westwards.
Variegated Iris (*I. variegata*) has stems branched above the middle and mainly yellow or white flowers, the outer perianth segments violet- or reddish-veined. *Flowering:* May–July. *Distribution:* Central and south-east Europe.

Stinking Iris *Iris foetidissima* 30–90cm Fetid-smelling rhizomatous perennial with evergreen leaves, the basal 300–700 x 10–25mm. One to five dull purplish flowers tinged with yellow or sometimes completely yellow. Inner three perianth segments 25–40 x 5–9mm, erect; outer three 30–50 x 10–20mm, down-turned, each partly overlain by a petal- like stigma. Orange-scarlet seeds persist for the winter in the open capsule. *Flowering:* May–July. *Distribution:* South and west Europe.

Yellow Iris *Iris pseudacorus* 60–120cm Perennial with a thick, fleshy rhizome. Stiff, bluish-green leaves are sword-shaped with a conspicuous midrib, the basal 500–900 x 10–30mm. Solid, slightly flattened stem bears four to 12 pale to deep yellow flowers, the lower ones long-stalked. Flowers with six perianth segments, the inner three narrow and erect, 20–30 x 4–8mm, outer three broad, 40–60 x 15–27mm, each down-turned and partly overlain by a petal-like stigma. *Flowering:* June–July. *Distribution:* Most of Europe; wet places.

Wild Daffodil

Autumn Narcissus

Pheasant's-eye Daffodil

Iris aphylla

Stinking Iris

Yellow Iris

Crocus chrysanthus:
flower, 3 petals
removed

Sand Crocus

Eastern Gladiolus

Greater Duckweed:
whole plant

Crocus biflorus Spring-flowering perennial with a smooth corm. Three to five leaves are only 0.5–2.5mm wide, all basal and present when flowers open. One to three flowers are white to lilac-blue, often striped or tinged blue- or brownish- purple and white, lilac or yellow in the throat. Goblet-shaped perianth has six segments 15–45mm long united below into a slender tube 20–80mm long; stamens three. *Flowering:* February–March. *Distribution:* Southern Europe, from Sicily eastwards. Very similar **C. chrysanthus** has pale to deep yellow flowers with a purplish or brownish perianth tube. *Flowering:* January–February. *Distribution:* Balkan Peninsula to Romania.

Spring Crocus *Crocus vernus* Spring-flowering perennial with a fibre-covered corm. Two to four leaves are 4–8mm wide, present but not fully developed when flowers open. Solitary, goblet-shaped flower is white, purple or striped; six perianth segments 15–55mm long, united below into a tube 25–150mm long; stamens three; style deep yellow to orange-red. *Flowering:* March–May. *Distribution:* Endemic to central and southern Europe, naturalised in Britain; short turf and open woods, mainly in mountains.

Romulea bulbocodium Up to 10cm Plant with a smooth, hard corm. Two almost cylindrical basal leaves are 50–300 x 0.8–2mm; stem leaves up to five, shorter. Stem carries five to six flowers varying in colour from white to lilac or violet, greenish or with dark lines on outside, throat yellow within. Six perianth segments 20–35mm, united below into a slender tube 35–80mm long. *Flowering:* February–April. *Distribution:* Mediterranean region. Similar **Sand Crocus** (*R. columnae*) has perianth segments 9–19mm long, with dark veins within. *Flowering:* March–May. *Distribution:* Western Europe and Mediterranean; sandy turf near the sea.

Wild Gladiolus *Gladiolus illyricus* Up to 50cm An erect perennial with a fibre-covered corm. Sword-shaped leaves are 100–400 x 4–10mm, rather stiff and forming a flat fan. Stem carries three to 10, slightly irregular crimson-purple flowers in a one-sided spike. Six perianth segments in two whorls of three are 25–40cm, joined at the base to form a very short, curved tube, the upper segment twice as broad as the laterals; three stamens curve up under the upper perianth segments, anthers shorter than filaments. *Flowering:* June–August. *Distribution:* Southern and western Europe; dry heaths.

Field Gladiolus *Gladiolus italicus* Up to 50cm Closely resembles Wild Gladiolus but with leaf bases sometimes reddish-tinged. Flowers pinkish-purple, upper perianth segment broader and separate from the others; stamens with anthers longer than the filaments. *Flowering:* April–June. *Distribution:* Southern Europe; arable and waste ground. **Eastern Gladiolus** (*G. communis*) has darker purple flowers with the upper three perianth segments similar in size and pressed together. *Flowering:* April–May. *Distribution:* Southern Europe; dry ground.

Common Duckweed *Lemna minor* A free-floating aquatic plant consisting of a plate-like body 1.5–5mm across, obovate to rounded, the lower surface with a single thread-like root up to 150mm long. Minute flowers borne in a pocket on the margin of the plant. New plants may also be budded from the parent body. *Flowering:* June–July. *Distribution:* Throughout Europe on still water. **Fat Duckweed** (*L. gibba*) is grey-green or reddish-brown with a swollen lower surface. **Greater Duckweed** (*Spirodela polyrhiza*) has a flat, shiny body 5–8mm across, often purplish beneath and with five to 15 roots.

Crocus biflorus

Spring Crocus

Romulea bulbocodium

Wild Gladiolus

Field Gladiolus

Common Duckweed

Sweet-flag *Acorus calamus* Up to 125cm A perennial with parallel-veined, linear leaves with wavy margins, smelling of oranges when crushed. Hermaphrodite flowers are 2 x 1mm, greenish-yellow, packed tightly in a compact, up-curved spike; leaf-like spathe easily mistaken for a continuation of the stem. *Flowering:* June–August. *Distribution:* Naturalised in Europe, absent from the far north, the south-west and most of the Mediterranean; introduced from Turkey in the 16th century, as a medicinal plant; by rivers.

Bog Arum *Calla palustris* Up to 30cm A creeping perennial, with round to broadly ovate leaves, heart-shaped at the base, with sheathing stalks. Flowers are small, yellowish-green, densely packed together in a cylindrical spike not enclosed by the spathe which is leaf-like but white on the inside. Berries red, about 5mm. *Flowering:* June–August. *Distribution:* Northern, central and eastern Europe, westwards to Belgium and southwards to south-central Russia and southern Romania; marshy areas and edges of lakes.

Italian Lords-and Ladies: inflorescence

Lords-and-Ladies *Arum maculatum* Up to 25cm A perennial with long-stalked, arrowhead-shaped, shiny green leaves appearing in spring. Spike has small male flowers carried above females and maturing at different times, all hidden in base of yellowish-green spathe which withers before the red berries form; purple appendix long, cylindrical. *Flowering:* April–May. *Distribution:* Western, central and southern Europe, northwards to Britain; woods and hedgebanks, often on chalky soils. **Italian Lords-and-Ladies** (*A. italicum*) is larger, the leaves appearing in the autumn or winter, the spathe drooping at the apex, and the flower spike with a stout yellow appendix. *Distribution:* Southern and western Europe, northwards to southern England; hedgerows and disturbed ground.

Snake's-tongue *Biarum tenuifolium* Up to 40cm A perennial with linear to oblong or spoon-shaped leaves, occasionally stalked, either flat or wavy. Flowers are unisexual, males and females separated by a zone of sterile flowers; spike has a slender purple appendix, larger than the dark purple spathe which is tinged with green on the outside. *Flowering:* September–November, after the leaves, or April–June with the leaves. *Distribution:* Mediterranean, central and southern Portugal; rocky hillsides.

Mousetail-plant: inflorescence

Friar's-cowl *Arisarum vulgare* Up to 40cm A perennial with ovate to arrowhead- or heart-shaped leaves on long spotted stalks appearing in the autumn. Spike with small, unisexual flowers, males above females; tip of long greenish appendix projects from downturned apex of tubular spathe which is pale green, striped with reddish-purple and dark green to purplish-brown above. *Flowering:* March–May. *Distribution:* Mediterranean, central and southern Portugal; shady areas. **Mousetail-plant** (*A. proboscideum*) has leaves all arrowhead-shaped; spathe pale at the base, dark purplish-brown above, ending in a long thread-like process resembling the tail of a mouse. *Distribution:* Central and southern Italy, south-western Spain; shady places.

Dragon Arum *Dracunculus vulgaris* Up to 100cm A perennial, the leaves divided into nine to 15 elliptical to oblong-lanceolate, pointed lobes; long purple-spotted stalks sheathing. Spike with small male and female flowers and a dark purple appendix on a short, pale stalk; spathe greenish outside, dark brown-purple inside. *Flowering:* March–May. *Distribution:* Eastern and central Mediterranean to Bulgaria; cultivated and occasionally naturalised elsewhere; woods and scrub.

Sweet-flag

Bog Arum

Lords-and-Ladies

Snake's-tongue

Friar's-cowl

Dragon Arum

Lady's-slipper *Cypripedium calceolus* Up to 50cm A perennial, with three to four elliptical to ovate-oblong, slightly downy leaves. Flowers are 60–90mm across, reddish-brown, with a large yellow, inflated slipper-shaped lip; stamens and stigmas borne on a column, with two fertile stamens and three fertile stigmas. *Flowering:* May–June. *Distribution:* Widely distributed in most of Europe, but always rare; woods and meadows, on lime-rich soils.

Marsh Helleborine *Epipactis palustris* Up to 70cm A creeping perennial, with four to eight oblong-lanceolate, pointed leaves decreasing in size up the stem. Flowers are 15–20mm, wide open, seven to 14 in a spike; sepals three, purple or purple brown; petals whitish, pink-tinged, the labellum white, fringed; bracts lanceolate. *Flowering:* July–August. *Distribution:* Most of Europe, except far north and parts of Mediterranean; marshland and damp places. **Broad-leaved Helleborine** (*E. helleborine*) has broader leaves on a longer stem, flowers smaller, more pendant; petals pinkish-violet, the labellum bending under, making it appear round. *Distribution:* Most of Europe; woodlands and scrub, sometimes on seaside sand-dunes.

Broad-leaved
Helleborine

White Helleborine *Cephalanthera damasonium* Up to 60cm An upright perennial, with the leaves broadly ovate-lanceolate, oblong-ovate or lanceolate. Flowers are 15–20mm long, white or creamy-white, tubular, in a 12- to 16-flowered spike, bracts usually longer than flowers; sepals oblong; petals oblong-lanceolate, the labellum short, white, yellowish within. *Flowering:* May–July. *Distribution:* Southern, central and western Europe, northwards to England and southern Sweden; woods, shady places, usually on chalky soil. **Narrow-leaved Helleborine** (*C. longifolia*) has longer, narrower leaves, the upper linear; flowers more open, longer than bracts; sepals lanceolate. *Distribution:* Most of Europe; woods.

Narrow-leaved
Helleborine

Red Helleborine *Cephalanthera rubra* Up to 60cm An upright, glandular-downy perennial, often with a purple tinge. Leaves five to eight, the lower oblong- lanceolate to lanceolate, the upper linear-lanceolate. Flowers are up to 25mm long, open, up to 12 in a spike; sepals lanceolate, pointed, glandular on the outside; petals ovate-lanceolate, the labellum about as long as sepals, white, pointed, with a purple margin. *Flowering:* June–July. *Distribution:* Most of Europe, northwards to southern England and southern Finland; woodland shade, usually on lime-rich soils.

Violet Limodore *Limodorum abortivum* Up to 80cm A perennial saprophyte lacking any green pigment. Stems are violet, covered with short, scale-like sheaths. Flowers are 40mm across, opening wide, in loose spikes; sepals oblong-lanceolate; petals shorter, narrower, violet; labellum violet and yellow, 16–17mm, triangular with wavy margin and a 15mm spur. *Flowering:* May–July. *Distribution:* Central and southern Europe, north-westwards to Belgium; woodlands and shady grassland, on lime-rich soils.

Ghost Orchid

Bird's-nest Orchid *Neottia nidus-avis* Up to 45cm A yellowish-brown perennial saprophyte, the stem with sheathing scales. Flowers are about 15mm across, in a short spike; upper petals and sepals form a hood; labellum 8-12mm, two-lobed. *Flowering:* May-July. *Distribution:* Most of Europe, rare in the far north. Similar **Ghost Orchid** (*Epipogium aphyllum*) has shorter, pinker stems and up to seven, larger flowers; labellum three-lobed, upwardly directed. Distribution: Northern and central Europe, southwards to Pyrenees, Apennines, Greece and Crimea; woods.

Lady's-slipper

Marsh Helleborine

White Helleborine

Red Helleborine

Violet Limodore

Bird's-nest Orchid

Lesser Twayblade

Creeping Lady's-tresses

Greater Butterfly Orchid

Pyramidal Orchid

Common Twayblade *Listera ovata* Up to 60cm An upright perennial, with opposite, broadly ovate or elliptical leaves, and often one or two bract-like leaves further up the stem. Flowers are up to 10mm across, short-stalked in a loose spike; sepals green; petals yellowish-green, the top sepals and petals forming a loose hood; labellum 7–15mm, two-lobed. *Flowering:* May-July. *Distribution:* Most of Europe; woodlands, scrub and grassland. **Lesser Twayblade** *(L. cordata)* is smaller, the leaves ovate to heart-shaped; flowers about half as large, reddish inside; labellum purple. *Distribution:* Northern and central Europe; damp, often coniferous woods.

Autumn Lady's-tresses *Spiranthes spiralis* Up to 35cm A short perennial, with the next year's basal rosette of ovate-elliptical, pointed, grey-green leaves present by the current year's flowering stem. Flowers are 6–10mm, white, scented, six to 20 in a single spiral; lateral sepals diverging; upper sepal and the top two petals forming a tube, with the yellow-green labellum upwardly curved. *Flowering:* August-September. *Distribution:* Southern, western, and central Europe, northwards to Denmark; dry grassland. **Creeping Lady's-tresses** *(Goodyera repens)* is similar but creeping, with net- veined leaves; labellum white. *Distribution:* Europe southwards to the Pyrenees, Alps and Bulgaria; coniferous or mixed woodland.

Lesser Butterfly Orchid *Platanthera bifolia* Up to 50cm A variable perennial, with two nearly opposite, elliptical basal leaves; stem leaves two to five. Flowers are 15–20mm, white tinged with green, scented; lateral sepals spreading, upper sepal forming a hood with the upper petals; labellum long, with a long straight spur. *Flowering:* June–July. *Distribution:* Most of Europe, rare in Mediterranean; woods, meadows, heaths. **Greater Butterfly Orchid** *(P. chlorantha)* is larger, with greener, less fragrant flowers. *Distribution:* Much of Europe except the north, east and south-west.

Fragrant Orchid *Gymnadenia conopsea* Up to 65cm An upright perennial, with four to eight linear-lanceolate leaves, the upper bract-like. Flowers are 8–10mm, pink or reddish-lilac, fragrant, in a many-flowered spike; sepals spreading; upper petals forming a hood; labellum three-lobed with a long, thin, curved spur. *Flowering:* June–July. *Distribution:* Most of Europe except parts of the south; grassland, marshes, fens and scrub, usually on limy soils. **Pyramidal Orchid** *(Anacamptis pyramidalis)*, has a pyramidal spike of smaller, more purplish-red flowers smelling of foxes. *Distribution:* Western, central and southern Europe; grassland and scrub, on chalk.

Elder-flowered Orchid *Dactylorhiza sambucina* Up to 30cm A short perennial, with four to five leaves, the lower obovate-oblanceolate blunt, the upper lanceolate. Flowers are 14–20mm, pale yellow or purple, rarely bi-coloured, in a dense, cylindrical spike; lateral sepals spreading, upper sepal and petals forming a hood; labellum three-lobed with long down-turned or straight spur. *Flowering:* April–June. *Distribution:* Most of Europe, absent from Russia; meadows, scrubland and open woods.

Broad-leaved Marsh Orchid *Dactylorhiza majalis* Up to 75cm A perennial with four to eight oblong leaves, often covered in brown spots. Flowers are 12–24mm across, bright purple to reddish, with an entire or three-lobed labellum with a downward curving spur. *Flowering:* May–July. *Distribution:* Western and central Europe, Baltic and northern Russia; damp meadows and fens.

Common Twayblade

Autumn Lady's-tresses

Lesser Butterfly Orchid

Fragrant Orchid

Elder-flowered Orchid

Broad-leaved Marsh Orchid

Common Spotted
Orchid

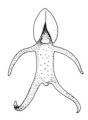

Monkey Orchid

Bug Orchid

Heath Spotted Orchid *Dactylorhiza maculata* Up to 60cm An upright perennial, with five to 12 leaves, the lower linear-lanceolate to oblong, often brown-spotted. Flowers are 15–20mm, white to pink-purple, in a dense spike; labellum broad, three-lobed, the central lobe very small; spur 3–11mm. *Flowering:* June–August. *Distribution:* Most of Europe, except much of south-east; moors, grassland, damp places, mainly on acid soils. **Common Spotted Orchid** (*D. fuchsii*) almost always has spotted leaves; flowers smaller, crimson-blotched; labellum deeply three-lobed, the lobes of equal size; spur 6–9mm. *Distribution:* Most of Europe, but absent from much of the south; dry grassland and open woods, mainly on chalky soil.

Early Purple Orchid *Orchis mascula* Up to 60cm An upright perennial, with three to five oblong-lanceolate to narrowly oblong, usually purple-spotted leaves below, and small leaf sheaths above. Flowers 12–16mm across, pink to purple, hooded, strong-smelling, in a loose spike; labellum shallowly three-lobed; spur cylindrical. *Flowering:* April–June. *Distribution:* Much of Europe; woodlands, scrub and grassland.

Military Orchid *Orchis militaris* Up to 45cm An upright perennial, with three to five oblong-lanceolate or ovate, flat leaves. Flowers are up to 20mm across, pinkish, in a short, conical to cylindrical spike, and resembling a helmeted soldier; sepals and upper petals form a hood, purplish labellum four-lobed; spur cylindrical, downwardly directed. *Flowering:* May–June. *Distribution:* Southern England and north-western Russia southwards to Spain, Italy, Bulgaria; open woods, scrub, grassland, on limy soils. **Monkey Orchid** (*O. simia*) is very similar, but the labellum has much narrower lobes and a small central tail, giving a monkey-like appearance. *Distribution:* Southern and western Europe, to southern England and Hungary.

Burnt Orchid *Orchis ustulata* Up to 35cm An upright perennial, with two to three oblong leaves at the base, one to three in lower half of stem. Flowers in a dense spike are 5–7mm across, dark brownish-purple hood becoming paler with age; labellum white or pink, purple-spotted, lobed; spur cylindrical, down- pointing. *Flowering:* May–June. *Distribution:* England and Russia southwards to northern Spain, Italy, Macedonia and central Ukraine; chalk downs, mountain meadows. **Bug Orchid** (*O. coriophora*) has linear or narrowly lanceolate leaves; flowers with a pointed purple hood and smelling of vanilla or bed bugs; labellum brown-purple edged. *Distribution:* Southern, central and eastern Europe.

Man Orchid *Aceras anthropophorum* Up to 60cm An upright perennial with oblong to oblong-lanceolate lower leaves. Flowers are up to 10mm, greenish-yellow in a narrow, many-flowered spike; hood red-streaked, four-lobed labellum 12–15mm, yellowish-green, strongly resembling the figure of a man. *Flowering:* May–June. *Distribution:* Mediterranean and western Europe northwards to England, Netherlands; grassland, scrub, on limy soil.

Lizard Orchid *Himantoglossum hircinum* Up to 90cm A stout perennial, the stems often with faint purple blotches. Lower leaves are elliptic-oblong, the upper smaller, pointed, clasping the stem. Flowers resemble lizards and are 15–20mm across, greenish-grey, purple-spotted, smelling of goat, in a loose spike; labellum 30–50mm, with two short lateral lobes and long central lobe, whitish with purple spots; spur short. *Distribution:* Southern to western Europe, England and Netherlands; grassland, scrub, dunes.

Heath Spotted Orchid

Early Purple Orchid

Military Orchid

Burnt Orchid

Man Orchid

Lizard Orchid

Long-lipped Serapias

Heart-flowered Serapias *Serapias cordigera* Up to 50cm An upright perennial, with five to eight lanceolate leaves, the basal sheaths usually purple-spotted. Flowers are 20–35mm, with a purplish hood, in a two- to ten-flowered spike; labellum at least twice as long as other petals, heart-shaped, hairy, deep purplish with black streaks. *Flowering:* March–May. *Distribution:* Southern and western Europe, northwards to France; grassland, sandy heaths, woods and dry bare places. **Long-lipped Serapias** (*S. vomeracea*) has unspotted basal sheaths; flowers 4–10mm; labellum narrow, red-brown. *Flowering:* March–June. *Distrtibution:* Southern Europe; woods and damp grassland.

Fly Orchid *Ophrys insectifera* Up to 60cm An upright perennial with seven to nine, linear-lanceolate, erect, pointed, shiny leaves up the stem. Flowers, which resemble small bumble-bees, are 12–16mm across, three to 14 in a loose spike; sepals green; petals blackish-violet, linear; labellum furry, blackish- violet, the central lobe elongated with a bluish patch at the base. *Flowering:* May–June. *Distribution:* Much of Europe except south-east, rare in the far south and the north; woods, scrub, grassland, on lime-rich soils.

Mirror Orchid *Ophrys speculum* Up to 30cm Resembles Fly Orchid but has oblong basal leaves and lanceolate, pointed stem leaves. Flowers are 12–16mm, four to eight in a loose spike; sepals green or yellowish; petals blackish-violet, ovate to lanceolate; labellum 13 x 15mm, dark purple, furry, with a fringe of coloured hairs, and a shining blue, yellow-edged centre. *Flowering:* March–April. *Distribution:* Mediterranean, central and southern Portugal; undisturbed grassland, woodland and hot dry areas.

Sawfly Orchid

Early Spider Orchid *Ophrys sphegodes* Up to 45cm A distinctive perennial with ovate-lanceolate, blunt basal leaves and lanceolate stem leaves. Flowers are 12–25mm, up to 10 in a loose spike; sepals ovate or lanceolate, green; petals triangular to lanceolate, usually green; labellum ovate-orbicular, the margins flat or folded back, the sides reduced to furry, brownish-purple lumps with blue, H- or X-shaped markings. *Flowering:* April–June. *Distribution:* Western, central .and southern Europe, northwards to southern England, central Germany, eastwards to the Crimea; lime-rich grassland. **Sawfly Orchid** (*O. tenthredinifera*) has pink sepals, round pink petals shorter than sepals and a large, purplish-brown, furry, two-lobed labellum with a wide, yellow, densely-hairy margin. *Distribution:* Mediterranean and Portugal; grassy, stony and hot dry areas.

Woodcock Orchid *Ophrys scolopax* Up to 45cm A variable perennial, with five or six lanceolate leaves. Flowers are up to 25mm, three to ten in a loose spike; sepals pink, oblong-ovate, lanceolate or triangular; labellum bent back, round, ovate or obovate, brownish-purple, furry, with a yellowish appendage at the tip, and a blue H-shaped or semi-circular marking. *Flowering:* March–April. *Distribution:* Southern Europe; scrubby hillsides, woods, grassland, on limy soils.

Calypso *Calypso bulbosa* Up to 20cm A strikingly handsome plant with a single, elliptical-oblong, short-stalked, conspicuously-veined leaf. Flowers are 20–40mm, pinkish-purple, in the axil of a small, linear bract; sepals and petals linear, spreading, ascending; labellum 10–20mm, slipper-shaped, whitish with pink or yellow spots or blotches. *Flowering:* May. *Distribution:* Northern Scandinavia and northern Russia; marshes and wet coniferous woods.

Heart-flowered Serapias

Fly Orchid

Mirror Orchid

Early Spider Orchid

Woodcock Orchid

Calypso

Field Equipment

Apart from sharp eyes, the basic equipment needed for observing and identifying wild flowers in the field is remarkably simple. When assembling your equipment the key word to keep in mind is 'portable'. It is neither sensible nor practical to take numerous items, especially bulky or heavy ones, into the field. At the end of the day their apparent weight will have doubled. With this in mind, only simple, essential items are described here.

The first item is a good quality hand-lens for observing fine details of the plant. It should have a magnifying power of at least x10 and you may find the type which incorporates a second lens of x15 or x20 very useful. You will also need a ruler or tape-measure to record any measurements you take. A slender-bladed knife or other fine-pointed instrument can be useful for *gently* prising apart overlapping organs in order to observe them more clearly. Always carry a notebook and pencil to record the details you have observed and perhaps to make simple sketches to aid your memory. This removes the need to pick the flower and take it home. As well as recording any measurements, leaf shape, petal number and so on, make a note of the general appearance of the plant. Is it straggling, or do the leaves or flowers droop? Remember also to check for more transient characters such as the scent, if any, of the flowers or crushed foliage. Make your notes as full and informative as possible since you may not be able to return to or find this particular plant again.

A camera can be a very useful means of quickly and accurately augmenting your notes. It need not be sophisticated as even the simplest model can provide an aide-memoire for future reference. However, if you do want to take good quality photographs a single-lens reflex camera will be suitable. You will certainly need a lens which allows you to take close-ups in order to adequately capture details. It is best to take several photographs. Try to show both the whole plant and close-ups of those details which will be of most help in identifying the plant later.

Try to resist the temptation to take a specimen – the plant may be rare and you risk breaking local, national or even international law (read the section on plants and the law in *Conservation*, on the next page). If you do remove a specimen be sure you do not uproot the whole plant or unduly damage it. Never take a specimen if the plant is the only one present. If you observe the plant carefully and make full notes it should not be necessary to take a specimen, and a colour photograph makes an acceptable substitute.

Finally you will need an identification manual or similar reference work with which to check the identity of your specimen. No matter how good your notes and photographs, it is always better to try to identify a wild flower on the spot, while the specimen in question can be checked. Some of the more extensive reference works are bulky and far too large to carry into the field. This guide is designed to be compact and light enough to slip into a ruck-sack or pocket.

Conservation

Conservation is nowadays a major topic of debate as concern for the environment has increased. The pressures on wildlife have reached a point where many species are under severe threat with some populations reduced, in extreme cases, to single individuals. Most attention from both conservation agencies and the public is focused on animals but wild flowers are equally if not more important. As well as providing food and shelter for animals, preventing erosion and moderating the climate, plants are central to almost all aspects of human life. Food, clothing, fuel and medicines are just a few of their products on which we rely. Some wild flowers are now protected from picking and collecting but this does not prevent other activities from continuing their decline and more is needed for protection to be effective. In Europe few truly natural areas of any great extent remain. Agriculture, building and development, and pollution are all factors in the degradation and destruction of habitats and there is now a greater emphasis on preserving entire communities rather than piecemeal protection for individual species.

While much of the responsibility for correcting the current situation must be taken by governments and international agencies, there are many simple but practical contributions which individuals can make towards conservation. Avoid picking, uprooting or trampling wild flowers. Encourage them to grow in your garden by leaving a corner uncultivated and do not, as some misguided individuals do, deliberately attempt to introduce flowers - of whatever origin - into the wild as this may cause unforeseen problems. Certain species, especially bulbs, have become endangered in the wild from over-collecting for sale through the horticultural trade. When you buy bulbs check that they were grown specially for the retail trade and do not come from a wild source.

Above all, take an interest in plants by supporting the activities of local botanical societies and conservation groups or by simply observing flowers in the wild. A clear understanding and appreciation of wild flowers is the best protection of all.

Plants and the Law

Most laws protecting wild flowers in Europe date from the last ten to 15 years and new laws, both national and international, continue to be enacted and proposed. Some name the species of wild flowers which are protected, usually from picking, cutting or uprooting. Others specify certain groups, such as medicinal plants, or cover certain types of threatened habitat. The Berne Convention of 1979 is a European-wide accord protecting 119 rare or threatened plant species and was revised in 1990 to cover 517 species. In the United Kingdom the Wildlife and Countryside Act of 1981 fully protects 62 wild flowers and ferns and makes it illegal to uproot any plants without permission from the landowner: there are similar laws in most European countries. The Berne Convention also provides protection for endangered habitats such as wetlands and again some countries have similar laws at national level. A new and encouraging development is the linkage of conservation and rural development laws which is begining to be made in some countries. Finally, the Convention on International Trade in Endangered Species of Wild Fauna and Flora (CITES) is a world-wide agreement signed in 1973 which regulates trade in wildlife, including about 50,000 species.

Where to see Wild Flowers in Europe

Even the least promising places are home to a surprising number and variety of wild flowers and it is very satisfying to discover those in your own area, but to see different species or habitats you will need to visit other regions. Some parts of Europe are famous for the diversity of their species or for containing specialised floras and a brief selection of major sites for wild flowers is given here. All are protected at some level to preserve their riches and any specific restrictions or regulations should be checked before visiting them.

SCANDINAVIA
Dovrefjell National Park, Norway Situated in the mountains of south-central Norway. A largely unforested area of uplands with extensive lime-rich heaths and an exceptionally rich flora of arctic and alpine plants.
Abisko National Park, Sweden Situated in the mountains in the extreme north of Sweden, close to the border with Norway. The climate here is surprisingly dry and sunny. Rich in lime-loving mountain plants, including some very rare orchids.

NORTH-WEST EUROPE
Upper Teesdale National Nature Reserve, England Situated in the northern Pennines. It comprises chalky grassland, high moorland, hay meadows and cliffs, with an exceptionally rich flora, especially on outcrops of 'sugar limestone', with a mixture of southern and northern species.
Fontainebleau Forest, France Situated just south of Paris. A large state forest with beech, oak and coniferous woodlands and many open, sandy and limestone areas. Exceptionally rich and varied flora with numerous orchids and chalk grassland plants.
Duinen Van Doorne Nature Reserve, Holland Situated on the coast of southern Holland. Mainly dune habitats with a full range from very young to old, wooded dunes. The flora has over 700, mainly dune and coastal, species.
Frankische Schweiz-Veldensteiner Forst Nature Park, Germany Situated north of Nuremberg. A partially wooded limestone area, with numerous cliffs and caves together with areas of chalk grassland. A lime-loving flora with a mixture of lowland and mountain species.

NORTH-EAST EUROPE
High Tatra National Park, Czechoslovakia and Tatra National Park, Poland A cross-border protected area covering most of the Tatra mountains. Heavily forested and with grasslands, cliffs and high upland areas. The rich flora includes many endemics and eastern European specialities.
Bialowieza National Park, Poland Situated in north-east Poland close to the border with the CIS (formerly the USSR). It consists mainly of remnants of ancient primary forest with an extensive flora of about 600 species. It is also very rich in fungi.

THE ALPS
Hohe Tauern National Park, Austria A dramatic high mountain area in western Austria with glaciers, pastures, woodlands and high mountain habitats. As would be expected, the flora contains many high mountain species.
Stelvio National Park, Italy and Switzerland A joint national park situated on the border to the east of St Moritz. Together the two protected areas form a huge haven for wildlife with woods, pastures, lakes and high peaks. The flora contains both lime-loving and lime-hating species as well as endemics.
Mercantour National Park, France and Argentera Reserve, Italy Two reserves situated on the French/Italian border in the Maritime Alps north of Nice. The extremely rich flora is a mixture of alpine and Mediterranean species with many bulbs and endemics.

SOUTH-WEST EUROPE
Pyrenees National Park, France and Ordesa National Park, Spain Two superb areas situated on opposite sides of the central Pyrenees. Both have extremely rich mountain floras

including both lime-loving and lime-hating species, together with numerous lowland woodland and grassland plants.

Picos de Europa, Spain An area of dramatic mountains in north-central Spain protected by nature reserve and National Park status. Notable for the superb species-rich hay meadows managed on traditional lines, and for the numerous mountain species, including endemics. A range of Daffodil species occur here.

Sierra Cazorla, Spain An extensive national reserve in limestone mountains in southern Spain. Heavily wooded, with pine and evergreen oak forests. Very rich in plants with numerous endemics and pre-glacial survivors.

SOUTH-CENTRAL EUROPE

Cevennes National Park, France Situated in southern France, west of the Rhone. An extensive area of limestone and more acidic hills which extend for a considerable distance to the west of the park. Very rich in a mixture of northern, southern and mountain plants, with orchids a speciality of the area.

Gargano Peninsula, Italy A large, hilly headland projecting from central Italy into the Adriatic, partly protected as a forest reserve and proposed as a National Park. Containing limestone pavement and grassland, crowned with the beech and oak woodland of the forest of Umbria, some 2000 species have been recorded here, including over 60 species of orchid.

SOUTH-EAST EUROPE

Mount Olympus National Park, Greece Situated close to the east coast of mainland Greece. A high mountain area running down to lowland maquis with extensive mid-altitude woodlands. In addition to the many endemics the extremely rich flora includes widespread Mediterranean and mountain species.

Samaria Gorge National Park, Crete An area of limestone hills with the spectacular Samaria Gorge at the centre. Partly wooded with mixed coniferous and deciduous forest, it is rich in the more widespread eastern Mediterranean plants as well as being noted for its endemic species. Bulbs are well-represented here.

Organisations and Addresses

Below are the names and addresses of various organisations which promote an interest in wild flowers, together with a brief note on the particular interests of each society.

Alpine Garden Society
Lye End Link, St. John's, Woking, Surrey GU21 1SW
Furthers the knowledge of alpine plants. There are various local groups.

Botanical Society of the British Isles
c/o Department of Botany, Natural History Museum, Cromwell Road, London SW7 5BD
The study of British wild plants.

British Naturalists' Association
48 Russel Way, Highham Ferrers, Northants NN9 8EJ
Supplements the activities of local natural trusts.

Fauna and Flora Preservation Society
8–12 Camden High Street, London NW1 0JH
The protection of wildlife worldwide.

Hardy Plant Society
Garden Cottage, 214 Ruxley Lane, West Ewell, Surrey KT17 9EU
Furthers interest in and culture of hardy plants.

Natural History Societies
There are many regional and local societies. Addresses usually available from local libraries.

Joint National Conservation Council (formerly Nature Conservancy Council)
Monkstone House, City Road, Peterborough, Cambridgeshire PE1 1JY
Embraces the regional conservation organisations of English Nature, Scottish Natural Heritage and Countryside Commission for Wales.

Royal Society for Nature Conservation
The Green, Nettleham, Lincoln LN2 2NR
Promotes conservation of nature.

Wild Flower Society
68 Outwoods Road, Loughborough, Leicestershire LE11 3LY
Encourages an appreciation of wild flowers.

Woodland Trust
Autumn Park, Dysart Road, Grantham, Lincs. NG31 6LL
To protect by ownership or re-plant areas of broadleaved woodland. There are regional groups for Scotland and Wales.

World Wide Fund for Nature–UK
Panda House, Weyside Park, Catteshall Lane, Godalming, Surrey GU7 1XR
Conservation projects on a world-wide basis, especially for threatened species and habitats. There are also Scottish, Welsh and Northern Irish regional branches.

Bibliography

There are many books and publications dealing with the various aspects of European wild flowers. Those listed below will lead you further into this extensive literature.

Clapham, A.R., Tutin, T.G. and Moore, D.M. *Flora of the British Isles* (3rd edition). Cambridge University Press, Cambridge. 1987

Dony, J.G., Jury, S.L. and Perring, F.H., *English Names of Wild Flowers* (2nd edition). The Botanical Society of the British Isles, London. 1986

Greuter, W., Burdet, H.M. and Long, G. (Eds). *Med-checklist*. 3 volumes. Conservatoire et Jardin botaniques de Genève, Geneva. 1984–1989

Grey-Wilson, C. and Blamey, M. *The Alpine Flowers of Britain and Europe*. Collins, London. 1979

Grey-Wilson, C. and Mathew, B. Bulbs. *The Bulbous plants of Europe and their allies*. Collins, London. 1981

Heywood, V. H. (Ed.) *Flowering Plant Families of the World*. Oxford University Press, Oxford. 1979

Jalas, J. and Suominen, J. (Eds) *Atlas florae Europaeae. Distribution of Vascular Plants in Europe*. 9 volumes. Helsinki University, Helsinki. 1972–1991

de Klemm, C. *Wild Plant Conservation and the Law*. IUCN - The World Conservation Union, Bonn. 1990

Lousley, J.E. and Kent, D.H. *Docks and Knotweeds of the British Isles*. BSBI Handbook No 3. The Botanical Society of the British Isles, London. 1981

Mabberly, D.J. *The Plant Book* (2nd edition). Cambridge University Press, Cambridge. 1990

Phillips, R. and Rix, M. *Shrubs*. Pan, London. 1989

Rich, T.C.G. *Crucifers of Great Britain and Ireland*. BSBI Handbook No 6. The Botanical Society of the British Isles, London. 1991

Stace, C. *New Flora of the British Isles*. Cambridge University Press. Cambridge. 1992

Tutin, T.G. *Umbellifers of the British Isles*. BSBI Handbook No 2. The Botanical Society of the British Isles, London. 1980

Tutin, T.G. et al (Eds). *Flora Europaea*. 5 volumes. Cambridge University Press, Cambridge. 1964–1981 (Volume 1 revised 1992)

Webb, D.A. and Gornall R.J. *Saxifrages of Europe*. Christopher Helm, London. 1989

Williams, J.G., Williams, A.E. and Arlott, N. *Orchids of Britain, Europe, with North Africa and the Middle East*. Collins, London. 1985

INDEX

Common Names

327

INDEX
Scientific Names

335